A Voice for Human Rights

D1122740

A Voice for Human Rights

MARY ROBINSON

EDITED BY KEVIN BOYLE

FOREWORD BY KOFI ANNAN
AFTERWORD BY LOUISE ARBOUR

PENN

University of Pennsylvania Press
Philadelphia

PENNSYLVANIA STUDIES IN HUMAN RIGHTS

Bert B. Lockwood, Jr., Series Editor

A complete list of books in the series is available from the publisher.

Copyright © 2006 University of Pennsylvania Press
All rights reserved
Printed in the United States of America on acid-free paper

10 9 8 7 6 5 4 3 2 1

First papeback edition 2007

Published by
University of Pennsylvania Press
Philadelphia, Pennsylvania 19104-4112

Library of Congress Cataloging-in-Publication Data

Robinson, Mary, 1944–
A voice for human rights / Mary Robinson ; edited by Kevin Boyle ;
foreword by Kofi Annan ; afterword by Louise Arbour.
p. cm. — (Pennsylvania studies in human rights)
Includes bibliographical references and index.
ISBN-13: 978-0-8122-2007-0 (pbk. : alk. paper)
ISBN-10: 0-8122-2007-2 (pbk. : alk. paper)
1. Human rights. 2. United Nations. Office of the High Commissioner for Human Rights.
3. Globalization. I. Boyle, Kevin. II. Title. III. Series.

JC571.R653 2006
323—dc22

2005042338

Frontispiece: Mary Robinson, UN High Commissioner for Human Rights, 1997–2002

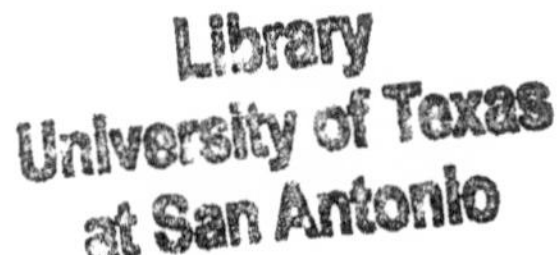

Contents

Foreword

WITHDRAWN
UTSA Libraries

The job of United Nations High Commissioner for Human Rights is not for the faint of heart. At times even well-behaved Governments view the occupant of the post as something of a nuisance, while those with something to hide will often denounce the High Commissioner's efforts as unwarranted attacks on national sovereignty. Civil society organizations, meanwhile, often expect miracles—as though the policies of hard-bitten dictators could be changed overnight by confrontational public comments, or for that matter by hidden persuasion, from an official whose power is entirely of the "soft" variety. And as if this wasn't enough, the High Commissioner must also run a sizable administration and navigate the political minefields associated with the Commission on Human Rights and its wide-ranging mechanisms. Equal parts lawyer and teacher, prosecutor and witness, hard talk and soft shoulder, the job, though little more than a decade old, is one of the most important in the entire United Nations system.

It was the need for such a forceful combination of qualities that led me, in 1997, to ask Mary Robinson to take it on. I was familiar with her distinguished career in Ireland as a lawyer and women's rights advocate. Her visits, as President of her country, to Somalia and Rwanda had coincided with my own efforts, in the United Nations Department of Peacekeeping Operations, to resolve the conflicts and alleviate the suffering in those countries. I was moved by her concern for the victims of violence. When I later sought someone to serve as High Commissioner for Human Rights, I remembered the eloquent compassion she had shown. Along with human rights advocates around the world, I was delighted when she agreed to take up this challenge.

My faith in her proved well founded. She brought to the task a leader's vision, a lawyer's precision, and a believer's conviction. Whether talking to Government officials or to the victims of violations, in large meetings or in more intimate settings, she was able to convey the very essence of human rights. She focused renewed attention on neglected issues such as economic and social rights and the right to development. She inspired her staff to new levels of accomplishment. And she never shied away from controversial issues. Hers was a clear voice for human rights where a clear voice was needed.

That singular voice resonates in the speeches and statements reproduced in this book. Steeped both in history and in the daily lives of today's oppressed, it reminds us why human rights matter and shows how a High Commissioner *can* make a difference. These speeches are her thoughts alone, in her own voice, but they challenge all of us to be less apathetic, more curious about the fate of others, and more engaged.

When Mary left the United Nations in 2002, she left the world a better place than she had found it. And her work for the cause of human rights continues. I hope this collection will reach the wide global audience it deserves.

Kofi Annan
United Nations Secretary General

Introduction

Mary Robinson, former President of Ireland and an outsider to the United Nations, was its High Commissioner for Human Rights from September 1997 to September 2002, a period of five years.[1] She was the second individual to be the "principal officer for human rights" in the United Nations. The first High Commissioner was José Ayala-Lasso (1994–97), a United Nations diplomat, who left the post to return to Ecuador as Foreign Minister. The third, Sergio Vieira de Mello, a highly experienced and highly regarded United Nations career official, was appointed in September 2002. He had served but eleven months before he was killed in a bomb attack on the United Nations headquarters in Baghdad. In July 2004 a new High Commissioner, Louise Arbour, former Canadian Supreme Court judge and prosecutor at the United Nations Ad Hoc Tribunals in The Hague and Arusha, took up the post.

The post of United Nations High Commissioner for Human Rights is therefore little more than ten years old. Mary Robinson's five years in the position were its formative years to date. Hers became one of the most influential voices on human rights of the last decade. The purpose of this book, which brings together a range of her addresses, speeches, and statements along with linking commentary, is to provide a systematic record of, and context for, the ideas, policies, campaigns, and initiatives so energetically pursued over that period by Mary Robinson and the staff she inspired. Such a collection will serve to honor the signal contribution she made as High Commissioner to the cause of universal human rights. But it will also, it is hoped, serve as an introduction to the international human rights cause and how that cause continues to be pursued inside and outside the United Nations.

This book is not a biography.[2] Nor is it an evaluation of Mary Robinson's term as High Commissioner.[3] Rather, it is an effort to tell the story of her five years in this important position through her own words. The texts of statements made, speeches delivered, and messages sent are a powerful historical resource in seeking to offer such an account. They cannot, however, capture the entire story. As High Commissioner, Mary Robinson traveled continuously, and in her meetings with victims of human rights violations and with local human rights defenders in many countries, she delivered numerous memorable and empowering messages that were by their nature unscripted and unrecorded. She was at her best without a script, speaking from the heart. Nevertheless, even though the bias in this selection of texts is to the formal record, her deep commitment to making a difference in the lives of ordinary men, women, and children—often the victims of conflict and violence, discrimination and abuse—shines through.

Her words assembled in this book are not simply from the archives of what has passed. They also remain relevant to the present and the future. That is because the mission of securing universal respect for human rights is a long-term project. Steps that have been taken and milestones reached in that mission are never defunct history. They remain part of a story that stretches back to the founding of the United Nations and are part of the context for today's efforts to advance further. It is striking how frequently Mary Robinson's speeches invoke the past, understood in these terms. Eleanor Roosevelt's injunction that the Universal Declaration of Human Rights 1948 must be heard "in small places, close to home" was a favorite quotation, for example. The position of High Commissioner rests, as does much else in contemporary human rights work, on the Vienna Declaration and Programme of Action of the World Conference on Human Rights of June 1993. This high point of international consensus after the Cold War led to indispensable understandings on the nature of human rights and the legitimacy of international concern over their violation. The World Conference documents figured prominently and inevitably in many of Mary Robinson's speeches.

In broad terms, the role envisaged for the post on its creation by the General Assembly in 1993 entailed three responsibilities: to give moral leadership on human rights to the world; to offer expert advice and support to human rights institutions at the international and national levels; and to improve the overall effectiveness of United Nations human rights activities. Communication is vital to all of these tasks. They require a High Commissioner in addressing a wide range of audiences variously to inspire, explain, or educate; to advocate, shame, or condemn; to persuade, encourage, or cajole—in short, to communicate. Apart from the significant but invisible role of "quiet diplomacy," such messages were conveyed through the written or spoken word; in media interviews, press releases, and video messages; on the OHCHR Web site or in publications; and at official and informal meetings, symbolic ceremonies, conferences, and lectures all over the world. Mary Robinson, as High Commissioner, energetically and skillfully used all such means and occasions to make human rights more visible. The texts gathered in this book reflect her passionate insistence that international human rights standards must be taken seriously by all. Whatever the occasion, formal or informal, her words convey that passion. They also convey what she saw as her primary mission to be a voice for the victims of human rights abuses.

Career

The possibility of real change requires the coincidence of a person and particular historical circumstances. And so it proved in respect of Mary Robinson's five years as High Commissioner. Her earlier career had prepared her well for the post and she took up the position at a time when a new reforming Secretary General of the United Nations, Kofi Annan, was set to bring human rights into the center of what the United Nations should stand for.

Born on 21 May 1944, Mary Robinson had an exceptional public presence in Ireland before taking up her United Nations position.[4] This encompassed a career in law, the academy, politics, and social activism that incorporated an international outlook and a belief in human rights from the outset. By the age of twenty-five she had gained a law degree at Trinity College Dublin and a master's in law from Harvard. In 1969 she was appointed as the youngest professor of law at Trinity College, and she was later to become its Chancellor, the first woman to do so since the Tudor monarch Elizabeth I.

Her espousal of women's rights and civil rights issues in the Irish and European courts, her involvement with social movements, and her twenty campaigning years as a senator in the Irish Parliament demonstrated a commitment to human rights activism that continued during her seven years as Ireland's elected President, 1990–97. The 1990s are now referred to in Ireland as the "Robinson years," a time of rapid economic improvement and movement toward a more honest and socially inclusive society. Mary Robinson was both the symbol of and a key influence on the shaping of present-day Ireland. Her concerns as President were not confined to Ireland. She led public opinion in looking out both to the Irish diaspora and to the stark contrasts in life chances between developing and developed worlds. Her visit as head of state to Somalia in 1992 and her personal campaign to alleviate famine there, along with her presence in Rwanda soon after the genocide of 1994, helped focus not only Irish but also world attention on collective responsibility for these appalling and avoidable tragedies.

When appointed High Commissioner by the General Assembly in 1997 on the recommendation of Kofi Annan, Mary Robinson was recognized throughout the world as an Irish leader of integrity and as an advocate and activist for global social justice and human rights. Her appointment was welcomed by many governments and was greeted with open delight by human rights and development groups worldwide. They hoped that her drive and passion combined with her visibility and status could make the post of High Commissioner a force to advance the UN's faltering commitment to the defense of human rights.

The goodwill, support, and hopes of the world's grassroots were to drive Mary Robinson in her new role. But she was also sensitive to the danger of dashing expectations. She could and did speak out over human rights abuses. But the limits of moral authority in the world were also constantly brought home to her. So also were the constraints imposed on her own freedom of action as an international official in the world of competing states and competing priorities that is the United Nations. She had no prior experience working in a large organization, and the bureaucratic procedures of a complex international body such as the United Nations were experienced first with shock and then with frustration.[5]

The potential of the United Nations to make a difference she never doubted, but impatience with the pace of progress and the inadequacy of the funds committed to human rights caused her, as her first four-year term came to an end, to announce that she would not seek a second term. She told the Commission on Human Rights that she believed she could "achieve more outside the constraints that a multilateral organization inevitably imposes."[6] The announcement caused a furor among many governments and human rights organizations who appealed to her to stay. At the request of Kofi Annan she agreed to continue as High Commissioner for a further year, sensitive to his point that it was short notice to find a qualified successor.[7]

The additional year was not one of marking time. It included the enormous task of leading the World Conference against Racism. It also included the epochal event of "9/11" in the United States. Her contributions to the World Conference and her concerns for global human rights in the aftermath of the terrorist attacks in the United States are recorded in this book.

The Mandate

The origins of the post of High Commissioner for Human Rights can be traced to the period of the drafting of the International Bill of Human Rights. It had been championed for many years by John Humphrey, the first United Nations permanent secretary for human rights.[8] The Commission on Human Rights endorsed the idea of a High Commissioner as early as 1967. It was also endorsed at the Vienna World Conference on Human Rights. Following the Vienna Conference, in December 1993, the General Assembly established the position of High Commissioner for Human Rights along with an office of the High Commissioner (OHCHR).[9] The High Commissioner would have the rank of Under-Secretary General and be described as the "United Nations official with principal responsibility for United Nations human rights activities." The first High Commissioner, José Ayala-Lasso, who had chaired the working group that hammered out the resolution, took up his duties in April 1994.

The drafting of the General Assembly resolution that contains the job description of the post resulted in consensus. But one consequence was that each regional grouping in the United Nations inserted its own wish list of what a High Commissioner should do. As a result, the particulars of the post proposed a vast list of potential responsibilities. Mary Robinson's task on her appointment was to make headway in addressing all of these while seeking to establish priorities among them.

The resolution's main thrust was to give a greater prominence to United Nations objectives in the promotion and protection of human rights in the post-Cold War world. Human rights activities had developed ad hoc in response to particular pressures and events over many years. The hope was that the new position of High Commissioner, located within the United Nations Secretariat, could shape the different institutions and procedures into a coherent and more effective program that would make a difference to the millions whose rights were violated on a daily basis.

The Kofi Annan Reforms and "Mainstreaming"

The possibilities of creating such coherence were significantly boosted by Kofi Annan's election as Secretary General in 1997 and his sweeping program of reform of the UN Secretariat.[10] Human rights were to be a priority and integrated or "mainstreamed" into all the activities of the United Nations, in particular the work of the four proposed Executive Committees responsible for all programs. The High Commissioner for Human Rights was to be tasked with leading the new mainstreaming policy. Mary Robinson's first major address after her appointment, the Romanes lecture in Oxford (see Chapter 1), in which she accused many in the United Nations of having "lost the plot" because of the failure to maintain human rights protection as a core purpose of the Organization, was seen as explicit support for the Annan reforms from the new High Commissioner. The speech was later reprinted by the United Nations and clearly helped to focus minds on the new priority for human rights.[11]

The new status for human rights within the United Nations, as she noted at the time, presented Mary Robinson's fledgling office with an enormous challenge as well as opportunity.[12] She spoke of her role as being "catalytic" to induce change in the Secretariat and UN agencies that would lead them to embrace human rights values, concepts, and principles in their programming and policies. Such thinking, supported by Kofi Annan, constituted a radical development in UN terms. Human rights had been perceived by many as a technical and legal field that was also politically charged and overall best avoided. The efforts made to overcome such perceptions, the efforts to advance integration of human rights into different UN policies and programs, and the considerable success achieved during Mary Robinson's term are reported on in different texts in the book.[13]

The New Human Rights Agenda: The Vienna World Conference on Human Rights

If Kofi Annan's plans to shake up the United Nations were one foundation on which Mary Robinson built, the other was the new understandings on human rights and the duties on the international community to uphold them that resulted from the Vienna World Conference on Human Rights.[14] At Vienna there was a conscious abandonment of Cold War positions on human rights and the international order that had polarized the world and had made effective international action on human rights abuses virtually impossible. A fresh statement of global values, which sought to link the concerns and approaches of all regions, found consensus support, as did a Plan of Action to implement them.

Perhaps the most important advance in the long term was the acceptance by the World Conference of the legitimacy of international concern over the human rights practices of all states. Human rights everywhere were declared to be in the international public domain, as was the need for the international community to treat human rights problems globally "in a fair and equal manner, on the same footing and with the same emphasis."[15] The universality, indivisibility and interdependence of all rights—economic, social, and cultural, as well as civil and political—were also affirmed. The Conference recognized the imperative of development in an unequal world and that the pursuit of development, human rights (including the right to development), democracy, and the rule of law were interdependent goals. Vienna also represented a significant positive step in the struggle for the recognition of the rights of women. The Conference called for new efforts to achieve gender equality and to eliminate all other forms of discrimination, in particular racial discrimination.

The substance of these understandings and commitments was to be incorporated into the General Assembly resolution setting out the job description of the new post of High Commissioner. Not the least of Mary Robinson's achievements was to ensure that this new vision for the cause of international human rights was actively pursued as the foundation of her Office's program of work.

Throughout the speeches in this book, her commitment to ensuring equal recognition of economic and social rights with civil and political rights is a staple theme. She was the first to argue that extreme poverty was in itself human rights violation and that the elimination of poverty was the central meaning of the link between the human rights obligations of all states and development. Her advocacy of the nexus between development and human rights and her highlighting of the impact of poverty on women provided highly influential analysis and advocacy for international agencies, governments, and human rights activists alike. Such thinking also connected directly with the new policy of mainstreaming human rights into the United Nations system. It gave that policy impetus in her newly established Office and in the cooperation pursued with other UN agencies and programs, notably the United Nations Development Programme.[16]

The fiftieth anniversary of the Universal Declaration of Human Rights was celebrated in 1998, during Mary Robinson's first full year of office. The anniversary provided her with opportunities in different parts of the world to bring the Vienna commitments and understandings on human rights to a global audience. It also provided her with the opportunity to remind governments of the implications of what they had agreed on in Vienna and that for too many people there was nothing to celebrate after fifty years of the promise of the Universal Declaration.[17] No single voice did more to ensure a continued focus on the human rights gains of Vienna and to link them to later steps in international cooperation, including the Millennium Declaration and the Millennium Development Goals.[18]

Building an Office

Mary Robinson's first concern, if her mandate were to be advanced at all, had to be the building of an office, OHCHR. In its first years the High Commissioner was physically located alongside the United Nations Human Rights Centre in Geneva, the name given to the secretariat that serviced the UN human rights machinery including the treaty bodies, the Human Rights Commission, and its Sub-Commission. The relationship between the Centre and the new post was predictably fraught with problems of hierarchy and function. The solution, a merger of the two structures, came with the Annan reforms. Later the Swiss Government gifted new premises, the refurbished and graceful Palais Wilson, the original seat of the League of Nations.

Establishing a professional office in Geneva and at UN headquarters in New York required sustained attention to organizational, management, personnel, and budgetary issues, tasks that were as demanding, unglamorous, and time-consuming as they were vital. But the results over her five years, of which Mary Robinson was very proud, was to create a more effective and professional staff some five hundred strong and with higher morale than when she began.[19] A major achievement was to successfully marry the internal secretariat functions with an external operational dimension for OHCHR that brought engagement with human rights issues beyond the inevitably remote processes of the United Nations to country and regional levels. That engagement was intended to connect the work of United Nations human rights bodies, their decisions, and their recommendations with people and institutions within countries and regions. This vision of a "joined up" system of human rights protection is conveyed in many of her speeches.[20]

Presence on the Ground

Human rights work within countries had begun to develop before the post of High Commissioner was established and took the form of human rights field presences in the rapidly developing peacekeeping and peace-building roles of the United Nations.[21] It was the beginnings of such placements in the early 1990s that convinced Amnesty International of the need for a new post on human rights responsibilities within the United Nations. Amnesty International's advocacy of the post of High Commissioner was influential at the Vienna World Conference where the idea was endorsed.[22] Under Ayala-Lasso, the first High Commissioner, the numbers of human rights specialists on the ground accelerated.[23] Mary Robinson embraced the new development, her first field mission, in December 1997, being to visit her staff in Rwanda, where she had been as Head of State in 1994. One early initiative, which became an annual event, was to bring together the heads of field operations in Geneva to build common strategies and better communications between Geneva and the field. In line with evolving UN thinking, she advocated and encouraged the increasing integration of such human rights presences into the main UN operations working within countries and at regional levels.[24]

Before the establishment of the position of High Commissioner, a trend had begun in states requesting technical and legal advice and assistance to establish national human rights protection and human rights training. The creation of the post of High Commissioner and the higher profile of human rights that followed Kofi Annan's reforms and Mary Robinson's appointment brought a dramatic increase in expressions of interest and in requests from states for such services. A large "technical assistance" program was established over her five years as High Commissioner and today represents a major contribution of the Office to human rights promotion and protection in the world.[25]

Building on the advisory services and field presences, she sought over her years in the post to extend the contribution of OHCHR to global protection by establishing regional advisers based in the different world regions. The aim was to encourage regional cooperation in the implementation of international human rights standards and to increase the responsiveness of the Office to local needs.[26]

The Search for Funds

A source of frustration, and one familiar to all United Nations activities, was the gap between the growing tasks assigned or taken on by OHCHR and the budget allocated to carry them out. Insufficiency of funds was one trigger that led Mary Robinson not to seek an extension of her term. OHCHR works, as the rest of the UN does, on a biennial budget allocation. The allocation from the regular budget to OHCHR for 2002–3 was US$47.7 million, corresponding to 1.8 percent of the total UN biennial budget of US$2.6 billion. The regular or statutory budget counted for only 34 percent of OHCHR's annual expenditure in 2001, with 66 percent, or US$42.8 million, coming from voluntary funds.[27] Voluntary funds are generated on a yearly basis by an appeal to states and foundations. While she lobbied for a larger slice of the regular budget, arguing that a share of less than 2 percent for human rights was unfair, Mary Robinson also initiated OHCHR's annual global appeal to donors to meet the needs of its burgeoning programs. It was a professionally managed, project-focused initiative that was combined with annual reporting back to the donors on the use made of their funds. Her fund-raising proved successful and was vital for OHCHR programs; it also strengthened the transparency and accountability of the Office. But she was not successful in securing a significant increase in the regular budget and changing the worrying reliance of a UN department for the greater part of its budget on voluntary contributions from, in the main, a few large donors.

Moral Leadership

The expectation of many countries and in particular human rights NGOs, of the new post of High Commissioner was not focused alone on organization, funding, or programs. They also wanted a moral voice that would give leadership to an international human rights community that was growing rapidly during the 1990s. They wanted an authoritative voice that would support grassroots and international efforts to move states to adopt and implement pro-human-rights policies and one that could galvanize the international community to take action on widescale human rights violations in the world. Mary Robinson sought to provide that leadership.

Despite the often scattershot coverage by global media of human rights issues, the wretched conditions and suffering of millions are for the most part ignored. That is the case with violations caused by political oppression, racial discrimination, or religious persecution and even more so where the daily denial of rights flows from poverty, food insecurity, and lack of clean water, sanitation, shelter, and education. The need to end oppression and to address the often structural sources of hopelessness in the lives of many were at the heart of Mary Robinson's leadership on human rights.

Denouncing human rights violations is rarely popular with impugned governments, armed opposition, or new culprits, such as multinational corporations. But Mary Robinson spoke out where it was necessary and whether the abuses occurred in developed or developing countries. At the same time she worked to change conditions of oppression and violation, engaging, for example, with countries through OHCHR programs to strengthen national capacity, human rights education, and protection. She built partnerships with civil society organizations and local human rights activists, and she played an influential role in encouraging businesses to become involved in the Secretary General's Global Compact on upholding human rights, labor, and environmental standards.[28]

Deadly Conflict

But at the same time, like other leaders of the international community, including the United Nations Secretary General, she also had to react to emergency events, in particular the sudden eruption of violence and conflict with their inevitable cost in large-scale human rights violation. Ayala-Lasso, the first High Commissioner, took up his position in April 1994, the month that the Rwandan genocide began. Engagement by OHCHR with gross violations dates from that unimaginable horror. Mary Robinson's term saw other crises and bloodshed, including in Chechnya, East Timor, the Great Lakes region of Africa, Sierra Leone, the Balkans, and the Middle East. Her efforts to ensure protection for victims and to press for the accountability of perpetrators in such conflicts are recorded in this book.[29] At the same time she sought greater commitment by all for the prevention of conflict as the true antidote to large-scale human rights violation. Prevention is a theme that links her reflections in this book on the different conflicts that OHCHR investigated and which she personally visited and reported on.[30]

The Organization of the Book

The edited speeches and other material in the book are organized thematically. This approach serves to underline continuity between the human rights challenges faced by Mary Robinson as High Commissioner and the challenges that face her successors. While the collection reflects her remarkable personality and her distinctive priorities, to a large extent the human rights challenges she tackled endure. A further advantage of a thematic approach is that it conveys vividly the enormous and diverse range of issues and initiatives that are now encompassed in the work of OHCHR. The sheer range of ideas, projects, and programs chronicled in these pages, many the legacy of Mary Robinson, offers also an in-depth introduction to the contemporary world of human rights theory and practice. The huge responsibilities given to the post are not widely understood, nor are the institutional and financial constraints under which the High Commissioner operates. This collection of texts should help also to bring out these dimensions.

After her time as High Commissioner had ended, and as she promised, Mary Robinson has continued in her independent capacity as a human rights activist to work for universal human rights. The final chapter of the book traces her thinking on globalization and human rights. The need to instill an ethical dimension into globalization, which for her requires as a minimum the incorporation of international human rights legal standards and principles, has become her present field of endeavor. Realizing Rights: The Ethical Globalization Initiative, which she now leads, represents an imaginative, and even a natural progression from her role as United Nations High Commissioner for Human Rights.[31]

I
A Vision for Human Rights

Chapter 1
A Personal Vision

Mary Robinson first spoke publicly about her vision for human rights and her ambition for her new post of United Nations High Commissioner for Human Rights two months after her appointment, when she gave the Romanes Lecture at the University of Oxford. She expressed forcefully her commitment to her entire mandate and to what would be her priority—the implementation of the human rights legal standards already agreed upon by the world community. She was equally forceful in calling upon the United Nations to take human rights seriously in all its activities and in her support for the reform program of the new Secretary General, Kofi Annan. Her commitment to reverse the historical neglect of economic, social, and cultural rights; to women's rights; to poverty elimination; and to development as central human rights concerns all emerge, as does her belief in the power of civil society to be the engine of change. The speech was thus a remarkable early statement of a vision of how human rights protection could be made to work, and it was a vision that remained consistent throughout her five years as High Commissioner.

In her first full year of office the world marked the fiftieth anniversary of the Universal Declaration of Human Rights. The Declaration is the foundation text of post-Second World War idealism and the entire international human rights movement. Her reflections on the Universal Declaration in Oxford and in a speech marking the fiftieth anniversary given in Tokyo confirm its influence on her own belief in universal and indivisible human rights. However, her distress at the continuing gross abuse of rights and freedoms throughout the world is also palpable. The Tokyo speech brings out her activist approach when she looks forward to building a global alliance to reverse the neglect of economic, social, and cultural rights and the right to development. A year later, on the award of the Erasmus Prize in Amsterdam, she addressed questions of human responsibilities and the challenge of gross violations in new human rights crises that had erupted in Kosovo, Sierra Leone, the Democratic Republic of the Congo, and East Timor.

"Realizing Human Rights: 'Take hold of it boldly and duly . . .'"
Oxford University Romanes Lecture 1997
Oxford, UK, 11 November 1997

On the morning I left Dublin, just two months ago, to begin my work as United Nations High Commissioner for Human Rights, Seamus Heaney gave me a beautifully bound copy of *The Golden Bough* inscribed with those encouraging words "Take hold of it boldly and duly . . ."

It seems fitting to repeat them here at Oxford and to do so as I avail of this first opportunity to reflect publicly on my new responsibilities. Until now I have been preoccupied with learning and doing, while recognizing that there was insufficient time to step back a little and think. The honor of delivering the Romanes Lecture for 1997 deprived me of any further excuse to postpone thinking.

It is a particular pleasure to return to this University and to follow in the footsteps of your distinguished Chancellor, who described himself to me as "last year's man." I would like to borrow from his Romanes Lecture the following reminder: "Oxford, both as a geographical entity and as one of the great academic communities of the world, is an irreplaceable national (and international) asset, and it is a duty upon us all to handle it carefully as well as imaginatively."[1] Thank you for placing this asset at my disposal at a very early stage of what I have described as a daunting challenge.

The deep sense of loss felt internationally on the death of Sir Isaiah Berlin reminds us of the true strengths of this academic community. I invoke his name too because he was, as Bernard Crick reminded us, in the words Berlin applied to Pasternak, "a soldier in the battle for human freedom."

Human freedom is that precious space secured by standards, laws, and procedures that defend, protect, and enhance human rights. We are all custodians of those standards. As the Vienna Declaration in 1993 stated, "Human rights and fundamental freedoms are the birthright of all human beings."[2] I do not propose to detail here the range of international instruments and mechanisms developed since 1948, but that body of substantive international human rights law is there because domestic protection of vulnerable individuals or groups is either absent or insufficient. Today, news reaches us faster than ever, and much of it concerns human rights violations. I chose the title "Realizing Human Rights" to put the emphasis on the problem confronting the international community, and for which I now bear some responsibility, of making human rights protection work.

The task is not easy, particularly because the expression "human rights" carries different meanings and resonates differently in various parts of the world and within countries depending on political preferences, ethnic association, religious views, and, importantly, economic status.

My own approach to human rights is based on an inner sense of justice. Perhaps that is part of me because I am from Ireland and have my roots in a past of struggle for freedom, of famine, and of dispersal of a people. Perhaps also it derives from my experiences as a lawyer and politician and, more recently, as a President privileged to visit and be a witness to profound suffering and deprivation in countries such as Somalia and Rwanda.[3]

I have been in listening mode over the past two months. In Geneva, and subsequently in New York, I met the Permanent Representatives of Governments in the five regional groups and had opportunities for bilateral discussion with senior members of a number of governments.[4] I have also interacted with representatives of nongovernmental organizations and with the academic community as part of the wider civil society engaged in human rights issues. As I listened, I learned that the gap in perceptions of what we mean by human rights is even wider than I had thought. It is a gap that must be narrowed if there is to be a shared commitment at the international level to further the promotion and protection of human rights.

The broad mandate of my office, created by the General Assembly resolution of 20 December 1993, entrusts me, I believe, with a particular responsibility to bridge that gap.[5] The means at my disposal are modest, the tools being mainly advocacy and persuasion. Nonetheless I take the very breadth of the mandate as the starting point, because it is clear that the gap in perception is widest when the term "human rights" focuses specifically on civil and political rights on the one hand or, at the other end of the spectrum, emphasizes the importance of the right to development. My responsibility as UN High Commissioner is to adopt and to foster a rights-based approach across the whole spectrum of civil, cultural, economic, political, and social rights; to promote and protect the realization of the right to development and specifically to include women's rights as human rights, as we were reminded by the 1995 Beijing conference.[6] It is useful to have a timely opportunity for an open and, I hope, frank debate on all of this. That opportunity presents itself.

The Universal Declaration of Human Rights

Next year we mark the fiftieth anniversary of the Universal Declaration of Human Rights. This Declaration, I believe, ranks as one of the great aspirational documents of our human history. It embodied the hopes and even dreams of people still scarred from two world wars, newly fearful of the Cold War, and just beginning the great liberation of peoples, which came about with the dismantling of the European empires.

The Universal Declaration proclaims the fundamental freedoms of thought, opinion, expression, and belief and enshrines the core right of participatory and representative government. But just as firmly and with equal emphasis it proclaims economic, social, and cultural rights and the right to equal opportunity. It was to be "a common standard of achievement for all peoples and all nations," and the rights and freedoms set forth therein were to be enjoyed by all without distinction of any kind, such as race, color, sex, language, religion, political or other opinion, national or social origin, property, birth, or other status. Twenty years after its adoption the basic tenets of the Declaration were endorsed in the Teheran Proclamation of 1968.[7] These rights and freedoms were developed in greater detail in two United Nations Covenants, the Covenant on Civil and Political Rights and the Covenant on Economic, Social and Cultural Rights, both of which entered into force in 1976.

The Universal Declaration is a living document. To commemorate it in the closing years of this millennium, the debate must give more priority to current complex human rights issues: the right to development, the recognition of the rights of indigenous peoples, the rights and empowerment of people with disabilities, gender mainstreaming, and issues of benchmarks and accountability in furtherance of these and other rights. There are also now many more participating governments than were present on 10 December 1948 and many more voices from the wider civil society. The challenge will be to engender a similar commitment to a shared vision so that such new rights concerns will form part of a renewal in our time of the vision of 1948. The challenge is to ensure that they are encompassed in the opening words of the preamble to the Universal Declaration: "Whereas recognition of the inherent dignity and of the equal and inalienable rights of all members of the human family is the foundation of freedom, justice and peace in the world . . ."

The Failure to Achieve

The international system's achievements to date in implementing human rights standards cry out for fresh approaches. As we prepare for the fiftieth anniversary of the Universal Declaration, I have told my colleagues that I do not see this as an occasion for celebration. Count up the results of fifty years of human rights mechanisms, thirty years of multi-billion-dollar development programs, and endless high-level rhetoric and the global impact is quite underwhelming.

We still have widespread discrimination on the basis of gender, ethnicity, religious belief, or sexual orientation and there is still genocide—twice in this decade alone. There are forty-eight countries with more than one-fifth of the population living in what we have grown used to calling "absolute poverty."

This is a failure of implementation on a scale that shames us all. So much effort and money and so many hopes have produced such modest results. It is no longer enough to hide beyond the impact of the Cold War and other factors limiting international action in the past. It's time instead for a lessons-learned exercise.

One lesson we need to learn and to reflect in our approach is that it is of the essence of rights that they are empowering. Poverty is a violation of numerous basic human rights. Furthermore, the increased recognition of the feminization of poverty makes it vital to link into the international protection of human rights the energies and approaches of the thousands of international and national networks of women's groups. This link between rights and empowerment is very much in my mind as I begin to identify my own priorities. One of these must be to respond to the directions of Secretary General Kofi Annan in his report last July on *Renewing the United Nations: A Programme for Reform* that "the High Commissioner will undertake an analysis of technical assistance provided by the United Nations entities in areas related to human rights and formulate proposals for improving complementarity of action."[8] The report also notes: "The Office of the High Commissioner should be able to provide its advice for the design of technical assistance projects and participate in needs assessment missions."

What the Secretary General had in mind were the various United Nations programs that, for example, assist democratic processes, strengthen good governance and the rule of law, support the reform of the judiciary and legal system, and train security forces. In addition, many United Nations programs affect economic, social, and cultural rights and the rights of the child. The analysis sought by the Secretary General will respond also to the admonition in the Declaration and Programme of Action of the World Conference on Human Rights in 1993, which "urges all United Nations organs, bodies and specialized agencies whose activities deal with human rights to cooperate in order to strengthen, rationalize and streamline their activities, taking into account the need to avoid unnecessary duplication."

The Vienna World Conference on Human Rights

Which brings me to the other international event we will mark next year: the five-year review of that World Conference on Human Rights convened in Vienna in the summer of 1993.[9] The Conference concluded by adopting a Programme of Action, which identified particularly vulnerable individuals and highlighted the need for continual review of measures taken to ensure adequate protection of the rights of these groups. Women, minorities, indigenous peoples, children, persons with disabilities, refugees, migrant workers, and prisoners were seen as particularly vulnerable. The Vienna Declaration and Programme of Action was endorsed by a resolution of the General Assembly, which also established the post I now occupy.

One of the prime movers in building the consensus in Vienna for that post was Ecuador's Ambassador and now Foreign Minister, José Ayala-Lasso. He was then handed the challenge of being the first High Commissioner. He moved prudently—building a more solid and durable consensus for the role of the post, beginning reform of the human rights secretariat in Geneva, and enlarging the activities of the new Office to include substantial field presences in the wake of the genocide in Rwanda, in Cambodia, and elsewhere. When the United Nations Decade for Human Rights Education was proclaimed by the General Assembly to begin in 1995, he initiated a plan of action for its implementation that I propose to build upon.

And what of the role of civil society? In his reform proposals last July, the Secretary General noted that "civil society constitutes a major and increasingly important force in international life," but he continued, "Yet despite these growing manifestations of an ever more robust global civil society, the United Nations is at present inadequately equipped to engage civil society and make it a true partner in its work." He urged "all United Nations entities to be open to and work closely with civil society organizations that are active in their respective sectors . . ."[10]

My predecessor saw the need to link more effectively with nongovernmental organizations. I too feel a particular responsibility, as the person charged through my mandate both "to enhance international cooperation for the promotion and protection of human rights" and "to coordinate the human rights promotion and protection activities throughout the United Nations system," to give leadership and with my colleagues to forge partnerships with, and channel the energies and effectiveness of, the broad constituency that constitutes the human rights community worldwide.

The Mandate of High Commissioner

It will not be easy to achieve. Commentators have noted that the High Commissioner's mandate was carefully worded and balanced—reflecting the concern of a number of governments that they were creating a post which might shine an unwelcome light on some neglect of their citizens' rights. Professor Philip Alston, in a recent article, described the quest to define the role of the UN High Commissioner for Human Rights as "neither fish nor fowl."[11] He points out that whereas the tasks given to the High Commissioner have continued to expand, including significant field operations, it has been necessary to supplement the inadequate resources from the regular UN budget by seeking voluntary special-purpose contributions. I share the broad thrust of his analysis. Indeed, recognizing that voluntary contributions from governments will continue to be an important source of funding for programs and activities, I am taking the step of writing to all governments so that support for our activities will be as inclusive as possible.

I am also very conscious of the difficult task of developing an appropriate balance between the use of consensual diplomacy and the moral voice on behalf of victims, which speaks out in defense of human rights. It helps to have only one agenda, the fulfillment of my mandate, and to recognize that there are many friends in the international human rights community ready and willing to help in meeting the challenge.

I would like to focus briefly on the coordinating role of the High Commissioner, which has been given new impetus in the Secretary General's reform-package proposals of last July. There is an oft-cited quote attributed to Ian Martin—the former Secretary General of Amnesty International—that the High Commissioner for Human Rights should wake up each morning thinking how best to protect human rights. I agree with him but would go further. The protection of human rights requires that every United

Nations staff member should wake with the same thought and work committed to that end.

Almost by definition and certainly according to its Charter, the United Nations exists to promote human rights. Somewhere along the way many in the United Nations have lost the plot and allowed their work to answer to other imperatives. This is the root cause of much of the criticism that is leveled at the Organization—you hear it couched in terms of complacency, of bureaucracy, of being out of touch, and, certainly, of being resistant to change. There is an opportunity now to recapture the lost purpose of the United Nations. I hope to contribute to this work under the leadership of Secretary General Kofi Annan by helping to shape a framework for action, which will result in an Organization driven by human rights standards.

Mainstreaming

I believe profoundly in the relevance to our global community of the human rights standards built up over more than fifty years. Not only are all human rights universal, indivisible, interrelated, and interdependent; they are also inherent in human nature and pertain to the individual. Realizing and implementing these human rights standards is a core value of the Secretary General's reform proposals. The language is explicit, and I quote: "Human rights are integral to the promotion of peace and security, economic prosperity and social equity"; and again, "A major task for the United Nations, therefore, is to enhance its human rights program and fully integrate it into the broad range of the Organization's activities."[12]

The first step has already been taken by assigning each entity in the UN system, with the exception of my Office, to one of four Executive Committees. These committees are the central tool in ensuring coordination in the system, focused on peace and security, humanitarian affairs, economic and social issues, and development operations. The Secretary General has asked me to participate in each of the four committees and to assess, in due course, whether this is a more effective way to "mainstream" human rights rather than having a fifth executive committee concerned with human rights.

In a practical way, human rights has become a core value in the work of the United Nations—human rights imperatives can and should be injected into every aspect of the Organization's work. It will require an integrated approach—for example, working with our colleagues in political affairs and peacekeeping—to understand that today's human rights violations are the causes of tomorrow's conflicts. And so on through the web of agencies tackling economic development, population activities, health, women and children, education, and refugees and displaced persons. And I do not exclude those agencies that appear purely technical. The International Telecommunications Union has a crucial role in ensuring that people in the least developed countries can join the information revolution. Article 19 of the Universal Declaration anticipates the Internet, enunciating the right to "receive and impart information and ideas through any media and regardless of frontiers."

As High Commissioner I have the responsibility to act as a catalyst by stimulating and coordinating action for human rights throughout the UN system, and to provide education, information, advisory services, and technical assistance in the field of human rights. The task, I am convinced, requires more than structural and organizational changes: it requires an approach of education and heightened awareness among the UN's most important resource, its staff. They need to become familiar with human rights standards and how these standards are applied in their own areas of responsibility. They need to understand the principles and ethics underlying these human rights standards and feel a sense of identification with this ethos. They should have a commitment to promote human rights and the ability to communicate and implement human rights standards in their daily work.

Changes are occurring. I have been impressed with new thinking and approaches on the need to develop the concept of a "strategic framework" in how we work in each country. This is a collegiate effort to encourage disparate elements of the United Nations to accept common goals and to coordinate their actions in order to achieve those goals. What human rights can bring to this discussion is a unifying set of standards—common reference points for setting the objectives, assessing the value of possible interventions, and then for evaluating the impact of the actions that are agreed. It will undoubtedly help me in fitting into and contributing to this integrated approach that my office is small and my resources modest. There is every incentive to coordinate.

The internal process, of what amounts to building up a culture of human rights throughout the UN system, will be our contribution to the review after five years of the Vienna Declaration and Programme of Action. That review requires stocktaking by governments of the extent to which they have implemented the international human rights standards. It will also engage regional and national human rights institutions, and the process will involve reporting to the Commission on Human Rights meeting in Geneva next spring and to the General Assembly in autumn.

Human Rights in Development

The timing is right. The five-year review of the Vienna Conference will give us reference points by which to assess what is working and what might work better. Clarence Dias and James Paul coined the expression "lawless development" as a succinct indictment of the shortcomings of international interventions over the past thirty years and as a broad hint that some solutions might be found in the application of international law.

In my introduction I hope I made clear my commitment to treat economic and social rights with the same priority as civil and political rights. They must be treated as interdependent and indivisible if either set is to be realized. I mention this because I fear that those who work in development agencies may not yet be sufficiently aware of their role in the realization of human rights.

A few weeks ago colleagues in my Office met with an Australian NGO which—in conjunction with counterparts in South East Asia—is formulating guidelines for the implementation of what it calls the "Rights Way to Development."[13] Their ideas are challenging.

This group is asking the right questions; for example: What are the real objectives of a World Bank loan for an infrastructure project or an intervention by the International Monetary Fund to stabilize a currency? For too long the objectives and the success or failure of interventions has been measured narrowly—according to the criteria of macroeconomics. I suggest tonight—as I suggested to the Bank and Fund recently in Washington—that their real purpose is to contribute to the realization of a number of human rights. In many ways both institutions are adapting to this broad objective using terms such as "human development," "human well-being," "human security," "basic needs" and "good governance." I prefer the language of the Universal Declaration and the two Covenants. The language there, unlike these surrogate terms, has the force of treaty law and directly empowers people. It tells people at the grassroots level that they have rights: rights to security, dignity, economic opportunity, and a better life for their children—not any vague and undefined entitlement to a favor of some kind bestowed by a government or an international agency.

Let me stress that I am advancing nothing that is new, nor is it the agenda of any particular ideology. I am simply advocating the implementation—in a consistent, coordinated, and coherent manner—of well-established legal obligations.

Rosalyn Higgins, one of this country's great international jurists and now a member of the International Court of Justice at The Hague, described international law "as a normative system, harnessed to the achievement of common values—values that speak to us all, whether we are rich or poor, black or white, of any religion or none, or come from countries that are industrialized or developing."[14]

The normative work is largely done. The international human rights standards are in place. The task for us all, given new impetus by the focus of next year, will be to implement them.

Let me return, in conclusion, to *The Golden Bough*:

If fate has called you,
The bough will come easily, and of its own accord.
Otherwise, no matter how much strength you muster you never will
Manage to quell it or cut it down with the toughest of blades.

As I wake up each morning thinking how best to protect human rights, I must also, and with modesty, rely on fate.

"The Universal Declaration of Human Rights: A Living Document"
Keynote Address to the Third Symposium on Human Rights in the Asia-Pacific Region
Tokyo, Japan, 27 January 1998

I am honored to give the keynote address at this symposium on human rights in the Asia-Pacific region, and to have the privilege of listening to participants who will contribute from the perspectives of the peoples of the region.

On 10 December 1998 we will commemorate the fiftieth anniversary of the Universal Declaration of Human Rights, which was adopted in the shadows of Auschwitz and Nagasaki and on the doorstep of the Cold War. Like all major anniversaries it provides an opportunity to take stock, to examine what has been achieved and to reflect on what needs to be accomplished in the future. It is fitting that this should take place in the same year as the five-year review of the World Conference, which was convened in Vienna in 1993, and as we approach the new millennium.

The celebrations, however, cannot take place amidst the fanfare of self-congratulation. Too much remains to be done in the field of human rights protection to rest on our laurels. The present-day victims of destitution and persecution are uppermost in our minds, as is the yawning gap between aspiration and genuine achievement.

A Visit to Cambodia

I have just come from Cambodia, where last week I visited the museum Tuol Sleng in Phnom Penh. It had been a school but became a place of torture and inevitable death for over sixteen thousand people during the Khmer Rouge period from 1975 to 1979. As I looked at the iron beds with torture implements, saw the graphic photographs of how they had been used, and walked past row upon row of photographs of young girls and boys, of old people, of people from every walk of life—civil servants, peasants, intellectuals, soldiers, students—as I saw the piled-up clothes and shoes it brought back so vividly my visit to Auschwitz, and when I came to Hiroshima in 1995, and the terrible aftermath of the genocidal killing in Rwanda which I saw on my first visit there in 1994. How often have we said "never again"? This, surely, is the strongest argument for the universality and indivisibility of human rights. It also reminds us of the need for eternal vigilance in safeguarding those rights.

The commemoration has another purpose. It is to remind the peoples of the world of the tenets of the Universal Declaration and, in so doing, to reaffirm and to renew our attachment to these fundamental principles and to this vision. For it is also, and perhaps primarily, through education that the aims of this great document can be fulfilled. That is why it is so important that countries include in their national plans of marking the anniversary a further commitment to integrating human rights education not only into school curricula but also into youth groups and continuing education projects. The commemoration compels us to reflect on the continuing relevance of the Universal Declaration to the political, social, economic, and cultural environment we live in. How can we transform its promise into a living reality for more people? Our achievements so far in this domain, when we remember the genocides and the continuing conditions of "absolute poverty" in the world around us, are a cause of shame. We must match our rhetoric with action.

Human Rights: Universal and Indivisible

When the Declaration was adopted by the General Assembly on 10 December 1948 it distinguished itself from other great constitutional documents—such as the Code of Hammurabi, the Magna Carta, the French Declaration of the Rights of Man, or the American Declaration of Independence—in two fundamental respects. First, it was the first international articulation of the rights and freedoms of all members of the human family. For the first time in the history of mankind nations had come together to agree on the content of the human rights of all human beings. They did so in the aftermath of the barbarities of the Second World War out of respect for the dignity of each human being and because they perceived the close connection between violation of human rights and national and international peace. The emphasis throughout the Declaration was on rights and freedoms applicable to every person everywhere.

Second, the Declaration—the "common standard of achievement for all peoples and all nations"—treated human rights as not only universal but also indivisible—that is, civil and political rights, on the one hand, and social, economic, and cultural rights, on the other—are both demanding of protection on the same plane and are interdependent and interrelated. In doing so, it laid the essential conceptual foundations of the international law of human rights; it charted the human rights agenda of the United Nations for this century and beyond and awakened the great forces in civil society to the cause of human rights.

Thus the Declaration proclaims in its Preamble that "recognition of the inherent dignity and of the equal and unalterable rights of all members of the human family is the foundation of freedom, justice and peace in the world." Economic, social, and cultural rights are set out with the same degree of affirmation and conviction as civil and political rights. Freedom of speech and belief are enshrined but also freedom from fear and want. Fair trial and the right of participatory and representative government sit shoulder to shoulder with the right to work, to equal pay for equal work, and the right to education. Both sets of rights are proclaimed as "the highest aspiration of the common people." That means all the people.

We must be honest, however, and recognize that there has been an imbalance in the promotion at the international level of economic, social, and cultural rights and the right to development. Extreme poverty, illiteracy, homelessness, and the vulnerability of children to exploitation through trafficking and prostitution are telling indictments of leadership in our world as we end this millennium. I have committed myself as High Commissioner for Human Rights to work, together, I hope, with a global alliance for human rights to redress that imbalance. This year, 1998, is a good year to begin to forge this alliance.

Today the Universal Declaration of Human Rights stands as a monument to the convictions and determination of its framers, who were leaders in their time. It is one of the great documents in world history. The *travaux préparatoires* are there to remind us that the authors sought to reflect in their work the differing cultural traditions in the world. The result is a distillation of many of the values inherent in the world's major legal systems and religious beliefs, including the Buddhist, Christian, Hindu, Islamic, and Jewish traditions.

The Declaration has exerted a moral, political, and legal influence throughout the world, far beyond the aspirations of its drafters. It has been the primary source of inspiration of all postwar international legislation in the field of human rights. All of the United Nations human rights treaties and resolutions as well as the regional human rights conventions—the European and American Conventions and the African Charter on Human and Peoples' Rights—have been directly inspired by the Declaration. Virtually every international instrument concerned with human rights contains at least one preambular reference to the Universal Declaration, as do many subsequent declarations adopted unanimously or by consensus by the General Assembly of the United Nations.

Its detailed provisions have served as a model for many domestic constitutions and laws, regulations, and policies that protect human rights. National courts throughout the world have had recourse to the provisions of the Declaration in the interpretation of provisions of national law or directly applicable international law. Parliaments, governments, lawyers, and nongovernmental organizations throughout the world invoke the Declaration when human rights are discussed.

The Declaration as Law and Inspiration

Many of the provisions of the Declaration have become part of customary international law, which is binding on all states whether or not they are signatories to one or more multilateral conventions concerning human rights. Thus, what started its existence as a solemn but nonbinding proclamation of rights and freedoms has, at least in some respects if not all, acquired through state practice the status of universal law.

Twenty years after its adoption, its tenets were authoritatively endorsed by the 1968 Proclamation of Teheran[15] and transformed into the provisions of the Covenant on Civil and Political Rights and the Covenant on Economic, Social and Cultural Rights, both of which entered into force in 1976. Most recently 171 countries participating in the 1993 United Nations World Conference on Human Rights reaffirmed their commitment to the Declaration in the Vienna Declaration and Programme of Action. They endorsed its inspirational role as in United Nations standard setting. The Universal Declaration inspired other world conferences, including the Beijing Platform of Action that emphasized again that women's rights are human rights. Indeed, one of the functions of the Office of the High Commissioner for Human Rights established by the General Assembly in 1993 is to promote and protect the rights and freedoms contained inter alia in the Universal Declaration of Human Rights. In short, the Declaration has, since its adoption, assumed the mantle of a constitutional instrument, giving specificity to the concept of human rights in the United Nations Charter and radiating its benign influence throughout the planet.

My vision of the Universal Declaration, however, strays beyond its legal and political influence. Nelson Mandela has recently reminded us that the Declaration was adopted only a few months after the formation of the first apartheid government. He said—and I quote:

> For all the opponents of this pernicious system, the simple and noble words of the Universal Declaration were a sudden ray of hope at one of our darkest moments. During the many years that followed, this document . . . served as a shining beacon and an inspiration to many millions of South Africans. It was proof that they were not alone, but rather part of a global movement against racism and colonialism, for human rights, peace, and justice.[16]

It is often said that rights that exist on paper are of no value. But paper, vision, commitment, and action are the powerful tools of peace. The pages of the Universal Declaration, as Nelson Mandela observed, have been a source of courage to the downtrodden by showing them that they are not alone! They also interrogate our sense of solidarity. Notwithstanding the cruel fact of the persistence of human rights violations throughout the world, this document has served and will continue to serve as a reminder that the world community cannot turn a blind eye to the suffering of the oppressed and the destitute and that it has a mandate to concern itself and, where possible, offer succor—beyond all frontiers.

One need look no further than the Preamble of the Declaration to realize that, while the world around us is evolving at a pace more rapid than at any other time in human history, the premises on which the Declaration is founded will remain valid and immutable forever. Test their relevance against the bitter realities of today's world events. The Preamble continues to articulate our response. It speaks of "barbarous acts which have outraged the conscience of mankind." It points out that "it is essential, if man is not to be compelled to have recourse, as a last resort, to rebellion against tyranny and oppression, that human rights should be protected by the rule of law." It reminds us of the connection between human rights observance and "friendly relations between nations." It ends with a phrase that goes to the heart of the commemoration of the fiftieth anniversary, that a "common understanding of the rights and freedoms is of the greatest importance for the full realization of this pledge." No one reading these phrases today can fail to be struck by their insight into the connection between denial of human rights and peace—domestic and international—and their enduring actuality.

But today's world is more complex than it was fifty years ago. There are now many more participating states than there were in 1948 and more strident and concerned voices from civil society. The agenda set by the Declaration is surprisingly apt for these new complexities—whether they are linked to the rights of indigenous peoples or to the right to development or discrimination on grounds of gender or on the basis of sexual orientation—but who could have imagined in 1948 that we would use the fiftieth anniversary of the Declaration as an opportunity to reposition these fresh concerns and others in our order of priorities?

Human Responsibilities

It is in this context that the search for global ethical standards and the work of the InterAction Council and others in focusing on human responsibilities bring fresh insights into the interpretation of the Preamble and Articles of the Universal Declaration of Human Rights as a living document.[17] It is right that we should focus more on duties and obligations, but I believe, it would be wiser to avoid the distraction of seeking a new declaration. Instead we need to recognize and recommit ourselves to the extent to which these values are implied in creating through the Universal Declaration of Human Rights "a common standard of achievement for all people and all nations," which can be reinforced by greater emphasis on them as valued for individuals and communities in all our civil societies. It is thanks to the Universal Declaration that human rights have established themselves everywhere as a legitimate political and moral concern, that the world community has pledged itself to promote and protect human rights, that the ordinary citizen has been given a vocabulary of complaint and inspiration, and that a corpus of enforceable human rights law is developing in different regions of the world through effective regional mechanisms.

I would venture to suggest that it has become an elevating force on the events of our world because it can be seen to embody the legal, moral, and philosophical beliefs held true by all peoples and because it applies to all. It is precisely this notion of "universality"—in the widest sense—which gives it its force. Its universal vocation to protect the dignity of every human being has captured the imagination of humanity. It is this vision which explains the enduring mission of the Declaration and its unsurpassable dominance as a statement of legal principles. We tamper with it at our peril.

Lord Acton, a famous British historian of the last century, said of the two pages of the 1789 French Declaration of the Rights of Man that they weighed more than whole libraries and than all of Napoleon's armies. The remark is also fitting for the Universal Declaration.

But I have a preference for a more poetic image inspired by Václav Havel. It is that of the tree which was planted for mankind as a symbol of justice in fertile soil following the end of a great cataclysm. It has gradually taken root and grown into a unique and enduring specimen. Much care has been taken to water the ground around it and to nurture its growth. Cuttings have been taken and planted throughout the world. We have watched it grow every day. Patiently. Slowly it has acquired impressive stature.

But like all living things, it has certain fragility. It is part of our heritage that we have been asked to teach others its history and purpose and to hand down the skills and commitment needed to sustain it. Its message will have to be understood and acted upon. Most of all, and in Havel's words, "it will need to be looked after with understanding and humility but also with love."

Acceptance of the Erasmus Prize
Royal Palace, Amsterdam, The Netherlands, 9 November 1999

Your Majesty, Royal Highnesses, Excellencies, Ladies, and Gentlemen,

It is a great honor for me to be the recipient of the 1999 Erasmus Prize.

It is difficult to know how to respond to the words of praise I have just heard and to the wording of the citation. However, the focus this year has been on collective responsibility. There is collective responsibility for the fact that I am here today! Perhaps the best response I can make is to thank you for this prize and to say that in honoring me you honor all those who defend human rights—often at great personal risk—and that I dedicate this prize to their name.

Prince Bernhard was kind enough to refer to my term of office as President of Ireland. I was elected on 9 November 1990, the first anniversary of the fall of the Berlin Wall, and my election symbolized for many the opening up of Irish society. Looking back, I can say that it was a most exciting time to serve as head of state of a country experiencing such momentous change as Ireland has seen in recent years. People find an air of prosperity and confidence about modern Ireland, reflecting the fact that success has been achieved through hard work, prudent management of the national finances, and the far-sightedness of investing in education, thus enabling the country's young workforce to reap the benefits of the technological revolution.

In 1625 Hugo Grotius wrote what was probably the first comprehensive treatise on international law, *On the Law of War and Peace.*[18] It is sobering to think that Grotius was seeking all those years ago to establish rules of behavior for nations and individuals and then to recall what terrible conflicts have occurred since his day. It is sobering, too, to consider the issues on the agenda of the two Hague Peace Conferences of a century ago—arms control, humanitarian law, the peaceful settlement of disputes—and to have to acknowledge that we are still far from finding lasting solutions to these problems at the end of this very violent century.

Hard questions are being asked these days about human rights. I welcome that. If human rights are to work, their rationale and effectiveness must stand up to the closest scrutiny.

Hard questions are being asked about the gap between the ideals of the human rights movement and the evidence appearing before us daily that shows how far respect for human rights is from being embedded in society. In this year alone we have witnessed gross human rights violations in Kosovo, East Timor, Sierra Leone, and the Great Lakes region, to mention only some of the worst instances. The placing of human rights center stage in political life must produce tangible improvements if there is not to be an erosion of credibility and a rise in cynicism.

I believe that the greatest challenges which lie ahead—securing peace and development, channeling the forces of globalization productively, coping with the rapidly changing world we live in—must all be grounded in respect for human rights. The message of human rights is clear. It says to the poor, the oppressed, the marginalized: "You are not alone. You are not powerless. You have rights which are universal and fundamental." Solid progress has been made over the past fifty years in standard setting. Now we face the even greater challenge of putting those principles into practice.

Responsibility and Rights

I return to the rubric under which this prize is awarded, which is collective responsibility. The Universal Declaration of Human Rights spells out the importance of this concept when it refers in the Preamble to the fact that "The peoples of the United Nations have in the Charter reaffirmed their faith in fundamental human rights, in the dignity and worth of the human person and in the equal rights of men and women and have determined to promote social progress and better standards of life in larger freedom." The Preamble goes on to say that "Member states have pledged themselves to achieve, in cooperation with the United Nations, the promotion of universal respect for and observance of human rights and fundamental freedom." These concepts of collective responsibility, and the determination to act collectively on the basis of those responsibilities, are also spelled out in articles 55 and 56 of the United Nations Charter.

As far as the individual's responsibilities are concerned, champions of human rights have recognized that, just as we possess rights simply by virtue of being human, so also we have responsibilities to those around us. There is an understandable hesitation to place too much emphasis on responsibilities and duties because unscrupulous regimes have been known to argue that duties to the state are more important than the rights of the individual. The drafters of the Universal Declaration considered listing parallel responsibilities or duties to match the rights they proclaimed, but they realized that this might qualify or relativize fundamental rights. So the issue of duties was encapsulated in one article, article 29, which states: "Everyone has duties to the community in which alone the free and full development of his personality is possible."

Article 29 makes it clear that our rights are not entirely unrestricted. It says: "In the exercise of his rights and freedoms, everyone shall be subject only to such limitations as are determined by law solely for the purpose of securing due recognition and respect for the rights and freedoms of others and of meeting the just requirements of morality, public order and the general welfare in democratic society." In my view, article 29 gives sufficient guidance as to the responsibilities of individuals and the balance that should be struck between individual freedom and the rights of our fellow human beings.

Human rights are all about collective responsibility. Their underlying message is that we belong to one global community and that we are responsible for what happens in that community. A few weeks ago, when the crisis in East Timor was at its height, the Irish poet Seamus Heaney said something that struck me as especially relevant. He said, "Everybody has felt the pity and the terror of the tragedy. But I think that we have also experienced something more revealing, which is a feeling of being called upon, a feeling of being answerable."[19]

That "feeling of being answerable" is a way of saying that we are responsible for the rights of others, and not just for our own rights. It is a key factor in the struggle to establish human rights in society. We have responsibilities, both as individuals and as members of groups, to the people we live and work with, to our country, to the global community. That is what motivates courageous women and men to speak out when governments abuse the rights of citizens. That is what makes us listen when nongovernmental organizations shed light on violations and shortcomings.

The onus on governments to discharge their responsibilities is clear. Governments may have ceded some of their powers to market forces over which they have little control, but they retain far-reaching powers over citizens. The human rights message to governments is: you should rule wisely and respect the rights of the ruled because these rights are not yours to give or take.

When they act responsibly, when they are guided by leaders with vision, governments have the power to do great good. I think of those postwar European leaders who recognized that the cycle of conflict on this Continent must be ended and joined together in the great enterprise that is the European Union. That is an outstanding example of collective responsibility, though the task of ensuring a peaceful Europe will not be complete as long as conflict rages in the Balkans.

We should not think of human rights as something abstract or for other people far away. Human rights begin at home. As Dag Hammarskjöld put it: "The great commitment all too easily obscures the little one. But without the humility and warmth that you have to develop in your relations to the few with whom you are personally involved, you will never be able to do anything for the many."[20]

The more I see of human rights in action, the more convinced I become of the value of collective action at the local, grassroots level. Reference has been made to my visit to Sierra Leone in June. One of the terrible aspects of the violence there, particularly in January and February of this year, was the systematic rape of young girls. But I was deeply impressed to meet a Sierra Leone representative of the Federation of African Women in Education (FAWE) who was counseling ninety rape victims in Freetown and who said her colleagues throughout Sierra Leone would take on this responsibility as peace was restored. It was out of recognition of the importance of grassroots human rights activity that my Office established a special fund last year, marking the fiftieth anniversary of the Universal Declaration, to create a kind of microcredit support for human rights work.[21]

Whether the description of me as "independent-minded and uncompromising but not one of life's natural mediators" is accurate or not is hard for me to say. The first part I can agree with; the second I must leave to others to judge. I am happy, though, to accept Prince Bernhard's description of me as "one of life's natural activists." As he said, human rights are too important to be negotiable.

Much of my work will, of its nature, be conducted privately with governments. I will not raise my voice to make public comments if quiet diplomacy will achieve results. But neither will I compromise or hesitate to speak out if the occasion demands. In my position as High Commissioner for Human Rights I have assumed a burden of listening: listening to the pain and anguish of victims of violations; listening to the anxieties and fears of human rights defenders. I will go on listening and will continue to speak out for those who have no voice or whose voice is ignored.

Let me conclude by quoting from Aung San Suu Kyi, who lives the values she advocates:

At the root of human responsibility is the concept of perfection, the urge to achieve it, the intelligence to find a path towards it, and the will to follow that path if not to the end at least the distance needed to rise above individual limitations and environmental impediments. It is man's vision of a world fit for rational, civilized humanity that leads him to dare and to suffer to build societies free from want and fear. Concepts such as truth, justice and compassion cannot be dismissed as trite when these are often the only bulwarks that stand against ruthless power.[22]

II
Fighting for Equality and Nondiscrimination

Chapter 2
The Struggle against Racism

The international struggle against racism has been perhaps the most important human rights campaign waged by the United Nations over its half-century existence. A mechanism that the UN has deployed over the last thirty years to engage the widest participation in its efforts to eliminate racism and racial discrimination has been programs known as Decades against Racism. In addition the General Assembly has launched World Conferences intended to reinforce the goals of the Decades. All three World Conferences, in 1978, 1983, and 2001, were dogged by political controversy. The most ambitious and successful of these was the third, held in Durban, South Africa, in August and September 2001. The 2001 World Conference against Racism, Racial Discrimination, Xenophobia and Related Intolerance (WCAR), despite huge difficulties, including the withdrawal of the United States and Israel, did agree on a far-reaching Declaration and Programme of Action. The Conference adopted important language on the shameful past of racism, including anti-Semitism and Islamophobia, and the continuing legacy of that past. It also set out a comprehensive long-term action program for the world, recognizing that the struggle against all forms of racism would be protracted in this century, as it proved to be in the last.

Mary Robinson was appointed Secretary General of the World Conference by the UN General Assembly in 1998. The General Assembly endorsed the documents agreed by the Conference in June 2002. Thus, for four of the five years of her tenure as High Commissioner she was engaged with the WCAR and its follow-up. Preparations included the organization of four regional conferences in addition to the main event in Durban. These regional conferences were intended to involve as many countries and civil society groups as possible in a global antiracism drive. An Anti-Discrimination Unit in OHCHR was established to give leadership to the antiracism campaign that was planned to be (and has been) pursued following the Conference.

The Durban Conference, a responsibility she inherited on her appointment, was perhaps the largest single challenge that faced Mary Robinson and OHCHR during her tenure as High Commissioner. It took place at a time when the global consensus on human rights achieved in the Vienna World Conference in 1993 had waned. She faced criticism over it. The Conference was marred by anti-Semitism, which took hold of some of the parallel events organized by nongovernmental organizations. She condemned these outbreaks in forthright terms and sought successfully to achieve a consensus on combating racism, although not before the United States and Israel withdrew. Whatever the criticism, no one doubted that she and her staff acted with energy and commitment to make this global consultation over how to effectively confront the evil of racism a considerable success.

After a long period of contentious negotiations between diplomats in the lead up to the World Conference, her opening speech in South Africa in July 2001 expressed her expectations. Success would be measured in the remedies and relief the Conference brought to the victims of racism. Her reflections following the Conference were delivered to the General Assembly along with the Conference official report nearly six months later. One of her innovations at Durban was the convening of a Youth Forum which produced a parallel declaration. Mary Robinson's efforts to include young people as the bearers of the goals of the conference in eliminating all forms of discrimination and her faith that they can achieve this shine through.

Mary Robinson was tireless before the World Conference in raising awareness and encouraging involvement, especially from global civil society in the fight against racial discrimination. Following the World Conference she was equally tireless in urging effective action to follow up its recommendations: Durban she repeated, must be a beginning, not an end. Her concern over anti-Semitism in Europe is reflected in her remarks to the Stockholm International Forum in January 2001 and in her letter to all European Union interior ministers in May 2002. A theme of her report to the General Assembly, the struggle against all forms of racial intolerance and the goal of a world which embraces both diversity and equality, are part of the antidote to terrorism following September 11, and is reflected in other speeches in this book.

"The Global Impact of Racism"
William J. Butler Human Rights Medal Address
University of Cincinnati, USA, 9 March 2000

Ladies and Gentlemen,

I am proud to be the first recipient of the William J. Butler Human Rights Medal. To receive an award in the name of such an outstanding human rights defender as Bill Butler is especially moving. All the more so when the person concerned is a friend of mine and a friend and supporter of the Office of the United Nations High Commissioner for Human Rights.

Bill Butler's commitment to the cause of international human rights is so well known that it does not need to be repeated by me. I would just like to say that whenever I have called on him on behalf of my Office, whether to attend the Ocalan trial or to act as my adviser, he has responded positively, notwithstanding the many demands on his time.[1] He has truly put his human rights beliefs into practice in a very tangible way. So to receive an honor in Bill Butler's name has a particular resonance for me.

I wish to thank the University of Cincinnati College of Law and the Urban Morgan Institute for Human Rights for honoring me in this way. It is a privilege to be associated with a law school which plays a unique role in the teaching of international human rights law in this country. I am pleased, too, to be taking part in the twentieth-anniversary celebrations of the Urban Morgan Institute for Human Rights. The Institute and the College of Law are providing an invaluable service by training and bringing forward the human rights defenders of tomorrow. I congratulate Bert Lockwood and all those involved in these celebrations for the achievements of the past twenty years.

Reference was made in the citation to my own background as a human rights lawyer as well as to my term as President of Ireland and the position I now hold, that of United Nations High Commissioner for Human Rights. Most of those present this evening are involved with human rights in one way or another. There are many reasons why people take an interest in human rights but I was struck by a quotation from Bill Butler's father-in-law, the renowned civil rights lawyer Arthur Garfield Hays, which was included in the Institute's prospectus. He said, "I hate to see people pushed around." I think that that simple sentiment is one which has motivated a lot of human rights defenders over the years. When you reflect on it, the idea of standing up for those who need help to defend themselves—and it is always the poor and the vulnerable who are on the receiving end—is not a bad way of describing what human rights are all about. Underlying it is the sense that everybody is entitled to his or her dignity and rights—and this, of course, is the central message of the Universal Declaration of Human Rights and the other great human rights documents. All who work for human rights, especially young people who are preparing to devote their lives to this kind of work, should retain a sense of anger at the spectacle of people being pushed around and a determination to do something practical to change that.

The civil rights movement of the 1960s is a good example of people standing up for their own rights and the rights of others. It is a particular pleasure to receive this award from the Honorable Judge Nathaniel Jones, who played an active role in the civil rights movement and in the fight against racism and apartheid.

The World Conference against Racism

Racism is, in fact, the issue I would like to focus my remarks on this evening. My mandate as High Commissioner for Human Rights is very broad, covering the whole range of rights, both civil and political, on the one hand, an economic, social, and cultural on the other. But the topic of racism is high in my thoughts because of my role as Secretary General of the third United Nations World Conference against Racism, Racial Discrimination, Xenophobia and Related Intolerance, a conference that will be held, fittingly, in South Africa from 31 August to 7 September 2001. Racism is also of overriding importance because there is a growing realization that racism, racial discrimination, xenophobia, and intolerance are the root causes of most of the conflicts and human rights violations that disfigure our world.

It is interesting to note that there has not been a world conference on the subject of racism for seventeen years. In the past, the United Nations convened two world conferences against racism. In 1978 the first World Conference to Combat Racism and Racial Discrimination reaffirmed the responsibility of the United Nations to victims of racial discrimination, as well as to those under colonial rule or alien domination. The second World Conference, held in 1983, recognized the importance of national legislation and judicial and administrative action to combat racial discrimination, and underlined the importance of defined recourse procedures for the implementation of antidiscrimination laws. Both conferences had the struggle against blatant forms of discrimination such as apartheid very much in mind.

What we are seeing today, regrettably, is that in spite of the victory over apartheid and the advances made in protecting minority rights, racism is on the increase in many parts of the world. That is what has prompted the holding of this third world conference. As we start a new century racism, racial discrimination, xenophobia, and related intolerance present enormous challenges to the international community. In the past decade alone the world has witnessed the recurrence of brutal conflicts, even genocide. The marvelous invention of a new medium—the Internet—is unfortunately also being used by some to transmit messages of hatred. No society is free from at least some people who are intolerant of difference, whether racial, ethnic, or religious, and whose intolerance finds violent expression.

In Europe, there are worrying signs of a rise in racism and xenophobia. Far-right groups are active, preaching the rhetoric of hatred and violence against those perceived as foreigners or different. In the former Yugoslavia thousands lost their lives, hundreds of thousands lost their homes and property, and we witnessed the brutal practice known as "ethnic cleansing." In Africa, terrible ethnic conflicts have taken an immense human toll in many countries, destroying lives and communities and arresting the economic and social development that countries in the region need so badly. In South America, discrimination against migrants and the many indigenous peoples who populate the continent is a serious problem. In the Asian region, there has been a big rise in the incidence of trafficking in women and children and in contemporary forms of slavery, which often have a racial or ethnic basis to them.

The Global Presence of Racism

As members of this audience are well aware, the United States is far from being free of the scourges of racism and racial discrimination. It is significant that in a recent poll where Americans were asked about the biggest challenge facing the nation in this new century, the highest number of respondents said relations between the races.

A particular issue that has drawn critical attention in recent times is the practice of "racial profiling" in policing, when a police officer may suspect a person of criminal behavior solely on the basis of race. This is a harmful presumption that encourages incorrect stereotypes about people.

The long-term impact of racism has a no-less-harmful effect. For example, economic indicators reveal how race-based disparities persist, with American Indians, people of Latin origin, and African Americans tending to experience higher rates of poverty when compared to white people in the United States. There are also active forms of discrimination in employment, housing, and consumer and credit markets. And religious intolerance is a source of underlying tensions in the United States, just as it is in many other parts of the world. One of the challenges facing next year's World Conference will be to analyze all of the factors—political, historical, economic, social, and cultural—that lead to racism.

Causes of Racism

What are the root causes of racism and xenophobia?

First, there are cultural and social dimensions involved. There is the fear and lack of knowledge or understanding of those who are perceived to be different. This is an area where education and awareness raising about diversity and the harmful consequences of racism can play a very important role.

Second, the legacies of colonialism and slavery have created in many countries conditions and conceptions that foster racism and xenophobia. As a result, many nations struggle with the modern-day impact of historical policies, practices, and attitudes based on racial difference.

Third, there is the economic dimension to racism. Economic prosperity induces job seekers to migrate to more prosperous countries or regions in search of a better life. This migration and movement can lead to racial tensions and xenophobia in the receiving country. Similarly, difficult economic times in societies tend to perpetuate racial or ethnic intolerance. There is a strong tendency to blame outsiders for domestic economic problems such as unemployment.

International Responses

Since its creation, the United Nations has placed a high priority on measures to combat racism and racial discrimination. There is now a comprehensive body of international human rights law and mechanisms in place. The UN Charter calls for "respect for human rights and for fundamental freedoms for all without distinction as to race, sex, language, or religion"—a sentiment echoed in the Universal Declaration of Human Rights. An important milestone was the adoption in 1965 of the International Convention on the Elimination of All Forms of Racial Discrimination, which has since been ratified by 155 states. The Convention established the Committee on the Elimination of Racial Discrimination, which is mandated to monitor and review the legal, judicial, administrative, and other steps taken by individual states to fulfill their obligations to combat racial discrimination. The Committee is a key monitoring body, which can help us to heed early warning signs and take preventive action before a problem becomes acute. Under the auspices of the United Nations, the International Covenant on Civil and Political Rights, and the Convention on the Prevention and Punishment of the Crime of Genocide have also been adopted.

In summary, there is broad acceptance by governments that all members of the human family have equal and inalienable rights, and commitments have been made to assure and defend these rights under international human rights law. Governments have repeatedly pledged to promote and encourage universal respect for and observance of human rights and fundamental freedoms for all, without distinction as to race, sex, language, or religion.

To have built up an impressive body of law against racism is an achievement. What we have to look at now is how the international community can be encouraged to ensure that these mechanisms are used effectively to combat racism. As we prepare for the World Conference, I will be looking to the different regions of the world to focus on themes of particular relevance and to come up with strategies. The United States can and should take a leadership role in this process by focusing attention on the Conference and by stimulating open debate. And it can set an example by embracing its own diversity, by fighting the trend toward a society divided between the haves and the have-nots, and by ensuring that the rights and freedoms of all Americans are protected, regardless of race, sex, language, or religion.

Issues before the World Conference

The General Assembly has called for an action-oriented Conference with concrete steps to be identified in the areas of prevention, education, and protection. This is certainly my approach. Let me outline some of the specific issues that will be addressed.

One issue is the question of recourse procedures open to victims of racial discrimination. Although the principles establishing nondiscrimination and the equality of all human beings have been accepted by governments and recognized in international law, the rights have yet to be assured by effective guarantees at the national level which allow individuals to have access to recourse procedures when their rights are violated. In many countries effective penal, civil, or administrative recourse procedures to victims of acts of racial discrimination have not yet been established. In those countries where recourse procedures exist, they are often little known, or they are complex and difficult to use effectively, or they require significant financial resources that are rarely available to those who suffer most.

Another issue will be how contemporary forms of racism, racial discrimination, xenophobia, and related intolerance manifest themselves. The Conference will consider inter alia discrimination against black people, Arabs, and Muslims; xenophobia; Negrophobia; anti-Semitism; and related intolerance, including discrimination against indigenous peoples, migrants, refugees, displaced persons, and the Roma population.

Racism has taken another contemporary form in the dissemination of racist and xenophobic material via the Internet. Web sites exist which publish racial hatred and which urge incitement to racial and ethnic hatred and action, even genocide. Hateful, racist messages are only a click away. The international community will wish to address the issue of harmful and hateful content in telecommunications, taking account of freedom of speech and opinion and access to information.

A further theme will be the disproportionate economic impact of racism and racial discrimination. Certain regions, countries, or entire communities are affected by racially based economic policies or discriminatory laws that have a widespread economic impact.

Involving All in the Fight against Racism

Combating racism, racial discrimination, xenophobia, and related intolerance remains our collective responsibility. A fundamental first step is that nations and the international community as a whole acknowledge the reality of multiracial and multiethnic nations. Only then can we endeavor to protect and promote all human rights for all. I would ask you to think in the period ahead about racism, to discuss concrete measures to fight racism and intolerance, to encourage the holding of symposia and seminars and the writing of articles about the many issues and problems associated with racism, racial discrimination, xenophobia, and related intolerance.

There is a fundamental need for civil society to be closely involved in the work of the World Conference. Human rights and the fight against racism are not just the province of lawyers. Everyone has a part to play in combating racism: nongovernmental organizations, community groups, religious groups, and the private sector. I welcome the active participation of these groups at the World Conference.

I look forward to your cooperation in this important task and to your continued action on behalf of human rights worldwide. People sometimes ask me if I do not get discouraged at the human rights abuses I witness in the course of my work. It is true that there is no shortage of violations, whether it is gross violations such as people being murdered or driven from their homes in East Timor and Kosovo, or children being mutilated in Sierra Leone, or the daily assault on the economic and social rights of a huge part of the world's population. But I draw encouragement from the fact that we start this century with human rights to the fore of international attention on a scale never known before. Human rights legislation has reached an advanced stage, and the mechanisms are largely in place. What is needed now is to move from standard setting to implementation, and I believe that this can be achieved as long as the will is there to do so.

I also draw encouragement from the award I have received here tonight. I accept it on behalf of all those who champion the cause of human rights. It will be an inspiration to me as I prepare for the World Conference against Racism and in my work as United Nations High Commissioner for Human Rights.

Thank you.

"Combating Intolerance"
Stockholm International Forum on Combating Intolerance
Stockholm, Sweden, 29 January 2001

Prime Minister, Distinguished Guests, Excellencies, Ladies, and Gentlemen,

I am honored to have been invited to address this Forum, and I pay tribute to the Government of Sweden for making it happen. It comes as no surprise to me that Sweden should lead the way in the fight against intolerance, given this country's remarkable record in giving the lead internationally on human rights and humanitarian causes.

The theme of this forum is especially appropriate after last year's Stockholm Conference on the Holocaust, and the program is impressive both as regards substance and in its forward-looking approach.

As the Secretary General, Kofi Annan, will emphasize when he addresses you, combating intolerance is central to the aims of the United Nations and engages all branches of the organization. The Preamble to the UN Charter states one of its top priorities as being "to reaffirm faith in fundamental human rights, in the dignity and worth of the human person, in the equal rights of men and women . . . and for these ends to practice tolerance and live together in peace with one another as good neighbors."

Humankind has made many advances over the centuries. The age we live in is one of revolutionary discoveries in the fields of science, medicine, and technology, which are improving our quality of life in ways that even the previous generation could not have imagined. But as we enjoy the improvements which human ingenuity has produced, we cannot but see that all manner of human rights violations remain commonplace in our supposedly advanced world. We are conscious, too, that the capacity to bring our race to the brink of disaster is not merely a theoretical possibility but something that actually happened, less than sixty years ago. The Irish poet Seamus Heaney, in the speech he delivered here in Stockholm in 1995 on receiving the Nobel Prize for Literature, put it well: "Our realism and our aesthetic sense make us wary of crediting the positive note. . . . The very extremity of our late twentieth century knowledge puts much of our cultural heritage to an extreme test. Only the very stupid or the very deprived can any longer help knowing that the documents of civilization have been written in blood and tears. . . ."[2]

Intolerance is a destructive force that has the capacity to ruin lives and threaten all of the advances the human race has made. I recall the words of Elie Wiesel at the ceremony of dedication for the Auschwitz memorial: "I speak as a Jew who has seen what humanity has done to itself by trying to exterminate an entire people and inflict suffering and humiliation and death on so many others. In this place of darkness and malediction we can but stand in awe and remember its stateless, faceless and nameless victims."[3]

In fact, our first duty in the face of intolerance, and particularly in the face of its most extreme manifestations—genocide and crimes against humanity—is to remember and bear witness. I applaud the initiative whereby a publication on the Holocaust was sent to households in Sweden. It is a painful book to read, but it is vital that young people who were not yet born when these terrible deeds took place should understand where intolerance ultimately leads. It is especially important to dwell on this at a time when synagogues in Europe are once again the targets of racist attacks.

The World Conference and Intolerance

But we must do more than remember: we have a solemn duty to do everything in our power to combat intolerance in all its manifestations. An excellent opportunity to do this is presented by the UN World Conference against Racism, Racial Discrimination, Xenophobia and Related Intolerance, which will be held in Durban, South Africa, from 31 August to 7 September of this year.

The first task of the World Conference must be to reach a thorough understanding of racism, racial discrimination, xenophobia, and related intolerance as they exist in this twenty-first century. An extensive range of preparatory conferences and regional expert seminars has been under way since last year and will continue up to the Conference proper. The meetings are considering many different issues, and their geographic spread is wide, ranging from Dakar to Teheran, from Santiago to Bangkok.

I hope that the preparatory meetings will enlighten us further about the nature of racism and xenophobia. I look to this Forum today to shed more light on the phenomenon of intolerance, which is a key factor in racism. Intolerance, prejudice, and racism are deep-rooted, complex forces. They take many forms: they can be based on difference of religion, nationality, social class, and gender. One thing is certain: discrimination on the grounds of racial difference is particularly strong.

All modern manifestations of intolerance and racism must be confronted. Previous UN Conferences have addressed the particular problems of indigenous peoples, national minorities, and migrants. These remain issues of serious concern. Other topics we will need to address at Durban include the plight of the Roma community—and indeed the traveler community in my own country, Ireland—ethnic conflict, gender and racism, and prejudice against refugees and asylum seekers.

We will need, as well, to examine the impact of globalization on racism and intolerance. As in so many other aspects of our lives, globalization has implications in this area also. One example is that cross-border crimes such as trafficking in persons are on the increase. Another is that population movements often lead to a rise in xenophobia. In this regard, I was struck by a recent statement by the NGO Working Group on Migration and Xenophobia, which highlighted the complex forces that are at work:

> In the experience of many NGOs, xenophobia and hostility against non-nationals both overlap with and are distinct from racism and racial discrimination. In some cases, discrimination is manifested on the sole basis of foreignness, even when racial and other characteristics make non-nationals indistinguishable from nationals. In other situations, the intersection of racism and xenophobia is manifested by the presumption that anyone whose physical characteristics are distinct from the idealized national norm is assumed to be foreign.[4]

What can we hope for from the World Conference?

I am looking for concrete results in Durban. My objective is to get the agreement of the international community on a ringing declaration against racism, racial discrimination, xenophobia, and related intolerance; a substantive plan of action with specific activities and time lines; and a process to review actions at the end of a set period. I look to Sweden and to every UN member state, to play a constructive role in ensuring that the Durban Conference succeeds in devising new, effective strategies to combat all forms of racism and intolerance.

Racism and Europe

When tackling such a difficult challenge, it is generally agreed that actions are required at international, regional, and national levels. The World Conference will set out the norms and standards which all countries should adhere to and map the way forward. In Europe, Sweden can play a powerful role over the coming months through its presidency of the European Union. More can and should be done in Europe to combat racism. At the European Conference against Racism in Strasbourg last October, I said that we should not be blind to the scale of racism and xenophobia in Europe today; I referred to such aspects as

the overall increase in intolerance toward foreigners, asylum seekers, and minorities;
discrimination against minority groups by law enforcement, immigration, and other officials;
discrimination in the workplace and the service sector;
the rise in support for far-right parties;
the emergence of racist attitudes in places where it had not been so evident before and in wealthy societies where there is no threat to livelihoods.

European attitudes strike me as paradoxical. Even leaving aside the equity issue and countries' obligations toward refugees and asylum seekers under international law, the economic arguments in favor of a more liberal approach are striking. Europe's birthrate has fallen sharply, and the age profile is steadily rising. For the purpose of its economic vitality alone, Europe needs more people.

Regrettably, many political leaders in Europe have turned their backs on this reality and have been at best lukewarm and at worst hostile in their attitude toward refugees and asylum seekers. I said in Strasbourg and I repeat here that leadership is needed on this issue from Europe's politicians. The message I send to them is this: a multicultural Europe is inevitable. Europe has no alternative but to embrace tolerance and diversity. I would go even further and say that tolerance is not enough; the goal should be to achieve full respect for the inherent dignity and equal and inalienable rights of "the other" in our societies—of minorities, indigenous peoples, migrants, and those of different color, race, or ethnic background.

Perhaps the greatest effort that will have to be made is at the national level. Here, too, Sweden can lead the way. I have been impressed with the approach of the Sweden 2000 Institute in identifying driving forces for diversity in Sweden. The Institute has examined the aging population and workforce. It has noted that the workforce will become more multicultural, posing a challenge to Swedish companies to view diversity management as a strategic issue that needs to be integrated in all parts of the processes and practices within a company.[5]

My call to each of the countries represented at this Conference is to focus over the coming months leading to the Durban Conference on a positive approach to diversity at each country's level. There needs to be more transparency, more honesty, more valuing of the contribution of those who will come from outside the country to contribute to the essential purposes of each country in achieving its full economic and social potential over the coming years.

Another Swedish example is the office of ombudsman. The international community admires the way Sweden developed this office. The notion of an independent arbitrator who stands up for the rights of the individual against the state has had enormous influence in strengthening human rights and has spread to many parts of the world in a relatively short time. Today Sweden has a highly developed structure of national institutions including a parliamentary ombudsman and ombudsmen responsible for ethnic discrimination, equal opportunities, and discrimination on the basis of sexual orientation, the disabled, and children.

Experience has shown that, even where sophisticated legislation and machinery exist to protect rights, the scope for discrimination and intolerance remains great. Neither Sweden nor any country can claim to be free from racism and discrimination. The World Conference against Racism is therefore an ideal occasion for each country to examine the record so far, including the effectiveness of existing legislation and arrangements to combat racism and to ask whether these are adequate to cope with new trends.

Ladies and gentlemen, the Visionary Declaration prepared for the World Conference and signed by more than seventy heads of state and government across the world calls for a recognition that we all constitute one human family. The Declaration says:

> [T]his truth encourages us towards the full exercise of our human spirit, the re-awakening of all its inventive, creative and moral capacities, enhanced by the equal participation of men and women. Instead of allowing diversity of race and culture to become a limiting factor in human exchange and development, we must refocus our understanding, discern in such diversity the potential for mutual enrichment, and realize that it is the interchange between great traditions of human spirituality which offers the best prospect for the persistence of the human spirit itself.[6]

World Conference against Racism, Racial Discrimination, Xenophobia and Related Intolerance, Opening Statement
Durban, South Africa, 31 August 2001

President Mbeki, Heads of State and Government, Secretary General, Excellencies, Ladies, and Gentlemen,

Today marks the start of an event which many people have worked long and hard for over many months. To all who contributed and especially to the people of Durban and South Africa, I say a warm "thank you."

We have come a long way to Durban. I recall the first formal event of the Conference eighteen months ago—an expert seminar in Geneva on Remedies Available to the Victims of Acts of Racism, Racial Discrimination, Xenophobia and Related Intolerance and Good National Practices in the Field. We have come a long way since then in building up our understanding of racism in the modern world. There have been four regional conferences, five expert seminars, and three sessions of the Preparatory Committee. There have been lengthy drafting sessions, and events of every description have taken place in every part of the world, with the focus on the themes of Durban.

We have come a long way psychologically and substantively too. Our journey to Durban has helped to shape thinking about who are the victims of racism and discrimination, what sort of remedies can be made available, and the best kinds of preventive measures. When the balance sheet is drawn up for the Conference, the greater understanding which has been achieved of the sources, causes of, and remedies for racism must weigh heavily in its favor.

This was never going to be an easy Conference. Asking people to face up to the problems of racism in their midst is not always welcome. There is a tendency to say "We don't have those problems in our country." It is always easier to point the finger of blame than to look hard at our own prejudices and biases.

And we should not be surprised that the negotiations have been difficult. The issues we are addressing here confront us at so many levels, nationally, regionally, and locally. They are among the most sensitive the United Nations and the international community have to deal with. It is worth remembering this over the coming week. We should remember, too, that we cannot solve all of the world's problems at Durban.

A theme I have been stressing is that we all belong to one human family. Families do not agree on everything. But they agree on certain fundamentals, and that is what makes families strong. What I am asking all of you is that we agree on the fundamental aims of this Conference, not that we try to sort out all the problems on the international agenda.

One thing that is clearer to me after the preparations of the past eighteen months is how badly we need new strategies to fight racism and intolerance in the modern world. To those who say we do not need a World Conference on this subject I say, "Look around you." How much misery, inequality, conflict is caused by racism and discrimination? From a human rights point of view, this Conference is crucially important. Equality and nondiscrimination are central to the pursuit of human rights. Success at Durban should be measured by whether or not the outcome brings effective remedies and relief to the victims of racism, racial discrimination, xenophobia, and related intolerance.

I have also learned how closely contemporary forms of racism are bound up with the past. I believe this Conference could mark a historic breakthrough in the struggle against racism if agreement could be reached on language that recognizes historic injustices and expresses deep remorse for the crimes of the past. If we can do that, it will connect with millions of people worldwide and affirm their human dignity. It will connect in the way that poetry connects and will be heard by that inner ear.

We must focus attention on outcomes and forward strategies. In some respects the journey proper will only begin after we leave Durban. That is when the real test will come of what we have achieved over these months of preparation and at the Conference.

Durban will only be a landmark if there is substantial text adopted here and meaningful follow-up. The task that we must achieve before we leave is to have a clear understanding about the follow-up which must be accomplished, about who is responsible for the necessary actions and how we can measure progress. I call on every government representative to ensure that the responsibilities of states in the fight against racism and discrimination are fully understood and acted on through national programs or plans of action. I call on intergovernmental organizations to play their part to ensure that the aims of this Conference are reflected in their own activities, and that they vigorously monitor the commitments that will be made here.

As far as the role of the United Nations is concerned, the participatory process has made it clear that the UN must not only continue its historic fight against discrimination but also intensify that struggle. We have heard at length from those who are hurting, from those who are the victims of injustice, and from those in quest of dignity and equality. I have already drawn firm conclusions from this, and I shall establish an antidiscrimination unit reporting directly to me to take follow-up action on the insights we have already gained, on the implementation of your recommendations, and to maintain common cause and mobilization with civil society. I shall be consulting with member states at the forthcoming General Assembly on how we can take forward processes to follow up in the regions on the practical proposals that have come out of the various regional conferences and expert meetings.

I cannot overstate the role of civil society in the follow-up process. I look particularly to non-governmental organizations, the international youth network, and civil society generally to take up the challenge of Durban and form a global alliance with governments to carry the struggle forward. The impression I have is that NGOs are indeed rising to the challenge and are aware of how vital is the fight against racism, racial discrimination, xenophobia, and related intolerance.

There are three things I would ask for in the week ahead from all parties and especially from delegates. The first is generosity of spirit; it is no small issue we are dealing with in Durban: it is no time to be small-minded. Second, I call for flexibility and a willingness to meet the views of others; progress can be made only on that basis, and the urgency of devising new strategies to combat racism and discrimination requires it. Third, I would appeal for a sense of vision; I remain convinced that this can be a defining moment for the international community and that we have the capacity at the start of this century to work for a better and fairer world order.

We can draw inspiration from the African concept of *Ubuntu,* that ancient term which embraces humaneness, caring, sharing, and being in harmony with all of the world. When he came to Geneva last April, Archbishop Desmond Tutu explained how the concept represents the opposite of being selfish and self-centered. *Ubuntu* empowers everyone to be valued, to reach their full potential while remaining in accord with everything and everyone around them.

This spirit is reflected in the Universal Declaration of Human Rights when it speaks of "the inherent dignity and the equal and inalienable rights of all members of the human family." The Universal Declaration proclaims "All human beings are born free and equal in dignity and rights . . . and should act towards one another in a spirit of brotherhood." Let that spirit inform our discussions over the coming week as we strive for a world where the principles of equality and nondiscrimination are honored, not merely in words, but in fact.

Thank you.

Elimination of Racism and Racial Discrimination
Statement to the Third Committee, Fifty-sixth General Assembly
United Nations, New York, 28 January 2002

Distinguished Chairperson, Distinguished Delegates, Ladies, and Gentlemen,

I am pleased to be with you today for the discussion of agenda item 117 and thank you, Chairman, for facilitating this debate. The elimination of racism and racial discrimination is a central tenet of the Universal Declaration of Human Rights. It is also one of the fundamental objectives of virtually every international human rights instrument adopted by the United Nations. The International Convention on the Elimination of All Forms of Racial Discrimination, the key human rights treaty in this field, has established widely accepted human rights standards to eliminate racial discrimination. My Office is committed to achieving universal ratification of this Convention and its effective implementation by all states parties.

Although the standard of nondiscrimination has been established as a bedrock principle of international law, the persistence of racism, racial discrimination, xenophobia, and related intolerance clearly demonstrates the need to look for new ways to address this problem with more resolve, with more humanity, and with greater efficiency. Last year the World Conference against Racism, Racial Discrimination, Xenophobia and Related Intolerance, of which I was Secretary General, helped focus the international community's thinking about where action to date has been insufficient and in what areas and in what ways we can do more to create just and fair societies free of racial discrimination.

As most of you know, the Conference involved nine days of intensive and frequently difficult negotiation. Even after the Conference, there was a difference of views or perceptions that principally concerned the placement of several paragraphs in the Durban Declaration and Programme of Action, and which delayed the issuance of the report of the Conference. Nevertheless, despite all of the obstacles that had to be overcome, the Conference was ultimately successful in negotiating a Declaration and Programme of

Action by consensus. The report of the Conference was issued and is now before you.

Conference Overview

The documents adopted at the Conference address a wide range of subjects. Common language was found on difficult issues relating to slavery, the slave trade, and colonialism, as well as the issues relating to the Middle East.

Agreement was reached on the need for national action plans, tougher national legislation, and more legal assistance to victims of racial discrimination. Improvement in the administration of justice and the reinforcement of national institutions to combat racial discrimination were also emphasized. In this regard, the importance of appropriate remedies and positive action for victims of racial discrimination was underlined.

A wide variety of educational and awareness-raising measures were adopted. Measures were also included to ensure equality in the fields of employment, health, and the environment. In this regard, the need to have accurate data collection and research was identified as an important prerequisite for taking corrective measures. Measures to counter racism in the media and through the use of new technologies such as the Internet were also included in the documents adopted.

The documents adopted specified that a victims-oriented approach was an important tool to eliminate racial discrimination. In this regard, specific reference was made to Africans and persons of African descent, Asians and persons of Asian descent, indigenous peoples, migrants, refugees, minorities, the Roma, and others. Durban also put the gender dimension of racial discrimination on the map, as well as the more general question of multiple discrimination. Finally, the importance of involving not only states but also a wide variety of actors, including civil society, NGOs, and youth, in the implementation of the Durban commitments was emphasized.

In reflecting on the World Conference, I believe it is important to note that the documents adopted in Durban are both historic and forward-looking. They provide a new and innovative antidiscrimination agenda and, as such, constitute an essential element of an emerging global dialogue on how to eliminate the scourge of racial discrimination from our world. Indeed, the World Conference texts have become all the more important in the aftermath of the horrific terrorist attacks here in New York on September 11. Their vision of a world which embraces diversity and stands for equality, is an antidote to terrorism.

The real issue today, then, is not to look back and dwell on how difficult the process was in Durban. We all knew it would be a difficult Conference, and it was. We all knew the issues involved were not ones that lent themselves to easy solutions, and difficult compromises had to be made. But we also knew that was precisely the reason why this Conference was so important, why we accepted the challenge to have it, and why we persisted in our efforts until we finally had agreement.

Following Up on Commitments Made

The real question now is the credibility of the international community in living up to the commitments made at the Conference today, tomorrow, and beyond. Now is the time for action. Now is the time for implementation. People in all parts of the world continue to suffer daily from racism, racial discrimination, xenophobia, and related intolerance. I am sure they are hoping that the United Nations and its member states will lead the way forward and help them to have the conditions for a better life, a decent life, and one free of discrimination. We should respond to these hopes and aspirations. We must make Durban a reality. We cannot let the victims of discrimination down at this crucial moment, after all our efforts to date. There is an enormous consensus around the world, amongst peoples and governments alike, on the need to do more to implement the principles of equality and nondiscrimination. The World Conference documents give us the tools to do this. But the best tools are only of value if they are put to use.

Distinguished delegates, after the debate on this item, you will be considering and eventually adopting a draft resolution on the World Conference. I would appeal to you to show the same resolve in adopting this resolution as you demonstrated at the Conference. In this regard, I would strongly urge you to adopt this resolution by consensus. Only such an approach would send a clear and unambiguous message that the international community is united in its determination to follow up on the commitments made in Durban, and to consolidate the gains made there.

I would also like to highlight that the Programme of Action contained in the report before you refers to the establishment of an antidiscrimination unit within OHCHR to follow up on implementation. This unit will have a number of important functions. Among its major tasks will be the mainstreaming of the Durban Declaration and Programme of Action in the activities of OHCHR as well as in those of other UN bodies and specialized agencies. The unit will also prepare the annual progress reports to the Commission on Human Rights and the General Assembly on follow-up to Durban, as well as undertake public awareness and information activities worldwide. In addition, the unit will provide input to OHCHR technical assistance programs designed to fight racial discrimination, including in the development of national action plans. The antidiscrimination unit will also be organizing seminars both in Geneva and on a regional basis, and establishing a database on best practices and national legislation to combat racism and racial discrimination.

I have taken the necessary steps already to establish this unit on an interim basis. It began functioning at the beginning of this year. However, budgetary support is required in order to ensure the long-term functioning of this unit. The interim antidiscrimination unit is a key element in the ability of OHCHR to do its part in implementing the Durban Declaration and Programme of Action, and it is therefore a priority for my Office to put it on a solid financial footing.

The Programme of Action also recommended the establishment of a group of five independent eminent experts, appointed by the Secretary General, on recommendation by the Chairperson of the Commission on Human Rights. The purpose of this body is to follow the implementation of the Durban Declaration and Programme of Action, in cooperation with my Office. This proposal will also require budgetary support in order to ensure that this new mechanism can be established, that it can meet as required, and that my Office can service it in an appropriate manner.

I would like to conclude my comments on the report of the World Conference by reiterating what I said at the conclusion of the Conference. Durban must be seen as a beginning and not an end. The Durban Declaration and Programme of Action will be meaningless unless governments follow through and act on them. This is why I appeal to you all that, at the end of this debate and after consultations have resolved outstanding issues, you should endorse the World Conference texts and adopt a consensus resolution that will allow the next phase of the struggle against racism, racial discrimination, xenophobia, and related intolerance to begin.

"United to Combat Racism: A Youth Vision"
Keynote address at the conclusion of Durban Youth Summit
Durban, South Africa, 27 August 2001

It is a pleasure for me to address you here in Durban at the closing ceremony of the Youth Summit. I congratulate those who have turned the dream of a Youth Summit into reality: the World Conference Non-Governmental Organization (NGO) Forum Secretariat, the International Youth Committee, and the South African Youth Task Team. Without their determination and hard work we would not be here together tonight.

I look forward to receiving the outcome of your discussions. I promise to read these carefully and to take account of your conclusions as I prepare for the World Conference. One of the ways in which your work here can be carried forward is to make it part of the United Nations Special Session on Children which will take place next month in New York. I will be meeting Carol Bellamy, the head of United Nations Children's Fund (UNICEF), here next Sunday, precisely to consider how to include the concerns raised here in the program of the Special Session.[7]

I hope that you have profited from being in Durban. The great advantage of an event like this is that it offers opportunities for young people from different parts of the world to get together, to compare notes, and to coordinate strategies. That is one of the reasons I strongly supported the holding of this Youth Summit. But most of all I wanted the voice of youth to be heard in Durban. I can tell from the reports I have been receiving about your discussions that you have indeed been addressing the whole range of issues we need to tackle.

This World Conference against Racism, Racial Discrimination, Xenophobia and Related Intolerance will be different. As well as tackling deep-rooted and well-known forms of racism, it will focus on new forms of racism that have appeared, such as racism in the media and on the Internet.

New categories of victims have been identified. As well as the "traditional" targets of racism, xenophobia and intolerance, such as ethnic, national, and religious minorities, the Conference will also be focusing on the special problems of refugees, asylum seekers, migrants, Roma-Sinti, the traveler communities, indigenous peoples, and Afro-descendants in all continents, as well as trafficked persons.

The Conference will turn the spotlight on people who suffer multiple discrimination. Children, the elderly, women, and people living in extreme poverty often carry a double or even a triple burden because they belong to a particular racial, social, ethnic, or religious group.

Racism is not a stand-alone problem. Race or origin can determine access to quality education, job opportunities, the house and the neighborhood you live in, your right to land, representation and participation in political life and public service, health care, and even life expectancy.

Every country in the world has issues of racism and xenophobia to grapple with. Now is the moment for governments to demonstrate their recognition of this, their understanding that the causes and roots are deep, and their collective determination to move the fight against racism and xenophobia onto a new plane.

The objective of the Conference is to have a strong Declaration agreed to by governments—one that recognizes the damage caused by past expressions of racism and that reflects a new global awareness of modern forms of racism and xenophobia—and a strong, practical Programme of Action. Every government should go away from Durban committed to a national plan of action to fight racism, and there should be a review of whether they have achieved their goals after a fixed time.

The fight against racism cannot be won without the wholehearted support of young people. South Africa is a good example. It would have been impossible to dismantle the apartheid system without the courage of South African youth. They helped change the history of their country.

You are all familiar with the story of Steve Biko, who gave his life for the cause of equality and nondiscrimination. Here was a young man who became a symbol of resistance to an oppressive regime and inspired millions.

Another young person we should remember today is Hector Peterson, the fifteen-year-old student who died on the first day of the Soweto uprising. He was marching with friends from the Soweto High School against the imposition of Bantu education when police opened fire and he was shot. I visited the memorial to Hector Peterson when I came here as President of Ireland and again last March. On both occasions I was moved by the thought of such a young person's sacrifice and the example he set for all of us.

We can draw inspiration from many other countries too. For example, next week we will hear from someone whose experience should encourage us all to step up the fight against racism and discrimination. Mariama Oumarou is a seventeen-year-old girl from Niger who was sold as a slave at the age of fifteen. But she escaped and will be telling her story in Durban as one of the Voices of Victims.[8]

What these young people have in common is that they inspire us. They show us the reality of racism, racial discrimination, xenophobia, and intolerance and how they can blight peoples' lives—and how it is possible for young people to take a strong stand against these scourges.

During the preparations for the Durban Conference I saw for myself how enthusiastic young people are to support the aims of the Conference. I also saw how they can make their presence felt. It happened at the regional preparatory meeting for the Americas in Santiago de Chile last March. In the middle of the official speeches a young Argentinean woman, Viviana Figueroa, commandeered the microphone from the President of Chile to express the feelings of the indigenous people who were not included in the drafting process.

I would also like to welcome the youth delegation from Guyana, who bravely convinced shops, businesses, schools, sports clubs and the police force to turn their buildings into "race-free zones." We need more initiatives like this as a follow-up to the Conference in order to make the outcome of Durban a reality for everybody. In the June edition of our World Conference Newsletter that focused on children and youth, we described a range of positive initiatives which I recommend to your attention. You can find these—and lots more information—on our Web site.

Young people can bring special insights to bear on the issues facing the World Conference because they are particularly vulnerable to conflict and discrimination. Millions of young people suffer discrimination both because they are young and for other reasons—for example, because they belong to minority, indigenous, or refugee groups. The discrimination they face may be because of the color of their skin, or because of their language, religion, or cultural traditions. Just ask South African youth of color about the uninvited-guest treatment they and their parents often receive when enrolling in educational facilities.

The discrimination young people encounter may be hidden and subtle. Often it is suffered in silence. This can have a profound impact on children's and young people's self-esteem and self-confidence. It can cause them to bottle up negative attitudes. This in turn can lead to resentment and negative attitudes building up over generations.

Young people may be preyed on and encouraged to be aggressors themselves. If they grow up in a racist environment, they can turn into racists. If they live in an atmosphere of violence, they can be used as weapons of ethnic and racial tension, even wars. They can be used to advocate violence, hatred, and destruction against religious or ethnic minorities. Young people have killed and been killed; they have raped and been raped; they have tortured and been tortured—often on ethnic or racial grounds.

The opposite is also true: if children and young people have role models that act without racial hatred and discrimination, they can themselves become advocates of tolerance and champions of diversity.

You are the people who can decide what world you want to live in: a world divided along the lines of race, gender, or national or ethnic origin, or a world in which we all see each other as members of one human family.

You can put pressure on governments and local authorities to implement measures aimed at combating racism.

You can take practical initiatives at the local level wherever you see racism at work.

You can encourage open and frank dialogue about racism, racial discrimination, xenophobia, and related intolerance. This Youth Summit is proof that young people take the issue of racism seriously. The discussions on your report cover many issues and will ensure that the honest and determined voice of youth will be heard not only in Durban but also far beyond.

You can champion respect for difference. I am glad to hear that in your meetings the point was made that our aim should be more than tolerance—it should be respect for and celebration of difference.

Racism and intolerance thrive on ignorance and fear. You can bring to bear open minds, new ideas, and unique perspectives. Your energy, dynamism, and openness to change bring us hope that you can succeed where previous generations have failed to find solutions.

Today I would like to urge all of you present here: "spread your wings" and build a global network of youth organizations and leaders committed to combating racism. Take advantage of your stay here in Durban to exchange experiences and build bridges. Most of you belong to youth organizations or NGOs. You have a central role to play in instilling respect for difference among your peers.

On 21 March last, the International Day for the Elimination of Racial Discrimination, I invited young people to "take the pledge" to promote equality, justice and dignity throughout their lives. I would like to repeat it here with you: "As a young citizen of the world community, I stand with the United Nations against racism, discrimination and intolerance of any kind. Throughout my life I will try to promote equality, justice and dignity among all people in my home, my community and everywhere in the world."

Letter to European Ministers of the Interior on the Rise of Anti-Semitism
Palais Wilson, Geneva, 3 May 2002

Dear Minister,

I would like to express my deep concern regarding the recent wave of violent attacks against the Jewish community in several European countries and other expressions of anti-Semitism. As you are no doubt aware, these deplorable acts have included anti-Semitic graffiti, the desecration of Jewish cemeteries, physical violence against persons, and vandalism and arson against synagogues and other Jewish symbols. These acts are among the most serious expressions of anti-Semitism in recent decades in Europe.

Although Europe has a long and tragic history of anti-Semitism, including the horrors of the Holocaust that resulted in the physical extermination of six million Jews during the Second World War, the postwar era European leaders have demonstrated their commitment to combating this evil. Notwithstanding this commitment, incidents of anti-Semitism are growing significantly in parts of Europe.

I have taken note with great interest of the appeal issued on 18 April 2002 by the Ministers of the Interior of Belgium, France, Germany, Spain, and the United Kingdom to reinforce the struggle against discrimination and anti-Semitism by the European Union. I am also aware of the measures adopted by the fifteen countries of the European Union on 25 April 2002 to "step up preventive action and the fights against racist violence and anti-Semitism" during a meeting of the Council of Ministers of Justice and the Interior in Luxembourg.

I support the measures announced by the European Union to take strong and decisive action to end this disturbing wave of attacks against the Jewish community and to prosecute vigorously those who have committed illegal acts.

My Office stands ready to assist you in such efforts, and I am available to meet with you and other representatives of the European Union to this end.

Yours sincerely,
Mary Robinson
High Commissioner for Human Rights

Chapter 3

Women's Rights Are Human Rights

As High Commissioner, Mary Robinson gave every emphasis possible to the advancement of women's rights as human rights concerns. As with the post of High Commissioner, an important advance for women stemmed from the Vienna World Conference in 1993. Under the slogan "women's rights are human rights" a clear commitment was made to give priority to confronting the inequality, discrimination, and violence suffered by the world's women. After that Conference a new policy of "mainstreaming" women's rights was adopted throughout the United Nations system and the General Assembly adopted a Declaration on the Elimination of All Forms of Violence against Women on 20 December 1993, the same day that it created the post of High Commissioner for Human Rights.

Placing women's rights and gender concerns at the heart of the human rights agenda was a personal priority for Mary Robinson. This is reflected, for example, in her speeches in 2000 and in the events held to review the progress made in the five years since the adoption of the Declaration and Platform of Action of the Fourth World Conference on Women held in Beijing.

Her speeches in Afghanistan and South Africa highlight conditions that endanger the rights of all but which disproportionately impact on women—namely religious extremism, armed conflict, and poverty. In doing so she recognizes both the suffering and the strength of women. Honoring the impact that women can have on their communities, through events such as Rural Women's Day and its laureate scheme, was but one of many ways she sought to get across the message of the need for women's empowerment, and their centrality to the success of development and reconstruction programmes, as well as to human rights dialogue in general.

"Women's Rights Are Human Rights"
Address to the Afghanistan National Workshop on Women's Rights
Kabul, Afghanistan, International Women's Day, 8 March 2002

Minister, Sima Samar, My Afghan sisters, *Kha haray Afghan azziz* (Dari), *Mehraban khor may* (Pashto),

Today, all over the world, women and men are marking International Women's Day with a particular focus on the women of Afghanistan. What a joy and privilege it is to join so many Afghan women at this special seminar in Kabul.

During decades of civil conflict, the women of Afghanistan demonstrated impressive courage and endurance. You worked hard to look after families and neighbors. You found ways to farm the land and were inventive in the search for income. Many of you had to seek refuge from conflict or drought or from massacres, rapes, abductions, repression, or the bans on education and employment. Yet you found ways to set up home schools and clinics or worked with the United Nations and nongovernmental organizations to bring relief to others. Some of you took additional risks by speaking up—and in some cases paid a heavy price for it. You have worked as teachers, doctors and nurses, law professors, and elected representatives—and have proven that you can ensure the survival of entire families in the harshest of circumstances.

Now that peace and stability can be restored in Afghanistan, it is Afghan women at home and abroad who must speak up about rights and protection from abuse that they have been denied for too long. The Secretary General of the United Nations has said that "true peace and recovery will not come to Afghanistan without a restoration of the rights of women."[1] Only you can decide how best to address, without renouncing your inalienable human rights, the traditional taboos that make it difficult to tackle violence against women in all its forms. One contribution my Office hopes to make is in developing with the authorities and civil society here a program of human rights education. Genuine human rights education must involve those who want to learn more about their human rights. Women must become involved in the planning of human rights education initiatives.

The Struggle for Women's Equality and Human Rights

Women's rights are human rights. So natural, so obvious—yet it has taken decades of struggle by women and their advocates to have this principle accepted and increasingly respected around the world. The strides that women have made are impressive, but the challenges remain enormous. We need to commemorate their achievements today, on International Women's Day, but we should also use this occasion to renew our commitment to the respect and promotion of the rights of all women everywhere. This year when the thoughts of the international community are particularly centered on Afghanistan, we must highlight our solidarity with the women and girls of Afghanistan and our commitment to the restoration of their rights.

Equality of rights for women is a founding principle of the United Nations, laid down over fifty years ago in the preamble of the United Nations Charter. The provisions of the Charter regarding equal rights of women have been further refined and developed in a great number of international human rights instruments. The first and most important of these is the Universal Declaration of Human Rights.

According to the International Covenants on Civil and Political Rights and on Economic, Social and Cultural Rights, states parties should undertake to ensure equal access of men and women for the enjoyment of all rights set forth in each Covenant. The Convention on the Rights of the Child prohibits sex-based discrimination, and the provisions of the Convention on the Elimination of Racial Discrimination and the Convention against Torture are also clearly relevant to the promotion and protection of women's rights.

The international human rights instrument which specifically addresses women's rights is the Convention on the Elimination of All Forms of Discrimination against Women adopted by the General Assembly in 1979 and legally binding on 168 states parties. Afghanistan has signed but not ratified this Convention. The Convention identifies many areas where discrimination against women is widespread, such as political rights, marriage and family, and employment. The Convention also recognizes directly the need for a change in attitudes, through education of both women and men, to accept equality of rights and to overcome prejudices and practices based on stereotyped roles.

The Convention requires states to embody the principle of gender equality in their laws and policies, to adopt legislative and other measures—including sanctions—prohibiting discrimination, and to establish legal protection for women through tribunals and other public institutions. States party to the Convention are also required to undertake positive measures to ensure the full development and advancement of women so that they might enjoy and exercise their rights on the basis of equality with men.

Last year the adoption of an Optional Protocol to the Women's Convention marked the establishment of yet another protection mechanism for women's human rights. Women from countries who accede to the Optional Protocol can submit allegations of violations of their rights to the United Nations if they have not been able to find justice at the national level.

The 1995 Beijing Fourth World Conference on Women adopted a Declaration and Platform of Action which provide a detailed articulation of steps needed for implementation of the human rights of women and of the Convention on the Elimination of All Forms of Discrimination against Women.[2]

Women in Situations of Armed Conflict

War affects everyone—women and men, boys and girls. Yet everyone experiences conflict differently and conflict impacts on everyone, including women and men, differently. History has shown what today's conflicts continue to demonstrate: women and girls are particularly affected by sexual and gender-based violence in wartime.

However, and as the situation of Afghan women and girls proves, women are not only victims in times of armed conflict. Women also play a crucial role in efforts to rebuild the economic, political, and social fabric of societies torn apart by conflict. Women are particularly active in peace movements and are involved in many grassroots peace-building and reconciliation efforts. During conflict, women have often assumed societal roles and responsibilities that go far beyond their status before the war. Yet, time and again, women who were actively involved in rebuilding local economies or in civil society efforts have been ignored during formal peace negotiations.

In recognition of these challenges to women in wartime and in postconflict peace building, the Security Council, in October 2000, adopted resolution 1325 on women, peace, and security.[3] The Security Council emphasized the need to include gender issues in all United Nations efforts on conflict prevention and resolution, peace building, peacekeeping, rehabilitation, and reconstruction efforts. It called for respect for human rights of women and girls, attention to violence against women, and an end to impunity through the prosecution of those responsible for crimes related to sexual and other violence against women and girls. The Security Council also urged increased representation of women, in particular at decision-making levels.

Violence against Women

Yet, the human rights of women and girls continue to be violated also in peacetime. Violence against women, whether in the family, in society, or perpetrated and/or condoned by the state, is pervasive in all societies. Causes of violence against women are linked to sexuality, cultural ideology, patterns of conflict resolution through violence, doctrines of privacy, and government inaction.

The Challenges in Afghanistan

Before I turn to the challenges facing you in Afghanistan, I would like to refer to the Joint Declaration of the Special Rapporteurs on Women's Rights, Ms. Marta Altolaguirre, Ms. Radhika Coomaraswarmy, and Ms. Angel Melo, our sisters from Asia, the Americas, and Africa, that was issued today to celebrate International Women's Day.[4] The Special Rapporteurs referred to the diversity among women and the right of people in community and with other members of their group to enjoy their own culture and the particularities in the different regions regarding the application of women's rights. However, states must not invoke any custom, tradition, or religious consideration to avoid their obligations with respect to the elimination of violence and discrimination against women. All women have the right to live in freedom, equality, and dignity.

And, Minister Samar and other colleagues, that is exactly what you are demanding. At two meetings held in Brussels in December, the Afghan Women's Summit for Democracy[5] and the Roundtable on Building Women's Leadership in Afghanistan,[6] Afghan women talked about their demands and priorities. You asked for participation in decision-making at all levels. You talked about access to education, to health services, or to housing. You emphasized that it would be difficult for women to contribute effectively to the reconstruction of Afghanistan if ways are not found to ensure access to employment, to land and water, or to credit for income-generating activities.

You have asked to be consulted at every stage in postconflict reconstruction because without the full involvement of women, durable peace and stability is not possible. The women and men of Afghanistan will have to work together and bring every contribution to bear to build peace and development for the future. The young will also need to be brought into the process, which must engage the energies of the young men and women and boys and girls who have often known nothing other than conflict and poverty. Afghanistan cannot afford the exclusion of any group or minority from the reconstruction effort.

When Afghan representatives met in Bonn and reached an agreement on how to proceed with peace building, they promised that women would participate in the Interim Authority and in the Emergency Loya Jirga. Mr. Karzai signed the Declaration on the Essential Rights of Afghan Women, which had previously been adopted by Afghan groups. Afghanistan had already committed itself to respecting internationally agreed human rights for both women and men when it ratified the International Covenant on Economic, Social and Cultural Rights; the International Covenant on Civil and Political Rights; and the Convention on the Rights of the Child.

The Human Rights Commission

The Bonn Agreement provides for an independent Human Rights Commission to be set up. Tomorrow my Office will organize a workshop, with participation of Afghan women and men, to assess how we may best support the establishment of a national human rights commission for Afghanistan. Experiences of other national human rights commissions have found that effective promotion of respect for human rights requires that such a body should have a comprehensive mandate covering all rights, not only the right to life and security or to freedom of thought or from arbitrary detention. It is essential that women participate fully in the process to establish the commission. It is essential that women be fully represented in the composition of the commission. The mandate of a national human rights institution should also cover, for example, the rights to education, food, health, and housing. It should be involved also in promoting and protecting the rights of all ethnic groups, of women, of children, and of people with disabilities. In addition to a comprehensive mandate, a national human rights commission needs sufficient resources and the ability to be independent and to listen to all Afghans and their concerns. By helping the Interim Authority to set it up, the international community can ensure that the protection and promotion of the human rights of women will take place in Afghanistan through the efforts of Afghan women and men.

Dealing with the Past

The international community must be ready also to help Afghans ensure that justice is done, to ensure that impunity for past human rights violations will not set the stage for a repetition of the horrors of the past. Those who have suffered from gross human rights violations must have the right to tell their stories so that peace and reconciliation can be set upon strong foundations. The women and men of Afghanistan must decide how to move forward, but they must also be supported, enabled, and encouraged to bring about change in every way they are ready to attempt.

We have realized—thanks to the efforts of the many women and men who have struggled for many years for the cause of women—that the concept of women's rights as human rights does not call only for a focus on nondiscrimination and equal rights of women with men. It is also essential to the achievement of sustainable development. Above all, respect for women's rights as human rights requires the simple acknowledgment that women and girls are entitled to enjoy their human rights not only because they should be equal to men and boys but also because they are human beings.

Minister Samar, my sisters, I have understood well the concerns that you have elaborated here during these three days of discussion. I hear loudly your continuing calls for equal access and enjoyment of all your rights: your right to information, to education and training, to services that promote reproductive health. These are just a few of the messages that I will take back with me and share with my many networks and resources, with your many, many supporters. Your friends, men and women, in civil society from the subregion, region, and world stand behind you ready to assist you in any way we can.

Be bold and aim high. There is now no stopping you.

Good luck. *Mafaq bashed* (Dari). *Kamyaba ussay* (Pashto).

"Women, Human Rights and Sustainable Development in the 21st Century"
Speech at the Gala Dinner for African Women Leaders
Pretoria, South Africa, 31 August 2002

Thank you, Ms. Mbeki.

It is a pleasure to be back in South Africa, and with such an impressive group of women from this continent. I would like to thank Zanele Mbeki for giving me this opportunity to address you as I come to the end of my term as United Nations High Commissioner for Human Rights.

It is hardly a secret that during my five years as High Commissioner and in my previous position as President of Ireland, Africa—all of Africa, all of this beautiful continent, north, south, east and west, and all its peoples—has been close to my heart. And I hope it will not be a surprise that in the work I plan to do in the future, Africa will be a focus.

Let me recognize our South African friends for the important contribution they have made by hosting a number of international summits. Last year it was the Durban World Conference against Racism, Racial Discrimination, Xenophobia and Related Intolerance. This year it is the Summit on Sustainable Development in Johannesburg. As Secretary General of the Durban Conference and an active participant at the Johannesburg Summit, I have a true understanding of the enormous workload and responsibility that have fallen two years in a row on the government and people of South Africa. Such efforts at global dialogue are not expected to end with everyone agreeing on everything. But one thing agreed on by all at Durban was the open generosity and wonderful welcome offered by South Africans to their visitors from all parts of the world. I am sure that after the Johannesburg Summit there will be equal agreement.

In Durban, with the help and support of women and men from around the world, we recognized the multiple forms of inequality that can affect women. The Durban Conference acknowledged that women are often discriminated against both because of their gender and because of their race, language, ethnicity, or religion. The Durban Declaration and Programme of Action calls for an end to the racial and gender discrimination experienced by women. We owe that success in great part to African women—starting with a group of women ambassadors from African countries in Geneva and continuing with the able leadership of Dr. Nkosazana Dlamini Zuma, President of the Durban Conference.

African women have an opportunity at the current World Summit for Sustainable Development to remind the world that denial of the human rights of women is one of the greatest obstacles to the achievement of sustainable development. The Millennium Development Goals include the promotion of gender equality and empowerment of women. It is not only a goal in itself but one that will be crucial to the achievement of progress on most of the other goals set as we entered this new century.

Respect for the human rights of women will be crucial in achieving the objectives of the Johannesburg Summit. On every continent women suffer from unacceptable discrimination that limits their access to, and control over, productive resources. In every country women are underrepresented in the decision-making process, denied an equal opportunity to shape the environmental and development policies that determine whether development will take place and, if so, whether it will be on a sustainable basis. And yet the failure to achieve sustainable development has as great, and in many cases a greater, impact on women than on men.

Women's Human Rights

In my remarks this evening I should like to offer *un tour d'horizon* of women's human rights achievements, possibilities, and challenges; and I would like to place these in the perspective of all our preoccupations at this Summit, sustainable development.

We often talk about the right to development, about the right of every individual to enjoy the full range of civil, economic, political, social and cultural rights that will allow all persons to develop their own capacities to their maximum potential. But it is only recently that we have acknowledged the simple fact that "women's rights are human rights." So natural, so obvious—yet it has taken decades of struggle by women and their advocates to have this principle accepted and, happily, increasingly respected around the world. The progress that has been made is impressive, but the challenges before us are enormous.

Equality of rights for women is a founding principle of the United Nations, set down over fifty years ago in the Charter of the United Nations. These provisions have been further refined and developed in a great number of international human rights instruments. The first and most important of these is the Universal Declaration of Human Rights. It is fitting that the name we associate with the adoption of that instrument, a milestone in the history of the cause of human rights, is that of another great woman, Eleanor Roosevelt. So let us not forget that at every stage of the battle, women have been involved in the human rights cause, and that the rights of women encompass the right to freedom from want.

The international Covenants on Civil and Political Rights and on Economic, Social and Cultural Rights require states parties to undertake to ensure equal access of men and women to the enjoyment of all rights set forth in each Covenant. The Convention on the Rights of the Child prohibits sex-based discrimination, as do other core human rights instruments. Every country in the world has ratified at least one of these treaties. Every country in the world has voluntarily accepted the obligation to respect, protect, and promote the right of women to be free from discrimination in the enjoyment of human rights. In Africa, article 18 of the African Charter on Human and People's Rights obliges states parties to ensure that *every* form of discrimination against women is eliminated, while asserting the duty of every individual to preserve positive African cultural values in the spirit of tolerance, dialogue, and consultation.

The international human rights instrument that specifically addresses women's rights is the Convention on the Elimination of All Forms of Discrimination against Women (CEDAW), adopted by the General Assembly in 1979 and legally binding on its now 170 states parties. Over 90 percent of African countries have ratified this Convention (and all but one have ratified the Convention on the Rights of the Child). The CEDAW Convention identifies many specific areas where discrimination against women is widespread, such as political rights, marriage and family, and employment. The Convention addresses specifically, in article 14, the discrimination suffered by rural women and their right to participate in the elaboration of development policies, and to have access to health services, information and education, and agricultural resources. It also recognizes specifically the need for a change in attitudes, through education of both women and men, to accept equality of rights and to overcome prejudices and practices based on stereotyped roles. The adoption in 2000 of an Optional Protocol to the Women's Convention, providing an individual complaint mechanism, represents another gain for advancement of women's human rights. The 1995 Beijing Fourth World Conference gave us a detailed set of steps needed if the Convention on the Elimination of All Forms of Discrimination against Women is to be fully implemented.[7]

There have been in Africa and elsewhere significant legislative changes that implement international commitments and enhance women's opportunities. There is the constant advocacy by women's groups everywhere that uses international standards to push for change. There are many interesting partnership projects on sustainable development involving women, governments, and international donors.

Women and Poverty

The struggle for women's equality through pushing for implementation of legal standards has to be linked to the struggle for sustainable development in an unequal world. I am often asked: "What do you think is the worst human rights problem in our world today?" I reply: "Extreme poverty." Extreme poverty means a denial of the exercise of all human rights and undermines the dignity and worth of the individual.

It is now widely accepted that unless the problems of poverty are addressed, there can be no sustainable development. The draft Plan of Implementation for the World Summit on Sustainable Development acknowledges that eradicating poverty is the greatest global challenge facing the world today.

It is painfully clear that the inequities within and between developed and developing countries are not diminishing but growing. Extreme poverty is the lifelong experience of millions of people, and the numbers are growing. Recently the President of the World Bank, in discussing world poverty, said:

> Poverty remains a global problem of huge proportions. Of the world's 6 billion people, 2.8 billion live on less than US$ 2 per day, and 1.2 billion live on less than 1 dollar a day. Six infants of every 100 do not see their first birthday and 8 do not survive to their fifth. Of those who do reach school age, 9 boys in 100 and 14 girls do not go to primary school.[8]

Behind such shocking statistics lies the reality of underdevelopment and powerlessness of human beings and human communities. Poverty is a global phenomenon, challenging communities in the North as well as the South. But there is no denying that the greatest burden of extreme poverty is in Africa. To give but one illustration: in sub-Saharan Africa twelve countries had net enrollment rates in primary school of less than 50 percent in the 1990s. It is estimated that the number of children out of school could be as high as fifty-four million by 2015, the date when the Millennium Declaration agreed that all children everywhere will complete primary education.

We know that women's poverty is directly related to the absence of economic opportunities and autonomy; lack of access to economic resources, including credit, land ownership, and inheritance; lack of access to education and support services; and minimal participation in the decision-making process. Poverty can also be a factor in forcing women into situations in which they are vulnerable to violence and exploitation. A concern throughout my time as High Commissioner has been the pernicious traffic in women and girls in all parts of the world. Indeed, just two weeks ago I visited Cambodia and urged greater urgency in that society and in the region in tackling human trafficking.[9] It is a trade that is directly linked to poverty and the powerlessness of poor women and children.

The Human Rights Approach to Poverty Eradication

Human rights is about the empowerment of the poor. The most fundamental way in which empowerment occurs is through introduction of the concept of rights itself. Once this concept is introduced to the context of policy-making, the rationale of poverty reduction no longer derives merely from the fact that the poor have needs but also that they have rights—entitlements that give rise to legal obligations on others. By introducing the dimension of international legal obligation, the human rights perspective adds legitimacy to the demand for making poverty eradication a primary goal of policy-making. The human rights perspective in policies aimed at poverty reduction recognizes that poverty signifies nonrealization of human rights and, therefore, that the adoption of a poverty reduction strategy is not just desirable but obligatory on the part of the states that have ratified international human rights instruments.

Human rights norms and standards contribute to the empowerment of the poor, including women living in poverty, because they emphasize the notion of accountability, the principles of universality, nondiscrimination, and equality; the principle of participatory decision-making; and the recognition of interdependence of rights. A human rights approach to poverty eradication will have all these features as its essential characteristics.

The right to equality and the principle of nondiscrimination deserve particular attention in addressing the issue of women living in poverty. The poor are often victims of discrimination on various grounds, such as their birth, property, national and social origin, race, color, gender, and religion. As discrimination may cause poverty, poverty also causes discrimination. In addition to their gender, women living in poverty are also subject to discriminatory attitudes by governmental authorities and private actors because they are poor. If governments are responsible for such discrimination, they are under an obligation to immediately prohibit and cease all discriminatory laws and practices. If discriminatory attitudes toward women are caused by traditions, often deeply rooted, governments must adopt and enforce laws prohibiting such discrimination by private actors. In both cases the twin principles of equality and nondiscrimination require governments to take special measures in order to provide to their most vulnerable, discriminated, and socially excluded groups, including poor women, effective protection against discrimination by governmental authorities as well as by private actors.

Perhaps the most important point is that the human rights approach emphasizes the accountability of policy-makers and other actors whose actions have an impact on the rights of people. Rights imply duties, and duties demand accountability. It is, therefore, an intrinsic feature of the human rights approach that any poverty-reduction strategy should include institutions and legal/administrative provisions for ensuring accountability.

I have enthusiastically welcomed the adoption of the New Partnership for Africa's Development (NEPAD) precisely because it represents an important step by Africans to address issues of development while acknowledging the importance of accountability.[10] NEPAD's emphasis on peer review, I would argue, must be accompanied by mutual accountability that involves both African states and the rest of the world. This principle is equally relevant to the discussions at the Johannesburg Summit. I hope also that the principle of gender equality will be recognized as fundamental to the success of NEPAD and the institutions of the new African Union.

Women's Participation in Public Decision-Making

At the Rio Earth Summit and the Beijing World Conference on Women, the global community stressed the importance of women assuming positions of power and influence, not only because their points of view and talents are needed, but also as a matter of their human rights.

Agenda 21 of the Rio Conference and the Beijing Platform for Action in particular recognized that women have an essential role to play in the development of sustainable and ecologically sound consumption and production patterns. However, and in spite of the many impressive examples among you today, women remain largely absent at all levels of policy formulation and decision-making in natural resource and environmental management. Their experience and skills in natural resource management remain too often marginalized in policy-making and decision-making bodies.

And where women have managed to break through to the political stage, stereotyping, including that perpetrated by the media, often confines women in political life to issues such as the environment, children, and health and excludes them from responsibility for finance, budgetary control, and conflict resolution. We must find ways to ensure that women like you, leaders who play an active role in the pursuit of sustainable development, become the rule rather than the exception.

I was in East Timor last week, a beautiful country whose people have suffered so much to be born as a nation. It was a very positive thing to learn that one-fourth of those elected in 2001 to the Constituent Assembly were women.

Nevertheless, let us recall the statistic globally: according to the United Nations Development Programme, in only sixteen out of the almost two hundred countries in our world does women's representation exceed 25 percent in the national parliament. Or in average women accounted for 11 percent of parliamentarians world wide in 1999 compared with 9 percent in 1987. Such gender disparities in public positions carry a clear message: progress is not inevitable and there is much more to be done.

The draft Plan of Implementation for the World Summit on Sustainable Development calls on governments to promote women's equal access to and full participation, on the basis of equality with men, in decision-making at all levels. Let us ensure that this language remains in the final document.

Impact of HIV/AIDS on Women's Poverty and Empowerment

HIV/AIDS provides a striking example of the interrelationship between health, human rights, and sustainable development. AIDS and poverty are now mutually reinforcing negative forces in many developing countries and are impediments to economic growth and sustainable development in the hardest-hit areas.

As you know, women are disproportionately affected by the epidemic, sometimes as a consequence of sexual violence. They suffer the highest rate of infection in certain countries, while they also bear the burden of caring for ailing family members and a growing number of orphans. Women often do not have the power to insist on safe and responsible sex practices and have little access to information and services for prevention and treatment. Around the world, women's enhanced physiological risk of HIV infection is compounded by economic deprivation; by lack of employment opportunities; by poor access to education, training, and information; and by sociocultural norms and practices.

The promotion and protection of human rights contribute to reducing vulnerability to HIV infection by addressing root causes, including stigma and discrimination. National human rights institutions in Ghana, India, and South Africa have launched activities that promote and protect HIV/

AIDS-related human rights in their countries. The Southern African Development Community (SADC) Parliamentary Forum has set up a Standing Committee on HIV/AIDS, which is developing strategic work plans to address HIV/AIDS-related issues. Promoting gender equality through increased respect for women's rights will be a crucial part in the development of any successful strategy against the epidemic.

Women's Equal Rights to Land and Property

One of the specific rights of women to which the UN Commission on Human Rights has been paying particular attention in recent years is the denial of women's equal right to land, housing, and property. Access to housing or inheritance is linked to poverty, and discrimination suffered by women in this regard is a factor in the overrepresentation of women among the poor. Gender discrimination in access to land and other productive resources is not only a factor in keeping women in poverty but also a major obstacle to bringing about sustainable development. Addressing discrimination against women in these areas can be a particularly daunting challenge, as gender disparities can result from the impact of a complex web of multiple legal systems (statutory, customary, religious, etc.), of social practices based on tradition, and even of the inadvertent consequences of well-intentioned development policies and programs.

Yet, the experience of some African countries shows that such problems can be addressed. African women and men, working together, have introduced legal reforms that target the discrimination suffered by women in this area of crucial importance to poverty and development. In Tanzania land legislation has explicitly recognized women's equal rights to land, including clauses (for example, on consent and information) to protect women's interests and prevent their exclusion from the land.

Some countries have also provided for representation of women in bodies taking decisions involving land; other forms of affirmative action are helping to ensure that women play a role in the taking of decisions. Uniform laws on succession can also address the discriminatory treatment of inheritance under traditions and customary laws that are still widely applied in many countries and prevent widows—and sometimes also daughters—from inheriting. Policies that deny credit to women without the consent of a male relative, or because they rarely hold family assets in their own name, must be reformed. Women must be recruited to serve as agricultural extension workers and given access to the information and inputs that can improve agricultural productivity.

These are issues that can be addressed by determined intervention, through appropriate formulation of legislation and policies and through awareness-raising campaigns that increase women's knowledge of their own rights. The examples of good practice that are available from many African countries provide useful suggestions on how improving respect for the equal right of women to land and other property can also reduce poverty and deliver more sustainable forms of development.

Violence against Women

Armed conflict impacts severely on progress to sustainable development, including in Africa, but not least in Africa. War affects everyone—women and men, boys and girls. Yet everyone experiences conflict differently and conflict impacts on everyone, including women and men, differently. History has shown what today's conflicts continue to demonstrate: women and girls are particularly affected by sexual and gender-based violence in wartime.

Conflict is not the only source of violence against women that impedes sustainable development. When the World Bank launched a major project to collect information on the views of poor people, one of the results that many found surprising was the extent to which poor women identified domestic violence as one of their greatest concerns, and an important obstacle to their escaping poverty. Violence within the family and in society is a barrier to the empowerment of women and their increased participation in public and economic life.

As President of Ireland, I supported rape crisis centers in my own country. As High Commissioner for Human Rights, I have seen the effects of violence against women in victims of trafficking in Cambodia, in victims of rape and forced marriage in Afghanistan, and in many other women of too many countries. I have also seen the strength of women who have overcome abuse and exploitation to play a role in the development of their communities.

Violence is regularly inflicted on many women, a shameful ongoing gross violation of human rights that takes many forms and plagues all societies. Governments must act on their special responsibility to protect women from sexual, physical, and psychological violence, a duty which is too often neglected or ignored. We cannot accept without rebellion that girls may drop out of school in fear of their teachers and classmates, that boys and men may believe themselves entitled to impose their will on women, and that women believe that their male relatives have the right to punish them. Above all, we cannot accept that women around the world should continue to be in many cases justifiably afraid of the treatment they will receive, from the legal system and the authorities that should protect them, if they dare to denounce their aggressors.

As Radhika Coomaraswarmy—the Sri Lankan independent expert who reports to the UN Commission on Human Rights on Violence against Women—has said, many practices that violate the rights of women have avoided human rights scrutiny because they are seen as cultural practices that deserve tolerance and respect. Even the forms of abuse that everyone recognizes as domestic violence can be difficult to condemn if tradition and culture allow men to abuse women or insist that family privacy is more important than the rights of the women or children who are abused.

Dear friends, you, the women leaders of this continent, are the ones who need to speak up about the rights and the protection from abuse you are denied—and only you can decide how best to address the traditional taboos that make it difficult to do so. Afghan women have already done this.

Only you can work out what will be the best strategies in each of your communities to address the problems and to build upon your strengths to claim your own rights. Ratification of the CEDAW Convention and other legal standards on gender equality and on the rights of women provide a reference in the search for sustainable development policies. Many of you already know about the human rights that the world has long agreed should be enjoyed by every woman—and every man. Others will want to know more. This is not something that women can be "taught" but something they must "learn." As I have already said, when referring to poverty, the most fundamental way in which women can be empowered is the introduction of the concept of rights—and that applies to the adoption of all development and environmental policies as much as to the fight against poverty.

I would like to pay tribute to the role many of you play, as women and as leaders in your own governments and civil societies. As I have said to other groups of women leaders around the world, we are the fortunate ones, free to be here and express ourselves. We must recommit ourselves to those who are not so fortunate and help them to secure their future. Women, like men, must be given a chance to develop their full potential. The girls and boys of today, and those of tomorrow, have the right to live in societies that give priority to the elimination of poverty and the pursuit of sustainable development. It will not happen without increased respect and protection of the rights of women. The women and men of Africa have the right to contribute to the process of sustainable development, and the obligation to do so. The international community has the duty to support you in your efforts.

World Rural Women's Day Message
Palais Wilson, Geneva, 15 October 1999

We have come here today to celebrate World Rural Women's Day and to pay tribute to the many courageous and creative women around the world, in particular to this year's six laureates from Burkina Faso, Bolivia, Honduras, Albania, Ireland, and Latvia. All are women who have exhibited outstanding leadership in improving the quality of life in rural communities and in claiming their right to development, peace, and leadership.

Rural women make a tremendous contribution to food and agricultural production. They also play a crucial role in determining and guaranteeing food security and well-being for the entire household. Equitable, effective, and sustainable agriculture and rural development cannot be pursued without an explicit recognition of these realities. In a global atmosphere of increasing poverty, food insecurity, rural out-migration, and environmental degradation, all potential actors in development must be given the support and access to resources they need to pursue sustainable livelihoods and strategies for a better life. Within this context, women's empowerment will be central to raising levels of nutrition, improving production and distribution of food and agricultural products, and enhancing the living conditions of rural populations.

Rural women comprise more than one-quarter of the total world population. Five hundred million women live below the poverty line in rural areas: women produce 60 to 80 percent of basic foodstuffs in sub-Saharan Africa and the Caribbean. Women perform 30 percent of the agricultural work in industrialized countries. They head 60 percent of households in certain regions of Africa, as well as meeting 90 percent of household water and fuel needs.

Poverty isn't just about lack of material possessions. What is sometimes far worse is the exclusion that comes with extreme poverty—having no voice, no standing, and no role in a community. The promotion of women's rights means the promotion of freedom, justice, and the peaceful resolution of disputes; of social progress and better standards of living; of equality, tolerance, and dignity.

We are only now beginning to understand more fully that true freedom is made up of a complex tapestry of rights, all of which must be addressed equally and protected. As the world celebrates this day, let us spread the message that women's rights are the responsibility of everyone.

The role of the United Nations as the guardian of women's rights must go beyond rhetorical support. Practical and creative measures to realize the human rights of women—civil and political rights; economic, social, and cultural rights; and the right to development—are a priority for my Office and must be for every part of the United Nations.

Let us reaffirm our commitment to promoting and protecting the full enjoyment of basic human rights for all women. Women's equal dignity and human rights are affirmed in the basic declarations and instruments of the international community, but these rights have yet to be realized in practice. Women must be empowered to be leaders and agents of change, because only in that way can they make a real difference.

I extend my warm congratulations to the six laureates being honored here today, for their commitment and endurance, for their hope and their courage, and to the many women and men who have worked by their side.

Fighting for women's rights is a positive struggle, which recognizes the quality of women's contribution to every aspect of the community. I therefore invite everyone here today to renew their energies in undertaking practical and creative initiatives to achieve full respect for the human rights of women.

Realizing Women's Human Rights, the Challenges
Opening remarks at the UN Panel on Beijing+5 Review Conference
United Nations, New York, 8 June 2000

My appreciation goes to DAW and UNIFEM for cosponsoring this panel.[11] My thanks to the panelists for bringing together their voices to speak on the challenges before us in realizing women's human rights, to the representative from CEDAW who will chair the panel, and, finally, to the staff in my office who contributed to making this event possible.

The Fourth World Conference on Women and the Beijing Declaration and Platform for Action together represented a landmark in the cause of achieving human rights for all women.[12] The five-year review of the Beijing Declaration and Platform for Action currently under way provides us with the opportunity to evaluate the facts on what progress has been made. The first aim should be to consolidate the progress made up to and at Beijing. There must be no moving away from commitments made.

The Beijing Platform for Action notes, "unless the human rights of women, as defined by international human rights instruments, are fully recognized and effectively protected, applied, implemented, and enforced in national law as well as in national practice in family, civil, penal, labor and commercial codes, and administrative rules and regulations, they will exist in name only."

Protecting the human rights of women has become a central objective of the United Nations, and the outcome of the five-year review of Beijing will be crucial to continuing successful efforts to protect women's human rights.

It is clear that respect for human rights is essential if we are to reach the strategic objectives in all the critical areas set out in the Beijing Platform for Action. Ensuring that human rights makes its contribution will require the identification of the means by which respect for human rights can be integrated into the work under each critical area. It is also important to bring closer together the work on human rights of the Commission on the Status of Women, the Commission on Human Rights, the Committee on the Elimination of Discrimination against Women, and the other human rights treaty bodies.

Continued Discrimination against Women

A lot of ground has to be made up. The rights of millions of women continue to be denied, year after year. The fundamental right to equality has been affirmed and reaffirmed repeatedly in conferences and other public forums in which governments participate. Yet in an overwhelming number of countries, laws remain in force that perpetuate discrimination with regard to personal status, economic status, marital status, and recourse against violence. And it is not only the existence of these laws on the statute book that acts against women. Discrimination in the enforcement of the law, denial of equal opportunity in education and employment, denial of property and inheritance rights, exclusion of women from political representation, deprivation of sexual and reproductive rights, and the use of social forces and physical violence to intimidate and subordinate women all constitute fundamental violations of the human right to equality as well.

The Beijing+5 review presents an opportunity to reflect on the meaning of a human-rights-based approach to women's issues and lives. It is an opportunity to strengthen the language and thinking around the various treaty bodies and their role in monitoring the implementation of women's human rights, as well as that of the mandates entrusted to the specialized mechanisms. It is an opportunity to underscore, within the international community, the importance of developing and implementing systematic performance standards to measure the extent to which states discharge their obligations for the protection and promotion of women's human rights.

The Responsibility to Act

The question of responsibility for ensuring the protection of rights has been an issue at this Review Conference. Clearly, as a matter of law, responsibility lies with the state. Within that responsibility, the state must ensure that its national laws and development policies give effect, not just to the commitments made in the Beijing Platform for Action, but also to its international legal obligations to respect and protect human rights, and to do so without discrimination. Each sovereign state is part of an international order, created in the Charter of the United Nations and developed subsequently through both law and practice.

The state is not the sole actor. The impact of globalization, the patterns of economic development, migration, and armed conflict all require the integrated response which the Beijing Platform for Action skillfully attempted to produce. I would be concerned at any movement away from this. The effective protection of human rights requires the NGO sector, the government, and the international community to work together—indeed, that is one of the findings of the review; it is vital to ensure its continuance. Governments should draw up national plans of action together with representatives of civil society, who should also cooperate with the government in the implementation process.

Justifications advanced for inequality on the basis of national, cultural, religious, and historical considerations have often placed the human rights of women in danger. I would cite as examples of particular concern the fact that certain states still refuse to recognize marital rape and do not condemn so-called honor killings, or which deny access to reproductive health services to prevent the death of so many women. Violations of such an egregious nature cannot under any circumstances be acceptable. States must adopt not only measures of protection but also positive measures in all areas so as to achieve the effective and equal empowerment of women.

If they fail to protect and promote women's civil, political, economic, and social rights, governments create situations in which violations can occur. This will lead to sexual and economic exploitation of women in both the home and the community and within local, national, and global economies. States have often failed in their attempts to provide basic economic and social rights to all people, particularly to women, and have further entrenched sex-based divisions. Basic rights, such as to food, shelter, education, reproductive health, sustainable living, and peace, have been denied to a large percentage of the world's population, of which women comprise a large portion. Putting the right to development and economic, social, and cultural rights at the top of the agenda for the promotion and protection of human rights is both necessary and timely. There is growing recognition of the importance of all rights—civil, cultural, economic, political, and social—and of the fact that economic, social, and cultural rights have not been sufficiently emphasized over the years.

Role of National Human Rights Institutions

One of many ways to move from rhetoric to action is by strengthening and supporting the role that national human rights institutions can play in the promotion and protection of women's human rights. An example is the recent workshop organized in Fiji with the Asia-Pacific Forum on the role of national human rights institutions in advancing the international human rights of women.[13] Some of the conclusions were the following:

The Workshop expressed deep regret and concern at reports of the increasing incidence of violence against women and children in the region.

Participants urged governments to ensure that all international standards relating to the rights of women are effectively implemented and widely disseminated across all levels of society, with particular emphasis on youth. The Workshop called on governments to cooperate with NGOs in the preparation of their reports to CEDAW and to draw on NGO expertise in fulfilling their obligations to comply with the Convention.

The Workshop called on governments to create and/or strengthen national mechanisms for the advancement of the rights of women. It also called on governments to integrate gender perspectives into legislation, discussions that underpin industry and trade agreements and global initiatives considered by government, public policies, educational curriculum and other relevant programs and projects and to incorporate such measures within constitutional frameworks.

The Workshop welcomed the establishment of national institutions for the promotion and protection of human rights in many countries of the Asia Pacific Region. Participants called on the UN General Assembly to recognize the important role of national human rights institutions in the promotion and protection of the rights of women.

For the Beijing+5 review to be successful, it must address the failings and shortcomings which exist and come up with innovative strategies to implement full equal rights for women. The legal base is there in the principles of equality and nondiscrimination, which form an integral part of international law. And the standards have been set out in detail in the Beijing Declaration and Platform for Action. The challenge is to implement these agreed standards in practice.

Human rights are directly relevant to how we shape our future. The challenge we face is to build on the achievements of Beijing. That means assessing if governments have lived up to their promises of five years ago. It means taking stock of the pace of ratification of relevant international conventions and treaties, of institutional measures to advance women and remove discrimination, and of steps taken to tackle violence against women and poverty among women.

This panel presents an opportunity to reflect on the meaning of a human-rights-based approach to women's issues and lives, and to the challenges ahead for realizing women's human rights. It is an opportunity to underscore, within the international community, the importance of developing and implementing systematic performance standards to measure the extent to which states discharge their obligations for the protection and promotion of women's human rights.

I look forward to hearing the views of our distinguished panel.

Thank you.

Chapter 4

Eliminating Religious Discrimination and Intolerance

Religion or belief as a ground for discrimination against individuals and groups, especially minorities, has been a relatively neglected topic for the international human rights movement. The General Assembly adopted a Declaration on the Elimination of All Forms of Religious Intolerance and Discrimination in 1981. It has been the normative framework since that date for many initiatives. In 1993 the Commission on Human Rights established a Special Rapporteur to be concerned with the implementation of the 1981 Declaration and to respond to complaints from those persecuted on grounds of their faith or beliefs. In her Oslo lecture below Mary Robinson sets out these developments in protection and explores the spiritual foundations of human rights in the different religious traditions.

As High Commissioner, she sought to involve the religions in the human rights movement, including in the World Conference against Racism held in Durban in 2001. She had also sought to develop dialogue with Islam on universal human rights. At the request of the President of Iran she hosted a seminar on Islam and human rights in 1998 and supported a second such event held by the Islamic Conference in 2002.

"Sacred Rights: Faith Leaders on Tolerance and Respect"
Book Launch
Palais Wilson, Geneva, 15 June 2001

Excellencies, Representatives of Faiths, Ladies, and Gentlemen,

I am happy to welcome you to Palais Wilson as we launch the book *Sacred Rights: Faith Leaders on Tolerance and Respect.* I am particularly pleased that Bawa Jain, the Secretary General of the Millennium World Peace Summit of Religious and Spiritual Leaders, is able to be with us this evening. Thanks are due him for his commitment in ensuring that the book was published. I think that it is a very attractive book, both in appearance and layout and also in its thoughtful and thought-provoking content. The range of spiritual and religious leaders who have contributed is wide, starting with His Holiness Patriarch Alexy II and ending with His Excellency Sheikh Fawzi al-Zafzaf.

This book illustrates that, across the broad range of religious faiths, the human person enjoys a certain sacred status or dignity, and this applies to every member of the one human family. The sacredness of the human person and the oneness of the human family provide in religious perspective the basis for the human rights of every individual and for the religious rejection of discrimination or intolerance on the basis of race or gender or any other particular difference. This unanimous condemnation of racism by religious leaders the world over should strengthen the hearts and actions not only of their own followers but even of those without religious conviction and who may have seen religious difference as at least compounding racial and other divisions in the past.

We must recognize that difference has often been perceived as a threat. The stranger, or in some language the other, has prompted fear of the unknown. In many cultures this has led, and still leads, to exclusion and discrimination. Religion has been used as a pretext to separate communities and to stir up distrust of those regarded as different. Great wrongs have been done in religion's name; wars have even been fought in religion's name.

But we also know the power of faith, which has moved people to stand up for human rights and against injustice. I think of Martin Luther King Jr., Dietrich Bonhoeffer, Archbishop Desmond Tutu.

I see our task as being not merely to be tolerant and accepting of difference but to champion diversity. In order to move beyond what Chief Rabbi Jonathan Sachs calls the merely passive refusal to exaggerate or exploit differences, it is necessary, as he suggests, to understand and respect differences. This can be a slow and painful task of education, particularly in situations where historical divisions and their emotional overlay still persist. The great religions, with their tradition in education, can contribute enormously to this educational task, both through their own teaching as already touched on in this book and, more profoundly still, by the living examples of that teaching in their structures and practices.

The Patriarch of Ethiopia points out that for many religious traditions human diversity is God given, not only to be respected and understood but to be celebrated. This is also the message of the General Secretary of the World Council of Churches. Difference should be seen as a gift. Gender difference is in some ways a very obvious gift, and in religious traditions it is regarded as of clearly divine origin and blessing. This has not, however, prevented gender from being at times a source of painful oppression rather than a source of joyous celebration. The emergence of different racial and ethnic groups has an even more ambiguous history, and the celebration that should follow respect and understanding has only recently begun.

In religious terms, celebration of difference implies a celebration of the diverse gifts of different peoples and their cultures and of their creator. The Emir of Kano quotes in confirmation from the Qu'ran: "Oh mankind! We created you from a male and female, and have made you nations and tribes that you may know one another. Loa! The noblest of you, in the sight of Allah, is the best in conduct." In similar vein, the Reverend Billy Graham quotes from the Christian Scriptures about God's determination to bring into His eternal Kingdom people "from every tribe and language and people and nation."

Solidarity is a concept we need to embrace in our increasingly interdependent, multicultural world. Pope John Paul II emphasizes this approach: "The Church . . . feels itself in solidarity with all those who are victims of discrimination for racial, ethnic, religious or social reasons."

The richness of religious traditions provides much food for further reflection and, above all, for effective action toward the abolition of racism and all forms of prejudice and intolerance. The sense of joy in and celebration of human difference is the positive and liberating dimension of campaigns against racism which religions and their leaders are equipped to promote. One idea which may be worth considering is for the religions and faiths to organize—in addition to or in conjunction with the International Day for the Elimination of Racial Discrimination—an annual interreligious and international day of celebration of human diversity. This would, of course, include clear condemnation of racism and its associates, but the primary emphasis would be on the enriching character of human diversity, with special reference and outreach to those suffering discrimination in a particular region of the world.

Throughout the preparations for Durban, my aim has been to engage all sectors of society in the process so that the decisions and outcome of the Conference are truly representative. That is why I warmly welcome the engagement by religious and spiritual leaders. Their thoughts and beliefs will be an inspiration for all concerned with fighting racism, discrimination, xenophobia and related intolerance. By bringing these contributions together, this book will serve as an enrichment of our preparations for the Durban Conference.

"Human Rights, Hope and History"
Oslo Conference on Freedom of Religion or Belief
University of Oslo, Norway, 13 August 1998

I am grateful for the liberating experience of coming here to Oslo, leaving behind the day-to-day pressures of practical promotion and protection of human rights, in order to reflect with you on one of the most basic freedoms of all: the freedom of religion and belief. It is fitting, during this special anniversary year of the Universal Declaration of Human Rights, to look back to the vision of fifty years ago.

Human Rights, History, and Hope

The Universal Declaration may, like other major documents, assume such a significance in itself that its historical antecedents and cultural biases are ignored or forgotten. For all its fine achievements and continuing potential in the service of a more just and equitable human society, the Declaration has to be understood as the fruit of a long and complex history. Many of its particular provisions—including that of immediate concern to this conference, freedom of religion and belief—were bitterly disputed, and not just in intellectual and parliamentary debate but on the battlefield.

The developing phase in the history of human rights over the last fifty years of interpretation and implementation of the Declaration has opened it up to new perspectives and challenges in cultural conditions much more diverse than its Western roots had offered. Václav Havel, in a challenging speech delivered last March in Geneva at a special event to mark the fiftieth anniversary, noted:

> The emphasis placed in that document on human rights helped to put an end to the bipolar division of the world. It added momentum to the opposition movements in the communist countries who took the accords signed by their governments seriously, and intensified their struggle for the observance of human rights, thus challenging the very essence of totalitarian systems.

Later he spelled out his personal vision:

> I am convinced that the deepest roots of that which we now call human rights lie somewhat beyond us, and above us; somewhere deeper than the world of human covenants—in a realm that I would, for simplicity's sake, describe as metaphysical. Although they may fail to realize this, human beings—the only creatures who are fully aware of their own being and of their mortality, and who perceive their surroundings as a world and have an inner relationship to that world—derive their dignity, as well as their responsibility, from the world as a whole; that is from that in which they see the world's central theme, its backbone, its order, its direction, its essence, its soul—name it as you will. Christians put it quite simply: man is here in the image of God.
>
> The world has markedly changed in the past fifty years. There are many more of us on this planet now; the colonial system has fallen apart; the bipolar division is gone; globalization is advancing at a dizzying pace. The Euro-American culture that largely molded the character of our present civilization is no longer the predominant. We are entering an era of multi-culturalism. While the world is now enveloped by one single global civilization, this civilization is based on coexistence of many cultures, religions or spheres of civilization that are equal and equally powerful.[1]

The values and validity of the Declaration will, one hopes, be deepened and extended by these challenges. It is, after all, a living document written in the present tense. It is intended to be revisited and enriched by the insights of each generation.

The Declaration is now as much a matter of hope as of history. There is the hope that it will prove equal to the cultural and political challenges.

There is above all the hope for a human community that through the fuller realization of these rights will flourish in the justice, peace, and unity of deeper diversity. After another half-century of human rights endeavor it may be that hope and history will more closely rhyme.

The Long-Contested Right: Freedom of Religion and of Belief

In the difficult historical pursuit of human rights, their articulation, and implementation, a critical element has been the close affiliation between religion and ethno-political identity. This was very marked in Europe, where it issued in a particularly savage series of religious wars, the remnants of which are still with us. But it was not peculiar to Europe or to its major religions. Tolerance and protection of the religiously different have been rare enough practices in the history of humanity. So article 18 was one of the crucial articles in the vision represented by the Universal Declaration and is worth quoting in full: "Everyone has the right to freedom of thought, conscience and religion; this right includes freedom to change his religion or belief, and freedom, either alone or in community with others and in public or private, to manifest his religion or belief in teaching, practice, worship and observance."

The subsequent 1981 UN Declaration on the Elimination of All Forms of Intolerance and of Discrimination Based on Religion or Belief spells out in considerable detail the further implications of article 18 for which the Special Rapporteur has been created and which are being addressed in this conference.[2] For now I wish to stress the contested history forming the background to the cool and classic expression of religious freedom in article 18. That stress calls attention to how far we have come in this as in other areas. At the same time it sounds a note of warning about how long and how difficult the journey may yet be. The hope of humanity for the flourishing in communion which the ancient Hebrews called *shalom* lies, at least in part, in the universal and effective implementation of freedom of religion and belief. It may not be presumptuous to add that the hope for religion's flourishing is also closely associated with the acceptance of this principle.

Person as Foundation; Community as Context

The language of human rights, as the phrase goes, betokens both its personal and social dimensions. A language is at once a social construction and a personal possession. The search for personal freedom and social equity has found its voice, its language in the creative discernment of the freedoms and rights of persons-in-community. Discovery and construction came together in gradual articulation. The basis of this discovery/construction is the dignity and worth of the individual person, independently of social status or wealth, of personal gifts or achievements. This individual person is also and inescapably a social entity, so that the rights and freedoms have social dimensions themselves and encounter inevitable social limitations.

The basis in personal dignity which the Universal Declaration and other UN human rights instruments indicate—and religious bodies such as the Second Vatican Council strongly endorsed—has, of course, a certain Western philosophical and even religious tone. Yet its capacity to be translated into very different languages and cultures is undeniable even if much of the work of translation has yet to be carried out. This translation involves cultural dialogue in which the understanding of the role and relationships of the human person may be discovered anew without the threat of final, mutual incomprehension. The postmodern emphasis on particularity, with its critique of the covert and often overt imperialism of Western universals, is valuable in alerting Western people and institutions to the parochialism of their own achievements. For this imperialism, to which universal language and institutions are so readily prone, is a parochialism with the power to impoverish or destroy other particulars and their creative potentials. Such imperial tendencies, so often indulged politically and economically, culturally and religiously, are not irresistible.

A basic task for the defenders of human rights, and in particular for the defenders of religious liberty, is the fostering of the dialogue between cultures and religions. For religions generally the dignity of the human person is intimately related to the awareness and understanding of God, in whose image accordingly human beings are created.

Conversation with and between the Religions

Because the dignity of the human person is for religious people closely influenced by their religious beliefs, the dialogue with religions by people with responsibility for promoting human rights, including freedom of religion and belief, is in need of development. The insight of the religions themselves into human dignity and its relation to rights and above all their insight into religious freedom will help to enrich and promote the idea and the ideal of freedom of belief. The conversation between the religious themselves may be even more important. In his promotion of the idea of a global ethic the Swiss Catholic theologian Hans Küng has been using almost as a slogan the phrase: "No peace between the nations without peace between the religions."[3] And the Parliament of Religions meeting in Chicago in 1993 sought to further the cause of genuine dialogue between the religions.[4]

The cause of a global ethic may be interpreted and pursued in many different ways. In whatever way it is interpreted and pursued it has much in common with the promotion of human rights. And given the traditional close connection between religion and morality, the conversations with and between the religions must create a sphere of common understanding that will enhance the prospects of global acceptance of human rights and of a shared global approach to many major moral problems. Fruitful conversations between the religions require a freedom and equality which only a wholehearted acceptance of freedom of religion and belief can guarantee.

For these reasons I was truly honored last March when, in his speech during the session of the Commission on Human Rights in Geneva, the Foreign Minister of Iran invited me to arrange for commentaries from an Islamic perspective or viewpoint on the Universal Declaration of Human Rights. It was an invitation I accepted readily. It has led to a process of close consultation with the Organization of Islamic Conference and individual countries of the Islamic world with a view to bringing a group of experts in Islamic law together in Geneva during November. It is hoped that they will provide the enrichment of their insights into the universality of the rights set out in the Declaration, as well as the duties to the community which article 29 reminds us everyone has, and in which alone the free and full development of his personality is possible.

The Gift and Threat of Fundamental Belief

The particular difficulties surrounding freedom of religion and belief and which, for so long, have inhibited inter-religions conversation no doubt have to do with the very profound issues and attitudes involved in religious belief or unbelief. Confronting questions of the meaning of existence, human and cosmic, of the ultimate source and destiny of human living and loving, the very questions of religion, the stances taken and responses attempted penetrate believer and unbeliever very deeply. In many ways such depth of questioning and response is liberating. Serious believer and unbeliever acquire a sense of proportion in face of the endless and trivializing distractions of the consumerist society.

Contact with the great mysteries of life sets a person free from so many of the minor entrapments. For believers in particular, faith is understood at its best as progressively liberating into aspects of the truth and only the truth sets free. For unbelievers, or rather those who accept some alternative fundamental belief to that in a God, there is a sense of liberating truth. That is the gift of fundamental belief—liberation in truth. The threat is that of a belief or unbelief which the agent believes he possesses in its fullness and therefore must impose on others. The fundamentalist believer or unbeliever becomes a substitute God. He is at once dominated by his version of belief and seeks to dominate others in turn. This is the domination which occurs in sectarianism, proselytizing, and the other destructive religious and antireligious practices which have so often disfigured our world. The call of believer and unbeliever alike is to resist the degeneration of fundamental beliefs from their liberating potential into fundamentalist and dominating caricatures. Only in this way will authentic religious freedom be upheld.

Religious Freedom and Social Privations

Human rights form a unity. They belong together in a unified protection of humanity. Where other rights are violated, freedom of religion and belief will not thrive. So it is clearly with freedom of expression and assembly, and all the other political and civil rights. This is no less true of social and economic rights. Their neglect and violation impinge on the proper exercise of personal rights including, freedom of religion or belief.

The major religions, while concerned with ultimate questions, frequently present themselves as protectors and promoters of human dignity. They see themselves in particular as defenders of the deprived, the poor, the discriminated against. So their religious freedom is a freedom in society not merely to belief and worship but to uphold the cause of the deprived. In these circumstances they must ensure that their own internal practices are not discriminatory on grounds of gender or race or class. They have to learn from the good practice of wider society as well as teach it.

The Republic of Conscience and the Kingdom of God

In the Jewish and Christian traditions one of the great metaphors for the fulfillment of humanity and the world is that of the Kingdom of God. Translators nowadays tend to prefer terms such as the "reign" or "rule" of God to avoid the territorial or sexist overtones of "Kingdom". What is really in mind is the presence of God, of the creative, healing, liberating, transforming reality recognized by Jew and Christian as the ultimate mystery. This God is in search of free human response in love to the real mystery also called love and to one another. In that free and loving communion fulfillment is attainable. The freedom essential to loving is freedom to know the truth and to respond to it. It is freedom of conscience. To borrow Seamus Heaney's phrase, only in the Republic of Conscience is the Kingdom of God available. Freedom of religion and freedom of belief are basic to that republic and to all humane societies:

> At their inauguration, public leaders
> must swear to uphold unwritten law and weep
> to atone for their presumption to hold office—
> and to affirm their faith that all life sprang
> from salt in tears the sky-god wept
> after he dreamt his solitude was endless.[5]

Seminar on Enriching the Universality of Human Rights: Islamic Perspectives on the Universal Declaration of Human Rights—Personal Impressions

Palais des Nations, Geneva, 29 November 1998

Colleagues, Distinguished Experts, Excellencies, Ladies, and Gentlemen,

These past two days have been extraordinary. We have listened to presentations from you, our eminent experts, dealing with a wide range of crucial human rights topics from the perspective of Islam, and we have had very interesting exchanges of views. I, for one, have learned much. I have been very enriched by the opportunity to listen to the discussion, debate, and exchange of views.

As you know, when planning this seminar we agreed that, because of the complex nature of the subjects, the academic character of the debates, and the short time available, we would not attempt to adopt final conclusions or recommendations. I believe that decision was a correct one. There will be other opportunities, other contexts, other structures of debate and participation in the future. This was a beginning—a very enriching beginning.

However, I also believe that the importance of the discussions which have taken place and the understanding which has been built up merits some response reflecting what has transpired here. And thus I would like to share with you my own personal impressions of these two days. These thoughts are my own and do not engage you individually nor the seminar as such.

I have learned of the fundamental principles of Islam relating to the dignity of the human person, to the search for justice and the protection of the weak, solidarity, and respect for other cultures and beliefs. In all these discussions, no one expressed doubts about the Universal Declaration of Human Rights nor denied the legitimacy or universality of international human rights standards. And we have heard of the relevance of international standards, including the Universal Declaration, to promoting and protecting human rights on the national level.

Our attention has been called to the way in which human rights are actually lived. The principles of Islam relating to human dignity and social solidarity are a rich resource from which to face the human rights challenges of today. Islamic concern with human dignity is old; it goes back to the very beginning. It is also dynamic, as it confronts the challenges of today.

Our discussions have not only referred to Islam. They have also brought out a central challenge to the human community as a whole and to those interested in respect for human rights in particular: How big have we made the Arc of the Universal Declaration? Is it wide enough to encompass all humanity, or is it reserved for a privileged few?

I do not wish for a moment to minimize the serious situation of human rights in many countries or the need to act, as many of you have emphasized. But I found that we have been looking forward during this seminar, with each seeking how, in her or his own way, the challenge of protecting human rights today can be met.

In organizing this seminar I wanted to show that the United Nations was open for dialogue and ready to listen to those who seek better protection for human rights. This seminar has been part of a process which has opened a channel of communication. That channel should stay open, and I believe we should now reflect on how best to carry it forward. As I explained when I intervened, this seminar is complete in itself, in the sense that it has been based on an agreed procedure. It has been my intention to publish the proceedings of this seminar. I welcome the encouragement from you as experts that the proceedings should be published, and the date of 10 December of this year would be a symbolic one.

Finally, I want to express my appreciation to you, the experts and guests, to the Organization of the Islamic Conference, to the governments which have supported this process and to the individuals, including my own colleagues, who have invested time and effort in making this seminar a reality.

I recall during my first session of the Commission on Human Rights as High Commissioner that the Chairman challenged the Commission to make a difference. It was a good challenge. In a sense it was implicit in us all coming together for this seminar that we would try to make a difference. I believe that this seminar has made a difference. It will not be without its critics, and that is good: criticism is in itself a learning process and a fruitful and helpful one. But I believe that by having this seminar, by exchanging papers and views as experts, by having and listening to your contributions, that we have made a difference.

I thank you all.

Chapter 5
Combating Other Discrimination and Exclusion

The Universal Declaration of Human Rights set out the ideal of nondiscrimination on any ground Over the years excluded and vulnerable groups have sought to invoke human rights principles in their struggle to be recognized. As High Commissioner, Mary Robinson espoused many such causes, including the rights of sexual minorities.

The Disabled

The initiative to press for a human rights approach came from the disabled themselves, a cause also pressed by Ireland. As President of Ireland, Mary Robinson had championed the rights of disabled people. As High Commissioner, she continued that commitment.

Refugees

Human rights are in principle not linked to citizenship but to common humanity. But all States have the right to deny the entry of noncitizens into their territory. The right to seek asylum and the duty of States to admit those who qualify as refugees is one exception admitted by States to their control of entry. The enormous increase in the numbers of refugees across the world fleeing from conflict, persecution, and human rights abuse is a constant and visible reminder of human suffering in the contemporary world. Their protection is the responsibility of another United Nations agency, the High Commissioner for Refugees, with whom Mary Robinson's Office worked closely. As she notes below, the Refugee Convention of 1951 was "one of the first human rights treaties."

Migrants

The rights of migrant workers, who are compelled by poverty to leave their homes, and their vulnerability to discrimination and exploitation have been defined as human rights concerns mainly over the last decade. The linkage between racial discrimination, xenophobia, and migration was one focus of the World Conference against Racism. Mary Robinson and the OHCHR were part of a campaign linking many NGOs, religious communities, and UN agencies to achieve the necessary number of ratifications by states to make an ambitious scheme of protection—the Convention on the Rights of Migrant Workers and Their Families—part of international law. She describes herself as the cheerleader of the campaign and proposed a competition between States to become the twentieth State to ratify and thereby bring the Convention into force. The Convention came into force after receiving the required twenty ratifications on 1 July 2003.

Victims of Trafficking

Trafficking in human beings and particularly in women and girls for the sex industry is among the most distressing and underreported of human rights abuses. In addition to supporting the Council of Europe in its negotiations toward a regional convention, OHCHR produced Recommended Principles and Guidelines on Human Rights and Human Trafficking in 2002. States are encouraged to use the Guidelines in drawing up their own legislation and to encourage consistency of approach and international cooperation in combating trafficking. Mary Robinson had commissioned the Guidelines in 1999 and spoke out frequently over trafficking throughout her period as High Commissioner.

People Living with HIV/AIDS

The concern with the human rights of HIV/AIDS sufferers was a particular priority of the OHCHR during Mary Robinson's tenure. The plight of AIDS victims was probably mentioned more frequently in her speeches than any other subject. The High Commissioner worked closely with UNAIDS. OHCHR and UNAIDS developed the UN Guidelines on HIV/AIDS and Human Rights and campaigned together to have States adopt them.

THE DISABLED

"Honoring Human Dignity and Worth"
Address at the Kennedy Foundation International Awards Ceremony
Seattle, USA, 2 August 2000

Ladies and Gentlemen,

I am honored to have been invited to address you on the occasion of the international awards ceremony organized by the Kennedy Foundation. Your invitation caused me to reflect again on that part of the Preamble to the Universal Declaration of Human Rights which states that "the peoples of the United Nations have in the Charter reaffirmed their faith in fundamental human rights, in the dignity and worth of the human person."

What do we mean by that phrase "the dignity and worth of the human person"?

I think it is encapsulated in the spirit behind the awards to be made this evening. It also requires close attention to language: because language itself can either reinforce or undermine dignity and worth. I have a personal preference for the term "intellectual disabilities," which connotes for me great courage and abilities of the individual and other family members in coping with specific disabilities and living the fullest quality of life possible—in other words, being accorded full dignity and worth as a human being. However, I propose to use the terms "intellectual disabilities" and "mental retardation" interchangeably this evening, as some of you will identify with that latter term and imbue it with the same emphasis on the dignity and worth of the person concerned.

People with Intellectual Disability

Working on behalf of people with intellectual disabilities is a lifelong task—for the relatives and carers directly involved, for the professional staff and specialists who practice in the field, for the friends and supporters of organizations such as the Kennedy Foundation who devote so much time and effort to the cause. I am reminded of President Kennedy's saying, "What really counts is not the immediate act of courage or valor but those who bear the struggle day in day out."[1]

It is right to take time on an evening such as this to pay tribute to those deserving of praise and recognition. The recipients of tonight's awards have all displayed remarkable commitment. They are deserving of our gratitude and respect, not only for what they themselves have achieved but because they represent a spirit of dedication and service without which it would not be possible for people with intellectual disabilities to achieve their full potential.

I welcome the opportunity, as United Nations High Commissioner for Human Rights, to reaffirm the importance of placing the issue of intellectual disabilities in a human rights context. Article 1 of the Universal Declaration of Human Rights proclaims that "all human beings are born free and equal in dignity and rights." Equality and the related principle of non-discrimination are central to the mission of the United Nations.

I believe that one of the most hopeful developments of the age we live in is the growing acceptance of the fact that everyone in the world has certain fundamental rights—irrespective of where they live, whether they are rich or poor, what color they are, what religion they practice, what ethnic group they belong to, or what disabilities they cope with. These rights are spelled out in detail in the thirty articles of the Universal Declaration of Human Rights. They range from the right to equality before the law to the right to adequate health care and an adequate standard of living.

However, I am well aware that in practice many people are still unable to live full lives free from suffering, whether purposely inflicted or arising from neglect. Establishing that persons with mental retardation are entitled to the same basic human rights as the rest of the population is important. Ensuring that they actually enjoy those rights remains a major challenge. In fact, the international human rights instruments not only define the rights to which all of us are entitled, they also require governments to progressively realize human rights to the limit of available resources.

Persons with intellectual disabilities belong to the most vulnerable sections of society and, as such, are owed special care and attention by governments. But often they do not receive either. Lack of resources may be a problem in many countries, but that is not the only obstacle. Even in resource-rich societies adequate funding may not be made available. And it is not unusual to hear of the mentally retarded being treated callously and even cruelly and their fundamental rights abused.

International Standards

International attention focused on the rights of those with disabilities is a recent development. But the pace has been speeding up over the past decade, coinciding with our greater understanding of the issue and advances in medical science. The ground was laid by the 1971 UN Declaration on the Rights of Mentally Retarded Persons.[2] Two further landmarks in the international community's approach were, first, the Principles for the Protection of Persons with Mental Illness and for the Improvement of Mental Healthcare,[3] adopted by the UN in 1991, and second, the Standard Rules on the Equalization of Opportunities for Persons with Disabilities,[4] adopted two years later. These instruments have provided a common standard for all countries and have raised the international profile of this issue.

In 1995 the UN Committee on Economic, Social and Cultural Rights adopted General Comment No. 5 on the subject of Persons with Disabilities.[5] The term "disability" was given the widest definition, being described as covering "a great number of different functional limitations occurring in any population. . . . People may be disabled by physical, intellectual or sensory impairment, medical conditions or mental illness. Such impairments, conditions or illness may be permanent or transitory in nature." The Committee concluded that member states had paid very little attention to the rights of persons with disabilities in their reporting and agreed with the Secretary General when he said, "most governments still lack concerted measures that would effectively improve the situation of persons with disabilities."

The Responsibility of Governments

So what are the responsibilities of governments?

First, there must be a clear recognition of the special needs of the most vulnerable people in our society. Some five hundred million people in the world suffer from disabilities of one kind or another, and their situation is not always acknowledged.

The second point is one that I already mentioned, namely that measures must be taken to promote the realization of the rights of those with mental retardation and other disabilities. It is not enough for governments to refrain from actions that could have a negative impact—the obligation is there to take positive action to reduce structural disadvantages and give appropriate preferential treatment to vulnerable groups so as to ensure full participation and equality.

Third, adequate resources should be made available. That means adequate income support, and access to adequate food and housing, to decent medical care, and to education. Nor does the responsibility of governments end with the public sphere: there is a duty to exercise proper supervision and regulation in the private sector also, through legislation and raising awareness about the rights, the needs, the potential, and the contribution of people with intellectual disabilities.

Fourth, all forms of discrimination should be combated. There is, unfortunately, a long history of discrimination against those perceived as being "different." The tools to fight this are, once again, a combination of legislation and awareness-building.

Finally, particular attention should be paid to those suffering dual or multiple disabilities, as is often the case. Especially vulnerable people such as children require special attention, as the Convention on the Rights of the Child makes clear.

I would urge the people of the United States to give a good example to the world of how to respond to the needs of those with mental retardation. The place of the United States in the history of human rights is well known. I think of the inclusion of the Bill of Rights in your Constitution, which has proved to be a model for many other nations. And I think of the key part played by Eleanor Roosevelt in the drawing up of the Universal Declaration of Human Rights. National legislation to protect the rights of the mentally retarded and those with disabilities has been on the statute books in the United States for almost forty years.

But more can and should be done. There is a responsibility to ensure that all have access to facilities that can improve the quality of life. That responsibility extends to the millions who live in poverty here in America and cannot afford proper health care or assistance for their loved ones.

I am glad to say that my country, Ireland, is making significant progress in this field, as was demonstrated last year when Ireland received the Franklin Roosevelt International Disability Award. This award is given to a country which has made noteworthy progress toward ensuring the full participation of persons with disabilities. It was accepted at a ceremony in New York by

President McAleese. Ireland has also been leading the way in international efforts to promote the cause of the human rights of persons with disabilities at the United Nations Commission on Human Rights in Geneva.

Our responsibilities extend beyond national boundaries. It is a truism to say that we live in a global village, but it is the case that in this age of the information revolution we are better informed about what is happening in other parts of the world than we have ever been. We know the desperate poverty in which millions of people live. We know that clear linkages exist between poverty, malnutrition, and retardation. We do have a duty toward that wider global community, and we must not shirk that duty.

The Special Olympics

One shining example of international cooperation is the Special Olympics, which has brought such pleasure to so many and which goes from strength to strength. As the slogan for the Special Olympics underlines, it is about more than winning, more even than competing: it is about people with disabilities being acknowledged as useful and productive citizens who are accepted and respected in their communities.[6] In a similar spirit, Very Special Arts has enabled those with disabilities to surprise and delight us with the depth and creativity of their abilities.[7]

To give an example of a person with disability making a difference, a few weeks ago I met a remarkable man called Gerard Paul Fougerouse, who has traveled to many parts of America highlighting the situation of people with disabilities. He has written an inspiring story about his travels called *The United States in a Wheelchair.*[8] The reason for his visit to Geneva was to tell me that he plans to make a journey to South Africa in his wheelchair, drawing attention to and arriving for the World Conference against Racism, Racial Discrimination, Xenophobia and Related Intolerance in September 2001.

In conclusion, I would like to say that those being honored tonight come from all of the categories of individuals who contribute to improving the lives of those with intellectual disabilities. There are the scientists and educationalists who expand the boundaries of our knowledge. There are the carers, whether relatives, friends, or professionals, who deserve our gratitude but even more our practical support. And there are the advocates, often those with firsthand experience of loved ones affected by mental retardation. All are worthy winners.

Let me finish by quoting again from John F. Kennedy. In 1963, not long before his death, he signed into law the Maternal and Child Health and Mental Retardation Bill. He said then: "We can say with some assurance that, although children may be victims of fate, they will not be victims of neglect."[9] Those words set a standard for all of us to follow.

Thank you.

"The Human Rights Dimensions of Disability"
Opening remarks at the launch of the final phase of the OHCHR Disability Study
Palais des Nations, Geneva, 14 January 2002

Excellencies, Ladies, and Gentlemen,

It is a pleasure to welcome you today to the launch of the final phase of the study that I commissioned from the Research Centre on Human Rights and Disability of the National University of Ireland Galway to prepare. I am deeply grateful to Theresa Degener and Professor Gerard Quinn, the authors of the draft report, for the substantial work they have done. After my remarks they will share with you their initial findings on the current use and future potential of the United Nations human rights instruments in the context of disability. This day-long discussion will provide valuable responses and insights from representatives of governments and of UN agencies and programs.

Equality and its corollary principle of nondiscrimination are touchstones on which the guarantees of international human rights law have been built. The struggle to advance equality through the elimination of all forms of discrimination remains a fundamental element of the promotion and protection of human rights for all.

International Steps on Myth and Disability

Discrimination against persons with disability has been a neglected issue as compared to progress in combating other forms of discrimination. However, that neglect is being reversed. The key to change in attitudes and policy toward the disabled has come about through the recognition of the human rights dimension of disability. At the international level this recognition came in 1993, when the Vienna Declaration of the World Conference on Human Rights affirmed that all human rights and fundamental freedoms are to be guaranteed for all, and included an explicit reference to persons with disabilities and their right to active participation in all aspects of civil society. In 1993, also, Standard Rules were adopted unanimously by the General Assembly providing all countries with concrete guidelines on how to deliver that promise of equal rights to persons with disabilities.[10]

In 2001, at its fifty-seventh session, the Commission on Human Rights invited my Office in cooperation with the Special Rapporteur on Disability to examine measures to strengthen the protection and monitoring of the human rights of persons with disabilities.[11] The United Nations Economic and Social Council later endorsed the Commission's resolution.[12]

In response to that request I decided to strengthen the work of my Office on disability and to reinforce its expertise in this area. We designed a project that will, inter alia, provide a conceptual framework for the recognition of the human rights dimension of disability. The first outcome of the project is the draft study on human rights and disability being presented for discussion today. I am confident that this study is a significant first step toward building practical recognition of the human rights dimension of disability issues.

It will be important at this stage to intensify efforts at advocacy, in order to bring home to those with disabilities that there are valuable tools to help them in the international human rights system. Advocacy can take many forms. I had the pleasure of launching a state-of-the-art publication last month on *Advocacy—A Rights Issue* for the Forum of People with Disabilities in Dublin.[13] The launch, appropriately, took place in the Mountjoy Women's Prison, to put emphasis on the particular problems of people with disabilities in confined places.

A Possible International Convention

At its last session the General Assembly adopted a resolution (resolution 56/168 of 19 December 2001) which is a landmark in the history of the disability movement.[14] That Resolution establishes a Committee that is tasked with elaborating an international convention to protect and promote the rights and dignity of persons with disabilities. The Committee is directed to adopt a holistic approach in bringing together the work done in the fields of social development and human rights and nondiscrimination. The General Assembly has thus responded to the call of various disability groups for a legally binding human rights instrument. I welcome this reaffirmation of the importance of the disability issue in the international context.[15]

If this resolution brings us hope, we should still remain conscious of the challenging task the drafting of an international instrument will entail and the long road ahead before the international community agrees on a satisfactory convention. The Resolution, and the drafting of a convention, should not overshadow the need—right now—to ensure that the existing human rights provisions that are directly or indirectly linked to disability are used to advance the human rights of persons with disabilities.

It is the existing human rights norms and standards and their relevance to disability that are explored and analyzed in the draft study to be discussed today. We will also hear from Bengt Lindqvist, the Special Rapporteur of the Commission for Social Development. He has, since 1993, assessed the implementation of the Standard Rules and will be able to share with us the challenges faced in the implementation of the Rules at the national and international levels.

In summary, our approach should be twofold:

to ensure that existing instruments and mechanisms are both well known and used in the most effective manner to enable the full enjoyment of all their rights by persons with disabilities; and

To ensure that human rights are at the core of the proposed new convention and that the drafting efforts will be directed at providing the highest human rights standards in the promotion and protection of the rights of persons with disabilities.

I am confident that our meeting today will help to maintain, and indeed to increase, the international momentum on the recognition of persons with disabilities as full members of society and as holders of rights that are theirs to exercise. I am looking forward to an interesting, enriching, and challenging discussion.

REFUGEES

Marking the Fiftieth Anniversary of the Refugee Convention
Ministerial Meeting of State Parties
Office of the High Commissioner for Refugees, Geneva, 12 December 2001

It is an honor to speak to you at the close of your Plenary Session. I was very glad this morning to have the opportunity to listen to the introductory statements launching the Conference. All of us were moved by the statement by Her Excellency Vaira Vike-Freiberga, the President of Latvia, who reminded us that at the heart of our concern lies the individual and the need for all of us to reach out a helping hand to those forced to flee their homes and their country.

This fiftieth anniversary of the 1951 Convention provides a crucial opportunity for stocktaking. It has come at a critical time for refugees and asylum seekers worldwide—sadly, the theme of "Respect" has not been honored to the extent it should, and the challenge now is to reinvigorate the international commitment to protection. All that I heard this morning served to convince me further that we are coming to recognize the common aims and principles that link the fields of refugee protection, human rights protection, and protection in times of conflict—international humanitarian law.

The Achievements of the United Nations High Commissioner for Refugees and of the 1951 Convention

The achievements of the Convention and UNHCR have been enormous and should be recognized. In the 1951 Convention, the international community enshrined the protection principle and the principle of non-*refoulement.* It created for the first time a functioning system to tackle the protection needs of those who flee persecution. What was designed as a measure to deal with the refugee crisis arising from World War II has proved enduring. As High Commissioner Ruud Lubbers noted this morning, the 1951 Convention, together with its 1967 Protocol, has become in effect a universal charter on refugee law. In the shadow of the appalling acts of September 11 and the humanitarian crisis in Afghanistan, UNHCR stands yet again at the center of world affairs.

Flexibility

The Convention has proved its flexibility since its adoption in 1951 with only one revision of geographic and time limitations by protocol in 1967. It continues to map the contours of protection needs in 2001. But we have learned that the Convention faces new challenges. It has proved successful in adapting to earlier challenges. One example is that of gender-based persecution. Gender is not included in the Convention; indeed, it was not considered at all in the course of drafting. Since that time, however, the mainstreaming of women's rights has gathered pace. This is an area in which refugee law was ahead of most disciplines.

Path-Breaking

The Convention was path-breaking when it was adopted fifty years ago. In fact, it represented the earliest implementation of the Universal Declaration of Human Rights, whose anniversary we marked two days ago on Human Rights Day. The Convention was in a real sense one of the first human rights treaties.

In addition to the principle of non-*refoulement*, the Convention included a nondiscrimination clause. It guaranteed basic economic and social rights, for example, to education, social security and public assistance, and employment on the same basis as other nonnationals. It also recognized civil rights including access to the courts and freedom of religion.

The Refugee Convention, although not endowed with enforcement machinery, was the first treaty to have built into it a formal link to an international supervisory body—UNHCR. We can perhaps see here the seeds of the supervision systems established under human rights treaties in later years.

Contribution to Human Rights Law and International Law

The 1951 Convention has made a major contribution to general international law and human rights law principles. Provisions such as the definition of the term "refugee" and the guarantee against forcible return to territories where persecution is feared (non-*refoulement*) have become principles of public international law. The San Remo Declaration of 8 September 2001 (under the auspices of the International Institute for Humanitarian Law) is the latest in a long line of authorities confirming that non*refoulement* has the status of customary international law.[16]

Protection against *refoulement* has also come to be recognized in human rights law. The obligation to protect individuals against torture and other severe ill-treatment has developed into a prohibition on states removing persons to a territory in which a real risk of such ill-treatment exists. This principle—recognized by the European Court of Human Rights and the Human Rights Committee—was later explicitly incorporated into the UN Convention against Torture.

The mutual influence of human rights jurisprudence and refugee law is a welcome recognition of the interlocking purposes of human rights and refugee protection. UNHCR itself has recognized this relationship. In its annual Note on International Protection this year, UNHCR speaks of the 1951 Convention as being rooted "quite directly in the broader framework of human rights instruments of which it is an integral part, albeit with a very particular focus."[17]

Many challenges remain for those who seek to extend protection. As Mr. Lubbers said this morning, those challenges should be jointly addressed through effective partnerships. My Office is committed to addressing how OHCHR can be of service to all parts of the humanitarian community in the work of protection in the field.

Threats to Protection

The appalling acts of September 11 will have profound implications for the work of the United Nations, including both my Office and UNHCR. Of first concern must be the humanitarian crisis in Afghanistan and the surrounding countries with the associated massive displacement of men, women, and children.

It is against this background—what UNHCR has termed the world's worst refugee emergency—that some have voiced their doubts as to the sustainability of the refugee system. I share the concern at the possibility of reduction in protection in the aftermath of September 11. Even before the crimes of that day, refugees and asylum seekers had been viewed in some quarters with ever-increasing suspicion. Now the fear is great that simple assertions of "national security" will operate to deprive many needy persons of protection.

While claims are made that the Convention must come second to national security, a few points should be recalled. First, the Refugee Convention was not adopted at a time of starry-eyed idealism. As Professor Goodwin-Gill pointed out at the joint OHCHR-UNHCR seminar on refugees and migrants for Human Rights Day, the drafters of the 1951 Convention framed its terms at a time of great international insecurity. The Berlin blockade was in progress, and the Cold War was entering into being. In such a context the Convention was not overly generous to refugees to the detriment of state interests—the realism and careful balances all throughout its text point to its continuing relevance today, just as it addressed the concerns of an insecure world in 1951.

In recent years some European states, in questioning the Convention, have expressed fears of being "swamped" by asylum seekers and have used this as a ground for restriction of access to their territories and asylum systems. But the stark fact is that Iran and Pakistan host twice as many refugees as all the nations of Western Europe combined, and Pakistan is not even a party to the Convention. These figures highlight the vital importance of addressing urgently the issue of burden-sharing.

Some states now seek to override or ignore the provisions of the Refugee Convention. We should ask: Have they fully considered the possibility that in so doing they may be breaching their domestic law? Constitutional questions, for example, have been raised in the courts of a number of countries in recent years over measures mandating restriction of fundamental rights of refugees—either through deportation or through detention where such deportation may not be possible to carry out. The absolute necessity for strong procedural protections and strict judicial scrutiny in such cases was emphasized by the courts.

Conclusion

As the fiftieth year of the Refugee Convention is celebrated, let us put the emphasis back where it should always be—on protection. It is this basic aim and principle that provides the link between international human rights law and refugee law, and also international humanitarian law. Closer integration of these fields around the concept of protection offers the best possibility of filling the gaps—what refugee lawyers term the "gray areas"—of protection.

The Refugee Convention remains vital and indispensable. Let me leave you with the words of the World Conference against Racism, Racial Discrimination, Xenophobia and Related Intolerance held earlier this year in Durban, South Africa. I can think of no more fitting conclusion for my message for this occasion or for the challenges facing us today than to recall the solemn promise by states in the World Conference Declaration:

> We affirm our commitment to respect and implement humanitarian obligations relating to the protection of refugees, asylum-seekers, returnees and internally displaced persons, and note in this regard the importance of international solidarity, burden-sharing and international cooperation to share responsibility for the protection of refugees, reaffirming that the 1951 Convention relating to the Status of Refugees and its 1967 Protocol remain the foundation of the international refugee regime and recognizing the importance of their full application by states parties.

Thank you.

MIGRANTS

"Ratify the Migrants Convention Now!"
Remarks to the Panel on Migrants
Palais des Nations, Geneva, 15 April 2002

Distinguished Members of the Panel, Ladies, and Gentlemen,

This parallel event at the fifty-eighth session of the Commission on Human Rights has been convened with one purpose in mind: to give a boost to the need for ratification of the International Convention on the Protection of the Rights of All Migrant Workers and Members of Their Families. I am here as a cheerleader of the campaign. Like all of you, I care deeply about the subject. Migration has always been part of the human condition, not something new. But our era of globalization has stimulated large-scale movement of people and will continue to do so. As migration flows increase around the world, the need for a new human rights protection regime for migrants becomes ever more urgent. The Convention will open a new chapter in the history of efforts to establish the rights of migrant workers in international law and ensure that those rights are protected and respected.

The Convention needs twenty ratifications to enter into force. Nineteen instruments of ratification or accession have already been deposited with the Secretary General. One more to go! We had hopes that the twentieth might be received by the opening date of this Commission session. That has not happened; but let us not give up hope. We could suggest that those states considering their future adherence to the Convention organize a "competition" among themselves as to who might be number twenty. By speeding up their domestic procedures to subscribe to this important human rights treaty, one of them will win the honor of becoming the twentieth state party. Its name will be identified forever with helping the projection of a vision into reality—bringing into force a new legal mechanism for the international protection of migrants.

A Competition to Ratify

Last week there was great excitement when the sixtieth ratification of the Statute of the International Criminal Court was deposited in New York. How soon can we celebrate another such event when the twentieth ratification of the Migrant Workers Convention is deposited? Indeed you may have noticed that there were six ICC instruments of ratifications deposited at the same time, and all were treated as the sixtieth! So on that precedent we could get more than the minimum ratifications needed. And we do need more than the minimum number of countries to become parties. We are campaigning for universal ratification.

Let me express my appreciation of the work of the Global Campaign for the ratification of the Convention. My Office is, of course, a part of the campaign. The campaign has made a tangible difference in getting us this close to an operative convention. The cooperation it has generated for ratifications has involved UN agencies, the Special Rapporteur, Gabriela Rodriquez, other experts, religious communities, and NGOs, all of whom are represented in this meeting today. It exemplifies a global alliance for human rights in action, and it is the way we should be working for human rights for the future.

The Working of the Convention

Within six months from the entry into force of the Convention, the OHCHR as secretariat will organize the first meeting of the states parties to elect the ten members of the Committee on Migrants, the monitoring mechanism of the Convention. Members will serve in their personal capacity for a term of four years.[18]

States parties will have the obligation to report regularly on the steps they have taken to implement the Convention. The reports are expected to indicate problems encountered in implementing the Convention and to provide information on migration flows. After examining the reports, the Committee will transmit such comments as it may consider appropriate to the state party concerned. Close cooperation between the Committee and international agencies, in particular the International Labor Organization, is foreseen in the Convention and I am delighted to see Constance Thomas from the ILO on the platform today.

I hope that states parties who ratify will also make the declarations necessary for the entry into force of the individual complaint procedure under article 77 of the Convention. Ten such declarations are necessary for this purpose and I note that none has been made so far.

Ladies and gentlemen, poverty and the inability to earn enough or produce enough to support an individual or a family are major reasons behind the movement of work-seekers from one state to another. These are not only characteristics of migration from poor to rich states; poverty and opportunity also fuel movements from one developing country to another where work prospects seem—at a distance, at least—to be better.

There are other reasons why people go abroad in search of work. War, civil strife, insecurity, or persecution arising from discrimination on the grounds of race, ethnic origin, color, religion, language, or political opinion all contribute to the flow of migrants. As we know too well, migrants in turn may find themselves the target of discrimination or xenophobia in the host countries. This aspect of the subject was a major focus of the World Conference against Racism in Durban last year. We should remind states that ratification of the Migrants Convention was one of the commitments they made in the Plan of Action of the World Conference. I can assure you that my Office will bear in mind that promise in our own campaign to see the Durban Plan of Action implemented. The World Conference texts also gave us important and positive language on the need to cherish the diversity of the human family, language which should be invoked in working to foster harmony and tolerance between migrant workers and the rest of the society in host states.

On 18 December 2001, International Migrant's Day, the Secretary General, in urging ratification by states noted, that "the fate of many migrants lies in stark contrast to the aspirations reflected in the Universal Declaration of Human Rights, human rights norms and labor conventions."[19] I support the Secretary General's appeal for ratification of the Convention and remind states that the "race" to become the twentieth state party is still open.

Thank you and keep up the good work!

VICTIMS OF TRAFFICKING

"Combating Trafficking in Human Beings—A European Convention?"
OHCHR/Council of Europe Panel Discussion
Palais des Nations, Geneva, 9 April 2002

Mr. Chairman, Fellow Panelists, Ladies, and Gentlemen,

I would like to begin my short presentation by thanking the Council of Europe for organizing this event in cooperation with my Office. The subject matter of this panel—a possible trafficking convention for Europe—is one that interests me greatly, and I am very pleased to be here with you all today. The setting is also particularly appropriate. The Commission on Human Rights has been at the forefront of the fight against trafficking and has given important direction and support to my Office in this area.[20]

I am also pleased to note the sponsorship of this event by the IGO Contact Group on Human Trafficking and Migrant Smuggling.[21] The Group is now one year old and can already point to a number of significant achievements and I would like to take this opportunity to congratulate all its members on their important work.

The Nature of the Problem

The sheer scope of the problem of trafficking almost defies description. Every year, hundreds of thousands of people—perhaps even more—are tricked, sold, forced, or otherwise coerced into situations of exploitation from which they cannot escape. These individuals are the commodities of a transnational industry which generates billions of dollars and, almost without exception, operates with virtual impunity.

Despite recent encouraging developments at the national, regional, and international levels, little has changed for those caught up in this sordid trade. Attempts to deal with trafficking have, thus far, been largely ineffective. This is not a positive evaluation, but it is, I believe, an honest one.

More people are being trafficked than ever before. The pool of potential victims in this part of the world, as in all others, is growing rapidly because of widespread inequalities, lack of employment opportunities, violence, discrimination, and poverty. Increasingly restrictive immigration policies on the part of many wealthy states force individuals desperate for work into the arms of unscrupulous traders. Traffickers are able to operate with impunity because of inefficient law enforcement compounded, in some cases, by official corruption. The global sex industry, which generates billions of dollars for governments as well as for organized criminal networks, is allowed to flourish without constraint.

The Trafficking Cycle

What more can we do? I believe that first of all we must recognize the complexities involved. Trafficking is not one event but a series of constitutive acts and circumstances implicating a wide range of actors. It is essential that antitrafficking measures take account of this fact and that efforts are made to address the entire cycle of trafficking. This will involve, first and foremost, improving our information base so that we know exactly what we are dealing with. It will also involve ensuring an appropriate legal framework and an adequate law enforcement response at the national level; protecting and supporting trafficked persons; improving cooperation and coordination between countries; and identifying and responding to those factors which increase vulnerability to trafficking and which sustain demand.

In developing detailed responses to each stage of the trafficking cycle it is essential that we keep certain very basic policy principles in mind—guiding principles which can also provide us with a way of measuring the success of antitrafficking initiatives. Many of you are aware of the work of my Office in this area. I am pleased that I will shortly be releasing a set of International Principles and Guidelines on Human Rights and Human Trafficking. The Principles and Guidelines are the product of my Office's involvement in this issue since 1999. They have benefited from a wide consultation process involving most of the organizations represented here today, including the Council of Europe. OHCHR will be using the Principles and Guidelines as a framework for our own work, and I will be offering them to states, intergovernmental organizations, and others as a possible tool in their fight against trafficking.

Human Rights and Trafficking

For my Office, the key principle has always been the primacy of human rights: human rights *must* be at the core of any credible antitrafficking strategy.

What does it mean to make human rights the center of our antitrafficking work? For me, it means, first and foremost, acknowledging that trafficking and related practices such as debt bondage, forced prostitution and forced labor are violations of the basic human rights to which all persons are entitled. These include the rights to life and to equality, dignity, and security; the right to just and favorable conditions of work; the right to health; and the right to be recognized as a person before the law. These are rights which we all possess—irrespective of our sex, our nationality, our occupation or any other difference.

A human rights approach also demands that we acknowledge the responsibility of governments to protect and promote the rights of all persons within their jurisdictions. This responsibility translates into a legal obligation on governments to work toward eliminating trafficking and related exploitation. Passivity and inaction are insufficient. Tolerance or complicity is inexcusable.

Finally, for me as High Commissioner, a human rights approach to trafficking means that all parts of the international system should integrate human rights into their analyses of the problem and into their responses. This is the only way to retain a focus on the trafficked person, to ensure that trafficking is not simply reduced to a problem of migration, a problem of public order, or a problem of transnational crime.

The Proposed European Convention

What does all this mean for a possible European Convention on Trafficking? I would like to use this opportunity to publicly express my support for such an initiative. A further strengthening of legal commitments at the regional level is, I believe, an essential part of the global solution to the trade in human beings.

At the same time, we need to make sure that mistakes of the past are not repeated and that a new treaty represents a net advance for trafficked persons and their rights. This will be achieved if the European states agree to make human rights the foundation and reference point for the new Convention.

The following points could also usefully be kept in mind:

First, a new regional Convention on Trafficking should build on what we already have. Almost two years ago the international community finally agreed on a definition of "trafficking." That definition, now contained in the Palermo Protocol, supplementing the United Nations Convention against Transnational Organized Crime, should be integrated into any new legal instrument on this subject.[22]

Second, in order to promote uniformity and minimum standards, the protection and assistance provisions of the Palermo Protocol should be incorporated into the proposed European Convention as basic obligations. Protection and support are too important to be made optional.

Third, the Convention should explicitly protect trafficked persons from prosecution for the illegality of their coerced entry or residence, or for the unlawful activities they may undertake as a direct consequence of their situation.

Fourth, the possibility that trafficked persons may be in need of international refugee protection should be explicitly acknowledged.

Fifth, the Convention should recognize that the problem of child trafficking is a distinct one requiring special attention. The best interests of child victims must be considered paramount at all times. Children should be provided with appropriate assistance and protection. Full account should be taken of their special vulnerabilities, rights, and needs.

Sixth, the Convention should promote safe and, as far as possible, voluntary return. Trafficked persons should be offered legal alternatives to repatriation where it is reasonable to conclude that such repatriation would pose a serious risk to their safety and/or that of their families.

Seventh, the Convention should guarantee, to trafficked persons, the right of access to adequate and appropriate remedies.

Finally, the proposed Convention should require states to address the factors that increase vulnerability to trafficking, including inequality, poverty, and all forms of discrimination. It should also address demand as a root cause of trafficking.

Ladies and gentlemen, it is necessary for us all to confront the uncomfortable fact that so far, we have not succeeded in eliminating this trade in people for profit. We have not even managed to stem the tide.

A European Convention on Trafficking is a potentially important part of the solution. We have the opportunity in Europe to develop a treaty which will provide an example for other regions to follow. However, the chance will come only once. We must work together to get it right.

Address to the National Assembly of Cambodia
Phnom Penh, Cambodia, 21 August 2002 (excerpt)

Your Highness, Excellencies,

I want to raise with you one problem which I know is of concern to all of us. That is the repugnant trafficking in human beings. Every day, in many countries of this world, women and children are bought and sold, transported against their will, and forced into lives of prostitution, pornography, slave labor, and utter misery. The lives of these unfortunate human beings are ultimately cut short because of the diseases and dangers to which they are subjected.

Trafficking in Southeast Asia

Unfortunately, Southeast Asia is a major center for such trafficking. You will be aware that every year more than two hundred thousand women and children are "trafficked" in this region. In Southeast Asia the problem of trafficking is a cross-border phenomenon. Cambodia is a source, as well as a transit and receiving country. Vietnamese girls and women are trafficked into Cambodia, while Cambodian children, women, and men are sent to Thailand and other countries to do the most degrading work. Cambodia is also confronted with in-country trafficking. The flow is mainly from rural areas toward urban centers, tourist sites, and border vicinities. Most of the in-country trafficking occurs for purposes of sexual exploitation. It is linked to prostitution and mainly concerns women and children.

The pool of potential victims in this part of the world, as in all others, is growing rapidly because of widespread inequalities, lack of employment opportunities, violence, discrimination, and poverty. Traffickers are able to operate with impunity because of inefficient law enforcement, compounded, in some cases, by official corruption.

Southeast Asia is not the only region where this shameful trade is practiced. Recently a study was published on trafficking in southeastern Europe. The trade there displays the same characteristics of exploitation and abuse of women and children as in this region. The OHCHR, in partnership with UNICEF and the Organisation for Security and Co-operation in Europe, undertook the study.[23] The same organizations are working together and with governments in the region to bring an end to trafficking.

Cambodian Initiatives

Part of the answer lies in tougher laws. In November 2001 Cambodia signed the Protocol to Prevent, Suppress and Punish Trafficking in Persons, Especially Women and Children, supplementing the United Nations Convention against Transnational Organized Crime.[24] I encourage and urge you to ratify this Protocol as soon as possible. I note with satisfaction that your Assembly has approved the ratification of the Optional Protocol to the Convention on the Rights of the Child on the Sale of Children, Child Prostitution and Child Pornography.

I am aware of the many initiatives and programs that Cambodia has undertaken to prevent and combat trafficking, including in cooperation with my Office and other United Nations and international agencies. These are all commendable. However, more needs to be done.

Just last week the Ministry of Justice of Cambodia completed a draft of a revised law on trafficking and sexual exploitation. I read with concern the remarks of the Minister of Women and Veteran's Affairs, Madame M. U. Sochua, on the occasion of a consultation on the new draft, that trafficking is increasing, and increasing dramatically in Cambodia.

The women and children who are subjected to this inhumane cruelty are not foreign to us. They are our sisters and daughters. They are our children. This trafficking in them must stop. In today's world there is no place for this. It must be stopped, stopped completely.

A Personal Appeal

I want to ask you today to work with me, to work with the United Nations and the international community to bring human trafficking to a halt. I am issuing today this "Appeal from Phnom Penh" to all those countries in the region which are concerned with this scourge, to work together, to take every necessary step, to leave no stone unturned, to end this vicious and inhuman trade.

In the context of the UN Inter-Agency Project on Trafficking in Women and Children in the Mekong Sub-Region, I urge the governments to adopt National Plans of Action to combat trafficking. This will involve ensuring an appropriate legal framework and an adequate law enforcement response at the national level, protecting and supporting trafficked persons; improving cooperation and coordination between countries; and identifying and responding to those factors which increase vulnerability to trafficking and which sustain demand. I am pleased to note that Cambodia has already adopted a Five Year Plan of Action against Trafficking and Sexual Exploitation of Children, covering prevention, protection, recovery, and reintegration strategies, and that specific responsibilities are entrusted to various Ministries. It is important that similar commitments are extended to women and other victims of trafficking. The effort must now be on strengthening implementation of the Plan through concerted action at the national and regional levels.

My Office has developed Recommended Principles and Guidelines on Human Rights and Human Trafficking. I commend these to you as a useful tool in the fight against trafficking. I am pleased to announce that these Principles and Guidelines have been translated and are available in Khmer. I urge the National Assembly to ensure that the new draft law on trafficking takes a rights-based approach and reflects Cambodia's international human rights obligations as well as the Principles and Guidelines.

Human Rights must be the core of any credible antitrafficking strategy. A human rights approach also demands that we acknowledge the responsibility of governments to protect and promote the rights of all persons within their jurisdictions. This responsibility translates into a legal obligation for governments to work toward eliminating trafficking and related exploitation. A responsive and effective judiciary, adequately sensitized to the problem of trafficking and its human rights dimensions, is essential to secure accountability for traffickers and justice for victims.

Efforts to raise public awareness are very important in combating trafficking. An intensive media campaign is necessary to alert people to the evils involved. But in addition there must be economic and social development programs for women and children who are at risk. Such preventive measures can save potential victims.

Those who have the misfortune to be trafficked are not criminals, they are simply victims. They should be provided assistance to overcome the trauma they have lived through, as well as other options to live decent lives where their fundamental rights are respected. There is a clear distinction between victims of trafficking and illegal migrants. They should not be confused. I can only say that I regret the Cambodian court verdict of 5 August, which charged victims of trafficking with illegal migration and issued them prison sentences.

Firm and continued political will to break the trafficking cycle must underpin action in all the above areas.

Your Highness, Excellencies, I thank you once again for your warm hospitality. I wish you all, and the Cambodian people you represent, the peace and happiness which this country so deeply deserves.

Thank you.

PEOPLE LIVING WITH HIV/AIDS

World AIDS Day Statement

House of Commons, London, UK, 30 November 2001

May I begin by saying what an honor it is to be back here at the House of Commons today. As we recognize World AIDS Day, I welcome the opportunity to meet those of you who are at the forefront of the struggle against the epidemic: people living with HIV and AIDS, honorable Members of Parliament, AIDS service organizations, NGOs, and members of the media.

I am grateful to the National AIDS Trust and the All-Party Parliamentary Group on AIDS here in London for cohosting this meeting. The Trust has shown impressive leadership in its tireless efforts to promote a better understanding of HIV and AIDS, and to prevent its further spread and impact. I congratulate you on the launch of your media campaign against AIDS-related stigma and discrimination.

The All-Party Group is a model for how parliamentarians can work together to ensure an effective national response, based on respect for human rights. In the United Kingdom this is being achieved through successful public education initiatives, needle exchange programs, condom distribution, and voluntary HIV testing measures. The national response in Britain has recognized the links between AIDS, poverty, and development around the world and the responsibility the international community has in addressing these links.

HIV/AIDS is one of the greatest human rights and health challenges facing us today. We are all-too familiar with the statistics: an estimated thirty-six million people are infected worldwide; twenty-two million have already died; around fourteen thousand people are infected every single day around the world. These are staggering figures. But what they don't reveal are the countless individual stories of people whose rights are denied as a result of their HIV status; of the children orphaned by AIDS; of women who suffer discrimination, such as health worker Gugu Dlamini, who was stoned to death for having disclosed her HIV status; and of the HIV-positive men and women living in poverty without basic health services or access to medication, treatment, and care.

This year's World AIDS Day must be a rallying cry to all of us to show that we do care about the children, women, and men behind the statistics. It must be a challenge to us to work together as partners—as teachers, human rights activists, health care workers, politicians, businesspeople, and religious leaders—to confront the taboos associated with HIV/AIDS. Together we can challenge the attitudes and beliefs that lead to discrimination and inequality. We must encourage open and inclusive discussion on the difficult issues surrounding the AIDS epidemic, including discrimination based on gender, sexual orientation, race, poverty, and HIV and AIDS status.

The good news is that we know what works. We know that by improving respect for human rights we can go a long way to curbing the spread and alleviating the impact of the epidemic. This requires us to uncover and address the root causes of vulnerability to HIV infection. It means empowering women and girls to make decisions about their own sexuality. It means ensuring the right to freedom of expression, information, and association for individuals infected with and affected by HIV and AIDS. It means ensuring equal access to medication and effective health services. It means respecting the rights of all people—irrespective of their sexual orientation—to freely associate and express themselves. As UNAIDS Executive Director Peter Piot has stated, "this is not only the right thing to do: experience over the past twenty years tells us it is also the only pragmatic, practical solution to containing the spread of the epidemic and alleviating its impact."[25]

As you will know, Secretary General Kofi Annan has named the fight against HIV/AIDS as a priority issue for the international community. Important commitments have been made already. I would like to draw your attention to these.

At the General Assembly Special Session on AIDS in June 2001, states committed themselves to the realization of human rights as an essential part of the international response to the epidemic. They agreed on goals and targets based on human rights law and principles in four areas: prevention of new infections; provision of improved care, support and treatment for those infected with and affected by HIV/AIDS; reduction of vulnerability; and mitigation of the social and economic impact of HIV/AIDS. States also agreed on the need to address the factors that make individuals vulnerable to HIV infection, including poverty, lack of education, discrimination, lack of information and commodities for protection, and sexual exploitation of women, girls, and boys.

At the World Conference against Racism, states recognized HIV/AIDS status as a source of discrimination and expressed their concern that people infected with or affected by HIV/AIDS belong to groups vulnerable to racism, racial discrimination, xenophobia, and related intolerance. They agreed to strengthen national institutions to promote and protect the human rights of victims of racism who are also infected with HIV/AIDS, as well as to ensure access to HIV/AIDS medication and treatment.

Member states of the WTO recently adopted a Declaration on the TRIPS Agreement and Public Health which sends an important signal on the need to balance intellectual property rights against public health priorities for developing countries.[26] The Declaration stresses the need for TRIPS to be interpreted in a manner that supports states' right to protect public health and to promote access to medicines. The Declaration mentions in particular HIV/AIDS, malaria, and tuberculosis—all diseases that disproportionately affect developing countries.

And many states have made pledges to the Global Fund to Fight HIV/AIDS, malaria, and tuberculosis. This fund should allow additional resources to be mobilized to assist developing countries in addressing the challenges raised by these diseases.

All of these commitments encourage respect for the human rights of those infected with and affected by HIV/AIDS. My Office is working closely with UNAIDS to build on these commitments and to promote an effective and sustainable human rights response to the epidemic. Our approach is based on the following three elements:

The first element is ensuring respect, protection, and fulfillment of the human rights of people infected with, affected by or vulnerable to HIV, based on the principles of nondiscrimination, equality, participation, and accountability. This includes, for example, empowering women and girls by ensuring respect for their human rights, and particularly their right to make decisions about their own sexuality. It means ensuring that policies related to HIV testing are based on informed consent, on a confidential basis and accompanied by appropriate counseling.

The second element is creating the social and economic conditions to enable individuals and communities to exercise prevention, treatment, and care options when they are available. This means ensuring the right to freedom of expression, information, and association for all people, and in particular for those most affected by HIV and AIDS. This means ensuring that access to affordable HIV medication, care, and treatment is available on an equal basis.

The third element is addressing the needs of particularly vulnerable groups, including men who have sex with men, injecting drug users, women and men in prostitution, children, migrants and trafficked persons, minorities, indigenous peoples, and prisoners—as well as of the individuals and communities responding to the epidemic.

In order to achieve these objectives, OHCHR is working to increase accountability on HIV/AIDS-related human rights. Together with UNAIDS, we published the International Guidelines on HIV/AIDS and Human Rights as a tool to assist states in designing, coordinating, and implementing practical and effective national HIV/AIDS policies and strategies.[27]

I am delighted to note that the All-Party Parliamentary Group has used the Guidelines to analyze the British response to the epidemic and to recommend ways for the government to do more to protect and promote the human rights of people living with HIV and those vulnerable to it. The Group's inquiry into the United Kingdom's response to the International Guidelines sets a good example for others to follow. As the inquiry itself concludes, "only by considering the structural reasons for the spread of the virus and its effects, only by addressing the human rights of people vulnerable to the virus, only by striving to change the social and cultural factors that drive HIV will the world be able to confront, and ultimately stop, this devastating epidemic." Considering the horrific toll this disease continues to take on people in every country every day, the importance of this goal should not be underestimated.

III
Dimensions of the Mandate of High Commissioner

Chapter 6

Human Rights Defenders

Mary Robinson was hugely popular with NGOs and human rights defenders not least because her activist background as a lawyer, politician, and human rights campaigner meant that her sympathies and her perspectives were usually close, if not identical to, theirs on many controversies. On her many field visits she invariably sought out and encouraged grassroots activists, often speaking out publicly about their concerns and grievances as well as raising these in her official meetings.

A major gain for those working for human rights during her period in office was the adoption in 1998 of the Declaration on Human Rights Defenders after years of protracted and often polarized debate within the United Nations. To this was added the appointment in 2000 of a Special Representative of the Secretary General, Hina Jilani of Pakistan, with a mandate to monitor the implementation of the Declaration. During Mary Robinson's tenure as High Commissioner her constant encouragement and defense of civil society organizations, including human rights and development NGOs and youth and women's organizations and her insistence on their being heard were not appreciated by every government. But she saw the need to acknowledge their increasing influence within countries and in international affairs and to involve them constructively as partners in the struggle for equality, peace, justice, and development. She also recognized that human rights defenders were especially at risk after September 11 when antiterrorism measures were misused by some governments to clamp down on dissent and criticism. "Peaceful activities or the lawful exercise of rights must never be equated with terrorism," she declared in a speech in Dublin.

"New Protection for Human Rights Defenders"
International NGO Seminar on the Protection of Human Rights Defenders
Bogota, Colombia, 20 October 1998

Distinguished Delegates, Ladies, and Gentlemen,

It gives me great pleasure to be here with you at this important seminar on the protection of human rights defenders.

Seven months ago I opened the thirteenth session of the Working Group on Human Rights Defenders of the Commission on Human Rights entrusted with the elaboration of a draft Declaration on Human Rights Defenders.

I appealed to the participants to bear in mind the fundamental aim of this exercise: to support and strengthen the protection of human rights defenders around the world, who looked to the United Nations with great hope and expectation. The Declaration is now awaiting final approval by the General Assembly.[1] I am happy to recognize in this room potential beneficiaries of this Declaration who are at the forefront of efforts to promote and protect human rights, speaking and acting for those who have no voice and helping those seeking fairness and justice.

Role of Human Rights Defenders

As part of civil society, human rights defenders have always been the driving force of democracy, the rule of law and respect for human rights, and, accordingly, the counterweight to the power of the state. I would like to take this opportunity to pay tribute to the work of these men and women whose sacrifices have made possible most of the advances in the field of human rights protection, including the forthcoming adoption of the Declaration. Defenders play a crucial role in defending women's rights, promoting and protecting children's rights, struggling against impunity, and fighting racism, xenophobia, and religious intolerance. Their presence and work are most essential in situations of armed conflict or internal violence. Also—and we tend to forget this key element at the international level—local nongovernmental organizations are irreplaceable in explaining to individuals that they are the holders of rights and freedoms enshrined in international and national human rights instruments and that it is perfectly legitimate to campaign in favor of those rights.

Yet, these same individuals and groups are themselves often the victims of human rights abuses. They suffer from repression, intimidation, physical violence, and even murder, as the daily reports from around the world sadly bear witness. Indeed, in just over a year in office as High Commissioner, I have been deeply concerned about the large number of cases in which human rights defenders have been kidnapped or, alas, killed in the course of their courageous work. I have noted how many representatives of NGOs who come to see me in Geneva have asked if I could help to protect them when they returned home to continue their work. The Declaration will provide valuable and long-awaited recognition, protection, and support to those individuals, groups, and organizations.

The Declaration

At the same time, obviously, the Declaration will not resolve all the problems and difficulties faced by human rights defenders. Its adoption will, however, enable the international community to acknowledge the legitimacy of their work. The very first article of the draft Declaration states, "everyone has the right, individually and in association with others, to promote and to strive for the protection and realization of human rights and fundamental freedoms at the national and international levels." It is important to stress that the scope of the Declaration will not be limited to human rights groups or organizations. It will also extend to all individuals who, in their own countries, speak out routinely against human rights violations, particularly lawyers, journalists, trade union leaders, election monitors, educators, or all anonymous individuals committed to the promotion and protection of human rights.

The purpose of the draft Declaration is to clarify and reinforce human rights already recognized in existing international instruments. In order to do so, it refers to the right to set up human rights nongovernmental organizations, to defend the human rights of others, to meet and to communicate with other defenders, and to solicit, receive, and utilize resources. It also embodies the freedom of human rights activists to publish and make known their views and their right to criticize the human rights situations in their countries, to make proposals to improve them, and to have an effective and unhindered access to international bodies. Even more important for me is that the draft Declaration reaffirms that each state has a prime responsibility and duty to ensure, through legislative, administrative, and other steps, that the rights and freedoms referred to in the Declaration are effectively guaranteed.

We should certainly acknowledge that adoption of the Declaration on Human Rights Defenders is not an abstract goal. In today's world, thousands of human rights defenders are needed to help those whose rights are violated and to seek justice for those who suffer from unfairness in our societies. Yet, as I mentioned earlier, many face danger every day. It will therefore be essential to ensure that the rights and freedoms set out in the Declaration are put into practice in all countries and regions. Next year it will be up to the Commission on Human Rights to decide the steps needed for monitoring the implementation of the Declaration and assessing on a regular basis its effectiveness.[2] The Sub-Commission, treaty bodies, special procedures, and other mechanisms will all have to give due regard to the Declaration within their respective mandates.

The Declaration should be understood as a foundation for further progress in establishing a productive relationship between human rights defenders, states, and the international community. In this regard, I have taken note with interest of the joint statement of fifty-eight nongovernmental organizations, which calls upon my Office to ensure that the realization of the Declaration is addressed across the entire United Nations system. Priority measures will have to be taken to ensure the widest possible dissemination of the Declaration by the United Nations and its specialized agencies, other intergovernmental organizations, and nongovernmental organizations.

Colombia

I would like to take the opportunity of my presence in this Seminar to refer to the situation of human rights defenders in Colombia. In April this year the Commission on Human Rights was shocked and dismayed to learn about the assassination of Mr. Eduardo Umaña, a prestigious lawyer and a committed human rights defender, the latest in a long list of victims among human rights defenders in this country. The Commission's Chairman, Ambassador Selebi of South Africa, expressed our shock and sorrow, and we observed a minute of silence in memory of the slain lawyer. Allow me to pay a tribute to Mr. Umaña and to all Colombians who have given their lives while defending the cause of human rights.

The stress experienced by numerous Colombian nongovernmental organizations that carry out their daily activities under impossible circumstances has to be fully acknowledged. I will certainly encourage the authorities to take additional measures to protect human rights defenders. Among the issues I consider essential to address in every country are the need to have appropriate legislative and administrative measures in place for the protection of human rights defenders, the need to ensure proper investigations into attacks on them to bring promptly to justice the perpetrators of such abuses, and the need to provide due compensation to the victims and their families.

The adoption of the Declaration on Human Rights Defenders on 10 December 1998 will be of symbolic importance and an appropriate way to celebrate the fiftieth anniversary of the Universal Declaration of Human Rights. Let us remember that every attempt to deter defenders is a denial of the universality and indivisibility of the rights laid down in the Universal Declaration. The Declaration on Human Rights Defenders will remind states of their obligations towards those defenders. The Declaration will also give all those concerned appropriate tools in the defense of human rights throughout the world. It will be a challenge for all of us to preserve this important advance for the years to come.

"Linking the National and the International: A Challenge for Human Rights Defenders"
The Dublin Platform for Human Rights Defenders
Dublin, Ireland, 17 January 2002

Introduction

It is a great pleasure to be here with you today for the first Conference organized by FrontLine—the International foundation for the Protection of Human Rights Defenders.[3] To my knowledge this is Ireland's first indigenous international human rights NGO, and I congratulate Mary Lawlor and all of you who have contributed to its creation.

The central topic of this conference—that of human rights defenders—is of high priority to me personally, and to my Office as a whole. My message is threefold. First, I wish to acknowledge the crucial role played by human rights defenders and to reiterate strongly the importance of effective protection for defenders all over the world. Second, I wish to note growing concerns about the restrictions that may be placed on human rights defenders and their organizations, under the guise of action against terrorism in the aftermath of the appalling acts of September 11. And third, I wish to highlight the importance of follow-up to the Durban World Conference against Racism and the role of human rights defenders in that follow-up.

The Importance of Human Rights Defenders

To call the role of human rights defenders "crucial" is simply not sufficient. They are integral and indispensable to the implementation of human rights standards nationally and internationally.

Human rights defenders hold a mandate of protection—but we cannot forget that protection also applies to them. Our emphasis must be on the protection of those who dedicate their lives to promoting and protecting human rights. This is more than a moral obligation: it must rank among the highest priorities for the international community in its efforts to promote and protect human rights worldwide.

And yet in more than half the countries of the world, human rights defenders are attacked or subjected to a wide range of pressure tactics. Action against them ranges from violence in the form of the most outright attacks on life, physical integrity, and personal security to more subtle and diffuse forms of violence. These may include legal restrictions on freedoms of association, assembly, information, or movement and so on. Human rights defenders have suffered also through the false association of human rights with criminal activities, armed opposition to power, terrorism, or foreign influence. The saddest calls I received of late are those telling me of the murder of a brave defender I have met, Digna Ochoa in Mexico.

It is not the case that such attacks occur only in far-distant states. Three Irish names very quickly dispel that notion: Rosemary Nelson, Patrick Finucane, and Martin O'Hagan. These three names remind us that human rights defenders can pay with their lives for their work for others.

Human rights defenders come in many different forms. The Declaration on Human Rights Defenders sees them as "individuals, groups and associations . . . contributing to the effective elimination of all violations of human rights and fundamental freedoms of peoples and individuals." But there is great breadth to the term.

Defenders may be political activists or public servants; they may gather information or publicize it; they may witness and give testimony; they may teach, sing, or perform on human rights themes or simply stand up as individuals for a more just society. Some of their names are familiar to us, but the majority are not. Their ranks include the greatest possible variety of actors—from a lone voice in a remote village to major international NGOs based in the world's largest cities. The names of the Red Cross, Amnesty International, Human Rights Watch, and others are part of the language of our times, but equally there are individual heroes such as Victor Jara, who used music and song to powerfully campaign for justice in Chile. His life and death have recently been commemorated in song by a homegrown voice of social conscience, Christy Moore.

We must include those, for example, who cooperate with United Nations human rights bodies and mechanisms or domestic courts and tribunals. Witnesses who come forward may be considered as human rights defenders: collaboration with human rights or judicial processes can lead to considerable personal risks, and these people must receive adequate protection.

Of course, some human rights defenders may not have knowledge of the international system for the protection of human rights or the Declaration on Human Rights Defenders itself. They may not even identify themselves as part of the movement for human rights and fundamental freedoms. But they do all share an instinct for what is right, an understanding of the duty to protect those in need, and a longing for freedom and security for all.

The Role of Human rights Defenders

The title of my speech—"Linking the National and the International: A Challenge for Human Rights Defenders"—highlights one of the crucial tasks performed by defenders. We must not lose sight of a very clear truth: all human rights begin and end at home, at the national and the local level. In a sense, my Office and the entire international human rights system exists almost as a backstop or support structure to that central focus of human rights concern.

Encouraging and supporting civil society at all levels is a priority for my Office. For the international system can succeed only where the fruits of conferences, judicial decisions, and the recommendations of international treaty bodies are translated into law, practice, and, ultimately, enhanced protection at home. NGOs and human rights defenders have a crucial role to play in guaranteeing human rights on the ground—where they matter. They are the vital bridge between the theory and the practice of protection.

The Declaration on Human Rights Defenders recognizes this role in promoting human rights and fundamental freedoms and in safeguarding and strengthening democracy and democratic institutions and processes. Through investigating and bringing to light human rights abuses, human rights defenders develop and secure democracy.

Through insisting on respect for universal standards in their local environment, human rights defenders act as a conduit for international standards. Indeed, sometimes the mere presence of an individual to monitor and witness can provide effective protection against the gravest of human rights abuses. I am thinking of Peace Brigades International and other such persons who in a very real way extend protection through mere presence.

Human rights defenders also enhance the international system for the protection of human rights. Through civil society and human rights organizations at the local, national and regional levels, the universality of rights becomes more tangible—in essence you localize international standards while also feeding back into the international system, enriching shared universal values with the particular approaches, experiences and emphases of your region.

Protection of Human Rights Defenders

There is growing recognition at the international level of the importance of human rights defenders. The first major acknowledgment came with the adoption by the UN in 1998 of the Declaration on the Right and Responsibility of Individuals, Groups and Organs of Society to Promote and Protect Universally Recognized Human Rights and Fundamental Freedoms. This text—known as the Declaration on Human Rights Defenders—is a fundamental one, laying down a set of principles and rules designed to ensure the freedom of action of all human rights defenders.

While stressing that the primary duty to promote and protect human rights and fundamental freedoms lies with the state, it is recognized that individuals, groups, and associations have the right and responsibility to promote respect for, and foster knowledge of, human rights. A core cluster of rights necessary to human rights defenders is set out: the right of assembly, association, communication, information opinion and expression, and access to participation in the conduct of public affairs.

Similarly, the familiar guarantees of effective remedies and emphasis on education and training—of the public and of officials—are reflected in the Declaration. But it also goes further and, in article 13, covers such issues as the freedom to solicit, receive, and utilize resources for the purposes of promoting human rights and fundamental freedoms. It is further provided, in article 12.2, that

> The state shall take all necessary measures to ensure the protection by the competent authorities of everyone, individually and in association with others, against any violence, threats, retaliation, *de facto* or *de jure* adverse discrimination, pressure or any other arbitrary action as a consequence of their legitimate exercise of the rights referred to in this Declaration.

Another major advance in the protection of human rights defenders was ensured by the request of the Commission on Human Rights to the Secretary General, in April 2000, to appoint a Special Representative to protect and promote the rights of human rights defenders in compliance with the Declaration. Ms. Hina Jilani of Pakistan, who is here today, has done Trojan work since her appointment to this position.

Of course, protection of human rights defenders cannot be the responsibility of organs of the United Nations alone. NGOs themselves must seek to strengthen and make more effective the protection of human rights defenders in innovative ways. The formation of FrontLine—the first international NGO with a mandate to protect the protectors—is a welcome development in this regard. But all NGOs should aim to further promote the Declaration on Human Rights Defenders as a major bulwark against interference with the actions of defenders. It must be made better known.

Post–September 11

September 11, 2001 is a day that has entered our collective memory. The terrorist attacks that took place that day in the United States must be characterized as a crime against humanity—because of the nature and scale of the attacks primarily aimed against civilians. Many aftershocks of those horrendous acts have been felt in the international system. Indeed, its full implications are not yet clear and will take time to emerge.

Of course, the situation of human rights defenders was insecure before September 11 in many parts of the world. However, there is growing concern that increased restrictions may be placed on them. In the past, some authorities have sought to equate human rights work with criminal activities, armed opposition, terrorism, or undue foreign influence such as spying. Many states are now adopting antiterrorist or security legislation and other measures. We have heard reports of some governments using the global push against terrorism as a pretext to clamp down on legitimate dissent and criticism of state action. Let me repeat that peaceful activities or the lawful exercise of rights must never be equated with terrorism.

In efforts to eradicate terrorism, it is essential that states adhere strictly to their international obligations in the field of human rights. My Office is seeking to guard against inappropriate interpretations by states of Security Council Resolution 1373 on the suppression of terrorism, by monitoring in different parts of the world how human rights are being affected by antiterrorism measures.[4] Thus in respect of Europe, a joint statement on human rights and terrorism was issued in November by the Council of Europe, the Organisation for Security and Co-operation in Europe (OSCE), and my Office.[5] We recognized that the threat of terrorism requires specific measures but called on states to refrain from any excessive steps which would violate fundamental freedoms and undermine legitimate dissent.

We are also keen to ensure that states have regard in their antiterrorism policies and legislation adopted after September 11, to the standards set out in the International Covenant on Civil and Political Rights regulating resort to emergency measures. The Human Rights Committee, which monitors compliance with the Covenant, has adopted a detailed and authoritative comment for the guidance of states on the protection of human rights in an emergency.[6] An initial step required of all states that resort to emergency measures is to notify other states parties through the Secretary General of the existence of an emergency and of its official proclamation specifying any of the provisions in the Covenant that have been derogated from.

In the present difficult environment, the value of the Declaration on Human Rights Defenders will now be tested. It is a major bulwark against interference or restriction on the activities of defenders. It is the concrete expression of the resolve of the international community to assist and stand up for those who use their voices for those who cannot speak for themselves. The Declaration must reach the small, local NGOs and individual defenders and give them new strength and resolve in their actions.

World Conference against Racism

One point I have consistently emphasized is that the antidiscrimination agenda of the World Conference against Racism is even more crucial today than when it was adopted three days prior to September 11, 2001. The promotion of the twin pillars of equality and nondiscrimination are central both to the human rights agenda and to efforts to combat terrorism and conflict all over the world.

At Durban human rights defenders had the opportunity to participate and also to interact with one another. Such interaction has allowed the creation of new networks of groups and individuals committed to common goals. This is but one part of the continuing development of a truly international civil society, and the formation of alliances that can advance protection—for the vulnerable and for those who seek to defend them.

Durban must be a beginning rather than an end. Renewed emphasis on the nondiscrimination agenda is required to combat xenophobia and the disturbing increase in the number of violent incidents of racism—already on the rise in many societies (including our own) before the tragic events of September 11. The human rights goal must be to attempt to break the cycle of hatred, of intolerance, and of violence. Human rights education is a powerful tool in this regard. It can serve as a counter to a culture of ignorance or intolerance. It provides and develops a space for participation; it drives a demand for responsive institutions of state, which in turn provide alternatives to conflict.

However, this is not the complete story: true equality—both substantive and, in the language of the Irish peace process, parity of esteem—must be sought if conflict is to be prevented. There can be no enjoyment of human rights by all where some are excluded by disadvantage, discrimination and prejudice. Human rights, development, and the rule of law act as counterforces to the destructive ideologies of hate that inevitably spiral into conflict and violence. The challenge we face has, I think, been well encapsulated in the motto of the Women's Support Network in Belfast. It describes itself as "a united voice affirming difference."

Civil Society and International Affairs

The World Conference texts recognize fully the importance of civil society in the elimination of racism. At Durban there was an unprecedented level of civil-society involvement in the Conference and parallel events. Those parallel events, the youth summit, the Voices for Victims forum, the extraordinary level of participation by civil society, all reflect the growing transparency and democratization of global gatherings. We are experiencing the welcome transition of UN conferences from diplomatic gatherings to open and global dialogue. This reflects two elements of what Secretary General Kofi Annan in a recent speech termed the fundamental principles by which the work of the UN must be guided: namely, that the UN must place people at the center of everything it does—enabling them to meet their needs and realize their full potential—and that all the actors of the international system must work together in pursuit of common goals.[7]

Civil society has a central role to play in global dialogue. Ensuring greater accessibility of the UN—that is, efforts to have more voices at the table—is part of this growing global dialogue. But I believe this also reflects the new reality of international affairs. It is no longer the case—if it ever was—that governments and states are the only actors of import on the international stage. In this era of globalization, cooperation between governments and civil society actors at all levels must be the new norm. All these factors mean that civil society actors and human rights defenders have a greater possibility than ever to influence and to contribute to the protection of human rights.

Concluding Remarks

There is a saying that if you desire peace, you must first cultivate justice. The work of human rights defenders all over the world to promote social justice, equality, and basic rights is peace-building in action.

I think of the words of Angelina Atyam, a nurse from Uganda and the mother of a daughter abducted by the rebel army in 1996. She reminds us: "Human rights defenders come in all forms. The majority are ordinary individuals who have a small public voice and low public profile. However, they keep the fire burning."[8] In her case, she keeps a fire burning on behalf of the parents of over five thousand children abducted by the Lord's Resistance Army in Uganda, who have not yet returned to their homes.

Every person who lives in freedom is a testament to the tenacity of those who fight for justice. In short, we enjoy freedoms because of their selflessness, courage, and sacrifice. To the lawyers, singers, teachers, carers, journalists, activists, doctors, witnesses, writers, and parents, and quite simply to each and every person from whatever background who takes a stand for human rights and for justice I say thank you. We all owe you a great debt. And I pledge to all human rights defenders the continued commitment of my Office to your protection.

We must ensure that human rights defenders—those who keep the fire burning—are free to carry out their crucial role. Truly, when we protect human rights defenders, we protect ourselves.

Chapter 7

Economic, Social, and Cultural Rights

A defining characteristic of Mary Robinson's term as High Commissioner was her commitment to change the status of economic social and cultural rights as the neglected clauses of the Universal Declaration of Human Rights. In her speeches and messages, she advocated their equal status with civil and political rights and freedoms requiring equal attention from all governments. The impending ratification by China of the International Covenant on Economic Social and Cultural Rights provided her with an opportunity to discuss the signs that the neglect of these categories of rights was being reversed, including in the courts, and to urge China to fully accept the Covenant. The study of the right to food requested by the World Food Summit and undertaken by OHCHR in cooperation with others is an example of both the integration of a human rights perspective within United Nations agencies and the contribution that a human rights analysis can make to the global problem of food security. Similar points can be made with respect to her analysis of the right to adequate housing and OHCHR cooperation with the United Nations Centre for Human Settlements (HABITAT).

"Promoting Economic, Social, and Cultural Rights"
Opening address at Beijing Workshop
Beijing, China, 21 November 2000

It gives me great pleasure to be with you during this visit, which is of high importance for my Office and, I believe, for the people of this country. Yesterday afternoon Mr. Wang Guangya, Vice Foreign Minister, and I signed a Memorandum of Understanding on our mutual agreement to cooperate in the development and implementation of technical cooperation programs. This Memorandum is the fruit of more than two years of discussion and engagement.

One of the four key areas addressed in the Memorandum of Understanding is economic, social, and cultural rights and the right to development. These are key priority issues for my Office, and I am glad that specialists and experts representing different institutions have come together to discuss them today. I would like to share with you what my Office is doing in this regard, and I would like to learn more about your concerns and to understand the political and institutional implications of your deliberations on the ratification of the International Covenant on Economic, Social and Cultural Rights. I am aware that just last month the Standing Committee of the National People's Congress considered the issue of the ratification of this instrument. I welcome this positive development.[1]

New Commitment to Economic, Social, and Cultural Rights

The good news is that greater recognition and attention are being given these days to economic, social, and cultural rights. The World Conference on Human Rights of 1993 closed the long-running and unproductive debate about the importance of economic, social, and cultural rights relative to civil and political rights. Within the human rights community it is no longer seriously questioned that economic, social, and cultural rights are indeed as much rights and as indispensable as civil and political rights in enabling human beings to lead lives of basic human dignity.

The gap between the language of recognition and the reality of respect and implementation of these rights still persists. However, there are unmistakable signs that this state of affairs is beginning to change.

Both the Commission on Human Rights and the Sub-Commission on the Promotion and Protection of Human Rights have increasingly devoted attention to economic, social and cultural rights-related issues. A number of new, special mechanisms of the Commission on Human Rights have been created in recent years, such as Independent Experts on the right to development, on extreme poverty, and on structural adjustment policies and foreign debt. There have also been established Special Rapporteurs on the right to education, on adequate housing, and on the right to food. Furthermore, United Nations bodies have begun to address the enjoyment of economic, social, and cultural rights in the context of other current topics, such as the right to development, globalization and poverty, as well as international trade, investment, and finance.

The wind of change has also been felt by the monitoring body of the International Covenant on Economic, Social and Cultural Rights, the Committee on Economic, Social and Cultural Rights. It has in recent times benefited from a number of material improvements enhancing its capacity to fulfill its work.

My Office has also increased our regional activities, including in support of the promotion of economic, social, and cultural rights. The Teheran Framework for technical cooperation on human rights in the Asia Pacific region is based on four pillars, one of which concerns strategies for the realization of the right to development and economic, social, and cultural rights.[2] The first regional intersessional workshop on the realization of the right to development and economic, social, and cultural rights was held in Sana'a, Yemen in February of this year. A further regional inter-sessional workshop on the impact of globalization on the right to development and economic, social, and cultural rights will be hosted by the Government of Malaysia in Kuala Lumpur in the near future.

In parallel, my Office has supported a series of activities under another pillar of the Asia Pacific framework of technical cooperation: the pillar of national institutions for the promotion and protection of human rights. The Asia-Pacific Forum of National Human Rights Institutions has focused on economic, social, and cultural rights at its last three annual meetings.

Other opportunities are presenting themselves in different parts of the UN family through the process of integrating human rights within the United Nations system. A rights-based approach contributes to the realization of economic, social, and cultural rights.

The nongovernmental community is strengthening its engagement with economic, social, and cultural rights. The NGO forum accompanying the 1993 World Conference on Human Rights in Vienna was a watershed event. The Vienna+5 NGO Forum in Ottawa in 1998 was a further heartening stage where economic, social, and cultural rights became a primary focus for the first time at a major international human rights conference.[3] Other recent examples of global action include the emergence of the Habitat International Coalition on the right to housing and land, and the Food First Aid International Action Network on the right to food and land.[4] But in spite of the growing recognition of the importance of economic, social and cultural rights, many challenges remain.

Clarifying the Scope of Economic, Social, and Cultural Rights

First, there is a need for further clarity concerning the scope and meaning of these rights. The UN treaty bodies have contributed significantly to the development of their normative legal interpretation, in particular, the Committee on Economic, Social and Cultural Rights. The Committee engages in a constructive dialogue with states parties in the context of the reporting procedure, which provides the opportunity to address issues and concerns that are specific to each state party. During the dialogue, the Committee endeavors to determine the specific needs of the state, interpreting each right in concreto in the light of the particular circumstances of the state.

Another way in which the Committee tries to enhance the understanding of economic, social, and cultural rights is by the adoption of General Comments on issues arising from the Covenant. To date, the Committee has adopted fourteen such General Comments which contain authoritative interpretations of provisions of the Covenant.[5] These address a wide range of issues, such as the objectives of reporting, the obligations of states parties under the Covenant, and the domestic application of the Covenant in the national legal order. The General Comments also cover substantive rights such as the right to housing; the right to food; the right to education, including primary education; and, most recently, the right to health.

The Committee organizes Days of General Discussion, during which experts in the field, scholars, practitioners, and interested intergovernmental and nongovernmental organizations join with members of the Committee to discuss substantive issues concerning economic, social, and cultural rights. These Days of General Discussion often result in the formulation of a General Comment.

Monitoring

A second challenge lies in the area of monitoring the implementation of rights. At the international level, the reporting procedure does not meet all needs. There is a need for supplementary procedures allowing for the submission of complaints by individuals and groups concerning alleged violations of economic, social, and cultural rights. The Committee on Economic, Social and Cultural Rights has been considering a draft optional protocol providing for individual complaints since 1990 and submitted a draft to the Commission on Human Rights in 1996. I have endorsed the adoption of such an optional protocol, which would do justice to the principle of indivisibility and interdependence of all human rights, and which would allow for the establishment of a body of international case law.[6]

At the national level, pursuing justiciability is crucial. Domestic standards and enforcement must make up for the lack of strength in the international system. My Office is planning to organize, pursuant to the Beijing Plan of Action,[7] a workshop next year on the justiciability of economic, social, and cultural rights for the judiciary of South Asian countries.[8]

As I have mentioned, I am encouraged that steps are being taken by the relevant authorities in China to ratify the International Covenant on Economic, Social and Cultural Rights. Ratification of the Covenant will have a global significance on two counts: first, because it affects one-fifth of the world's population; and, second, because China's ratification of the Covenant will send a strong message to all other countries which are not yet parties to the Covenant. I encourage the Chinese Government not to enter reservations when ratifying the Covenant on Economic, Social and Cultural Rights. Treaty bodies request at every consideration of country reports that states parties review the reservations they have entered with a view to removing them.

Trade Union Rights

I would emphasize the importance of labor and social security rights in the context of China's current economic agenda and its entry to the World Trade Organization. In particular, I urge that there should be no reservation to article 8 of the International Covenant when ratified, on freedom of association and trade unions rights. Grassroots and trade union initiatives could be empowering for employees. I welcome the new initiatives aimed at enhancing people's awareness of laws and regulations concerning labor relations, social security, and labor dispute handling procedures. The Employee Legal Aid Centers first set up in Shanghai three years ago and now opened in many locations in China are good examples of such initiatives.

The promotion of economic, social, and cultural rights is a challenge for all of us working in governmental and civil society institutions, as well as in international organizations. I am interested in hearing your views in this regard, in particular about challenges in the area of education and health, women's rights and the rights of internal migrants, the right to association and trade union rights. I hope you will discuss various dimensions such as rural and urban concerns, minority rights, and gender issues in the changing context of social and economic issues in China. I recall my similar meeting with Chinese experts two years back where I was very encouraged by insights and advice received. I hope today's workshop will again become a forum for a frank, open, and fruitful exchange of views on the topic of economic, social, and cultural rights in the context of this great country.

Thank you.

"The World Food Summit: Five Years Later"
Food and Agricultural Organization, Rome, Italy, 10 June 2002

The 1996 Rome World Food Summit in its Plan of Action invited my Office in collaboration with others to undertake a better definition of the rights related to food in article 11 of the International Covenant on Economic, Social and Cultural Rights. That task has been completed successfully. The process involved a wide range of consultations with individual experts, treaty bodies, specialized agencies, and programs, with Mr. Jean Ziegler, the Special Rapporteur of the Commission on Human Rights on the right to food, as well as with nongovernmental organizations.

The scope of the definition and the obligations it places on states are best captured in the General Comment adopted by the Committee on Economic, Social and Cultural Rights. General Comment No. 12 gives an authoritative interpretation of the right to adequate food.[9]

The World Food Summit also asked my Office to propose ways to realize rights related to food as means to achieve the commitments and objectives of the World Food Summit. From a human rights perspective, this concerns the implementation of the right by the primary duty holder, the state. We can report progress on this task as well. Some twenty countries have adopted constitutions which, in more or less explicit terms, refer to rights concerning food or a related norm. A smaller number have developed legislative means to ensure enjoyment of the right to food in a comprehensive way. My Report to the Summit illustrates this with the example of Norway.[10] There have been welcome examples also of judicial consideration and enforcement of the right in different countries, and an important decision of the Indian Supreme Court is referred to in the Report.[11] But much more effort is needed on implementation of the right at the national level.

The shocking reality is that although there are sufficient food resources in the world, we are not progressing at the necessary pace to reach the target set in 1996 by the World Food Summit and reiterated by the Millennium Declaration in 2000, of halving the number of hungry by 2015. This is morally and legally unacceptable. As we gather here it is estimated that nearly thirteen million people in southern Africa will face famine in the coming months. In addition, certain groups, such as HIV/AIDS-affected persons and women in rural areas, can have particular difficulties in coping as a result of discrimination or lack of accountability on the part of states. As we begin to discuss how to shape a more ethical globalization, it is clear that food security must be an overall priority.

Therefore, we must move beyond rhetoric and put the realization of the right to adequate food at the center of the new agenda. The focus has to be on implementation. I believe it would be helpful to work further on agreeing on practical guidelines that may help states to identify measures to implement this right. The World Food Summit: Five Years Later should give a fresh impetus to international action on the implementation of the right to food. It should adopt a multitrack strategy in which states, the UN, the private sector, NGOs, and civil society generally join efforts to make the commitments of the World Food Summit, as reinforced by the Millennium Declaration, a reality.

"The Human Right to Adequate Housing—Practical Aspects"
OHCHR/HABITAT Expert Meeting
Palais des Nations, Geneva, 9 March 1999

Ladies and Gentlemen,

I am particularly glad to welcome so many experts on housing issues as well as our colleagues from the United Nations Centre for Human Settlements (HABITAT) to discuss over the next three days the best ways to implement at the international as well as the national and local levels the human right to adequate housing.

The extensive cooperation between HABITAT and the OHCHR over the full and progressive realization of the human right to adequate housing provides a practical example of successful implementation of the Secretary General's goal, which is to incorporate human rights issues across the activities of the United Nations as a *shared responsibility* of all UN entities.

Few economic, social, and cultural rights are violated on the scale of housing rights. According to UN estimates, over one hundred million people are structurally homeless, with a further one billion or more forced by circumstances beyond their control to reside in entirely inadequate housing.

The Right to Housing: Legal Dimensions

Since the adoption of the Universal Declaration of Human Rights in 1948, the right to adequate housing has been recognized as an important component of the right to an adequate standard of living. It has also been confirmed in the leading human rights conventions as well as the International Labour Organization Recommendation No. 115 on Workers' Housing.[12]

Throughout the past decade resolutions reaffirming the right to adequate housing have been adopted by the General Assembly, the Economic and Social Council, the Commission on Human Rights, and the Sub-Commission on Prevention of Discrimination and Protection of Minorities. The latter body appointed a Special Rapporteur on promoting the right to adequate housing, Mr. R. Sachar, who in 1995 produced a comprehensive study on practical measures toward the realization of this human right.[13]

The legal recognition of housing rights also has regional dimensions under the auspices of the Council of Europe, the Organization of American States, and the Organization of African Unity. The 1996 revised European Social Charter included an independent provision with a view to ensuring the effective exercise of the right to housing.[14] States parties undertook to take measures designed to promote access to housing of an adequate standard, prevent and reduce homelessness with a view to its gradual elimination, and make the price of housing accessible to those without adequate resources. A "collective complaints procedure" enables NGOs and other recognized groups to present formal legal complaints to the European Social Charter's Committee of Experts alleging violations or noncompliance with the norms of the Charter.

The housing process demands a broad and holistic approach to housing rights. These include the right to popular participation throughout the housing development process; the rights to organize, assemble, and associate; legal protection from forced or threatened eviction or house demolitions; the right to security of tenure for all dwellers; the right to equality of treatment; the availability of impartial legal remedies in cases of alleged violations of housing rights; access to essential services including piped water, drainage, sanitation facilities, garbage removal, electricity, and heating (if necessary), etc. An effective approach contributing to the full and progressive realization of housing rights will develop ways and means of adequately addressing each of these elements of the larger right to adequate housing.

The international recognition of housing rights is not a substitute for endeavors designed to closely monitor actual achievements and failures in the struggle for the human right to adequate housing. A comprehensive approach within the United Nations system to address different aspects of the realization process of housing rights is also needed. Adequately funded and clearly defined initiatives and objectives by the international community involving activities designed to prevent housing rights abuse and to empower, educate, and train citizens about their entitlements to adequate housing as a human right, and the incorporation of housing rights themes within ongoing human rights operations at the field level could go a long way toward actually protecting this fundamental human right.

Governmental Responsibilities

All governments without exception have a responsibility in the shelter sector, as exemplified by their creation of ministries of housing or agencies, by their allocation of funds for the housing sector, and by their policies, programs, and projects. The national laws should prohibit any discrimination and provide legal security of tenure and equal access to land for all, including women and those living in poverty, as well as effective protection from forced evictions that are contrary to the law. Governments should also adopt policies aiming at making housing habitable, affordable, and accessible to all disadvantaged groups, including low-income groups.

Definition of "Adequacy"

Seven principles provide a context for defining housing "adequacy" and in determining the level to which the right to adequate housing is in place in any given society: legal security of tenure; availability of services, building materials, and infrastructure; affordability; habitability; accessibility; adequate location in terms of access to employment options; and cultural adequacy.

Poverty thwarts the enjoyment of the human right to adequate housing and is itself a violation of human rights. Poverty prevents people from accessing even the cheapest legal homes and forces them into slums and squatter settlements. People living in poverty stand a far greater chance of living in housing that degrades and often decimates their health, well-being, and often physical security. Moreover, if you are poor—anywhere in the world—your chances of being forcibly evicted from your home are infinitely greater than if you were middle-class. The odds of possessing legal security of tenure if you are poor are limited throughout the world. These examples show clearly that inadequate housing results in violations of human rights and that these abuses can be prevented and remedied if the right policies—targeting the poor—are implemented.

Human Rights Guidelines on Forced Evictions

One of the most blatant types of housing rights violation is the still very common act of forced evictions. Despite the extensive consideration given to stopping this practice over the past decade, millions of people are violently removed from their homes each year. According to the Centre on Housing Rights and Evictions (COHRE), a staggering fourteen million people are currently threatened by planned forced evictions.[15]

In 1997 an expert group meeting convened by our Office adopted the Comprehensive Human Rights Guidelines on Development-Based Displacement,[16] which seek to steer states away from the practice of forced evictions carried out in connection with development projects. In this connection the Guidelines provide that states should ensure that no persons, groups, or communities are rendered homeless or are exposed to the violation of any other human rights as a consequence of a forced eviction.

The Guidelines propose that states should fully explore all possible alternatives to any act involving forced eviction. All affected persons, including women, children, and indigenous peoples, should have the right to all relevant information and the right to full participation and consultation and to propose alternatives to eviction. In the event that agreement cannot be reached, an independent body, such as a court of law, tribunal, or ombudsman, may be called upon.

Security of Place

Since all human rights are to be treated equally, in an interdependent and indivisible manner, we should begin discussions on what could be called the right to security of place. This right exemplifies the convergence of civil and political rights and economic, social, and cultural rights and places three forms of security into an indispensable human rights framework. First, this right encapsulates the notion of security-protection of physical integrity and safety from harm and guarantees that basic rights will be respected. Second, this right incorporates all dimensions of human security—or the economic and social side of the security dimension. While third, the right to security of place recognizes the importance of tenure rights (for tenants, owners, and those too poor to afford to rent or buy a home) and the critical right to be protected against any arbitrary or forced eviction from one's home.

This manifestation of security intrinsically links to housing rights concerns during times of peace and where housing rights issues arise in the midst of armed conflict and humanitarian disasters. I hope this gathering can discuss the notion of the right to security of place to determine how this might assist in improving the protection of housing rights everywhere.

Proposals for Action

In particular, I would like to support the following actions—all of which are obtainable, feasible, and necessary to giving housing rights the attention they deserve.

First, all key principles linked to housing rights shall be consolidated, and each manifestation of eviction, displacement, removal, or transfer shall be addressed through the guidelines on development-based displacement. The guidelines are also there for national implementation of the different aspects of the housing right: on property and housing restitution in the context of refugee and internally displaced persons' return and for international events and forced evictions. The Guidelines could be supplemented by a new General Comment by the Committee on Economic, Social and Cultural Rights on the rights of women and housing rights; a general recommendation on women, discrimination, and housing rights by the Committee on the Elimination of All Forms of Discrimination against Women; and a general recommendation on housing rights and racial discrimination by the Committee on the Elimination of All Forms of Racial Discrimination.

Second, the international community should adopt the Comprehensive Human Rights Guidelines on Development-Based Displacement. If approved in their current form, this new standard will provide a very useful series of international norms protecting people against the more ruthless side of the development process.[17]

Third, I would encourage further consideration of how to prevent housing rights violations. This subject is long overdue and of crucial importance if the Commission on Human Rights is to be seen to be treating all rights equally.

Fourth, I would encourage all states to appoint a National Housing Rights Officer with responsibility for all government policies, programs and plans on the implementation of housing rights. My Office will develop the capacity to provide technical assistance of various kinds to states wishing to pursue such appointments so that national plans of action geared toward the full realization of housing rights can be widely promoted.

Fifth, I would support the publication of a Comprehensive Compilation of National Housing Rights Legislation, with a view to assisting states wishing to adopt such laws and to provide a consolidated elaboration of these important, but often overlooked, local and national laws supporting housing rights.

Housing rights violations during periods of ethnic violence and armed conflict tend to be massive but often underestimated as a source of tension. Moreover, housing and property disputes in postconflict situations (Bosnia, Georgia, and Rwanda, to name several) present some of the most difficult challenges to policy-makers seeking to build peaceful, multiethnic societies.

Finally, incorporating a housing rights component into all field operations could perform a very useful function in giving housing issues the higher profile they deserve. A joint pilot project between HABITAT and my Office could prove a very practical way to formalize our UN Housing Rights Programme and to begin what will hopefully become a fruitful, much longer-term relationship with HABITAT, in which we together work in coordination toward the goal of ridding the earth of housing rights violations in our lifetime.

Chapter 8

The Right to Development

The General Assembly resolution establishing the post of High Commissioner included as one of the post's responsibilities "[to] promote and protect the realization of the right to development and to enhance support from relevant bodies of the United Nations system for this purpose." While a weak consensus has developed among countries on the recognition of such a right, there is little or none on how to implement it. In all her advocacy on questions of development and poverty and particularly on Africa, Mary Robinson promoted the right to development. She championed the New Partnership for Africa's Development (NEPAD), an African initiative that for her was an embodiment of the right to development in action. OHCHR gave support to the initiatives of the Commission on Human Rights on the right to development, in particular its Working Group.

This sample of addresses reflects her thinking on poverty and human rights, the right to development, Africa, and the UN Millennium Development Goals. The addresses reflect as well her efforts to advance thinking on rights-based approaches to development. (See also Chapter 18.)

Working Group on the Right to Development of the Commission on Human Rights
Opening Session
Palais des Nations, Geneva, 25 February 2002

Chairperson, Distinguished Delegates, Ladies, and Gentlemen,

My purpose in addressing you is to encourage you. I do so from a deep conviction that your work is of central importance.

At the follow-up to the World Conference on Social Development in June 2000,[1] I welcomed a new dialogue between development and human rights specialists, based on the affirmation of the right to development by all states—large and small, north and south. A few months on, the Millennium Assembly promised to make the right to development a reality for everyone. Now, two years on, we should be in a new and positive position in the third session of this Working Group to build on that consensus and propose positive insights and concrete ideas that, if accepted, the Commission could record as a real breakthrough on this vital right. Let us try to do so in order that our efforts over the next two weeks can be harnessed toward a practical outcome.

As we all know and know only too well, discussion on the right to development has been long a prisoner to political controversy. That should not, indeed cannot, continue if the Working Group truly wishes for success. While in this forum we proceed from year to year with a somewhat abstract dialogue, things are happening in the world, through which I would argue that the right to development is being recognized and realized in practice. The Working Group should take stock. It should take encouragement from the fact that many of the elements set out in the Declaration of 1986 are providing the building blocks of development programs, movements, initiatives, and ideas both ambitious and modest all over the world.[2] It will also find that my Office has been active in promoting the right to development through emphasizing these elements in numerous contexts, including in working with the Independent Expert, Arjun Sengupta.[3] My staff and I are confident that our efforts have borne fruit. We believe that we have demonstrated in the eyes of others the enduring merit and value of the1986 Declaration as a rich normative source for global social change and justice.

Allow me to recall some of those core elements of the Declaration: the centrality of all human rights, the principle of nondiscrimination, participation, accountability, international cooperation, and a multidimensional view of development that embraces, but goes beyond, economics. The most important and—indeed exciting—illustration I can offer of the application of these elements in a dynamic and creative relationship is the New Partnership for Africa's Development (NEPAD).

New Partnership for Africa's Development

As you will know, the New Partnership for Africa's Development was first developed by the leaders of South Africa, Nigeria, Egypt, Senegal, and Algeria. In July 2001 the OAU, in the context of proclaiming the new African Union, adopted NEPAD as the road map for development in all of Africa. NEPAD is significant because it is an African idea and will be an African-led program. It is significant also because it articulates a comprehensive vision of development, with a program of action that embraces initiatives on peace and security, democracy and political governance, as well as economic and corporate governance with a commitment to regional and subregional approaches to development. NEPAD is equally innovative in integrating into development plans as resources the rich cultural history of Africa and its contribution to the cultures of the global community.

African countries recognize that if the necessary higher level of debt relief, ODA, and longer-term private investment flows from their partners in the industrialized countries, are to come about, then in their own words, "accountable government, a culture of human rights, and popular participation"[4] are among the conditions. Detailed proposals on good governance are to be put in place by the NEPAD steering committee, which will involve peer review and a code of conduct. The task African leaders have set themselves is, of course, huge, but it has already evoked positive support and involvement from the G8 where NEPAD will be taken up in the June meeting in Canada.

I do recommend study by the Working Group of the NEPAD core text. You will find there, as I have illustrated, the practical application of all the elements of the right to development. The procedures and mechanisms of implementation are also worth study in considering questions of implementation of the right to development.

Ethical Globalization and International Cooperation

One objective of NEPAD is to end the marginalization of Africa through its integration into global economic and political processes. At the Global Social Forum in Porto Allegre and at the Economic Forum in New York last month I appealed for an ethical globalization.[5]

I noted that "Globalization is a reality; it is not new, and it is not going away. It is within our power, however, to ensure that it becomes a positive force for all the world's people."

Support for an ethical globalization is to be found in the Declaration on the Right to Development not least in the international cooperation provision in article 3.[6] Article 3 declares that states have a duty to cooperate with each other in assuring development and eliminating obstacles to development. We have seen the potential of international cooperation in the response through the Security Council to terrorism following September 11. Cooperation is key. I highlight two points.

First, international cooperation includes but is not restricted to development assistance. But the right to development is not a state right to development assistance. As NEPAD recognizes the right to development is about empowering individuals and communities. Governments of poor countries are the vehicles for the use of aid, and this carries with it important responsibilities. However, if the development goals of the Millennium Declaration are to be met, wealthy countries—OECD countries as well as large developing countries—have responsibilities also, including through meeting the UN development assistance goal of 0.7 percent of GDP. Few countries actually do so yet.

Second, international cooperation is an important element, as I have said, of ethical globalization. At Porto Allegre, I emphasized the need for states to examine the impact of agricultural trade agreements on the right to food and the right to development. Similarly, in implementing intellectual property agreements, I encouraged states to ensure at the same time the rights of people facing life-threatening diseases. The recent Declaration at Doha gives us room to hope that constructive approaches to economic globalization might be a realizable goal.[7] The right to development can and should provide the framework to achieve this goal.

Indicators and Benchmarks on the Right to Development

The next step on thinking on the right to development will require the compilation of an agreed list of core development indicators for civil, cultural, and political rights to measure such things as the administration of justice, political participation, and personal security. It will also require integrating the "rights element" into socioeconomic indicators, for example by desegregating health and education indicators to test for equality and nondiscrimination.

What we are looking for are tools for development, not weapons of critique—a set of time-bound targets for achieving the various components of the right to development against which the relative success of development programs can be judged. I encourage you to consider this as part of your deliberations over the next two weeks.

Development Compacts and the Right to Development

The Independent Expert, Arjun Sengupta, has demonstrated in his work a practical approach to the right to development with an emphasis on how to make this right a meaningful dimension of international economic relations and domestic policy. His proposed development compacts provide a good context and opportunity to develop thinking.[8] The Independent Expert has proposed a method for implementing the right to development immediately based on national development programming using a participatory model and international cooperation through development assistance. This model will elevate to the multilateral level what is already happening at the bilateral level. It also appears to me to be fully in line with the approach of the New Partnership for African Development. I encourage you to discuss his ideas seriously.

But I encourage you to go further. I encourage you to consider the best mechanism to elaborate the obligations attached to the right to development and the most appropriate means of translating universal standards into local benchmarks and indicators to ensure the transparency and objectivity that will be needed for the development compacts to work.

High Commissioner's Report to the Commission

My report to the forthcoming session of the Commission will be before you.[9] I thought to mention some points from it to underscore what I said at the outset, that my Office is constantly involved in activities under the six resolutions of the General Assembly and Commission that mandate our work on the right to development.

The report gives details of dissemination activities including the new training materials we have prepared with UNDP on human rights in development. We have a dedicated page on the OHCHR Web site on human rights and development. This is broken down into information links on the right to development, rights-based approaches to development, mainstreaming human rights, poverty, good governance, and globalization. That page also provides full coverage of the Working Group's meeting with all documentation placed on line.

On mainstreaming I should mention the MASCOT project, an abbreviation for support for mainstreaming human rights including rights-based development within UN country teams. Another project that is outlined is HURIST, a joint project with UNDP designed to define, test, and implement methodologies for integrating human rights standards and principles in sustainable human development.

The report to the Commission also notes that in November last the Office organized the First African Regional Dialogue on Human Rights, the African Union, and the New Partnership for African Development. The dialogue included as a topic "Human Right to Development."

I should mention also that in January 2002 I delivered a Presidential lecture at the World Bank in Washington at the invitation of Mr. Wolfensohn. Members will recall that the General Assembly had suggested that I should carry out a dialogue with the Bank on the right to development.[10] This lecture was a first phase of that dialogue which my staff has followed up on since. It is clear that there is the beginning of convergence of thinking between the Bank and OHCHR on the centrality of human rights to sustainable development. I confidently expect that that convergence will prove positive in deeper cooperation between us in the future.

Chairperson, this Working Group is one of the few opportunities within the United Nations devoted to discussion of development in all its forms—political, cultural, economic, and social. I urge you to use this opportunity to begin a process—heralded by the Millennium Declaration—to make the right to development a reality for everyone.

Development without human rights is meaningless. Poverty eradication without empowerment is unsustainable. Social integration without minority rights is unimaginable. Gender equality without women's rights is illusory. Full employment without workers' rights may be no more than a promise of sweatshops, exploitation, and slavery. Development without participation and accountability is undemocratic. The logic of the right to development is inescapable.

We can move forward only if there is consensus, and we can move further if the consensus is stronger. I would therefore ask that the conclusions of your work confine themselves to that which can be agreed with conviction. I do believe that the new thinking represented by NEPAD should be a source of inspiration and encouragement to all of us.

"Challenges for Human Rights and Development in Africa"
Celebration of International Human Rights Day
Addis Ababa, Ethiopia, 10 December 2001

Excellencies, Ladies, and Gentlemen,

Introduction

I have come to Addis Ababa on this Human Rights Day for a dialogue, and especially to listen. I am very glad to have had the opportunity to participate in this afternoon's Panel, and I learned a lot from the discussion it generated.

Today, 10 December, marks the date in 1948 when the General Assembly of the United Nations proclaimed the Universal Declaration of Human Rights. The Declaration, which set out ideals and targets calling for recognition and respect for all human rights—civil, political, economic, social, and cultural—for all human beings in the world, can claim to be the most influential text ever adopted by the United Nations.

It is true that most of Africa was not represented in the United Nations at that time. But I recall Nelson Mandela's account during his trial of first hearing of the proclamation of the Universal Declaration in 1948. It filled him with hope at a dark time for his people when the Nationalist government of South Africa was consolidating apartheid. When African peoples achieved self-determination and joined the United Nations they embraced the Universal Declaration. They went on to reflect its principles in their own African Charter on Human and Peoples' Rights. They also ratified the main international human rights instruments. African countries have helped shape many of those instruments. Indeed, it is not well-known history that it is to newly independent Africa, and more broadly the developing world, that we owe a number of the major innovations in the international legal protection of human rights of the twentieth century.

It was the determination of the new African and Asian nations of the United Nations in the 1960s to end apartheid in South Africa that shaped the long UN campaign against racism. When you view the struggle for equality as underscoring the entire human rights movement—as I do—this critical role assumes yet more importance. That struggle led to the International Convention on the Elimination of All Forms of Racial Discrimination, of 1965, one of the cornerstones of the international human rights treaty system. The struggle against apartheid at the international level also laid the foundations for the current capacity of the UN machinery to intervene and intercede over many other human rights violations across the world. This is a debt the world owes to Africa but which is not often recognized.

We also owe our thinking on the relationship between development and human rights largely to countries of the South and their determination to make the ideals of human rights relevant to their situation. When the newly independent countries of the 1960s and 1970s joined the United Nations, they took the promise of universal human rights principles and insisted that they were applied to the conditions of their peoples. Despite serious problems of governance, and often of corruption, the belief was there. In 1981 Africa recognized the right to development as a basic human right in the African Charter on Human and Peoples' Rights. From their efforts came the UN Declaration on the Right to Development of 1986. From that deeply influential statement—adopted in Cold War conditions—has come the current thinking of a rights-based approach to development that seeks to bring about the promise of universal human rights and dignity.

But turning to the contemporary world, I had a sober message for Human Rights Day. This has been a difficult year for human rights. After so many high hopes that the turn of the millennium would herald a new era of respect for fundamental freedoms, we are faced with the sobering realization that there is as much, if not more, work to do now to make human rights a reality for all.

The World Conference against Racism, Racial Discrimination, Xenophobia and Related Intolerance held in Durban concluded three days before September 11. The World Conference was the latest event in a long campaign by the world community to rid itself of the scourge of racism and discrimination. The terrorist attacks of September 11 shocked the world. All people who cherish life and abhor violence motivated by hatred condemn those attacks unreservedly. In 1999 the OAU adopted the Convention on the Prevention and Combating of Terrorism.[11] Let us hope that the Convention will be ratified soon and implemented.

It has been suggested in some quarters that human rights considerations must take a backseat in the struggle against terrorism. I cannot share in that line of thinking. Human rights must be observed, especially in times of crises. We can and must fight terrorism while observing human rights. However, the long-term antidote to terrorism is a world where the ideals of the Universal Declaration of equal human dignity for all without any discrimination have been achieved.

Poverty and Human Rights

Africa has been struggling to overcome not only racism but also poverty. It is the subject of extreme poverty and racism, the relationship between them, and the challenges they pose to all of us that I want to address. Poverty and racism correlate and reinforce one another. The groups most marginalized by discrimination are also those that are trapped in poverty. This relationship was one of the themes addressed at the Durban World Conference.

I believe that the greatest challenge to the building of a real human rights culture in any society lies in tackling discrimination and the endemic poverty that continues to dominate the social landscape of many parts of the world. The Declaration and Plan of Action of the Durban Conference offer us tools to renew commitment to the eradication of both poverty and racism. My message is clear: we must work in partnership to implement the Durban commitments in full, starting now.

It is painfully clear that inequities within and between the developed and developing are not diminishing but growing. Extreme poverty is the life-long experience of millions and millions of people in our world. Extreme poverty means a denial of the exercise of all human rights and undermines the dignity and worth of the individual. The numbers are growing. Recently the President of the World Bank, in discussing world poverty, said:

> Poverty remains a global problem of huge proportions. Of the world's 6 billion people, 2.8 billion live on less than US$ 2 per day, and 1.2 billion live on less than 1 dollar a day. Six infants of every 100 do not see their first birthday and 8 do not survive to their fifth. Of those who do reach school age, 9 boys in 100 and 14 girls do not go to primary school.[12]

Behind such shocking statistics lies the reality of underdevelopment and powerlessness of human beings and human communities.

Poverty is a global phenomenon, challenging communities in the North as well as the South. But there is no denying that the greatest burden of extreme poverty is in Africa. To give but one illustration: in sub-Saharan Africa twelve countries' net enrollment rates in primary school of less than fifty were achieved in the 1990s. It is estimated that the number of children out of school could be as high as fifty-four million by 2015, the date set in the Millennium Declaration when all children everywhere will complete primary education.

The Committee that monitors the implementation by governments of the UN Covenant on Economic, Social and Cultural Rights has thought hard about poverty and lack of rights. This treaty has been ratified by forty-six countries in Africa. The Committee recently made a statement that seeks to map out the linkages between poverty as a denial of rights, and rights as a means to combat poverty.[13]

In the past, poverty was often understood as insufficient income to buy a minimum of goods and services. A more comprehensive definition has now emerged which recognizes poverty's broader features that impact upon the basic ability to live in dignity. The Committee defines poverty as "the sustained or chronic deprivation of the resources, capabilities, choices, security and power necessary for the enjoyment of an adequate standard of living and other civil, cultural, economic, political and social rights."[14] This conveys much more effectively the powerlessness which lies at the heart of poverty.

Although the challenges of extreme poverty are many and complex, according to the Committee a human rights perspective can contribute at least three basic elements to poverty-eradication policies. These are the principles of indivisibility of rights, participation, and nondiscrimination. Indivisibility means that a human rights approach must encompass the entire range of rights, civil, political, cultural, economic, and social rights, as well as the right to development. They are all "indispensable to those living in poverty" as a means of ensuring a life of freedom and dignity.

Second is the principle of nondiscrimination. The Committee notes that "Discrimination may cause poverty, just as poverty may cause discrimination. Inequality may be entrenched in institutions and deeply rooted in social values that shape relationships within households and communities."[15] Only the guarantee of equality and nondiscrimination can redress that imbalance and protect vulnerable groups and individuals from the poverty trap.

And finally, the Committee lays emphasis on the right of the poor to participate. Participation brings with it empowerment, and is a major part of the answer to poverty. In the Committee's words, "a policy or program that is formulated without the active and informed participation of those affected is most unlikely to be effective." Those living in poverty must enjoy the right to participate in key decisions affecting their lives.

The process of making relevant operationally a human-rights-based approach to poverty reduction is at the beginning stage.[16] It will be crucial in development and poverty-reduction programs from this point onward. For example, the increased recognition of the feminization of poverty makes it vital to link into the international protection of human rights the energies and approaches of the thousands of networks of women's groups. The link between rights and empowerment assists once again in the identification of priorities for the reduction of poverty.

Racism and Poverty

The World Conference against Racism was the latest in a long line of United Nations efforts to address and to eliminate racism from the world. It was a remarkable coming together of states, NGOs, national institutions, and ordinary people. It was a difficult process, with sometimes impassioned negotiations. But it did succeed ultimately in adopting texts of importance, in agreeing on language on many complex issues—both of the past and present—highlighting that the scourge of racism and related discrimination or intolerance crosses all national and cultural boundaries. Most importantly, however, in the wide-ranging Programme of Action adopted, we have equipped ourselves collectively with a true blueprint for the future, a strong global antidiscrimination program that, if taken seriously, can result in real progress.

The end of apartheid and institutionalized racism was an enormous achievement. Let us recognize that. But at some point it was always going to be necessary to deal with its antecedents—colonialism and slavery. The World Conference against Racism proved to be the venue where these issues were confronted. It was painful for all, and it was not the last word. I would like to note some of the important statements made.

First, slavery and the slave trade, including the transatlantic slave trade, were appalling tragedies in the history of humanity. That slavery and the slave trade, especially the transatlantic slave trade, are crimes against humanity and should always have been so. And that slavery and the slave trade as well as colonialism are among the major sources and manifestations of racism and racial discrimination. Africans and people of African descent, Asians and peoples of Asian descent, and indigenous peoples were victims of these acts and continue to be victims of their consequences.

Second, the impacts of slavery, slave trade, and colonialism on poverty creation are enduring and should be addressed through targeted development initiatives.

Third, states, regional, and international organizations; financial institutions and organs of civil society should develop mechanisms to address aspects of globalization which may lead to racism, racial discrimination, xenophobia, and related intolerance.

The Conference also addressed the future. The Programme of Action recognizes

> the commitment and the determination of the African leaders, to seriously address the challenges of poverty, underdevelopment, marginalization, social exclusion, economic disparities, instability and insecurity, through initiatives such as the New African Initiative and other innovative mechanisms such as the World Solidarity Fund for the Eradication of Poverty.

This recognition is followed by a call upon—among others—the United Nations and its specialized agencies to provide, through their operational programs, new and additional financial resources, as appropriate, to support these initiatives.

Let me now turn to the connections between poverty and racism. I have already noted that these are self-perpetuating and mutually reinforcing. Those trapped in poverty often lack the legal rights that would empower them and protect them from arbitrary or inequitable treatment. They are therefore more vulnerable to discrimination and racism.

The reverse link—the effect of racism in promoting poverty—is also emerging. Recent studies are shedding more light on the long-term impact of racial discrimination in economic and social terms. We now find that poverty indexes broken down by race and ethnic group often correlate strongly with other human development indicators such as access to health services, education, and employment. But this is also the case with other forms of discrimination. The latest World Development Report confirms that "discrimination on the basis of gender, ethnicity, race, religion or social status can lead to social exclusion and lock people in long-term poverty traps."[17] In short, exclusion and marginalization lead to and exacerbate already existing conditions of poverty and inequalities.

Poverty and Racism—The World Conference Declaration

These insights are also to be found in the Durban Declaration.[18] That Declaration noted that "poverty, underdevelopment, marginalization, social exclusion and economic disparities are closely associated with racism, racial discrimination, xenophobia and related intolerance, and contribute to the persistence of racist attitudes and practices which in turn generate more poverty." The reverse was also recognized by the Declaration: the "negative economic, social and cultural consequences of racism have contributed significantly to the underdevelopment of developing countries and, in particular, of Africa."

The Conference resolved, "to free every man, woman and child from the abject and dehumanizing conditions of extreme poverty to which more than one billion of them are currently subjected, to make the right to development a reality for everyone and to free the entire human race from want."

States were urged to enhance their policies and measures to reduce income and wealth inequalities and to take steps to promote and protect economic, social, and cultural rights on a nondiscriminatory basis. I echo that call and underscore that if poverty and racism are to be eliminated, we must take renewed action on all rights.

Rights-Based Approach to Development

Part of the task of making Durban effective must be the further consolidation of a rights-based approach to development, of which the rights-based approach to poverty eradication is a part. I acknowledge that the process of making operational a human-rights-based approach to poverty reduction is in the early stages, but it will be crucial in development and poverty-reduction programs from this point onward. It is clear that there is convergence between human rights thinking and other approaches to poverty and development. The challenge is to use a common analysis and multidisciplinary and multisectoral approaches to achieve both development and poverty reduction.

These issues were understood by the Millennium Summit, the largest-ever gathering of world leaders, which refocused our attention on these relationships. In the Millennium Declaration, the General Assembly explicitly recognized the link between the realization of the right to development and poverty reduction.[19] It pledged to "spare no effort to free our fellow men, women, and children from the abject and dehumanizing conditions of extreme poverty, to which more than a billion of them are currently subjected."

In short, as the Declaration on the Right to Development of a quarter of a century ago taught us, human rights and development must be addressed in tandem—one is not possible without the other.

The Challenges of Globalization

In this age of globalization, we hear much of the "common village," and that the world is becoming a better place for all who live in it. The truth of the matter is that globalization has in the past acted as a double-edged sword: it has improved the lives of many; it has also added even more economic power to those who are already powerful; but it has led to further marginalization of many regions of the world, not least Africa.

The impact of globalization on Africa must be of concern to us all. In his annual report to the United Nations General Assembly in 2000, the Secretary General made a passionate plea for the world to "include Africa." Exclusion and marginalization are recipes for poverty and inequality. Importantly, they lead to conflicts with very serious implications for a whole range of human rights: civil, political, economic, social, and cultural. As noted by the World Conference, although globalization offers many opportunities, it can also aggravate poverty, underdevelopment, marginalization, social exclusion, cultural homogenization, and economic disparities along racial lines.

To avoid these negative consequences, I believe that a new ethical globalization must be pursued. Globalization must confront the inequalities it is currently exacerbating. Institutions of governance—including international governance—must ask and provide answers to questions such as Are we effectively and progressively guaranteeing for all people the right to health, to adequate housing, to sufficient food, to education, to justice, to freedom of expression and personal security?

But ethical globalization can do more than halt the negative impact of world integration. It can be harnessed to help the world's poorest, most marginalized countries to improve the lives of their citizens. A World Bank study—Globalization, Growth and Poverty: Building an Inclusive World Economy—was released last week.[20] It highlights that these questions are especially important in the wake of September 11 and the worldwide economic slowdown, which is expected to hit the poor particularly hard.

The study puts forward a seven-point plan to help developing countries take advantage of the benefits of globalization, while avoiding its risks. Among other measures, it calls on poor countries to improve their investment climates and put in place better social protection to support poor people in adapting to and taking advantage of opportunities in a changing economic environment. It calls upon rich countries to open their markets to exports from developing countries and to slash their large agricultural subsidies, which undercut poor-country exports. It also argues for a substantial increase in development assistance, particularly to address problems in education and health. It is clear at this stage how ethical globalization—through measures such as these, which are based on respect for human rights—can advance the eradication of poverty and underdevelopment. We must campaign to make it happen.

African Initiatives: Strengthening Institutions

Priority must be given to the strengthening of already-existing institutions and the building of new ones. I will speak in a moment about the plans of NEPAD and the AU, but side by side with these laudable plans, the importance of strengthening existing systems must not be forgotten. Here, I refer to the implementation of the African Charter on Human and Peoples' Rights, the strengthening of the role of the African Commission, and in particular the establishment of the proposed African Court of Human and Peoples' Rights. The number of ratifications of the Protocol for the establishment of the Court still stands at only four. I strongly urge all states parties to the Charter to demonstrate their commitment to the protection of human rights through speedy ratification of the Protocol. I also refer to the implementation of the Grand Bay Declaration of 1999, especially as it calls for the strengthening of national systems for the promotion and protection of human rights, including national human rights institutions.[21]

Homegrown African Responses: NEPAD and the AU

I mentioned the Secretary General's plea to the world to "include Africa." But in fact, Africa is leading on many of these issues.

What the Constitutive Act of the African Union and NEPAD have done is to put beyond a shadow of doubt that Africa and Africans want to focus on changing the economic life conditions of their peoples within the context of democratization and adherence to human rights and the rule of law. Human rights and democracy cannot thrive in extreme conditions of poverty; on the other hand, the absence of democracy, human rights, and the rule of law is more likely to lead to exclusion, inequality, conflicts, and poverty. As I have said before, the motto should be "bread and the ballot box," not bread alone or the ballot box alone; it cannot be any other way.

Working as Partners under African Leadership

I mentioned earlier that the world owes a debt to Africa for its role in building international human rights protection, which is not often enough recognized. Now the opportunity for partnership offers one way to begin to redeem that debt.

In the UN Millennium Summit, there was a resolve by the leaders of the world to tackle the special needs of Africa. The Declaration provides in part that "We will support the consolidation of democracy in Africa and assist Africans in their struggle for lasting peace, poverty eradication and sustainable development, thereby bringing Africa into the mainstream of the world economy."

As I pointed out, this recognition was also reflected in the Durban Declaration and Programme of Action—first, that the leadership of Africa on any initiative is crucial; and second, that the world must work in partnership with African leaders to advance our common goals. In the same way, I see the role of my Office as partner in this process, which must be driven by African needs, as identified by Africa itself.

This understanding—that we must build real partnerships, and that we must listen to the needs of Africa as expressed by its leaders and ordinary people—is part of the background to the new African Dialogue.[22]

Another aspect in the construction of partnerships is a new initiative of my Office: the building of regional and subregional strategies for the promotion and protection of human rights. An important part of this regional strategy is the appointment of regional advisers within the UN Economic and Social Commissions. Regional advisers will be based in Bangkok, Beirut, and Santiago. In Africa there will be four subregional advisers—one to be based in Addis Ababa. The purpose of this outreach is to make sure that the services of the Office are readily accessible in different parts of the world, and to ensure that our initiatives and programs of technical cooperation are built in partnership with those involved and respond to needs identified at home. These advisers will help to fill the gap in communication that has sometimes hindered our cooperation in the past. I encourage you to discuss with them your own ideas on how best my Office can work with you. I am strongly committed to developing this partnership.

OHCHR's African Dialogue

Last month my office convened the First African Dialogue under the theme "Human Rights, the African Union and the New Partnerships for Africa's Development (NEPAD)". The Report of the Dialogue is being distributed widely.[23] The primary objective of the Dialogue was to bring together African experts from states, the regional human rights bodies, national institutions, academic and research institutions, regional and international organizations, and leaders in civil society to help us interpret the Constitutive Act of the African Union and NEPAD. This will enable the United Nations to develop programs that are informed by and clearly reflect Africa's own needs, aspirations, and strategic plans for social, economic, and indeed political development.

I am convinced that this is the right approach. We must create true partnerships with African peoples and institutions, together with external friends of Africa, if real change is to take place in the material conditions of the people and enduring democratic foundations are to be strengthened or built. The immediate priority for us is to engage with the OAU/AU secretariat and the relevant NEPAD implementation structures in order to discuss and agree on specific areas and issues for cooperation. OHCHR is actively involved in working with other United Nations agencies in Africa under the coordination of the Economic Commission for Africa to ensure that our response to NEPAD will reflect the needs expressed by Africa and Africans.

Conclusion

Excellencies, ladies, and gentlemen, in conclusion I appeal to you as Africans and to Africa to take forward your vision and plan of action for the African Union, NEPAD, the African Defence Force process. Make them the real weapons for tackling poverty, inequality, discrimination, intolerance, HIV/AIDS, racism, ethnic and other differences, conflicts, and all other scourges that have held this and many other parts of the world to ransom. Let us all, my Office, other UN agencies, the OAU/AU, governments, and organs of civil society commit ourselves to work together, in partnership to make human and peoples' rights a reality in the lives of African peoples and all other peoples of the world. The agenda we all hold in common—the continuing search for equality and human development—can be reinvigorated by the commitments made at the Durban World Conference against Racism.

Strong action on this front holds great promise. We must now match our clear mandate with an equally clear determination to act. With the advent of the African Union, NEPAD, and other innovations, we are potentially closer to the elimination of poverty, discrimination, and inequality in Africa. We stand closer to the final realization of what Secretary General Kofi Annan has called Africa's third wave: a wave of peace rooted in democracy and human rights. My Office—and I personally—look forward to continuing to build partnerships and working with African institutions and organizations in pursuit of this, our common goal.

"The United Nations Millennium Development Goals—A New Challenge for International Cooperation"
Brown University, Providence, Rhode Island, USA, 11 May 2002

I want to discuss a new United Nations program that seeks to address the greatest source of global insecurity—that of the gulf between North and South between the majority poor and minority rich worlds. The story begins with an extraordinary meeting of world leaders at the United Nations in September 2000 where the Millennium Declaration was adopted unanimously.

As well as committing to a set of universal principles and values to guide their future cooperation, states adopted a bold agenda to promote democracy, good governance, human rights, and improved global security. The specific commitments I want to discuss concern tackling poverty and underdevelopment. States committed themselves to sparing all members of society from the "abject and dehumanizing conditions of extreme poverty" and "to making the right to development a reality for everyone." The Declaration includes ambitious objectives to fulfill these promises. In summary, these are, by the year 2015, to halve world poverty and hunger, to control killer diseases, to achieve universal education, and to reverse environmental degradation.

These goals cannot be realized if we continue on the current path. Large-scale intellectual, financial, and other resources must be committed by the international community, and there must be new partnerships created that engage the private sector.

The Financial Needs

Yesterday morning I listened to Chancellor Gordon Brown of the United Kingdom put figures on what would be needed to achieve these goals. He reminded us that the Zedillo Report estimates that an extra $50 billion will be required each year until 2015.[24] He noted that the UN Financing for Development Conference at Monterrey led to pledges from the United States and the European Union to raise, from 2006, $12 billion a year more for education, health, and anti-poverty programs.[25] He continued:

> Today, as this Special Session issues our call to action—a call we hope will be heard and heeded by all governments, and resonate far beyond these walls and these borders—I want to propose what is a new deal for the global economy, that is also a new deal for the world's children: that in return for developing countries pursuing corruption-free policies for stability and for creating a favorable environment for investment, developed countries should be prepared to open up trade to developing countries for everything but arms and to increase vitally needed funds to achieve the agreed Millennium Development Goals.
>
> And so, I suggest a new development compact grounded in new rights and new responsibilities—where no country genuinely committed to good governance, poverty reduction, and economic development, should be denied the chance to achieve the 2015 goals through lack of resources.[26]

Millennium Goals and Targets

Clearly, the political will is strengthening, and so the planning and implementation must reach a new level. Hence, the United Nations has engaged in a comprehensive internal effort to ensure that it is in a position to make the optimum contribution to change course.

This has entailed the identification of the Millennium Development Goals (or MDGs) as a set of eight specific targets to eliminate poverty and promote development. These are the eradication of extreme poverty and hunger; the achievement of universal primary education; the promotion of gender equality and empowerment of women; the reduction of child mortality; the improvement of maternal health; the reversal of HIV/AIDS, malaria, and other diseases; the promotion of environmental sustainability; and the development of a global partnership for development.

Within these goals, priorities have been set. For example, to ensure that all children have the opportunity to receive complete primary education by the year 2015; that the rate of HIV infection in young people is cut by 25 percent by the year 2010; and that rich countries provide more opportunities to poorer countries in the realms of access to markets, debt relief, and development assistance. The targets are limited in number and communicate clear objectives.

All parts of the United Nations system—UN funds, programs, specialized agencies including the World Bank and IMF—are called upon to cooperate, support, and contribute their knowledge, expertise, and skills to make UN interventions as effective as possible. This is a vital campaign, and it will extend not only to other multilateral groups but also to civil society, non-governmental, private sector, and foundation partners. The campaign also involves two decisive global conferences: The International Conference on Financing for Development, held in Monterrey, Mexico, in March 2002; and the World Summit for Sustainable Development, to be held in Johannesburg, South Africa, next August and September. While the Monterrey Conference focused on the mobilization of resources for development priorities, the Johannesburg Summit will concentrate on creating a new agenda with effective strategies and partnerships to achieve human development goals.

Some of you will be aware that the Secretary General has enlisted Professor Jeremy Sachs of Harvard University as his Special Adviser on the Millennium Development Goals. He will work with the Chair of the United Nations Development Programme, who acts as "campaign manager" and "score keeper." The Monterrey Conference endorsed the efforts of the United Nations to undertake a global information campaign on the goals. So you will hear more about this exciting if daunting initiative from now on!

Human Rights and Poverty Alleviation

The Millennium Declaration endorses the role of human rights not only in the promotion or encouragement of its development goals but also in the assessment of the achievement of those goals. It also makes an important link between extreme poverty and the right to development.

A global partnership for development as opposed to compartmentalization is the way to go forward. My Office, in consultation with various partners, is currently developing draft guidelines on the integration of human rights into poverty-reduction strategies. The ultimate objective is to enhance the effectiveness and sustainability of those strategies. Working with development partners has shown the congruence between the realization of both human rights and the MDGs. For example, international human rights law recognizes that many human rights cannot be implemented immediately and must be realized progressively and subject to available resources. Accordingly, the precise human rights obligations of the state can vary over time in relation to the same state (progressive realization). Achievement of MDGs is based on an appreciation that these goals cannot be achieved overnight, and that any strategy for helping to meet development objectives is dependent, to one degree or another, on resource availability.

What is the value added of human rights for development? I would answer that the universal human rights framework provides a platform for the empowerment and participation of the individual, standards to ensure nondiscrimination in achieving the development goals, and the accountability of states. Human rights principles serve not only as the tools to meet these development goals, but also as indicators of progress toward their achievement and ultimately the objectives to be attained. We would recommend a stronger emphasis on the international human rights standards for each Millennium Development Goal. We are proposing that reporting on country implementation of the Millennium Development Goals and other implementation activities should include identification of actions taken by governments to fulfill their international human rights treaty obligations for each goal, and the identification of the most vulnerable groups in relation to each goal. This approach would take advantage of the powerful system of international obligations created by the major human rights treaties, which most countries have ratified.

Human rights expertise can also make a contribution to capacity building at a national level, in strengthening the rule of law, and in supporting democratic institutions. Such work, termed "technical assistance," is a major part of the activities of my Office in many countries.

Universal Primary Education

Let me illustrate what a human rights analysis offers by reference to Millennium Development Goal 2—the achievement of universal primary education. From a human rights perspective, education can be seen as a right characterizing the indivisibility between civil and political, and economic, social, and cultural rights. The reason is simple: education is both a human right in itself, but also an indispensable means of realizing other rights. Education also constitutes an indisputable bridge between the Millennium Development Goals and human rights—it is the primary vehicle by which economically and socially marginalized children, girls as well as boys, and adults can lift themselves out of poverty. We must recognize that education is one of the best financial investments that states, and the world as a whole, can make.

The human right to education has been recognized in a number of international human rights instruments, including the International Covenant on Economic, Social and Cultural Rights. Thus, legally binding standards exist and so does a well-developed monitoring system. In addition, in 1998 the United Nations Commission on Human Rights, the body which to an important extent decides on the human rights priorities of the United Nations, appointed a Special Rapporteur on the right to education, Professor Katarina Tomaševski. The Special Rapporteur has the task to report on the status, throughout the world, of the progressive realization of the right to education, including access to primary education. To this end, regular dialogue takes place with a wide range of actors, including the World Bank and other financial and development institutions.

The existing legally binding standards go far beyond merely recognizing the right of all human beings to education. They also define and lay down the prerequisites for realizing the right to education, which provides a valuable entry-point and basis for the millennium development goal programming, methodology, implementation, and evaluation. The prerequisite is that primary education be compulsory and available free for all. Everyone, without distinction as to race, sex, color, or national or ethnic origin, must enjoy the right to education. Applying a human rights approach to achieve universal primary education would therefore mean to incorporate guarantees and affirmative actions in development strategies to ensure nondiscrimination and the equal enjoyment by all of the right to education.

Concluding Remarks

I should draw my remarks to a close. Let me repeat that the Millennium Development Goals can be achieved. That needs repeating because the scale of deprivation of human rights and human needs can be expressed in such a way as to induce a feeling of powerlessness. But we should resist that feeling by recalling that we have made progress. International cooperation and national action have made a difference to the human condition over the last half-century in many ways:

Life expectancy in developing countries has increased by a third, from forty-six to sixty-five years between 1960 and 1999.

In 1999 seventy-one countries enjoy a life expectancy at birth of more than seventy years, up from fifty-five countries in 1990.

Around 80 percent of people in the developing world now have access to improved water supplies.

Between 1970 and 1999 the adult literacy rate in developing countries rose from 48 to 73 percent.

On human security one can note that in the 1990s more than one hundred developing and transitional countries ended military or one-party rule, with between two-thirds and three-quarters of people in those countries now living under relatively pluralist and democratic government systems.

Of course, there is the debit side of the balance sheet of human development. HIV/AIDS is a dramatic tragic example. In the last decade the number of people infected has doubled from under 15 million to more than 34 million. The overwhelming burden of the disease is shouldered by developing countries. The point of the Millennium Development Campaign is to make a difference for AIDS sufferers for the 1.5 billion people who are not expected to survive to age sixty or the more than 850 million adults who are illiterate 60 percent of whom are women, or the 325 million children who are out of school.

I hope that your academic programs can encourage in students an awareness that along with the fruits of globalization should come a sense that we are all responsible in some way for helping to promote and protect the rights of our neighbors, whether they live on the next street or the next continent. The Universal Declaration of Human Rights is not simply a charter of rights but speaks of duties in very broad terms. Article 29 of the Declaration reminds all that "Everyone owes duties to the community." We need in this new century to understand that the community is no longer just our nearest neighborhood or country alone but the global community as well.

Chapter 9
Human Rights Education

The mandate of the High Commissioner is to promote and protect all human rights for all people. The central meaning of promotion is education. Human rights education (HRE) has been pursued by the United Nations for decades through information and publication campaigns with limited success. A new idea that grew out of the Vienna World Conference of 1993 was to approach the subject in a more systematic and professional way. This led to the International Decade for Human Rights Education proclaimed by the General Assembly for 1995–2004. The High Commissioner for Human Rights was given the role of coordinator of the Decade and its associated Plan of Action. However, it proved difficult to engage governments fully in the Decade or find the funding necessary to drive it forward. A consistent theme in Mary Robinson's thinking was the contribution that human rights education and knowledge could make to the empowerment of people and the ultimate goal of prevention of violation. One modest objective of the Decade was to disseminate the Universal Declaration in as many languages as possible. OHCHR's efforts to do so earned it a place in the Guinness Book of Records. *In 2000 the Office launched an on-line human rights education database and a resource and documentation center on HRE materials.*

"The Universal Declaration of Human Rights Is the Most Universal Document in the World"

Press release, 10 December 1999

The Office of the High Commissioner for Human Rights has been awarded the Guinness World Record for having collected, translated, and disseminated the Universal Declaration of Human Rights into more than three hundred languages and dialects: from Abkhaz to Zulu. The Universal Declaration is thus the document most translated—indeed, the most "universal"—in the world.

In the words of the High Commissioner for Human Rights, Mary Robinson: "This project bears a special symbolism. It immediately brings to us a sense of the world's diversity; it is a rich tapestry with so many different languages and peoples. But, at the same time, it shows that all of us, in our different forms of expression, can speak the 'common language of humanity,' the language of human rights, which is enshrined in the Universal Declaration of Human Rights."

This project, developed in the framework of the United Nations Decade for Human Rights Education (1995–2004),[1] provides an example of what global partnership for human rights is about. It was made possible thanks to the cooperative efforts by many partners within and outside the United Nations system: OHCHR and its field presences; the UN Department of Public Information (DPI) and many of its information centers and services around the world; the International Telecommunication Union (ITU); the United Nations Development Programme and its field presences (UNDP); UNESCO with some of its National Commissions and Regional Office; various governments and their Permanent Missions to the United Nations; selected universities and linguistic institutes; numerous international, regional, and local nongovernmental organizations; and the Government of the Republic of San Marino, who generously sponsored the final phase of this project.

Most of the linguistic versions of the Universal Declaration of Human Rights are now available on-line through the Office's Web site: *www.ohchr.org*

"Promoting Human Rights Education"
Celebration of Human Rights Day
Palais Wilson, Geneva, 11 December 2000

Excellencies, Distinguished Guests, Ladies, and Gentlemen,

This year we are marking Human Rights Day in Geneva with an event, which falls into two complementary parts. This morning's discussion focused on the culture of peace. The focus of this afternoon's meeting is human rights education and how it can contribute to a culture of peace. I welcome everyone to the discussion. At the outset I would like to stress my belief that respecting human rights is the surest basis on which to build a culture of peace and that I consider human rights education to be an indispensable means of ensuring respect for human rights.

The importance of human rights education has long been recognized. The prominence accorded to it at the Vienna World Conference and the fact that the United Nations decided to establish the International Decade for Human Rights Education are evidence of this.

Why is it so important? In the first place, the right to education is itself a fundamental right. And human rights provide the essence of a quality education.

At the most basic level it is clear that knowledge of one's rights is a prerequisite to establishing and defending those rights. But human rights education is more than that. In the words of the General Assembly Resolution establishing the Decade, human rights education is intended to be "a lifelong process by which people at all levels of development and in all strata of society learn respect for the dignity of others and the means and methods of ensuring that respect in all societies."[2] The key word there is "lifelong": the educational process is not confined to one phase of our lives but continues throughout our existence.

Beginning with Children

It is important that the need to respect the dignity and rights of every individual be understood as early as possible. Children should be the focus of particular attention. Children tend to have an open mind about the world; for example, they will play and live with children of a different race or color without attaching importance to difference. Prejudice and intolerance are not natural to children; they are learned responses. So it is vital to convey the importance of human rights to children in the classroom, in the home, and in all of their activities. Learning by example is as important as the civics class: children derive many of their attitudes from parents and friends. So each of us has a part to play.

Young people have great reserves of energy, creativity, and enthusiasm, which should be drawn on. Texts and materials geared to children's needs are essential. My Office, UNESCO and other agencies, and NGOs have made big advances with promotional and educational materials, and we should continue to do all we can to get the message across. I might mention that the Universal Declaration has been translated into over three hundred languages and that OHCHR has even been awarded a Guinness World Record on that account! But we must remember that there are many competing demands on children's attention, especially these days through computers and the Internet. Human rights education must be able to compete in the high-tech stakes.

The Needs of Adults

In adult life the need for human rights education is also great. This takes on a special urgency in societies in conflict and in societies, where gross violations have been committed. I have been to many such societies and what has greatly impressed me is the thirst for information about human rights that I encounter. Whether it is the Democratic Republic of Congo, East Timor, or Colombia, the urge to know more about human rights and how they can be meaningful in people's lives is very strong. The message I constantly get is that ordinary people, especially those caught up in conflict situations, see human rights as a basis on which to build a better life.

The Disappointing Results

In spite of the many benefits of human rights education, governments have not put as much emphasis on it as I would like, nor have they directed adequate resources to HRE. The results of a mid-term review of the International Decade for Human Rights Education, carried out by my Office, were disappointing.[3] If it were a school report card it would read "Considerable room for improvement." It may be that governments harbor residual fears that human rights are threatening. That would be a very shortsighted approach. All the evidence shows that human rights, by empowering people, strengthen democracy and social cohesion and greatly benefit societies. Governments have nothing to fear from human rights education—quite the reverse. Multilateral agencies, too, should not be afraid of the rights-based approach, and I am happy to see more and more of them embracing it.

Anyone familiar with human rights knows that it is a complex subject and growing even more complex by the day. The array of covenants, conventions, protocols, and other treaties is formidable, the literature on the subject vast. This is another reason why human rights education—which should translate those documents into people's daily lives—plays such an important role.

Human rights education operates at different levels. At the local level, the objective is to provide individuals with practical knowledge about human rights and mechanisms for their protection. At the national and international levels, human rights education promotes values, beliefs, and attitudes that inspire action in upholding human rights. Human rights education thus encourages all—from the individual to the international community—to take action to defend human rights and prevent abuses.

What OHCHR Can Contribute

There are many ways in which my Office and other UN agencies can assist action at the national level. We can assist human rights education, training, and public information efforts by providing materials, fellowships, and scholarships. We can and do urge the drawing up of national plans with the involvement of as wide a range of civil society as possible. We have provided guidelines for such plans. We can lend support and advice to national human rights institutions, which can serve as good focal points for all kinds of local education projects. We can organize seminars and workshops on particular human rights themes or issues, and we can demonstrate how international norms can be implemented domestically.

Training Professionals

The training of those engaged in careers in which human rights play a central or especially sensitive role is particularly important human rights education work. Judges, lawyers, and other members of the legal community fall into that category, and the need for human rights training adapted to their particular duties is clear. That is true also of law enforcement agents and immigration officials, as well as professionals involved in health and social services. My Office has worked on the preparation of training materials for many different professions including police, social workers, judges, lawyers, and prison officials. But we should remember that human rights issues arise for people in many walks of life, for example, local administrators who deal with members of minority communities.

An encouraging development is the expansion of interest in human rights seminars and workshops. To give an example, independent national human rights institutions have held a series of meetings on specific topics over the past year, ranging from the annual meeting of national institutions in the Asia Pacific region in New Zealand, which looked at strategies for realizing economic and social rights, to a meeting in June of the recently formed Caribbean Ombudsman's Association, where the role of independent institutions in promoting accountability, good governance, and sustainable development was discussed. One such workshop that sticks in my mind took place during my visit to Mongolia in August last and had as its focus the role of parliaments in protecting human rights.

The ACT Program

Individual support projects can be helpful too. One such is the Assisting Communities Together, or ACT, program, an OHCHR initiative that we implement in partnership with UNDP. ACT gives financial support—usually on a modest scale—to human rights initiatives on human rights education conceived and implemented at the grassroots level.

In Croatia, for example, the Center for Peace, Legal Advice and Psychological Assistance in Vukovar prepared sixteen radio programs on international human rights standards with a focus on women's and children's rights, which proved to be very popular and provoked a large number of phone-ins. Many of those who called wanted more information on their rights, and victims of human rights violations felt encouraged to communicate. This, in turn, spurred on local NGOs to learn more themselves about the promotion and protection of human rights.

In Togo, the NGO Amis des Enfants created theatrical plays, which addressed issues such as the exploitation of children, violence against children, trafficking of children and the promotion of the status of the girl child. They expected four hundred children to attend the performances, but in the event more than eighteen thousand came.

These are but two examples of the impact which can be made with even a small amount of funding—and further proof of the demand for information on human rights.

Education against Racism

Next year's World Conference against Racism, Racial Discrimination, Xenophobia and Related Intolerance in Durban provides an excellent opportunity to step up our efforts to educate about human rights. The World Conference has the potential to be a powerful mechanism for prevention of human rights violations and for addressing the root causes of such violations. As governments, international agencies, and NGOs make their preparations, we must not forget the role of young people. The World Conference is an occasion to educate in a very real sense about the evils of racism and discrimination and the great benefits that come from tolerance and respect for diversity.

I intend to involve children and young people closely in the World Conference against Racism and would appeal to all present to contribute to this effort. In order to get the message home, it is my intention to write to every Minister of Education in the world to seek their support for the objective of engaging young people with the World Conference.[4] I hope that UNESCO will join me in this initiative so that it will be a joint approach, just as we had a joint approach to heads of government this year on the mid-term review of the International Decade for Human Rights Education.

Four years remain of the International Decade for Human Rights Education. Progress has been made in some respects, but much more could be done. What is required is the will and the focus to do it, and the responsibility rests with all of us.

"Human Rights Education in Primary and Secondary Schools"
Opening Address at Beijing Workshop
Beijing, China, 8–9 November 2001

Your Excellency, Vice Premier Qian, Dear Friends,

It is a pleasure for me to welcome the Chinese authorities, the participants and the resource persons gathered in Beijing for this Workshop on human rights education in primary and secondary schools. As the United Nations High Commissioner for Human Rights, I attach great importance to this workshop, which is taking place in a country where one-fifth of the world's population is living. I fervently hope that our exploration of human rights education in this workshop will mark the beginning of long-term and successful cooperation between us in this vital area.

On many occasions and in different parts of the world, I have stressed the importance of human rights education as a nonviolent and long-term contribution to the building of just societies in which the human rights of all are valued and respected. When it proclaimed the United Nations Decade for Human Rights Education (1995–2004), the General Assembly defined human rights education as a "life-long process by which people at all levels of development and in all strata of society learn respect for the dignity of others and the means and methods of ensuring that respect in all societies."[5] Accordingly, human rights education efforts should be directed at all people—children as well as adults—since all members of society have a role to play in promoting and protecting human rights.

Human rights education is also a vital component of any strategy to combat racism and related intolerance. This is one of the messages to be found in the Declaration of the World Conference against Racism that recently concluded in Durban in September 2001. The Declaration reminds us that by promoting respect for human rights, human rights education can prevent discriminatory attitudes and behavior. It can also sensitize people to existing bias and prejudices, promote a change in discriminatory practices, and reinforce appreciation of cultural diversity.

The importance that the international community gives to human rights education was reflected in the proclamation of the United Nations Decade for Human Rights Education. We are now over halfway through that Decade. The disappointing and worrying reality we must face is that there are still very few effective human rights education strategies and programs established within countries. That must mean that the majority of children in the world must complete their education without being exposed to education on human rights.

Mid-Term Review of the Decade on Human Rights Education

Last year my Office undertook, in cooperation with UNESCO and others involved in the Decade, a mid-term global evaluation of progress made toward the achievement of the Decade's objectives. That evaluation revealed that, for the most part, effective human rights education strategies have yet to be developed. Within the school system relevant curricula and textbook development and revision, human rights training of school personnel, and development of extracurricular activities are not undertaken on a regular basis. At the university level, human rights are rarely a focus, apart from the programs of specialized human rights institutes. Some progress has been made in the training of professionals, for example those working in the administration of justice, but less so with regard to officials working in the social and economic fields. In different countries public-awareness campaigns have been organized. But the potential role of the media, artistic expression, and new information technologies remains largely unexplored. In many cases the broad range of human rights education activities reported was not part of an overall strategy. The activities were rather ad hoc conferences, training courses, and seminars and were rarely evaluated. There is obviously much work to be done by all parts of society if we are to achieve comprehensive human rights education.

We must start in schools. Effective inclusion of human rights education in schools can be a first important step toward the development of an overall country human rights education plan. Such plans have been called for by both the General Assembly and the Commission on Human Rights. The Decade's mid-term evaluation has highlighted that such national plans for human rights education should be comprehensive (in terms of outreach), participatory (in terms of involvement of all relevant actors), and effective (in terms of educational methodologies). In this regard, priority should be given to sustainable approaches, for example the training of trainers, and the integration of human rights into all relevant training and educational curricula. Given the respective potential and capacities in this field, national-level strategies should be developed, implemented and evaluated through partnerships within and among governmental and nongovernmental actors, working together in a spirit of mutual respect.

Almost two years ago, at a human rights education workshop held in Seoul, the participants, including ten officials from China, discussed problems, needs, achievements and possible strategies toward the effective incorporation of human rights education in the school system.[6] Today's workshop will build on those discussions in order to define some concrete steps toward a country strategy for China at both the central and provincial levels. A number of international and national resource persons, with first-hand experience in human rights education in schools, are among us in order to facilitate this process. I would like to thank them for their participation.

This Workshop will look at the many ways in which human rights education can be promoted within the school system. It will look at such issues as the appropriate provision for human rights issues in curricula and textbooks; preservice and in-service training for teachers on human rights and human rights education methodologies; the organization of extracurricular activities, both at the school level and reaching out to the family and the community; the development of educational materials; the establishment of support networks of teachers and other professionals from groups such as human rights groups, teachers' unions, nongovernmental organizations, and professional and parents' associations.

It is important to keep in mind that human rights education in schools should take into account the developmental stage of children and their social and cultural contexts in order to make human rights principles meaningful to them. Teachers, administrators, outside resource persons, and parents should be involved in this process as well as the students themselves. The "human rights climate" that exists in the classroom and the school is also important: it should be based on reciprocal respect between all parties involved.

An important task for all the participants of the workshop is to identify concrete follow-up activities so that in the not-far future human rights education can be fully incorporated in Chinese schools. This is challenging work for a short workshop of one and a half days. I trust in your diligence and dedication to come out with concrete proposals. I wish to reaffirm to the Chinese Government the commitment of my Office in supporting your efforts in this regard.

Chapter 10
Children's Rights

The Children's Convention, the United Nations Convention on the Rights of the Child, has been ratified by almost all countries of the world, a significant exception being the United States. Mary Robinson campaigned for the universal protection of all children using the Convention as her frame of reference. She worked closely with the UN agency dedicated to children, UNICEF, with the ILO, and with others. OHCHR's own responsibilities included servicing and supporting the innovative Committee on the Rights of the Child, which oversees implementation of the Children's Convention. One of Mary Robinson's last major commitments as High Commissioner was the Children's Summit held in New York in May 2002. This was a follow-up to the Summit for Children of September 1990 that brought an unprecedented number of world leaders together to pledge a better deal for children. However, as she pointed out, many of those pledges remained unfulfilled a decade later.

Worst Forms of Child Labour Convention
Eighty-Seventh Session of the International Labour Conference
Geneva, June 1999

I welcome the fact that a Convention concerning the Prohibition and Immediate Elimination of the Worst Forms of Child Labour is to be adopted by the International Labour Organization. This will at the least represent an important first step in the vital task of protecting children who are at once the most valuable and the most vulnerable members of society.

Child labor and its harmful consequences have been a matter of deep concern to the international community for many years. Children continually find themselves victims of exploitation through labor. One of the worst forms of forced labor is bonded labor, which can amount to little more than slavery. The increasing extent and serious effects of this worldwide phenomenon, which has emerged as one of the dominant human rights issues of our time, calls for an overall strategy and integrated and concerted action by governments, the United Nations, and other competent bodies. The current efforts to develop new standards to put an end to the worst forms of child labor are therefore particularly welcome.

At this year's session of the Commission on Human Rights, my Office initiated a special dialogue on children.[1] The resultant discussion was one of the most useful sessions of the Commission and broke new ground in that it placed special emphasis on social and economic exclusion of children.

An essential element is that the Convention applies to all children under the age of eighteen. This will provide a legal framework for the implementation and monitoring of concrete programs of action to eliminate the worst forms of child labor.

I welcome the fact that the new ILO Convention specifically refers to the Convention on the Rights of the Child. As you know, the Convention is a comprehensive international instrument for the promotion and protection of children's rights. This year marks the tenth anniversary of the Convention, and it is therefore particularly appropriate that a new Convention should be adopted which builds on this basic international agreement regarding children. Many provisions of the Convention on the Rights of the Child have, of course, a direct bearing on the issue of child labor. I would mention in particular article 32, which recognizes each child's right to be protected against economic exploitation and having to perform work likely to interfere with the child's education, or to be harmful to the child's health or physical, mental, spiritual, moral, or social development.

The new Convention addresses the terrible and growing problem of child soldiers. I would prefer the text to call for the prohibition of all participation by children in armed conflict, rather than to refer only to forced or compulsory recruitment. The Commission on Human Rights dialogue heard clear evidence that soldiering exposes children not only to the grave peril of death and injury in combat, but also to the likelihood of criminal trial and punishment—including the death penalty—to arbitrary detention, imprisonment, and execution for desertion and refusal to fight, not to mention illness, malnutrition, sexual exploitation, and many other hazards. I am looking forward to a more positive outcome when the issue of children in armed conflict is discussed in the Working Group on the Optional Protocol to the Convention on the Rights of the Child. I urge all states to attend this important meeting.[2]

I would also have preferred more specific language on the gender dimension of this question, with particular reference to the different implications for both girls and boys.

Once adopted, the Convention on the Worst Forms of Child Labour should be immediately ratified by all states and implemented in full. My Office will continue to work closely with the ILO so as to accord the highest priority to the task of preventing and combating the exploitation of children. It is only by uniting all the strength of the international community that children's rights will become a reality and that it will be possible to effectively fight the scandal of the abuse, exploitation, and violence still affecting millions of children throughout the world.

Optional Protocol on Involvement of Children in Armed Conflict
Message on the adoption of the text of the draft protocol
Palais Wilson, Geneva, 28 January 2000

The world is today one step closer to sparing its children the savagery of war. Last Friday, 21 January, a panel, or working group, of the United Nations Commission on Human Rights completed the elaboration of a draft Optional Protocol to the Convention on the Rights of the Child to establish eighteen years as the minimum age for participation in hostilities. The draft Optional Protocol would also prohibit the compulsory recruitment by governments who subscribed to it of persons below eighteen years and ban recruitment or use in hostilities of persons under eighteen by nongovernmental armed groups. The document raises the standards contained in article 38 of the Convention on the Rights of the Child and represents a willingness to take stronger measures to keep children out of armed conflicts.

I wish to express my deep appreciation that the working group has successfully completed its mandate by adopting by consensus the text of the draft Optional Protocol. Working group participants showed much flexibility: indeed, the draft protocol constitutes a significant compromise between the divergent positions of various delegations. When I addressed the working group, I expressed my belief that the question at issue was not the difference between sixteen, seventeen, and eighteen years of age, but rather the distinction that needed to be made between children and adults. I feel the new draft instrument confirms this important distinction, even if it does not go as far as some would have wished.

I welcome the spirit of cooperation, which prevailed in the working group, and I wish to express my appreciation to both governmental and nongovernmental representatives for their hard work toward adoption of a draft Optional Protocol. This is an achievement that comes just in time to mark the tenth anniversary of the entry into force of the Convention on the Rights of the Child. I look forward to the speedy adoption of the Optional Protocol by the international community as a whole and its entry into force so as to make it an effective instrument to protect children in armed conflicts.

Violence against Children, within the Family and in Schools
Day of General Discussion, Committee on the Rights of the Child
Geneva, 29 September 2001

Thank you, Mr. Chairperson. Members of the Committee on the Rights of the Child, Invited Guests, Ladies, and Gentlemen,

I am pleased to address you on this Day of General Discussion. Such an opportunity for reflection, discussion, and analysis of the procedure of the Committee on the Rights of the Child and that of other treaty bodies is an innovation of considerable value for the effective working of the treaty system and ultimately for the better protection of human rights.

I know that Committee members welcome the opportunity for informal dialogue with UN partners NGOs and especially those government representatives who will join the discussion. I am glad to welcome them all. I know that several of the human rights mandate holders who deal with related issues have expressed their regret at being unable to accept the Committee's invitation to take part in this year's discussion. But I am glad to see that the newly appointed Special Rapporteur on the sale of children, child pornography, and child prostitution, Juan Miguel Petit, is joining you today.

The theme of last year's Day of Discussion, continued this year, is violence against children.

Last year the Committee's focus was on state violence. This year, the discussion will be on violence in the family and school. These contexts are less often examined, but they are nevertheless fundamental.

Mention of the subject of violence must bring to everyone's mind the events of September 11 and the terrorist attacks in the United States. I had the opportunity to visit New York last week. I was able to go along with a colleague from our New York office to Ground Zero. I had the opportunity to meet with some of those involved in the rescue services and some of those offering counseling and comfort to the bereaved. As far as we are aware, all those killed were adults. But being there in the aftermath of the attack, what struck me was the sense of the vulnerability of all of us, adults and children, to violence and the need we all have for physical and psychological security.

The World Conference against Racism, held in Durban, concluded just two days before the US attacks. One relevant observation on Durban is the extent to which it emerged that ethnicity—like gender—can be a factor making many children particularly vulnerable to violence. Young people raised their voices in Durban through the Youth Forum and asked us to redouble our efforts, for children and with children, to end the violence they suffer.

Violence against children can stem from numerous causes and contexts. But whatever its source two points need to be emphasized: first, children can be more vulnerable to lifelong consequences of the violence they experience; and second, violence against children is always a violation of their rights. International human rights treaties impose legal obligations on states—and these are clearly violated when state agents are the ones who breach human rights norms. But the human rights of children are also violated when the state fails to live up to its obligation to protect children from violence suffered at the hands of others.

Violence and the School

When the 191 states parties to the Convention on the Rights of the Child accepted to be bound by the provisions of its article 28, they agreed to "take all appropriate measures to ensure that school discipline is administered in a manner consistent with the child's human dignity." Yet, in too many cases, discipline is still invoked as the justification for treating children in ways that we would consider absolutely unacceptable if applied to adults. This is a matter in which great progress could be achieved quickly with enough political will and determination. Many states have yet to enact appropriate legislation banning unacceptable forms of so-called discipline—including corporal punishment and other sanctions that humiliate rather than correct. Other states must ensure that existing legislation is extended so as to cover private establishments as well as public ones. In addition, among the many states that have appropriate legislation in place, efforts must be increased to ensure that it is enforced in practice. In all cases, states must involve children in their initiatives including the creation of nonviolent systems of discipline in the school. They should increase their efforts to provide appropriate training to teachers and school administrators. There is also a need to increase public debate and awareness, especially among parents, not only about the unacceptability of harsh methods of school discipline but also about the effectiveness of alternative nonviolent approaches.

Discipline is needed in schools. The evidence shows that when it is properly designed and administered, children are the first to appreciate and welcome clear guidance on acceptable as well as unacceptable behavior. Teachers and school administrators must be able to ensure that children are not victimized by other students. The provisions of articles 28 and 29 of the Convention that guarantee to every child the right to an education directed at the development of her or his personality, talents, and mental and physical abilities to their fullest potential cannot in practice be secured where the school becomes a place to be feared, rather than enjoyed.

When large proportions of students live in fear of bullying by their classmates, when they are taught or learn to value violence, or when they feel threatened by a school climate that tolerates violence and vandalism, their right to learn and to prepare for a responsible life in a free society is denied. And we should note that they do not get a second chance. Where school students are more likely to suffer violence and abuse because of their gender or because they are the target of racial, religious, xenophobic, or similar discrimination, then their rights are doubly violated. Educators have a major role to play, not only in ensuring that their own behavior is not violent or discriminatory, but also in ensuring protection to the girls in their class, as well as to the immigrant or minority children or to kids who for some reason are different from the others in the classroom—all may be particularly vulnerable to violent abuse.

Violence and the Family

The second theme you are discussing today is violence against children in the family. This is sometimes seen as an even greater challenge to the human rights community and to all societies. Articles 5 and 18 and other provisions of the Convention require states to give full recognition and support to the responsibilities, rights, and duties of parents with regard to their children. However, other provisions, and in particular article 19, also impose a clear obligation on states—an obligation that as a general principle has long been recognized in most societies: that is, to take all appropriate measures to protect children from all forms of violence and abuse while in the care of parents and guardians. Some people, perhaps learning for the first time that the international community has given clear recognition to children as subjects of human rights, are tempted to see these two sets of obligations not as complementary, but as in conflict.

We must work hard to explain to parents and communities everywhere that recognizing the human rights of children does not amount to denying rights to parents. Thus the right to family privacy most often cited in this context extends to children as much as to adults. There is nothing new about the constant need to reconcile the different rights of several parties in any given situation and setting limits to the exercise of rights when they conflict with the rights of others. This everyday process of balancing or harmonizing rights does not amount to denying rights. There is nothing new in accepting that the state has an obligation to protect children from violence even within the family—what seems new to some is the acknowledgment that children enjoy that right to the same extent as any adult. If we are serious in believing that children have rights, we cannot accept the right of anyone to treat them in a way that would be considered intolerable, and a criminal offense, if inflicted on a spouse in the home or on a stranger in the streets.

Children cannot but be most deeply affected by violence that they suffer within their own families. Research has taught us that no other violation of their rights is as difficult for children to voice and to denounce as violence within the family. Many suffer silently because to do otherwise would be unthinkable. While collecting reliable statistics is extremely difficult, we must face the facts that, sadly, it is very likely that a greater number of children are victims of violence and abuse within their own families and homes than in any other setting. We know that no other abuse has a greater potential impact on the development of the child. We know that while gender discrimination has an impact on the pattern of abuse and vulnerability, both boys and girls are affected. And we understand the need for responses to such violence that will best ensure physical and psychological recovery and social reintegration of the victims. I might add that we must also ensure that racial or related discrimination does not influence prevention and intervention efforts. But we are also aware that no other form of violence is as difficult to monitor, as complex to prevent, and as wrenching to remedy.

Just as in the case of schools, to call for an immediate end to the victimization of children within the family does not amount to denying the need for discipline in the child's formation. It does, however, require states to go beyond the enactment of legal measures. In addition, states need to ensure through public education and awareness-raising campaigns that there are changes brought about in social and cultural perceptions of the acceptability and effectiveness of alternative forms of discipline. At the same time states need to ensure that support and assistance are available to parents and family members who may find it difficult to deal appropriately with their children, especially in situations of psychological or economic stress. Children, too, need to have easy and appropriate access to advice and help. Professionals working with and for children should have the necessary specialist training and resources. They should also be encouraged to work together, with the common emphasis being on prevention.

We need to make sure that protecting children against *all* forms of violence is seen as an even greater priority of the international community, fully involving all parts of the UN system. I am certain that the outcome of today's discussion will help to inform the outcome of the General Assembly Special Session on Children when it takes place next year. But we are also very aware that it is at the national level that action must be taken to change the daily lives of children. It will be up to me, but also to all of you participating in today's meeting, to take the Committee's recommendations back to our own organizations and to ensure that they are studied and used to improve the way in which we fight against the violence suffered by children. My Office will bring the recommendations adopted on these themes to the attention of all human rights mandates, and will continue to cooperate in the follow-up efforts that will be needed for today's discussion.

I wish you all success and look forward to the outcome of your deliberations.

Address to the General Assembly Special Session on Children
United Nations, New York, 9 May 2002

Chairperson, Excellencies, Ladies, and Gentlemen,

In September 1990 world leaders gathered at the United Nations and made a "solemn commitment to give high priority to the rights of children, to their survival, and to their protection and development."[3] A decade later, you are here again to adopt a new series of goals—mindful that many of the goals and targets adopted by the World Summit for Children have still to be met. There is a need to link that Summit's commitments with the Millennium Development Goals, many of which go to the heart of issues you are here to discuss: the eradication of hunger among children, universal primary education, reducing child mortality, and combating HIV/AIDS, malaria, and other diseases.

This Special Session is the opportunity to take stock of the progress made. It should serve as a spur for greater political support, for increased resources, and for more dynamic social mobilization to achieve all unmet goals.

The adoption of the Convention on the Rights of the Child in 1989 reflected an international consensus on a new vision of children—no longer as mere objects of protection who have needs, but as human beings who enjoy rights. The core idea of the Convention—that children's rights are human rights—is central to the matters being considered at this Special Session. The Convention, adhered to now by 191 states, is one of the great success stories of multilateral diplomacy and of the human rights movement. But the challenge before us remains significant, and the gaps in implementation remain painfully obvious.[4]

A human rights approach to the well-being of children requires states to make every effort to eliminate all forms of discrimination against children. Yet, discrimination against children, especially girls, is still prevalent around the world and affects their enjoyment of every right. I have vivid memories of my visit to Kabul last March, which provided a striking example of how development efforts must address gender discrimination if they are to succeed. None of us will ever forget the joy in the faces of the girls who had finally returned to school after years of denial of this most fundamental right.

Just two days ago the Security Council heard the powerful testimonies of three children affected by war.[5] No one is better placed to remind us that the impact of conflict is a profound violation of their rights. We need to do everything we can to ensure children's protection and to realize their rights.

Next week, here in New York, the historic first session of the new Permanent Forum on Indigenous Issues will provide a further opportunity for implementing the antidiscrimination agenda adopted at last year's World Conference against Racism, as it applies to indigenous children. Many other forms of discrimination must also be addressed, including that suffered by children from poor families, from rural and remote areas; those living with disabilities; or those belonging to minorities.

A rights-based approach to action for children requires children, parents, and local communities to be empowered to participate in the defense of their own rights. Human rights education must therefore become a comprehensive, lifelong process and start with the reflection of human rights values in the daily lives and experiences of children, including in the school curricula.

While every issue under discussion at the Special Session relates directly to the Convention on the Rights of the Child, there are particular aspects that are of concern to my Office. According to the Special Session of the General Assembly held on HIV/AIDS, respect for human rights is directly linked to reducing the spread and impact of HIV/AIDS on children.[6] A rights-based approach, including increased access to medication, is central to mitigating the economic and social impact of the pandemic. The empowerment of adolescent girls, and their knowledge of reproductive rights, is an essential element in responding effectively to HIV/AIDS.

Children involved with the criminal justice system also have rights. Yet, in too many cases the right of children to be treated in a manner consistent with human dignity—taking into account the child's age and the objective of constructive reintegration in society—is disregarded.

We increasingly recognize that violence against children, in all its forms, is a violation of their rights. My Office has committed itself to support the Secretary General's study on violence against children requested by the General Assembly.[7] The Commission on Human Rights at its recent session recommended the appointment of an independent expert on this issue.

This Special Session must yield concrete action toward the full implementation of the rights already recognized by the international community. The Convention on the Rights of the Child is nearly universally ratified. Our task now is to bring these standards home—home to every school, hospital, law court, workplace, and family in the world.

I urge you to keep in mind the human rights framework that already exists for the protection of the rights of children. This includes the work of the Committee on the Rights of the Child and the Special Rapporteurs on the sale of children, child prostitution, and child pornography and on the right to education. The mainstreaming of children's rights has meant that many of the thematic Rapporteurs who are dealing with issues ranging from torture to food, report on issues affecting children. The growing community of independent national human rights institutions and the emergence of new coalitions of civil society organizations—including children's NGOs and networks—offer fresh possibilities for taking forward the struggle for children's rights.

Chairperson, Excellencies, ladies, and gentlemen, in adopting the Convention on the Rights of the Child, the General Assembly established an agenda for action. By making it the most widely ratified of all human rights treaties, states made a commitment to that agenda. As a lawyer, I understand this is a legally binding commitment by states. But as a parent, I understand it more deeply as a morally binding commitment to our children, and our children's children.

Children have brought us their own vision of the commitments the international community should undertake in "A World Fit for Us" which they worked on during the Children's Forum.[8] I wish you every success as you work, together with children, to implement this agenda. They have asked for a world in which their rights and dignity will be respected and their voices heard.

Chapter 11
Minorities and Indigenous Peoples

Recognition and protection of minority rights had been left aside during the drafting of the Universal Declaration of Human Rights. It took until 1992 for states to agree on a Minorities Declaration, a set of principles on human rights and minorities, as well as to accept duties to recognize and protect them. One major contribution of Mary Robinson was to ensure that ethnic and other minorities as well as indigenous peoples came within the purview of the World Conference Against Racism and its ambition to eliminate all forms of racial oppression and discrimination. The struggle to achieve recognition and protection for indigenous peoples similar to that of minorities remains work in progress. But an important development was the creation of the Permanent Forum on Indigenous Issues within the United Nations. OHCHR was the lead UN agency in the establishing of the Forum, and Mary Robinson as High Commissioner, was also coordinator for the International Decade of the World's Indigenous People (1995–2004).

Message on Minorities' Rights Day, India
Palais Wilson, Geneva, 18 December 1998

It is a great honor for me to have this opportunity to send you a message on the occasion of Minorities' Rights Day, in celebration of the adoption of the United Nations Declaration on the Rights of Persons Belonging to National or Ethnic, Religious and Linguistic Minorities.[1]

As we turn back the pages of history and remember the atrocities committed in the past, often against innocent people whose only fault lay in belonging to the wrong religious, cultural, or linguistic groups, we have learned the importance of building bridges between different groups, and of promoting better understanding and mutual tolerance between individuals and communities. Harmonious relations among minorities and between minorities and the majority are a great asset to the multiethnic and multicultural diversity that is Indian society. Positive relations between groups should be considered for their potential to contribute to pluralistic cohesion and harmony rather than a source of division and alienation, leading to tensions and conflict.

The celebration of Minorities' Rights Day recognizes the contribution minority groups can make to the enrichment of society. Tolerance, understanding, and above all the respect of the rights of persons belonging to minorities are crucial in ensuring coexistence, harmony, and peace both within the state and beyond. The international community has given strong direction on the need to preserve the identity of minorities and to protect and promote their rights. Although several international human rights instruments refer to ethnic, linguistic, cultural, or religious groups, the United Nations Declaration on the Rights of Persons Belonging to Minorities is the first and only instrument which addresses the specific rights of minorities in a separate document. The text of the Declaration, while ensuring a balance between the rights of persons belonging to minorities to maintain and develop their own identities and characteristics and the corresponding obligations of states, ultimately safeguards the territorial integrity and political independence of the nation as a whole.

Today is an occasion to seek new ways of building bridges with minorities. It provides an occasion to fuel new initiatives to promote tolerance, understanding, and friendship among all groups and all individuals in society. Living together while respecting differences is one of the major challenges facing each one of us today and for the years to come.

I wish you every success on this occasion.

Protection of Minorities and Other Vulnerable Groups
Message to a Regional Seminar of Experts for Central and Eastern European States
Warsaw, Poland, 5 July 2000

Excellencies, Distinguished Participants, Ladies, and Gentlemen,

The protection of minorities and other vulnerable groups and the strengthening of national capacity for their protection have been on the agenda of the international community for nearly a century now. It is worth recalling the minority protection system of the League of Nations, which was anchored in the foundation principle of equality of treatment in law and in fact for persons belonging to minorities.[2] The jurisprudence of the World Court solidified the principle of equality as a fundamental tenet of contemporary international law.[3]

Following its establishment, the United Nations declared the protection of minorities to be one of the central purposes of its human rights program. The International Convention on the Elimination of All Forms of Racial Discrimination, the International Convention on the Elimination of Discrimination Against Women, the International Convention on the Rights of Migrant Workers and Their Families,[4] and norms on the human rights of indigenous populations all have in view the principle of equal treatment of human beings in law and in fact and the need to ensure the application of that principle.

The United Nations Declaration on the Rights of Persons Belonging to National or Ethnic, Religious and Linguistic Minorities, adopted in 1992,[5] and regional instruments of the OSCE and the Council of Europe[6] have sought to undergird the legal protection of minorities and vulnerable groups. Their faithful implementation, in letter and in spirit, remains a key challenge before us.

Successive United Nations Decades to Combat Racism and Racial Discrimination have had in view the protection of minorities and other vulnerable groups. The First World Conference to Combat Racism and Racial Discrimination (1978) urged all states to abolish and prohibit any discrimination among their citizens on the ground of their ethnic or national origin and to protect and promote the human rights of persons belonging to national and ethnic minorities.[7]

The Conference recommended that states adopt specific measures in the economic, social, educational, and cultural fields and in the matter of civil and political rights, in order that all persons may enjoy legal and factual equality and that discrimination between majorities and minorities be eliminated.

The Conference urged also that states recognize a list of specific rights of indigenous populations. These included the right to carry on within their areas of settlement their traditional structure of economy and way of life, to maintain and use their own language, to receive education and information in their own language, and to disseminate information regarding their needs and problems. The Conference called on states receiving migrant workers to eliminate all discriminatory practices against such workers and their families by giving them treatment no less favorable than that accorded to their own nationals.

The Second World Conference, in 1983, recognized that throughout the various regions of the world there is a diversity of peoples, cultures, traditions, and religions that encompassed, in many instances, various minority groups.[8] It declared that there was a need for constant effort and continued vigilance on the part of all governments to avoid any form of racial discrimination based on race, color, descent, or national or ethnic origin.

The Conference underlined that national and local institutions, adapted to the needs and conditions of each country, can play an important role in the promotion and protection of human rights, in the prevention of discrimination and the protection of the rights of persons belonging to national and ethnic minorities, indigenous populations, and refugees.

The Third World Conference against Racism, Racial Discrimination, Xenophobia and Related Intolerance will be held in South Africa in September 2001.[9] It will register, at the start of this century, humanity's determination to achieve a world of equality in law and in fact, of human dignity, and of universal respect for all without discrimination on grounds of race, gender, nationality, social origin, or birth. If the twenty-first century is to be the century of human rights, then it is absolutely vital that the battle for equality be won across the globe. I should like to use this occasion to call for a global mobilization of conscience in favor of the eradication of racism, racial discrimination, xenophobia, and related intolerance.

As you proceed with your deliberations I would invite you to consider questions such as the following, with a view to formulating assessments or recommendations for consideration at the World Conference:

A vision of the unity of the human family

Following the first mapping of the human genome, how can we instill in every child, every human being, a sense of the oneness of the human family so that each person can have a sense of belonging to the whole and none would feel excluded?

Inclusive national identities

How can every country in the world revisit and recast its vision of a national identity that embraces and encompasses all parts or groups of the population, that gives to everyone a stake in the future of her or his country?

Combating discrimination through promotion and protection of human rights

How can we spread the implementation of human rights across the globe so that the practice of rights—economic, social and cultural, and civil and political—can foster cultures of respect and tolerance in the framework of fundamental human rights?

Combating discrimination through the advancement of economic and social justice

How can we eliminate disparities in access to economic and social opportunities and thereby eliminate root causes of prejudice and discrimination?

Internal self-monitoring

How can each country establish institutions to monitor itself to detect potential problems and head them off before they deteriorate?

Preventive regimes

How can we act more effectively to prevent discrimination and other violations of human rights?

Education

How can we use the opportunities provided by modern means of communication and information to spread the messages of the oneness of humankind, of respect, tolerance, good-neighborliness? How can we instill a universal culture of human rights?

Institutions

How can we develop the role of institutions nationally, regionally, and internationally to guard against racism, racial discrimination, xenophobia, and related intolerance?

New problems encountered by minorities, indigenous populations, migrants

What are the contemporary problems faced by minorities, indigenous populations, and migrants, and what can one recommend for consideration by the World Conference next year?

Central and East European dimensions

What insights would you wish to place before the World Conference about Central and East European dimensions of the issues I have raised, and what positive forms of action would you wish to identify for consideration by the World Conference: positive experiences that it can commend to other regions of the world?

I ask you to reflect on these and related questions and issues, and I send you my very best wishes for a successful expert meeting.

United Nations Permanent Forum on Indigenous Issues
Statement at the opening of the Permanent Forum
United Nations, New York, 13 May 2002

Deputy Secretary General, Members of the Permanent Forum, Distinguished Delegates and Guests, Ladies, and Gentlemen,

I am glad to join other voices today to help you celebrate this historic achievement. I use the word "celebrate" deliberately. At a time when the international community and the United Nations are beset with so many challenges, this inaugural session of the Permanent Forum represents a challenge that has actually been met. This was the challenge, recognized by indigenous peoples a long time ago and acknowledged at the Vienna World Conference on Human Rights in 1993, to find space within the United Nations system for indigenous peoples themselves to address the serious issues affecting their communities.

It is satisfying that the achievement is a shared one—an achievement of both governments and indigenous peoples. The structure of this forum, consisting of both governmental and indigenous experts, reflects this partnership—which is even mirrored in the seating plan for the room. It will be important now to ensure that this sense of partnership and shared achievement continues. Ideally, you will succeed in giving new meaning to the official slogan of the International Decade of the World's Indigenous People: "partnership in action."[10] Much of the experience gained in the Working Group on Indigenous Populations will be relevant—and I would like to welcome the presence today of its distinguished long-time chair, Ms. Erica Daes

—but much will also need to be developed afresh.[11] I share your sense of anticipation and expectation, both as coordinator of the Decade and as an Honorary Chieftain of the Choctaw People.[12]

Mandate of the Forum

The Forum has another special feature that will define its development. Although it was born out of a resolution in the Commission on Human Rights (and I wish to acknowledge the leadership provided by Denmark in that process), the mandate of this body extends beyond human rights. This is important not only for the activities of the Forum but also for the innovative way it will need to be supported and financed within the United Nations system—a matter I will return to later. The Forum is mandated to cover economic and social issues, health and education, human rights, and development and, indeed, all relevant matters that are dealt with by ECOSOC. This means that we now have a common space for indigenous peoples where all the diverse parts of the UN family can meet, exchange information, and coordinate their efforts. This is a body that has the capacity to address indigenous issues in a truly holistic and comprehensive manner.

The range of potential matters for your attention is broad indeed. For indigenous peoples the question of land is a crucial issue, which goes to the heart of indigenous culture and identity. Closely related to this is the protection of the environment. In many places the preservation of natural resources is linked to the survival of peoples. The processes of national development and poverty reduction need to be viewed from the indigenous perspective. This is clearly true for peoples who pursue traditional ways of life, but it is no less the case for those who, by choice or by reason of displacement, have established communities within urban environments. The approach to individual and collective rights will be instructive as we seek international consensus on the right to development. Indigenous peoples are the custodians of a vast array of traditional knowledge and rich and diverse cultural heritages that must be acknowledged, respected, and preserved. The right to one's own language is crucial in this regard. I know that the right to health is a fundamental issue in many communities where the demographics of life expectancy and infant mortality are often shocking when viewed in relation to the communities around them.

Children and Young People

Among many pressing issues, there are two that I would like particularly to draw to your attention. The first is the role of children and young people. We have just completed a Special Session of the UN General Assembly on children at which the children reminded us they are both our present and our future, and that we have important obligations toward them. If anything, this is even more true of indigenous children and young people. As we heard this morning, young people have clear ideas of their own and their ideas need to be attended to. I hope the members of the Permanent Forum will find ways to ensure that the voices of the young continue to be heard.

Discrimination

The other issue is discrimination. Indigenous peoples around the world remain subject to high numbers of incidents of racism and intolerance. Indigenous women often suffer multiple layers of discrimination. The extent of this racism and discrimination was recognized explicitly at last year's World Conference against Racism in Durban. Indigenous issues were accorded a separate chapter in the Programme of Action agreed on at that meeting. This Forum can play a role in follow-up of that Agenda.

There are many issues for you to address. But, fortunately, there are also many resources within the United Nations system at your disposal. This brings me to another key aspect of your mandate: you are charged with providing expert advice and recommendations to the UN's programs and agencies and with promoting coordination of activities in relation to indigenous peoples within the UN system.

This will require you to develop an understanding of how the UN system functions, learning where its strengths lie and where it has limitations. I am pleased that this process has already begun with the technical assistance of UNITAR and the financial support of the Canadian government.[13] But the scope of your mandate, and its focus on the coordination of UN activity, also imposes an obligation on the United Nations system to provide appropriate structures for you to accomplish your work.

When the Secretary General appointed my Office as lead agency for the establishment of the Permanent Forum, one of our first priorities was to set in place a system of interagency consultation. It quickly became clear that this should constitute itself into a permanent mechanism for linking the Permanent Forum with the rest of the UN system.[14] I would like particularly to thank Mark Malloch Brown, Administrator of UNDP; Anna Tibaijuka, Executive Director of HABITAT; and Thoraya Obaid, Executive Director of the UN Family Planning Agency, for being with us here today—this group exists to assist the Permanent Forum.

Ensuring that this unique Forum works effectively will require innovation and flexibility. From our side, the UN system still needs to think creatively of ways of managing itself differently in relation to the Permanent Forum. There is clearly a need for a permanent secretariat to service this body. The recommendations that you, the members, make in that regard will greatly assist us in determining how the Forum should be supported.

Finance

Your views should also serve to guide governments in deciding how the Forum should be financed. At present, the ECOSOC resolution mandates that the financing of the Permanent Forum shall be provided from "within existing resources" and through "such voluntary contributions as may be donated." I want to be frank on the matter of financing. The members of the Forum will need to consider carefully the recommendations they wish to make. To date, in the absence of regular budget financing, virtually all of the nonconference service costs associated with supporting the Forum have been drawn from precious unearmarked funds within our human rights budget.

I do not regret these expenditures, as I believe the Forum will become an important mechanism for advancing the human rights of indigenous peoples. But this avenue of financing is not sustainable. I know that this was not what member states intended when they created this important body. In the absence of regular budget funding, extrabudgetary contributions become critical, and I express my appreciation to the governments of New Zealand and Ecuador as the first states to make such contributions. But stable, permanent funding of this Permanent Forum is absolutely necessary for its effective functioning and success.

Ladies and gentlemen, in discussing the Permanent Forum there is a natural tendency to focus on what the UN system can do for indigenous peoples. This is understandable. But I think it is important that we give at least equal weight to what indigenous peoples can do for the United Nations. I was moved last week by a young Maori boy's spiritual invocation at the beginning of an event. Today we have been privileged to receive the traditional welcome of the Haudenosaunee. Beyond their traditional knowledge and cultural accomplishments, the indigenous peoples of the world are possessed of a unique spirituality, vision, and sense of community. If the members of the Permanent Forum can find a way to share some of the wisdom and worldview of their peoples with the United Nations family and with the wider international community, then this may prove to be their most important and enduring achievement.

I wish you every success, and pledge you every support, in the weeks and months ahead.

Chapter 12

Human Rights after Conflict

Concern for the protection of human rights in times of actual or threatened conflict and the need to take conflict prevention seriously were recurring themes in many of Mary Robinson's public statements as High Commissioner (see also Chapters 14 and 19). The texts here concern the aftermath of conflict and transitional justice issues. These include the protection of civilians, combating impunity, the need for accountability over gross violation of the past, rebuilding the rule of law, and the vital role of local civil society groups in repairing the effects of conflict. OHCHR's involvement in post-conflict reconstruction, including supporting truth and reconciliation processes, is recorded in her words on the Balkans, Indonesia, East Timor, and Peru. Mary Robinson visited these countries as High Commissioner to express solidarity with victims and to identify what her Office could best contribute to rebuilding lives.

"Building the Rule of Law after Conflict"
Vienna, Austria, 26 June 1998

Excellencies, Ladies, and Gentlemen,

It is a privilege for me to have the opportunity to address this Conference dedicated to the role of the rule of law in postconflict situations. Allow me to congratulate the organizers on the convening of this important meeting. I see it as an example of mainstreaming human rights by the United Nations Office at Vienna, a process that is currently developing throughout the United Nations system.

We have gathered here five years after the Vienna World Conference on Human Rights, a Conference that charted a course of action for the international community and that continues to serve as our guide. During this year, the international community both commemorates the fiftieth anniversary of the Universal Declaration of Human Rights and reviews the progress achieved in the implementation of the Vienna Declaration and Programme of Action.

This conference addresses a major challenge: how to respond effectively to conflict situations which are the most frequent source of grave human rights violations, and which destroy the lives of individuals, groups, and entire nations. To an outside observer, the rule of law may appear to be useless in situations of conflict, when force dominates the scene, so that adherence to it may not seem significant for redressing such situations. This Conference will endeavor to show how wrong such views are.

Ladies and gentlemen, the post-Cold War era has created new opportunities but has also brought new threats. In many cases, long-simmering problems left unresolved but suppressed in the past by authoritarian regimes have erupted into bitter hostility and even civil war. The situations in Somalia, the former Yugoslavia, Rwanda, and Burundi provide only a few tragic examples in this regard.

A major change in the nature of contemporary conflicts prompts us to reconsider the role to be played by the international community as well as the methods it should apply. Internal conflicts constitute today's reality—as we all know—a marked change from the past. According to 1996 figures, there were forty major armed conflicts in thirty-four states, all of which were internal—none of an interstate nature.

As we have witnessed, internal conflicts quickly spiral into violence and, tragically, share a common characteristic: the severe and lasting damage they inflict on civilian populations. By one estimate of these conflicts, the ratio of civilian casualties to soldier casualties is about nine to one. Equally troubling, belligerents have resorted to strategies and tactics that deliberately target women, children, the poor, and the weak. This has given rise to waves of refugees and internally displaced persons as a result of internal conflict and violence, which have grown to more than twenty-five million. In conflicts of this sort, not only regular armies but also militias and armed civilians with little discipline and with ill-defined chains of command become involved. As a result, humanitarian emergencies are commonplace.

The increase in internal conflicts highlights the failure of state structures to work through serious political and social tensions while maintaining both public order and confidence that the process will bring about progress for people.

Prevention and the Rule of Law

This change in the nature and pattern of conflicts requires our thinking to adapt regarding the best response of the international community. We must commit ourselves to providing the tools that can avert violence through prevention, instead of making commitments to assist only after violence has taken its toll. Limited resources have been cited frequently as the reason for lack of effective early action. I believe our shortcomings have not been due to limited resources as much as limited political will. Now is the time to shift our priorities from reaction to prevention by focusing our efforts on averting conflicts through support for education, democracy, sustainable development, and human rights programs.

The Secretary General has urged that the next century must be "the age of prevention of human rights violations."[1] We must respond to this call. Preventing human rights violations has not only a moral dimension; in the vast majority of cases, by preventing violations we are addressing the root causes of conflict. The vicious cycle—human rights violations and conflict resulting in further violations—can be broken effectively only by restoring respect for human rights under the rule of law.

The World Conference on Human Rights reaffirmed the inseparable link between the principle of the rule of law and protection and promotion of human rights. It recognized that the absence of the rule of law was one of the major obstacles to the implementation of these rights. This conference should reflect on how the full potential of the rule of law can be utilized under particularly challenging postconflict circumstances.

We have ample evidence that societies governed by the rule of law are better equipped to manage conflict by peaceful means. The rule of law provides the foundation for the just management of relations between and among people. It is a pillar of the democratic process. It helps to ensure the participation of individuals in governance and the conditions for economic opportunity and equity. Thus, the rule of law is a basic premise for a stable political, economic, and social system.

Yet, the rule of law is not merely "Government by Law and not by Men." It must also be a rule *of law* and not just *by law*. For at the heart of the rule of law are the values protected by a legal system. Law established merely to give the appearance of legality to an autocratic regime cannot be perceived as a legitimate component of the rule of law; neither can law which allows the use of torture or the deprivation of educational or health-care opportunities. If this happens, the rule of law degenerates into formal mechanisms dependent on the will of rulers or—at the very least—simply serves to protect their interests.

Law that is "nonoppressive" is only one requirement of a "good" law. The legal system of a democratic state must go further by creating the conditions under which the dignity of human beings is fully respected. This means that the law must be rooted in human rights—and we must stress here—*all* human rights. Let us remember that equal ranking of all categories of rights—civil, cultural, economic, political, and social—is a keystone of the Vienna Declaration and Programme of Action. I am highlighting this imperative since, in postconflict situations in particular, when countries face economic problems, both national authorities and international financial institutions are inclined to reduce the response to acute social problems to the provision of basic humanitarian assistance and public philanthropy.

Meanwhile, the neglect of economic, social, and cultural rights and appropriate developmental policies leads to situations which prompted Anatole France's sarcastic observation: "The Law, in its majestic equality, forbids the rich, as well as the poor, to sleep under the bridges, to beg in the streets, and to steal bread."[2]

The protection of all human rights should be a basic criterion for the system of institutions and procedures constituting the rule of law at the national and local levels. It is vital that the individual claimant has access to just, swift, and effective remedies. We should not overlook the remarkable fact that the better a legal system protects human rights, the better its overall functioning will be.

Accountability and Impunity

The rule of law also ensures control by law over and accountability of rulers. This should include responsibility for human rights violations. Denying impunity to perpetrators is widely perceived not only as a moral postulate but also as an indispensable element of a sound political order. We can observe, after many years of hesitation, a growing understanding that impunity is one of the primary obstacles to lasting solutions to conflict situations.

The Vienna World Conference called upon states to abrogate legislation leading to impunity for those responsible for grave violations of human rights such as torture, and thereby provide a firm basis for the rule of law. The Dayton Agreement, the activities of the Truth and Reconciliation Commission in South Africa, and the truth commissions in some Latin American countries all bear witness to the practical dimensions of this problem that once was dealt with behind closed doors in political offices.

If the international community is serious in its desire to prevent conflicts, it must say "no" to impunity. It is my hope that the International Diplomatic Conference in Rome that is examining the establishment of an International Criminal Court will achieve this objective. A strong permanent international criminal court will send out a powerful message of deterrence to all in positions of power and leadership that they can no longer use terror tactics, systematic rape, ethnic cleansing, mutilation, and indiscriminate killing of noncombatants as weapons of war or for any other purpose. All individuals, regardless of official rank or capacity, are legally bound to refrain from committing such horrific crimes as genocide, war crimes, and crimes against humanity: this principle is rooted in the ancient laws and customs of almost all cultures and throughout history.

One of the aspects of the rule of law pivotal to human rights is the legal regime and the practice pursued during a state of emergency, a time when human rights are at particular risk. The international community should remain vigilant where there is the suspension of human rights, the prolonged duration of martial law, and attempts to maintain the institutions of martial law after its apparent formal abrogation. We must also be aware of the lasting negative consequences that the imposition of martial law may cause in the consciousness of rulers and civil society.

Rule of Law and Technical Cooperation

The rule of law is not only a legal principle: it is, in fact, also a program of work. The United Nations, through its technical cooperation programs, strives to address the following fundamental challenges: imperfect law; weakness of institutions established to guarantee just and effective application of law; and low legal awareness in the society, especially concerning the role of the legal profession. The approach seeks to reinforce constitutional and legal reforms; to build and strengthen national institutions, and to provide legal and human rights training for professional groups and the general public. It is vital that human rights and rule-of-law components are integrated into the activities of programs and agencies mandated in areas of development, humanitarian assistance, and peacekeeping to ensure effective national infrastructures for human rights and the rule of law.

Monitoring human rights developments is another important support in restoring the rule of law. My Office, in parallel with its technical cooperation activities, also offers such assistance through screening relevant developments at national and local levels. This activity provides both the government concerned and the international community in general with the information necessary to shape programs and projects most appropriate for a given context. My Office stands ready to cooperate with governments wishing to establish such activities in their countries.

We have to bear in mind that in conflict situations only a swift and professional response is adequate. Therefore, the United Nations should harness all actors by improving coordination both at the headquarters and field levels. It should also work more closely with civil society and with nongovernmental and academic communities. Only then can scarce resources be put to efficient use and effective assistance provided.

The rule of law, understood as being interlinked with human rights, can and should play a decisive role not only in the prevention of conflict situations, but also as an essential element in their peaceful resolution. There is no better bulwark against the recurrence of conflicts than respect for human rights—fully protected by the rule of law. I am encouraged by the fact that this has become increasingly clear and that the role of human rights in the work for peace and security, democracy, and development is understood. Now we must put all this into practice, beginning in 1998, as we carry out the five-year review of the Vienna Declaration and Programme of Action and mark the fiftieth anniversary of the Universal Declaration of Human Rights.

"Developing a Human Rights Culture in Southeast Europe"
Humanitarian Issues Working Group of the Peace Implementation Council
Palais des Nations, Geneva, 8 December 1999

Madame High Commissioner, Excellencies, Ladies, and Gentlemen,

The past year in Southeast Europe has shocked us all with images of cruelty and suffering recalling the darkest days of the wars in Bosnia and Herzegovina and Croatia a few years ago. Human rights violations of the gravest sort early in the year in Kosovo were followed by the NATO bombing campaign from late March to June, during which ethnically motivated massacres, torture, and forcible displacement had a devastating impact. Today, nearly half a year after the end of the NATO operation, we receive daily reports of brutality against Serbs and other minorities groups in Kosovo. There have been twenty-two killings in the last week alone—for example, the murder on a main street in Pristina of a Serb university professor and the vicious beatings of his wife and mother-in-law. All are part of a stream of numbing incidents of violence.

What can we say of progress made in the last year to instill and promote a culture of respect for human rights in this part of the world? Sadly, there is little concrete progress to report, and the temptation is strong to say that our hard work over the last seven years has produced only the most limited results.

For the sake of those whose rights are being violated, however, we must not abandon our efforts, but instead we must seek to come up with new strategies to try to alleviate the suffering in the region of the former Yugoslavia and to consolidate the situations in neighboring countries. I am heartened by the regional approach, which has taken shape in the form of the Stability Pact, and the critical importance accorded to respect for human rights and democratic principles as key elements for sustainable peace.[3] As we move into another difficult winter in the region, the work of UNHCR and other organizations in assuring the humanitarian needs of the populations of southeast Europe will be vital to saving lives. Humanitarian work, however, will have a lasting impact only if it is part of a campaign to promote and protect human rights generally.

The challenges to be overcome are daunting. Returns of refugees and displaced persons throughout the region continue to proceed at an unacceptably slow pace. During my visit to the region in May—for example in my discussions with government leaders in Croatia—I learned of the obstacles which exist at the community level to the return of minority populations. In my view, however, it is the responsibility of the holders of the highest political offices to confront prejudiced and xenophobic attitudes, and to promote through their words and example a culture of tolerance and understanding at all levels of society. The failure of police authorities to respond vigorously to an assault by organized groups against peaceful demonstrators in Zagreb in May was deeply troubling to me. In Bosnia and Herzegovina, which present perhaps the most difficult challenge in the region, resistance to the implementation of reformed property legislation continues to be a problem. In this regard I commend the energetic stance of the High Representative, Ambassador Petrisch, who has pushed new property laws through and recently dismissed local leaders who failed to facilitate returns. Such leadership, however, should come from national authorities—as well as from the international community.

Civil Society Actors

What I learned during my visits to the region in May and June is that perhaps the greatest hope for social and cultural transformation in southeast Europe comes from the courageous and visionary work of civil society actors—those who take stands which may not be the easiest paths to political power. I was inspired by the work of NGOs in the former Yugoslav Republic of Macedonia who distribute information on the legal rights of detainees; by NGOs in Albania which investigated human rights violations taking place in Kosovo; by NGOs in Bosnia and Herzegovina which are leading the battle against trafficking in women and children. In Belgrade, I was deeply impressed by the anguish expressed by NGO representatives who feared the consequences to their struggle of the NATO military campaign. These are the people who hold the key to a more stable future for the region, and they are the ones whom we must support and to whom we must closely listen.

My Office is now determined to pursue a program to promote human rights in southeast Europe on a regional basis, including through maintaining close links with representatives of civil society. In this regard I am pleased to report on a successful conference which we sponsored, together with the Council of Europe and the International Helsinki Federation, in Ohrid, Macedonia, two weeks ago, which brought together NGO representatives from Greece to Slovenia, from Romania to Italy, and throughout the region. We emphasized the three issues of gender equality, the right to return, and the prevention of torture and found them to be areas in which we can pool our resources and experience to more effectively improve respect for human rights on both a country-specific and a regional basis. This is the sort of strategic approach that I intend to emphasize, as my Office's contribution to greater stability in Southeast Europe in the months and years to come.

Gender

Let me focus on the issue of gender for a moment, since it is a good example of an issue that we can address from a regional perspective. A regionwide gender analysis reveals: not only that women's rights to physical integrity are violated widely through the pernicious phenomenon of trafficking, but also that women's capacities to *combat* the effects of trafficking are compromised by systemic lack of opportunity, and lack of participation, lack of political and economic power. In Bosnia and Herzegovina, for example, demobilized soldiers receive preferential treatment in employment programs, while female job seekers are left to contend for themselves. There may be arguments in favor of this type of policy, but the question presented is: What changes could be brought to society if men and women were to have an equal chance of participation in economic and political activities? This was one of the subjects discussed in Ohrid, and our response may help us find the way to more inclusive, democratic, and stable societies in southeast Europe. I am pleased that my Office is involved in the Stability Pact's Gender Task Force in partnership with the OSCE, the Council of Europe, and NGOs.

We plan to start or carry on a number of initiatives to strengthen the culture of human rights in the region during the next year. In Macedonia and Croatia, we are working with the governments on programs for human rights education, while in Albania and Bosnia and Herzegovina we are discussing projects to assist those governments in meeting their treaty reporting obligations in the field of human rights. In the Federal Republic of Yugoslavia we will continue our work with federal and republic authorities in a number of areas, including clarification of the fate of prisoners and detainees and of missing persons in Kosovo. We hope we can be of assistance in Yugoslavia in linking up human rights concerns arising in Kosovo with those in the rest of the country.

I have been emphasizing the importance of "a culture of prevention" to ensure that mistakes of the past are not repeated and that the world responds adequately to indications of impending conflict. This approach remains eminently applicable to the situation in southeast Europe, where conflict unfortunately will continue to be a realistic possibility in a number of locations in the foreseeable future. Prevention is vital not only to heading off conflicts but also, once they have broken out, to stopping them from spreading to neighboring countries.

Culture of Inclusion

To a culture of prevention, I would like also to add the importance of "a culture of inclusion" as a key element in our strategic approach to southeast Europe. Despite people's different backgrounds, nationalities, and beliefs, it is vital that we take all possible measures to bring all people into the decision-making processes in order to ensure that all persons in the region have a stake in the decisions that affect their futures. We can achieve this kind of inclusion through vigorous programs of human rights education and training, through sustained promotion of the rights to democratic participation and free expression. This approach, finally, will be the best way to support your efforts in the humanitarian field, to ensure freedom from want and freedom from fear.

Madame High Commissioner, I return to my emphasis on the representatives of civil society as key actors in our combined efforts to instill a culture of respect for human rights in southeast Europe. I recall the brave individuals who pursue a vision of a better future that might lie ahead for this part of the world. I recall, for example, the schoolteacher I met in May in the refugee camp at the swimming-pool complex in Tirana. Although she had lost everything when she fled Kosovo, she continued to teach the children in the camp, maintaining her vision of how the world *should* be even as everything was falling apart around her. Despite all the setbacks and the disappointments of the past years, I hope that we can maintain that same sort of vision for southeast Europe, committing ourselves through the strength of faith to a better future for all the people of the region.

"Universal Jurisdiction and Combating Impunity"
Foreword to the *Princeton Principles on Universal Jurisdiction*
Princeton, USA, 25 January 2001

This subject is of great relevance to all who work for human rights. I regard the search for ways to end impunity in the case of gross violations of human rights as an essential part of the work of my Office and an essential instrument in the struggle to defend human rights. I welcome the fact that you are holding these discussions with such a prestigious group in attendance and trust that the initiative of the Princeton Project can play a positive role in developing and clarifying the principle of universal jurisdiction.

In my daily work as High Commissioner for Human Rights, I see many situations involving gross, and sometimes widespread, human rights abuses for which the perpetrators often go unpunished. Torture, war crimes—including abuses involving gender-based violence—and enforced disappearances are but a few of these crimes. The recent increase in transnational criminal activity, encouraged by globalization and open borders, has added to the challenges we face in fighting against impunity for such abuses. Trafficking of persons, and of women and children specifically, is an issue of particular concern to my Office. These disturbing trends have given me cause to reflect on the possibilities for alternative means of securing justice and accountability.

Two important and complementary means currently exist for the implementation of international criminal jurisdiction: prosecution by international criminal tribunals and the domestic application of the principle of universal jurisdiction. As far as the former is concerned, I am encouraged by the increasing number of states that are signing and ratifying the Statute of the International Criminal Court, and I hope that this permanent Court will soon be a reality. Even before the Court's establishment, the ICC Statute has proved an invaluable tool in the struggle against impunity. The Statute codifies crimes against humanity for the first time in a multilateral treaty, and it enumerates certain acts as war crimes when committed in noninternational armed conflicts.

Through its cornerstone principle of complementarity, the ICC Statute highlights the fact that international prosecutions alone will never be sufficient to achieve justice and emphasizes the crucial role of national legal systems in bringing an end to impunity. The sad reality is that territorial states often fail to investigate and prosecute serious human rights abuses. The application of universal jurisdiction is therefore a crucial means of justice.

The principle of universal jurisdiction is based on the notion that certain crimes are so harmful to international interests that states are entitled—and even obliged—to bring proceedings against the perpetrator, regardless of the location of the crime or the nationality of the perpetrator or the victim. Human rights abuses widely considered to be subject to universal jurisdiction include genocide, crimes against humanity, war crimes, and torture. The principle of universal jurisdiction has long existed for these crimes; however, it is rapidly evolving as a result of significant recent developments. I believe that the Princeton Principles should acknowledge that this doctrine continues to develop in law and in practice.

One aspect that might be mentioned is the application of universal jurisdiction to other offenses in international law since this has been raised recently in various forums. The UN Declaration on the Protection of all Persons from Enforced Disappearances,[4] for example, provides for the exercise of universal jurisdiction for alleged acts of forced disappearances, a provision already contained at the regional level in the Inter-American Convention on Forced Disappearance of Persons.[5] The international community is currently also considering a Draft International Convention on the Protection of all Persons from Enforced Disappearance.[6]

Universal jurisdiction was discussed recently at the symposium on the challenge of borderless cyber-crime to international efforts to combat transnational organized crime, held in conjunction with the signing conference for the United Nations Convention against Transnational Organized Crime in Palermo, Italy.[7] Discussions in treaty negotiations have raised the question of allowing civil jurisdiction for conduct, which constitutes an international crime, in the context of the draft Hague Conference on Jurisdiction and Foreign Judgments in Civil and Commercial Matters. These negotiations are of concern to my Office, as they may have important implications regarding the access to courts for victims seeking remedies for human rights violations. The International Court of Justice is also considering issues related to universal jurisdiction in the ongoing case concerning the arrest warrant against the former Minister for Foreign Affairs of the Democratic Republic of Congo by a Belgian investigating judge, who was seeking his provisional detention for alleged serious violations of international humanitarian law.[8]

These developments suggest that new ground is being broken with regard to the application of the principle of universal jurisdiction. This is not to say, however, that the exercise of universal jurisdiction is an easy matter.

There are significant practical and legal challenges regarding the application of this principle. The obstacles to universal jurisdiction were recently elaborated by the International Law Association in its very informative report on the subject.[9]

Obstacles to the exercise of universal jurisdiction include the question of the application of sovereign immunity defenses. In this regard, the decision of the British House of Lords in the Pinochet case confirming that former heads of state do not enjoy immunity for the crime of torture under UK law was refreshing and, along with other recent cases, has seriously challenged the notion of immunity from criminal liability for crimes under international law committed in an official capacity.[10]

An additional area that I am particularly concerned about is the issue of amnesty laws. I stress that certain gross violations of human rights and international humanitarian law should not be subject to amnesties. When the United Nations faced the question of signing the Sierra Leone Peace Agreement to end atrocities in that country, the UN specified that the amnesty and pardon provisions in article IX of the agreement would not apply to international crimes of genocide, crimes against humanity, war crimes, and other serious violations of international humanitarian law. We must be cautious not to send the wrong message regarding amnesties for serious violations of human rights and international humanitarian law, and I believe that the Princeton Principles should express the position that certain crimes are too heinous to go unpunished.

The exercise of universal jurisdiction holds the promise for greater justice for the victims of serious human rights violations around the world. My Office will continue to monitor developments in this rapidly evolving area, including through the ongoing efforts of the Princeton Project to strengthen universal jurisdiction as a tool to end impunity. I encourage the wide dissemination of the Princeton Principles on Universal Jurisdiction.

"Transitional Justice: Defining the Quality of Indonesia's Future Democracy"
Indonesian National Commission on Human Rights, Komnas HAM
Surabaya, Indonesia, 22–24 November 2000

Chairperson, Minister, Fellow Speakers, Excellencies, Ladies, and Gentlemen,

It gives me great pleasure to visit Indonesia at this time. I am honored to be invited to address this workshop on the theme of "Transitional Justice: Defining the Quality of Indonesia's Future Democracy," organized by Komnas HAM, the Indonesian National Commission on Human Rights.

Since its establishment in 1993, Komnas HAM has played a pivotal role in the promotion and protection of human rights in Indonesia. My Office and Komnas HAM have established strong ties. We have worked together closely on activities undertaken by the growing family of national human rights institutions within the Asia Pacific region. Komnas HAM has generously shared its ever-widening experience throughout the Asia Pacific region and beyond. I was pleased that, a few weeks ago in the Philippines, members of Komnas HAM participated in a workshop supported by my Office, on economic, social, and cultural rights, which brought together national human rights institutions from all over the Asian region. Your Commission has also participated actively in the UN Commission on Human Rights meetings in Geneva, sending an important message about the role of independent national institutions to the international community and enriching that debate.

Today, in the presence of distinguished members of Komnas HAM, members of the government, and national and international human rights actors, I wish to acknowledge your invaluable support to OHCHR's technical cooperation activities within the Asia Pacific region. I am confident that we will deepen and strengthen these ties in the years ahead. I encourage Komnas HAM to continue its important work of promoting human rights at the national and the regional levels.

Indonesia, this vast and rich country, is, like other states in the Asia Pacific region, currently in a transitional phase as she puts in place the building blocks necessary to sustain the life of a democratic nation. I am well aware of the difficulties such a transition brings and applaud the determined steps being taken to meet these challenges.

As Indonesia works toward the establishment of a strong democracy, it is appropriate to ask, as indeed Komnas HAM has done with the holding of this workshop, What is the role of justice in the development of a secure, democratic future for Indonesia? What are the benchmarks of transitional justice that will define the quality of Indonesia's future democracy?

The first thing that I would stress, Chairperson, is that there can be no democracy without justice. And there can be no justice without full and complete respect for the rule of law. This applies in Indonesia, just as it does in every other nation.

Respect for the rule of law requires a commitment from all sectors of society—the judiciary, parliament, the executive, the law enforcement agencies, and the people. It requires a commitment that no one will be above the law, that accountability will be ensured, and that there will be no impunity for past or future crimes.

The objective should be a society that respects the human rights of everyone. That means the full range of human rights: economic, social, and cultural as well as civil and political. We are fortunate to live at a time when there is growing recognition of the importance of economic, social, and cultural rights. An important landmark was the affirmation at the Vienna World Conference on Human Rights that "all human rights are universal, indivisible and interdependent and interrelated." Earlier this year the

Commission on Human Rights stated that "the ideal of free human beings enjoying freedom from fear and want can only be achieved if conditions are created whereby everyone may enjoy his or her economic, social and cultural rights, as well as his or her civil and political rights." Social justice must be at the heart of the rule of law.

Enshrining Principles of Justice and the Rule of Law

Chairperson, how can Indonesia enshrine these principles in her path of transition to the establishment of a strong democracy?

In the first place, as I have said, it is imperative that the democratic process be based on a rights-based approach, which is all-inclusive and encompasses the entirety of society. This approach places the individual as a holder of fundamental rights at the center of our efforts. It is an approach that calls for the active participation of governmental and nongovernmental actors.

Second, we must recognize the centrality of a well-functioning justice system in a democratic society, a system in which independence and impartiality are honored, in which professionalism is paramount.

Third, although the judiciary rests at the heart of any national system of administration of justice and, as such, is at the forefront of the current transition in Indonesia, the justice system itself does not begin, nor does it end, with the judiciary. Law-enforcement officials, prosecutors, defense counsel, and prison officials all play central roles in the administration of justice.

Fourth, I attach great importance to independent national human rights institutions, which monitor and ensure compliance with international standards. Such bodies thrive best when appropriately resourced, trained, properly managed, and left outside the political realm.

The Role of Komnas HAM

At this juncture, Chairperson, I feel compelled to refer again to the work and role of Komnas HAM, which is critical in assisting, encouraging, and advancing the efforts of all elements of the justice system. With its important powers to initiate investigations, issue subpoenas, and begin mediation procedures, Komnas HAM has the tools necessary to lead the way for victims of human rights violations to follow up proceedings. By initiating procedures and addressing the most difficult cases, Komnas HAM ensures that respect for human rights and due process of the law is kept alive in the public conscience. In doing so, Komnas HAM plays a central role in developing a society steeped in the values of the rule of law, a society with justice at its core.

In addition to its regular range of activities that any national human rights institution can take, Komnas HAM has undertaken extraordinary activities which have served to underline the need for accountability and augment Indonesia's path to democracy. One such activity was the establishment of the Commission of Inquiry on the situation of human rights in East Timor, following the announcement of the results of the Popular Consultation, KPP-HAM. The establishment of this Commission was an act of great courage and was carried out with rigor. All over the world, human rights activists and professionals have commended the work of the Commission and the results of its findings.

Human Rights Courts Act

Chairperson, distinguished guests, I welcome the recent adoption by the House of Representatives of the Human Rights Courts Act. In particular, I am pleased to note that the Human Rights Courts will be authorized to try past cases of gross human rights violations. I also note that the Act contains provisions for identifying and prosecuting those individuals who bear ultimate responsibility for violations. It is worthwhile to observe that the Courts are also authorized to examine alleged human rights violations committed by Indonesian citizens outside the territory of Indonesia.

Investigation of Human Rights Violations in East Timor

In this regard, I am also aware of efforts by the government of Indonesia to investigate the gross human rights violations that took place in East Timor last year. I am encouraged by the discussions I held on this subject with your previous Chairperson, Attorney General Darusman, during my short visit to Jakarta in August of this year. I look forward to discussing the investigations with the Attorney General in Jakarta tomorrow, including my offer of technical assistance to support the prosecution process.

During my visit to East Timor in August, I was also heartened to learn of the collaborative efforts initiated by Indonesia and the United Nations Transitional Administration in East Timor (UNTAET), in particular in the areas of exchange of information and assistance in the investigations. This cooperation may prove to be a vital element in the overall efforts of Indonesia to strengthen her system for the administration of justice. In fact, I am of the view that such cooperation is the best way to effectively address the terrible violations that took place in East Timor last year.

Truth and Reconciliation Process

Chairperson, the experiences of many countries in transition reveal that justice and accountability can be further served by integrating other initiatives, those strictly falling outside the legal process, into the legal structure.

I speak of the truth and reconciliation framework that can, under certain conditions, effectively assist the process of healing and transitional justice.

The essence of a truth-and-reconciliation process is twofold. First, it is to document the past, to ensure that future generations know the truth about the facts—all the facts—with clarity and completeness. It is to ensure that the names of victims and individual stories of suffering are known and revealed. It is to ensure that, to the extent possible, perpetrators, including those who gave orders, and their motives are identified. The second essential element of this process is that of healing, of reconciliation, of atonement, of the coming together and achieving a common sense of closure and looking toward the common future.

The focus of this process must be on the community and society as a whole. This requires not only active participation of all sections of the community, but also the enjoyment of the benefits of this process by all.

I understand that a draft regulation on the establishment of a Truth and Reconciliation Commission for Indonesia has been prepared. I applaud and encourage the initiative of the Government of Indonesia in exploring the options for initiating such a process. However, I must emphasize that the truth-and-reconciliation process does not and must not mean impunity for those who are responsible for human rights violations. The judicial process and the truth-and-reconciliation processes must be carefully calibrated to be mutually supportive and to follow hand in hand.

Within the broad framework of the important ongoing initiatives for transitional justice, my Office is ready to work, in cooperation with other international partners such as the World Bank and UNDP, to assist Indonesia in taking steps to enhance the administration of justice sector. At the request of the Attorney General, my Office has elaborated a program of support to the administration of justice, which entails the training of ad hoc judges, prosecutors, and defense counsel. We are ready to provide further assistance as appropriate and refer to activities in the areas of human rights training and education as well as fellowships, in keeping with the understanding reached with the Ministry of Foreign Affairs/DEPLU. In this regard, I express appreciation for the manner in which officials of the Ministry of Foreign Affairs/DEPLU have met with my Regional Adviser, Mr. Justice Bhagwati, in recent days to discuss the modalities for the implementation of this technical cooperation project and for furthering a framework within which cooperative endeavors between OHCHR and Indonesia in the field of human rights can continue.

I wish you well in your deliberations today and tomorrow and every success for the workshop, which is an important initiative to address and deal with past abuses, while also looking to current and future efforts to strengthen the foundations of justice and democracy.

Thank you.

Opening of the National Parliament of the Democratic Republic of East Timor
Dili, East Timor, 23 August 2002

Your Excellency, Mr. Francisco Guterres, President of the Parliament; Distinguished Parliamentarians, Honored Guests, Ladies, and Gentlemen,

It is a singular honor for me to be invited to address you today in this, the first National Parliament of the independent state of the Democratic Republic of East Timor.

As you well realize, yours is both a great responsibility and an honor as you lead the people who elected you in the challenging task of state-building. I recall that when I last spoke here in Dili, in August 2000, I referred to the key role of political leaders, tasked with both the development and upholding of laws and the nurturing of a pluralist, tolerant, and nondiscriminatory society. I applaud you now for the manner in which you have begun to address these challenges.

At the outset, allow me to add my voice to those from all over the world who have congratulated you on the extraordinary work undertaken over the past two years in preparation for independence. A major undertaking in that period was the process of drafting a constitution. It is a matter of great satisfaction that the text incorporates some of the main international human rights principles and places specific emphasis on the Universal Declaration of Human Rights as a basis for interpretation of the Constitution.

I rejoice in the significant progress that has been made in rebuilding East Timor since my last visit. The change is testimony to the positive commitment on the part of the East Timorese people and its leadership to rebuild a nation. And to rebuild it not only through the reconstruction of the destroyed infrastructure, but also through the rebuilding of communities, families, and individual lives.

I am fully aware of your important responsibilities to those who elected you and the heavy parliamentary work program you face. But I believe you would be first to acknowledge that much work still requires to be done in the firm establishment of a society committed to the promotion and protection of all human rights for all people. Just after this meeting today I will have the honor to sign, with representatives of government, civil society, and the United Nations, a Human Rights Joint Communiqué, which sets out a master plan for the next steps which will be required. I invite you to study closely this text and to employ it in your own deliberations and program of legislative enactment.

Please permit me now to turn to some specific considerations:

I understand that the Government of East Timor is considering acceding to the core international human rights treaties and may present the instruments of accession on 27 September when the country becomes a member of the United Nations. This momentous initiative will undoubtedly reinforce the rebuilding process of East Timor and facilitate the incorporation of human rights into the foundation of the country's development.

Given the recent history of human rights violations against East Timorese people and denial of their fundamental freedoms, it is vital that East Timor embraces human rights at an early stage in its development and seeks to ensure that the country's laws, policies, programs, and institutions are founded on international human rights standards. Acceding to the international human rights treaties is one step in the process of developing a human rights culture. It is only by taking such definitive steps that human rights will be effectively guaranteed, protected and promoted in East Timor.

Distinguished Parliamentarians, as you carry out all work, I encourage you to keep in mind that human rights are universal, indivisible, and interconnected. This means that all rights—civil, political, economic, social, and cultural rights—are equally important and are all interrelated. It is therefore insufficient to respect some rights and leave others aside, or to speak out against some violations and remain silent in the face of others. I urge you, East Timor, to embrace all human rights and take measures to deepen the participation of the people as you build a nation based on the fundamental principles of human rights. As you go through this, special emphasis must be placed on vulnerable and marginalized groups in society, including women and children, along with the elderly and disabled, as well as religious and ethnic minorities.

As you embrace your responsibilities and continue to realize all human rights for all in East Timor, I can assure you that my Office, working with UNMISET, is ready to continue to cooperate with you to the largest extent possible.

In conclusion, I offer the best wishes of both myself and my Office. East Timor, as the newest member of the international community, is in a unique position to show the world how best to lay the foundations for a vigorous culture of human rights built on a democratic society. This is your challenge. We are your partners.

"Breaking Down the Walls of Silence"
Public hearing of the Truth and Reconciliation Commission
Lima, Peru, 4 July 2002

Compañeras y Compañeros,

It is a great honor to stand in solidarity with all of you today as you continue to confront and piece together the memories of your past.

I would like to congratulate Peru on having established this Truth and Reconciliation Commission and to acknowledge the commitment of the government to the Commission and to the future implementation of its recommendations. This Commission may count on the support of the Office of the High Commissioner for Human Rights in its journey of recovering Peru's historical memory.

I would also like to acknowledge the importance of these public hearings and the courage of the people who have come here today, both to speak and to listen. Perpetrators of human rights abuses often inculcate into their victims the belief that if they should dare to speak out, no one will believe them, or that no one will care. Their intention is to force silence upon those who most need to speak, and deafness upon those who most need to listen.

Today, at this public hearing, we are here to break that imposed silence—both as speakers and as listeners. We are all here to demonstrate to those who are still capable of committing human rights violations that the people of Peru and the international community do care. Today the focus of the public session is on those who have been falsely imprisoned and subsequently released. But we must also be mindful of those innocents who are still imprisoned as well as of those who did not survive their imprisonment.

I recognize that for survivors and family members of victims, speaking about the horrors of false imprisonment, arbitrary detention, disappearances, and torture often means to relive those moments.

Facing the truth is never an easy process for a society either. Often the "official story," or rather the official denial, has been effective in obfuscating the facts from which the fabric of truth must be sewn. How, for example, can one be expected to move forward if it is not clearly understood where one has been? Though this process of reconstructing memory can be painful for both individuals and societies, a meaningful national reconciliation can come only when there has been a full accounting and acknowledgment of the past.

National reconciliation is the motive for which governments and peoples go through the difficult process of recovering historical memory. National reconciliation is necessary for the consolidation of democratic institutions. Yet, in order for a society to reconcile, it must also nurture respect for the rule of law and human rights and form a comprehensive social understanding of the socioeconomic causes that gave rise to the violence in the first place.

Many new governments have created independent truth commissions, such as this one, which are devised to address the very broad and often enigmatic issues of truth, justice, and reconciliation. Because these issues hold different meanings for different people, fully addressing them to the satisfaction of all can be an enormous challenge. And because people have lived with impunity for so long, the mere possibility of truth and justice creates expectations that often cannot be met with the available resources.

Nevertheless, truth commissions can serve as an important tool in fighting the impunity that has languished in a society and sustained through years of political violence. It can do so by identifying the perpetrators when possible; signifying each actor's role in the perpetuation of the violence, and, by compensating as many survivors and family members of victims as possible.

While truth commissions cannot and should not replace the role of the courts in holding human rights abusers accountable, they can still play a profound role in facilitating the empowerment of survivors by breaking down the walls of silence.

Chapter 13
Business and Human Rights

Interest in the question of the human rights responsibilities of international corporations, whether such be legally enforceable or of moral weight only, has grown commensurate with corporations' increasing power and influence. Mary Robinson was an early and influential voice that sought to persuade business leaders to be concerned with the ethical dimensions of their increasingly global business environment. She was a crucial and skillful ally of Kofi Annan in building support for, and dispelling fears of, the Global Compact, the UN initiative launched in 2000 to encourage corporations to respect core human rights, labor, and environmental standards.

"Profitable Partnerships: Building Relationships That Make a Difference"
Business for Social Responsibility Conference
San Francisco, USA, 3 November 1999

It is a pleasure to return to San Francisco to address the annual conference of Business for Social Responsibility. At an early stage in my term as High Commissioner, I began to appreciate both the role business could play in respect of human rights and that business was increasingly interested in the subject. In the summer of 1998 I accepted an invitation to visit the Business for Social Responsibility office in San Francisco just to check them out. They passed with honors. I was impressed by small details: the concern for an environmentally friendly office; the multicultural and gender-balanced staff, their evident enthusiasm and commitment; and the sense of a team which had thought through its responses to complex ethical and moral issues.

I welcome the opportunity to take stock with you of where the debate on business and human rights has reached. In the past fifty years, the world has made progress in economic growth and wealth creation on a scale previously unimagined. This progress has been accompanied by significant improvements in human development indicators such as life expectancy, levels of education, and nutrition standards. The business sector has been and continues to be the backbone of this sustained progress.

There is perhaps no better example of how business moves this process forward than the revolution taking place here in California. The new technologies being created and developed here have accounted for the lion's share of US economic expansion in recent years and will undoubtedly play an increasing role in the years ahead.

But as we marvel at the power of business to generate ideas and products which in turn contribute to higher standards of living for many, we should not lose sight of other signs and indicators which make our view of the world more complex on the eve of a new millennium. Concerns are expressed by many people who believe that the system that has produced so much prosperity for some threatens many others.

As Mike Moore, the new Director General of the World Trade Organization, put it recently: "increasing numbers, not just in the United States, feel excluded, forgotten and angry, locked out and waiting for a promised train that may never arrive. They see globalization as a threat, the enemy. A central policy challenge for governments is to make the prosperity that flows from globalization accessible to people."[1] Let us hope the upcoming Seattle Ministerial Conference of the World Trade Organization will be able to contribute to the aims Mr. Moore has set for himself: an outcome which benefits the most vulnerable economies, a more open trading system that can contribute to better living standards and a safer world, and a WTO which can reflect the needs of all its members.

For there is still much debate as to whether making a bigger "economic cake" will lead to better living standards. There is little disagreement, however, about how much remains to be done to fight against poverty and the inequality of opportunities and development that continue to plague the majority of the world's people. Well-known statistics highlight these problems—three billion people live on less than two dollars a day. The growth in real per-capita income in the countries of sub-Saharan Africa from 1960 to 1995 was only twenty-eight dollars. The overall gap between the richest 20 percent of humanity and the poorest 20 percent doubled between 1940 and 1990. And if the gap between rich and poor countries is growing, so too is the phenomenon of poverty and exclusion within societies. In many developing countries, even those experiencing some increase in net national wealth, the gap between the poorest in society and the richest has been growing dramatically.

The Social Responsibility Movement

It is a pleasure for me to have the opportunity of raising these issues with a group of people who are looking ahead and asking the tough questions about the future—the leaders of some of the most successful and well-known corporations in the world who are also the leaders of the corporate social responsibility movement. Business for Social Responsibility (BSR) companies are on the vanguard of a process which has taken on incredible energy and direction over the past few years. I hope I will be able to hear also from you about the progress you've made and the challenges you face as you work to produce not only good products and services but also healthier societies.

This progress is due in large part to the work of organizations like BSR which are leading a fundamental reshaping of the way business is done. BSR's broad membership of influential companies, your extensive research and publications, as well as a wide range of training and technical assistance activities are invaluable resources for companies which have recognized that the triple bottom line of economic, environmental, and social performance is now being watched by shareholders and by wider society alike. I would not want to let this opportunity pass without expressing my admiration for the work of BSR's Chairman, Arnold Hiatt, who is one of the true pioneers of this movement. Arnold's commitment to this cause began as human rights begin, to borrow Eleanor Roosevelt's words, "in small places . . . close to home." Over twenty years ago Arnold did what every good business leader must; he thought not only about the needs of his customers but also about the needs of his employees and the wider community and their links to his company's success. He then convinced his board of directors that addressing in practical ways the needs of the community would not only be the *right* thing to do but would also be the *profitable* thing to do.

The Challenges to Human Rights

I am aware of other business leaders going the extra step needed, reaching beyond codes of conduct and external audits in efforts to construct industrywide inspection systems such as the Fair Labor Association (FLA), a monitoring group composed of industry and human-rights representatives that was created a year ago by a Presidential task force.[2]

But why does ensuring greater respect for human rights matter to you? My hunch is that I do not need to make the argument to this group. You already understand that consumers are increasingly well informed about how products are manufactured or produced and whether a company treats its workers well. You do not underestimate the extent to which investors are putting their money into socially responsible business funds. You recognize that without respect for human rights and the rule of law in our increasingly global village, you will eventually, if not already, find yourself trying to do business in unstable political and social environments where not only your employees' health and safety but also your opportunities for building new markets and continued growth are at risk.

So if we agree that human rights are important to business, we should ask ourselves: Are they being respected universally? The answer is clear and challenging: We have a lot of work to do. One need only consider the massive violations of human rights this year alone in places such as Kosovo, Sierra Leone, or East Timor to understand the enormity of the challenge still ahead. As terrible as these situations are, there are perhaps even more troubling violations of fundamental rights which are not part of the daily news because they have tragically become almost commonplace—the 12 million children who die each year under the age of five from preventable diseases, the 1.3 billion people who do not have access to clean water, the millions of women and girls throughout the world for whom primary education remains only a dream.

Having served as UN High Commissioner for Human Rights for just over two years now and seeing firsthand the state of human rights in all parts of the world, I am more convinced than ever that lasting progress requires first and foremost that governments live up to the letter of their commitments to human rights. Yet I recognize more now than I did two years ago that in many countries, due to severe lack of resources and in some places to the lasting effects of history, even the best intentions of governments will not be enough. Real progress will require innovative, mutually beneficial partnerships at all levels between governments, corporations, nongovernmental organizations, international organizations, and all others committed to a world where fundamental rights are guaranteed for all people.

What will happen if we don't do more? My fear is that unless concrete actions are taken now to effectively implement human rights in our interdependent world, the progress enjoyed by many countries over the last fifty years and the spread of democratic societies in all regions will not be sustainable.

That is why I draw such encouragement from the commitments that all of you have made to make the world a better place. And why I count on you to go further—to expand your network ever wider—and to look for new and innovative ways of achieving these common goals.

Turning Commitments into Actions

One of the most visible results of the increased attention paid to the links between business and human rights is the development of corporate policies and practices that address human rights issues directly. The evidence is to be found in internal ethical statements, corporate codes of conduct, sectoral agreements on issues such as child labor in the clothing industry, or wider codes such as Social Accountability 8000[3] and the new Sullivan principles,[4] which are to be commended.

The focus has rightly been placed on identifying and correcting business practices which result in clear violations of human rights standards such as child and forced labor, unsafe working conditions, and illegal transportation and dumping of toxic waste, to name some of the most evident practices which, unfortunately, have been only too common in the past.

I believe we are now moving into a crucial stage in what is an evolving process—namely, developing the systems through which the commitments made by companies to protect human rights, labor, and environmental standards can be monitored effectively to ensure compliance. Initiatives such as the Fair Labor Association may be the next step. In other words, ensuring that actions match commitments. This, by the way, is the main challenge which governments also face. Human rights standards are, by and large, now in place: implementation must follow.

This is no easy task. This afternoon the focus of one of your break-out sessions will be the topic of "Innovative Approaches to Monitoring." I was interested to read about the study of factory conditions recently conducted by the research organization IHS in Indonesia on behalf of Reebok, which will be discussed during this session.[5] What is particularly impressive in this case is Reebok's willingness to be open about the problems the study has brought out. It is an important example for other companies who are struggling with similar issues.

But even as significant efforts are being made to ensure that initiatives such as codes are rigorously complied with, some argue that even more must be done. It has been noted that the absence of uniform definitions among various codes and the variety of methods of implementation may result in ad hoc approaches that run the risk of being short-lived. Others have asked whether the business community will be able to mobilize across-the-board support for balancing global governance structures in favor of human rights, labor, the environment, and development.

The United Nations Global Compact

These were some of the issues UN Secretary General Kofi Annan hoped the United Nations could help to address when he proposed a "Global Compact" between the United Nations and the world business community earlier this year.[6] As many of you know, the Global Compact calls on business leaders to join forces behind a set of core values in the areas of human rights, labor standards, and the environment. In the area of human rights, corporations should ensure that they uphold and respect human rights and are not themselves complicit in human rights abuses. With respect to labor standards, businesses should make sure that they are not employing underage children or forced labor, either directly or indirectly and that, in their hiring and firing policies they do not discriminate on grounds of race, creed, gender, or ethnic origin. And in relation to the environment, companies should support greater environmental responsibility and encourage the development and diffusion of environmentally friendly technologies.

What makes these principles particularly important is that they already enjoy worldwide support, as embodied in the Universal Declaration of Human Rights, the International Labour Organization's Declaration on Fundamental Principles and Rights at Work,[7] and the Rio Declaration adopted at the 1992 Earth Summit.[8]

The Global Compact's immediate goal is to challenge the international business community to incorporate these universal values into mission statements; to change management practices to achieve these goals; and to share learning experiences. The three United Nations entities most directly involved in implementing the Global Compact, the International Labour Organization, the UN Environment Programme, and the Office of the High Commissioner for Human Rights, have joined forces to work together to promote the principles. A Compact-oriented Web site, dialogues among prospective partners, training exercises, and access to United Nations databases are among the mechanisms we are developing to make the Compact work.

My Office stands ready to support your initiatives. The approach we have adopted is a modest but, we hope, a catalytic one. We seek to encourage, stimulate and support corporate initiatives in this area and to work with organizations such as BSR to identify and recognize good practices. An idea your Chairman has been developing, and which I fully support, is to establish an award for a business practice that has made a real impact on ensuring respect for the human rights of employees or communities. I hope we will be in a position to work together to make such an award a mark of real achievement, similar to the Baldridge Award for quality here in the United States. I am excited by the proposal to weave into the award a prize that will support the work of human rights organizations in all regions.

But let me be clear: the Global Compact will be a truly useful tool only if it is able to produce something more than itself. This will require a process in which the interests of the UN system, the business community, and our nongovernmental organization partners converge around common goals. These goals must then be transformed into partnerships that contribute to achieving the UN's mandate of enhancing international cooperation to promote, as the UN Charter puts it "social progress and better standards of living in larger freedom."

I recognize the amount of work which will be required if the common framework of the Global Compact is to be used as a guide for innovative partnerships which produce real results both for business and for people. The UN's added value comes through the international standards themselves, an understanding of local and country situations and its ability to bring all relevant actors together to address common problems. But I believe it is the business community that will have to continue to drive this process forward.

Conclusion

If I could leave you with one thought: don't underestimate the role you can play in shaping the future of human rights as we approach the new millennium. Consider the information technology revolution and just imagine what your creativity and knowledge could contribute to improved access to education for all. Or how your ability to innovate could help ensure adequate distribution of food, energy, building materials, and health care—all of which would contribute to the realization of fundamental rights enshrined in the Universal Declaration and the International Covenants.

Your ability to make a difference was brought home to me recently. I read about Noah Samara, the Ethiopian-born founder of a company which is producing a digital radio made for developing markets that connects with various power sources, including solar panels. In addition to selling time to various broadcasters who will reach new audiences through the system, Mr. Samara will use 5 percent of his profits to provide free digital radios to the poorest villages in Africa and to provide basic information including educational and health programming. Mr. Samara says it best: "People need so many things in these areas—information on hygiene, how to be better entrepreneurs. . . . If we can do that, we will help them break through some of the hardest barriers."

This one initiative has the potential to make a real difference, to empower people not just in one community but in thousands. There is a lesson there: to look beyond your horizons; to put to their ultimate use the creativity and energy which you hold; and to build a future where human rights are a reality for all people.

I wish you every success for this year's conference.

Thank you.

"Beyond Good Intentions: Corporate Citizenship for a New Century"
Royal Society of Arts, Manufactures and Commerce, Inaugural World Leaders Lecture
London, UK, 7 May 2002

It is a pleasure to be here today with all of you, members and guests of the Royal Society for the encouragement of Arts, Manufactures and Commerce. I have long admired the range and scope of your activities. You will understand, however, that it is somewhat daunting to be invited to deliver the inaugural RSA World Leaders Lecture.

May I be bold enough to recall what I said when I was honored to receive the Albert Medal from your President, His Royal Highness, the Duke of Edinburgh, at an enjoyable ceremony at Buckingham Palace last November. I took some pleasure in noting the fact that the Royal Society, founded in 1754, drew inspiration from the Royal Dublin Society, founded in 1731.

Apart from that story, underscoring the intimate relationship between the two countries, it also reminds us of the great strength of a common tradition in the two islands, the space that existed for voluntary organizations outside of government to act for the public interest—to foresee a role for what is now called civil society—or a vibrant "third sector."

The question must be asked now on a global level. How can the RSA's mission—to create a civilized society based on a sustainable economy by stimulating debate, developing new ideas, and encouraging cooperation between the creative sources of British society—be harnessed to address the challenges of globalization?

As Secretary General Kofi Annan put it in his report to the UN Millennium Assembly, "We the Peoples":

> We must think afresh about how we manage our joint activities and our shared interests, for many challenges that we confront today are beyond the reach of any state to meet on its own. . . . We must form coalitions for change, often with partners well beyond the precincts of officialdom. No shift in the way we think or act can be more critical than this: we must put people at the center of everything we do.[9]

The Plight of Children

The evidence that new approaches are urgently needed to solve persistent global problems is all around us but all too easily overlooked. Consider the findings of a new report issued ahead of the special session on children, which begins tomorrow at UN Headquarters in New York.[10] I know some of you will be intimately aware of the grim statistics, but they bear repeating:

Of the 132 million children born every year, 10.2 million—or one in twelve—will die from preventable diseases: measles, malaria, diarrhea, and prenatal conditions.

As many as 150 million children from all regions of the world are malnourished.

Over 120 million will never go to school—the majority of them girls.

One of every five children between the ages of five and fourteen in the developing world will work, and half of those will do so full-time.

Clearly, despite the growth of the global economy and the world's commitment to a "first call for children," the reality is bleak. Why have we fallen short? At the heart of the problem is a lack of political will, a lack of accountability for failing to live up to international commitments, and in some countries, a severe lack of resources needed to make change. But I would propose that such shortcomings have also been due to a lack of imagination, an unwillingness to look for new solutions, and for new partners, to solve the problems of a new century.

Our efforts within the United Nations to confront the gaps in effective governance have increasingly sought to encourage the private sector and civil society in the kinds of creativity, innovation, and focus on good practice that have been the RSA's approach across the fields of business, design, the environment, education, and the arts throughout its long history. So I welcome this opportunity to share some thoughts on these issues and discuss with you the promise and the challenges of multistakeholder partnerships.

Beyond Good Intentions

The title I have chosen for my lecture today is "Beyond Good Intentions: Corporate Citizenship for a New Century." I chose this title for two reasons:

First, to repeat a point which I made at the Albert Medal ceremony last year: business leaders don't have to wait—indeed, increasingly they can't afford to wait—for governments to pass and enforce legislation before they pursue "good practices" in support of international human rights, labor, and environmental standards within their own operations and in the societies of which they are part.[11] The public increasingly expects corporations to act in a socially responsible way. But it is also a business-led debate, as the recent annual meeting of the Institute of Directors here in London illustrated.[12]

With globalization has come the growing sense that we are all responsible in some way for helping promote and protect the rights of our neighbors, whether they live on the next street or on the next continent. The Universal Declaration of Human Rights is not simply a charter of rights, but speaks of duty in very broad terms. Article 29 provides: "Everyone has duties to the community." What we need to do in the new century is to acknowledge that the community is no longer just our nearest neighborhood but the global community.

Practice Counts

Second, I wanted to indicate that good intentions clearly will not be enough. It is vital that the business community focuses not only on policies of good corporate citizenship but also on their implementation in practice. If the business community really wants to prove to a growing number of skeptics that globalization can be made to work not just for the privileged but also for the powerless, it is practice that matters.

Despite the progress made at the policy level in recognizing the links between profitable business and responsible social performance, many observers are still not convinced that company commitments are much more than window dressing in terms of the way business gets done around the world. Recent studies have shown that the business world has not succeeded in persuading the public that companies are serious about corporate social responsibility in practice.

Voluntary Action or Legal Regulation?

Research published late last year by *The Observer* newspaper reveals high levels of skepticism among leaders from the voluntary sector, education, local government, and media over companies' claims that they have improved their environmental and social performance.[13] These leaders believe strongly that only legislation is effective. They want laws to compel companies to act responsibly. This significant sector of public opinion is convinced that voluntary approaches, though strongly favored by the private sector, are piecemeal and largely ineffective because only limited pressure for change can come from consumers, investors, or campaigning groups.

On the environment, the debate is over whether or not business can "green itself from the inside." Environmental groups say it is not going to happen. Some of these groups are campaigning to have the Johannesburg Summit on Sustainable Development in August adopt proposals for an international convention to enforce responsible corporate behavior. They seek an international regulatory framework on corporate activities as the best way to ensure proper respect for environmental and social standards around the world.

I would argue that it is not a simple case of choosing between voluntary or regulatory systems to induce corporate responsibility. If indeed we believe that universal principles in the areas of human rights, labor rights, and the environment should become an integral part of business strategies and day-to-day operations, regulation alone will not be sufficient. It must be coupled with a concerted effort to stimulate good practices.

Regulation is crucial to minimize abuses and to enforce compliance with minimum norms. But regulation alone will not establish the business case for making necessary changes. To do so, we must provide incentives so that doing the right thing also makes good business sense. By focusing exclusively on regulation, business is driven toward the logic of managing the costs of compliance. The result is that society loses out on the power of business to innovate and establish new forms of behavior that are so desperately needed.

Millions of people who are denied their rights today want to enjoy them now, not in some distant future. To achieve that goal we will have to embrace every good idea, every committed partner, and every possible approach that can make a difference.

The Global Compact

One way of making progress is to engage the private sector in achieving public goals. Engagement between the UN and civil society in furthering international objectives is not new. Although civil society organizations and private enterprises have grown markedly in number, diversity, and influence over the past decade, they have been interacting with the United Nations since its founding. Many nongovernmental organizations, including representatives of business associations, participated in the San Francisco Conference of 1945.

Today, the UN is pursuing its engagement with the private sector on corporate social responsibility issues through a number of different avenues. One of the key initiatives is the Global Compact. Formally launched by the Secretary General in July 2000, the Global Compact calls on business leaders, trade unions and NGOs to join forces behind a set of core values in the areas of human rights, labor standards, and the environment.

Let me outline briefly what we are asking corporations to do in these three areas. With respect to human rights, corporations should, first, ensure that they support and respect human rights within their sphere of influence as set out in the Universal Declaration of Human Rights and, second, ensure that they are not themselves complicit in human rights abuses. On labor standards, businesses should uphold freedom of association and collective bargaining and make sure they are not employing underage children or forced labor, either directly or indirectly, and that in their hiring and firing policies they do not discriminate on grounds of race, creed, gender, or ethnic origin. And in relation to the environment, companies should support a precautionary approach to environmental challenges, promote greater environmental responsibility, and encourage the development and diffusion of environmentally friendly technologies.

Several hundred companies from a wide range of countries north and south, such as Russia, China, Argentina, South Africa, Germany, Norway, Indonesia, Thailand, the United Kingdom, and the United States, have responded to the Global Compact and are working with trade unions, civil society, and the UN to make its principles part of the strategic vision and everyday practices of companies in all regions. I have learned of local initiatives in discussion with business leaders of companies large and small in places as far apart as São Paulo, Brazil, organized by the Ethos Institute, and New Delhi, organized by the Institute of Indian Industry. It has been heartening to see women business leaders to the fore in these discussions.

What specifically are companies supporting the Global Compact being exhorted to do? As a first step, we are calling on them to:

publicly express support for the Compact and its principles in mission statements and annual reports;

post on the Global Compact Web site concrete examples of progress made or lessons learned in implementing the Global Compact principles; and

undertake activities jointly with the United Nations that advance the implementation of the Compact's principles or support wider UN goals such as poverty eradication.

The Global Compact is a voluntary initiative to promote good corporate citizenship. I want to stress that it is not, and must not be, a mere public-relations exercise. A commitment to the Global Compact has to lead to concrete actions in support of the core principles I have explained. Equally, when such actions are taken, a company deserves recognition.

Learning Forum or Monitoring?

But how will we know that real changes are happening? The Global Compact is developing a learning forum which will serve as an information bank of disparate experiences—some successful and some not—of company efforts to implement the Compact's nine principles. Through this learning approach we hope to develop the elements of good practice that address specific human rights, labor, and environmental issues relevant to all industry sectors. The idea is to move toward a system of performance-based good practices, reflecting the judgment of the broader international community, rather than the situation of asking companies simply to adhere to varied and often weak local standards and legislation.

It is too early to say whether this initiative will bring about large-scale improvements in business practices around the world. But I believe it is an experiment worth trying.

Many NGOs have argued that without monitoring mechanisms in place to ensure adherence to its principles, there can be little hope that the Global Compact will produce real change in performance by companies. The Global Compact does not substitute other approaches that rely on monitoring and enforcement. It is designed to complement such approaches by giving business and other sectors of society space to try out new ideas, and to make a difference through voluntary action.

But clearly, to maintain its integrity, the Global Compact needs to ensure high standards of participation. A significant step in this direction was taken earlier this year with the creation of Global Compact Advisory Council, which brings together senior business executives, international labor leaders, and heads of civil society organizations from across the world. The Council is the first UN advisory body composed of both public- and private-sector leaders. Its task is to assist the Secretary General in developing more precise standards of participation in the initiative.

Another step has been to strengthen links between the Global Compact and the Global Reporting Initiative (GRI). As you may know, the GRI was launched last month as an independent institution that will be based in the Netherlands.[14] It was established to develop, promote, and disseminate a generally accepted framework for sustainability reporting on the economic, environmental, and social performance of corporations and other organizations.

Social reporting has taken on significant importance in Europe and is increasingly seen as one important means to create the transparency through which companies can demonstrate that they are living up to their responsibilities. Companies endorsing the Global Compact principles now have in the GRI reporting guidelines an internationally recognized tool for fulfilling their Global Compact obligation to report on the steps they are taking to protect human rights, labor, and environmental standards.

The UN Human Rights Program and the Private Sector

What does the learning approach advocated by the Global Compact mean for involving the private sector in our human rights work at the United

Nations? Allow me to give you a few brief examples. At last year's World Conference against Racism, the Global Compact provided the framework for analysis and reflection on some very interesting initiatives by six companies from five continents on diversity, equality, and nondiscrimination in the workplace and surrounding communities. Secretary General Kofi Annan participated in a high-level dialogue on these issues with Global Compact-participating companies and other organizations on the opening day of the World Conference. A multistakeholder workshop looked at partnership approaches to fighting discrimination and fostering diversity, and a panel we cohosted with the ILO brought together trade union, company, and UN representatives to share experiences of implementing equal opportunity and diversity policies within organizations.

The resulting report of company experience, called *Discrimination Is Everybody's Business*, is available on the Global Compact Web site. I am pleased to note that the initiative has inspired a number of national-level initiatives between business and civil society that are getting under way this year.

My Office is also developing its role as a facilitator of dialogue with the private sector. In December 2001, for example, we hosted a workshop in Geneva between representatives of indigenous peoples and natural resource, energy, and mining companies.[15] There was a lively discussion at the workshop on the relationship between those companies and indigenous peoples concerning the questions of land, consultation, and revenue sharing, which led to recommendations for further study and joint action.

And this coming September the committee of independent experts charged with monitoring the implementation of the 1990 Convention on the Rights of the Child will hold a general day of discussion on "The Private Sector as Service Provider and its Role in Implementing Child Rights." The Committee has become increasingly aware of the significant role of private actors—be they corporations, foundations, nongovernmental organizations, or other institutions—in providing services which are vital in realizing the rights of children to, for example, education and health.

It will be an opportunity to gather and facilitate the exchange of relevant experiences on the development of public-private partnerships in providing services for children. The discussion will also seek to clarify how legal obligations of state parties to the Convention on the Rights of the Child are translated into practice when services for children are provided and/or funded by actors other than the state.

Challenges for the Future

These initiatives are intended to define more clearly the boundaries of corporate responsibilities for human rights and to identify good practices by companies in contributing to their realization. But they also raise many complex issues. While few would disagree that businesses are responsible for the safety and well-being of their employees, coming to grips with the responsibilities of a business outside its immediate operations but still within its "sphere of influence," as it is described in the first principle of the Global Compact, has not yet reached the same level of agreement.

Spheres of Influence

A new report by the Geneva-based International Council on Human Rights Policy has made a useful contribution to this issue.[16] It looks at the closeness of the relationship between a particular company and potential victims, and between the company and authorities which may abuse human rights. Clearly, the closer the company's connection to victims of rights violations, the greater its duty to protect. Employees, consumers, and the communities in which the company operates would be within a first line of responsibility.

But what happens when the company is more removed from the problem? The urgent debate over access to HIV/AIDS drugs in developing countries has highlighted the extent to which pharmaceutical companies have responsibility for the rights of people facing life-threatening diseases.

So we are finding that the nature of the product or service, the type and location of the relevant consumers, the size and power of the company, and the prevailing human rights situation in the countries where the company operates, in addition to the proximity to potential violations, must all be part of the responsibility equation.

Complicity

Turning to the second principle of the Global Compact—the obligation of companies to avoid complicity in human rights abuses—may I say that I do not underestimate the difficulties of defining the boundaries of business responsibility in this context. In order to draw those boundaries, it is important first to understand how the concept of complicity is being used today.

There can be no doubt that a corporation which knowingly assists a state in violating international human rights standards could be viewed as directly complicit in such a violation. For example, a company that promoted, or assisted with, the forced relocation of people in circumstances that would constitute a violation of international human rights could be considered directly complicit in the violation. The corporation could be legally responsible if it or its agents knew of the likely effects of their assistance.

But the contemporary notion of corporate complicity in human rights abuses is not confined to direct involvement in the execution of illegal acts by others. The complicity concept has also been used to describe the corporate position in relation to violations by government or rebel groups when the company benefits from these violations. Violations committed by security forces, such as the suppression of peaceful protest against business activities or the use of repressive measures while guarding company facilities, are often cited as examples of corporate complicity in human rights abuses. In legal terms, where human rights violations occur in the context of a business operation, the company need not necessarily cause the harm directly for that company to become implicated in the abuses.

Perhaps most challenging is the growing expectation that companies will raise systematic or continuous human rights abuses with the appropriate authorities. Indeed, it reflects the growing acceptance by the public, and by leading companies, that there is something culpable about failing to exercise influence in such circumstances. Whether or not such silent complicity would give rise to a finding of a breach of a legal obligation against a company in a court of law, it has become increasingly clear that the moral dimension of corporate action—or inaction—has taken on significant importance.

We have, I believe, made some progress in analyzing what is meant by the key phrases "sphere of influence" and "complicity in human rights abuses." These concepts shape the expectations on companies. They can also reflect legal requirements now and in the future.

Role of Government

But corporate responsibility is only part of the picture. What I want to stress again is that, although I am confident that initiatives such as the Global Compact can help to build consensus and reach practical solutions to contemporary human rights challenges, they do not imply that the role of government in ensuring respect for human rights has become any less important. Primary responsibility for the promotion and protection of human rights remains with governments. Voluntary initiatives are no substitute for government action.

Nonetheless, it is significant that parts of the UN human rights system which used to focus exclusively on the responsibilities of governments are now also addressing the role of the business sector. For example, a growing number of Special Rapporteurs and Independent Experts appointed by the UN Commission on Human Rights to study specific human rights issues around the world have sought to enhance contact and cooperation with the business sector in the course of their work. In addition, the Sub-Commission on the Promotion and Protection of Human Rights, an expert body of the intergovernmental Commission on Human Rights, is in the process of developing human rights principles for companies under the Universal Declaration of Human Rights and other universally accepted norms.[17]

UN Guidelines?

Some business representatives have argued for UN-approved guidelines of international standards for corporate practice. Why? First, because global business increasingly sees advantages in having standards that are applicable in all countries. Second, local companies supplying many customers on the international market are confronted daily with the demands of thirty or more codes, not all alike, and they lack the resources to respond. The argument is made that approval by the UN of one set of guidelines would give a level of authority that would make those guidelines the real standard and simplify and improve implementation. It has been stressed by some that it was important to use the Universal Declaration of Human Rights as a basis since business and government needed to have a shared ultimate reference point. At the same time, many others fear that new regulation in this field will hamper development or be used for protectionist purposes.

I would be the first to acknowledge that regulation internationally may be difficult, if not impossible, to obtain in the short term. But I believe that international standards will become more and more relevant in this context. Most of the debate centers on the existing human rights obligations generated by the Universal Declaration. The challenge is not to develop a new swathe of regulations rather, the task is to make the human rights norms proclaimed more than fifty years ago relevant, influential, and, most importantly, effective and enforceable in today's globalized world.

So where do we go from here? How do we address the current lack of ability in many countries to solve specific human rights problems through application of traditional sources of authority, and the need to engage other actors and institutions in society to work "collaboratively" toward solutions? What human rights challenges may lend themselves to new approaches? What role could the Royal Society for the Arts play in finding answers to these questions?

Let me close by suggesting three ways in which the RSA could be involved.

Within the Global Compact, we at the UN need partners committed to helping us take actions in support of the Compact's principles that can make a real difference in the lives of people. I would encourage all of you to consider how you could bring your own networks together to multiply these efforts at home and around the world.

By becoming part of the Global Compact learning forum, RSA members would have a new window into the challenges companies face in being both good corporate citizens and profitable. Perhaps you could consider sponsoring an event that could bring together academics, business leaders, and human rights advocates to share experiences and plan joint action around studying the challenges of corporate citizenship, specifically addressing human rights issues. The Global Compact and my Office would be pleased to support you in such an initiative.

Finally, I would urge you all to consider what in practice you could do to support international efforts in achieving the UN Millennium Development Goals. Take, for example, the technology gap between the developed and the developing worlds. You all know that this gap is widening by the day. Research and the development of new technologies are overwhelmingly directed at rich countries' problems. Think of the progress that could be made in addressing the crises of public health, agricultural productivity, environmental degradation, and demographic stress, which so many people have to face, if the business and academic communities were to offer their expertise and skills to address the problems of the poorest countries of the world.

These suggestions encapsulate the concept contained in the Universal Declaration that everyone has duties to the community. It can become one of the big ideas of this new century, an underlying principle that helps us shape the forces of globalization in the light of shared values. It can pave the way to an ethical globalization, which becomes a positive experience for all the world's people.[18]

IV
Building Human Rights Protection

Chapter 14

The High Commissioner and the United Nations Human Rights System

When the position of High Commissioner for Human Rights was established by the United Nations General Assembly, the responsibilities assigned to the post were considerable in number and extensive in scope. The range of subjects in the excerpts below, on which Mary Robinson reported annually to the General Assembly, underscores this point. The mission statement adopted by OHCHR declares that the High Commissioner's role was "to protect and promote all human rights for all." Kofi Annan's reform agenda for the United Nations that coincided with Mary Robinson's appointment as second High Commissioner brought human rights from the margins to the center of the United Nations organization. It added to the mandate the demanding and continuing challenge of integrating ("mainstreaming") human rights into all activities of the United Nations from development to peacekeeping.

The choice of priorities given such a broad mandate for what was a new Office, with limited financial means, was no simple matter. For Mary Robinson the advocate, a first priority, which remained such throughout her term, was to treat all categories of rights—civil, cultural, economic, social, and political—as of equal importance, to make their widespread abuse or neglect more visible and to identify and campaign for the removal of "obstacles" to their effective protection. She used her position and the moral authority it conveyed to be "a voice for the voiceless." That required speaking out on behalf of victims of human rights violations, advocacy with governments on behalf of victims, and urging governments to make greater efforts to live up to their human rights commitments. She saw human rights defenders and the broader civil society as her natural allies and worked consistently with them throughout her five years in the post. She worked with governments in many parts of the world, establishing agreements with her Office on practical steps to improve protection. She invested considerable effort in agreeing partnerships with fellow UN agencies instilling commitment to human rights ideas in UN programs especially at the country level.

The effective pursuit of such an agenda required a demanding program of travel to bring the human rights message to ordinary people everywhere and to encourage, in person, regional cooperation on human rights as well as the strengthening of country-level protection. But also she placed great emphasis on building up a professional Office in Geneva and New York, pioneering a professional approach to fundraising to make up the shortfall in the regular UN budget. Nor was the traditional demand on the Office to provide efficient support services to UN human rights bodies neglected.

In addition, there was the unexpected: the demanding responsibility that fell to the High Commissioner for Human Rights of responding to large-scale humanitarian and human rights emergencies resulting from the eruption of different political crises into violent conflict. In the early years there were the neglected conflicts of the Democratic Republic of the Congo, and Burundi, and those that received more international attention: Chechnya, Kosovo, East Timor, Sierra Leone, and the Middle East. These crises were followed by the epochal events of 9/11 and the Afghanistan conflict. All such crises were in their turn significant and daily concerns of the High Commissioner and her Office.

While the emphasis in the selection of texts in Part IV is on her efforts to strengthen and coordinate the UN human rights systems of protection and its links with regional and country protection systems, Mary Robinson's concern with large-scale conflicts and the human suffering they produce is also reflected. Similar themes are to be found in many of the statements and speeches throughout this book, as is her search for strategies to prevent gross violation and to ensure accountability of the perpetrators. Prevention was a major theme of her tenure as High Commissioner.

"Human Rights Today"

Faculty of Law, Catholic University of Leuven, Belgium, 2 February 2000

I am happy to have the opportunity to address this gathering and to speak about the state of human rights today and the role that the Office of the United Nations High Commissioner for Human Rights can play.

The position which I hold, that of United Nations High Commissioner for Human Rights, was established on the recommendation of the Vienna World Conference on Human Rights of 1993 and following a subsequent resolution of the General Assembly. The mandate of the Office has four essential components:

building global partnerships for human rights;
preventing human rights violations and responding to emergencies;
promoting human rights together with democracy and development as the guiding principles for lasting peace;
coordinating the systemwide strengthening of the human rights programmed.

The Secretary General's Reforms

I was fortunate in that I took up duty in 1997 at a time when reforms were being put in place by the Secretary General, Kofi Annan, to enhance the effectiveness of the United Nations and to fulfill his expressed wish to place human rights at the heart of the Organization's work.[1] Five areas were identified as being crucial to the UN's work. Executive Committees were established covering four of the five: peace and security, economic and social affairs, development cooperation, and humanitarian affairs. There is no committee specifically devoted to the fifth main area of work, human rights. But in a sense, human rights was accorded an even more central role in that my Office was directed to participate in all four Executive Committees, thus assuring the integration of human rights into all of the Organization's activities.

Cooperation between my Office and other UN agencies in the field is being strengthened. In recent years, human rights have been integrated more and more into the development process, for example through closer ties with the United Nations Development Programme. And the presence of human rights specialists is becoming a standard feature of peacekeeping and other UN postconflict operations.

I should explain that the role given to me as High Commissioner by the UN General Assembly is one of catalytic leadership, based on the recognition that human rights is the responsibility of most if not all United Nations organs, and not the exclusive domain of my Office. This is even more true given the policy set out by the Secretary General whereby human rights is a cross-cutting issue throughout the Organization.

The situation which the Office of High Commissioner finds itself in today is one in which we must be able to respond to a rapidly increasing demand. Our range of activities has, correspondingly, developed rapidly:

The number of OHCHR technical cooperation projects has increased to some fifty-five today.

The Office currently has officers in twenty-seven countries.

The Commission on Human Rights has appointed a total of thirty-four Special Rapporteurs with thematic or country mandates.

OHCHR is responding to requests from an increasing number of countries wishing to establish independent national institutions to promote and protect human rights or to develop national human rights plans of action.

These activities are additional to the traditional tasks of the United Nations in the field of human rights, in particular the servicing of the Commission on Human Rights, the Sub-Commission, and the treaty bodies. They are welcome proof of the strength of the human rights movement.

The Performance Deficit

Yet, in spite of the undoubted legislative and institutional achievements, it is plain to see that even the most fundamental rights of people are routinely denied in many countries around the world. The most extreme cases are those we read about or see on our television screens. Three particularly grave instances of human rights abuses occurred last year, in Kosovo, East Timor, and Sierra Leone. Today our thoughts turn to the civilian population of Chechnya who are caught between the actions of armed groups on one side and indiscriminate bombardment by the Russian army on the other. And many other violations are happening in which the world takes little or no interest—in the Great Lakes region of Africa, in Colombia, in Afghanistan. The list is long.

This gap between the ideals of human rights activists and the reality we witness should not be a cause of despair; rather, it should make us redouble our efforts to find strategies that will combat these gross abuses and embed a real culture of human rights in the world.

Strategies of Prevention

In order to achieve the goal of translating the ideals of those who drafted the Universal Declaration of Human Rights into a reality for all, I believe that we must pay more attention to preventive strategies. We go to considerable lengths in most aspects of our lives to prevent disasters, but in the field of international relations we often fail to heed warning signs and only move to action once a crisis has been reached.

Tackling the sources of racism and xenophobia is a good example of how prevention could head off conflict. I look to the countries of Europe to give a strong lead in the run-up to the World Conference against Racism.

I appeal especially to the young people here to play an active role in the fight against racism. Young people tend to be less conscious of difference of race, as well as being idealistic. Yet even among the postapartheid generation undertones of racism can be found. There is a challenge there to young people not to replicate the prejudice of past generations but to carry the torch of ethnic, religious, and racial harmony.

I see five types of preventive strategy, which are complementary and interrelated. All are predicated on my belief that strengthening the culture of human rights and respect for others in societies is the bedrock on which the issue of prevention is based:

first, greater regional cooperation;
second, more economic and social development programs which have human development as their chief focus and which are capable of improving the lot of the poorest people in the world;
third, accountability for gross violations of human rights;
fourth, strengthening capacity through support for participatory systems of government, democracy, the rule of law, the judiciary, and national human rights institutions;
fifth, human rights education.

Regional Cooperation

I am determined to develop my Office's support for regional and subregional cooperation in the human rights field. I will be putting emphasis on this in the preparations for the World Conference against Racism and hope that it can be a model for the future. Regional cooperation has many advantages:

By bringing together representatives of governments, national institutions, and nongovernmental organizations, it helps human rights to take root and to have a practical effect.

Regional cooperation is a valuable instrument to enable my Office to carry out its mandate to promote and protect human rights.

It encourages national capacity building.

Regional cooperation does not dilute the principle of universality; rather, it strengthens that principle through a better appreciation of shared universal values.

It promotes best practices for a region and acts as a buttress for preventive mechanisms.

Regional cooperation embraces the protection and promotion of all human rights, civil and political as well as economic, social, and cultural.

It brings together the agencies which play a role in promoting human rights, both within the UN family and among the regional organizations.

Additionally, regional cooperation is a useful catalyst for mobilizing civil society. An example of regional cooperation in action is Latin America where my Office was able to organize a useful workshop in Quito, Ecuador, last November.[2] At that meeting it was announced that my regional adviser for the Latin American and Caribbean region will be the former President of Chile, Patricio Aylwin. A former Chief Justice of India, Justice Bhagwati, has agreed to be my regional adviser for the Asia Pacific region, and I am appointing similar highly qualified experts in the other regions.

Economic, Social, and Cultural Rights

As well as the better-known civil and political rights, the Universal Declaration lists the fundamental economic, social, and cultural rights to which everyone is entitled. Yet, this set of rights gets a good deal less attention than civil and political rights. The rich countries rightly urge that civil and political rights be observed and are critical of abuses where they occur. But when it comes to economic, social, and cultural rights of poorer countries and the right to development, they have a good deal less to say. Yet, those rights are enshrined just as clearly in the Universal Declaration and in the international covenants and declarations of the United Nations as civil and political rights. Not only that, but the international community has repeatedly affirmed its support for these rights at numerous international conferences—at the Cairo International Conference on Population and Development, the Beijing Fourth World Conference on Women, and the Copenhagen World Summit for Social Development, to name only three.

The problems of extreme poverty and economic and social imbalances are getting worse, not better. The human rights so many take for granted—freedom of speech and religion, the right to a fair trial—cannot flourish where people are deprived of access to food, to health care, to education. And it is the abuse of these essential rights which leads inexorably to atrocities and gross violations. Gross violations do not suddenly happen; they start with minor discrimination. That leads on to worse forms of discrimination, which turn into exclusion and finally the ultimate exclusion whereby people are driven from their homes and murdered.

Focused, human-centered development programs have a key role to play in preventing atrocities. Yet, the readiness of rich countries to abide by their solemn undertakings to assist in development is weakening. Aid budgets are cut even though the developed world is enjoying unprecedented levels of prosperity. It is simply not credible to talk about human rights and prevention and at the same time to cut aid budgets.

The irony is that aid budget cuts are taking place just when it seems that the donor and agencies are learning some crucial lessons. There is a new focus on the human-centered approach to development that recognizes that improving the individual's lot is a more important objective than simply striving for better GNP growth.

One of my aims is to support the new awareness of the human dimension of development in the UNDP, the World Bank, and other development agencies, and to strengthen cooperation between my Office and these agencies.

Accountability

Accountability for atrocities is an indispensable weapon in preventing further human rights violations. A clear message should go out: nobody who commits atrocities should expect to get away with it, however much time it takes and however eminent the position he or she occupies. That is true whether the crimes are committed in the former Yugoslavia, in Cambodia, in Chile, or in East Timor.

I believe that movement toward the establishment of effective machinery to punish those guilty of crimes against humanity is irreversible. The adoption of the Rome Statute for the setting up of an International Criminal Court was a landmark and the logical next step following the work done by the Rwanda and Bosnia Tribunals. I welcome the adoption of the Rome Statute, and I urge governments to ratify it so that the Court can begin its vital work.[3]

Capacity Building

The fourth strategy I wish to emphasize is capacity building. There are clear linkages between participatory democracies and freedom from atrocities. The likelihood of conflict and gross human rights abuses is far greater where participatory democracy is absent. Most of the worst atrocities have happened where there are totalitarian regimes which refuse to answer to their citizens. It behooves us, therefore, to put resources into measures that support the establishment and consolidation of democracy, and to resource regional organizations to have preventive strategies in their regions.

Capacity building is a growing area of work for my Office. An example of the ways in which we can help is support for national human rights institutions. We have received requests from over forty countries wishing to establish human rights institutions. My Office will continue to put emphasis on helping and advising governments about national human rights institutions. I am under no illusions that these are automatic guarantors that human rights will be observed, but I believe they can play a valuable role.

Human Rights Education

And finally, there is human rights education. The first step in establishing a human rights culture is to know what your rights are, and there is still a great ignorance in many societies of even the basics of human rights. We are halfway through the UN Decade of Human Rights Education, and my Office is engaged in quite a number of initiatives aimed at tackling the information deficit. I see human rights education as an empowering instrument which enables individuals to understand and fight for their own rights and the rights of others.

All Actors Should Be Involved

Embedding human rights in society calls for the active involvement of all the different players—governments, international organizations, developmental bodies, nongovernmental organizations, human rights defenders.

In the global world we now inhabit, the role of business corporations is particularly important. Businesses can in some ways exert more influence on national economies than governments. That power can be a potent force for good or for ill. There are signs that business leaders are recognizing their responsibilities in this regard and that they are prepared to take positive action. I have just returned from the World Economic Forum meeting in Davos, where I met many business leaders who are interested in turning a new page in regard to human rights and who recognize that good ethics mean good business.

Universities and other educational institutions can also play a positive role for human rights, both through teaching and research and through the links which they have with the business community and with civil society as a whole. I have a vision of my Office working more closely with the academic community, particularly in the field of technology, science, and economics, so as to be able to face the undoubtedly formidable challenges that lie ahead. There are many areas of common interest: the implications of globalization, the role of the World Trade Organization, the North-South economic divide, the right to development, and the lack of access of poor nations to the technology and medical research which would halt the AIDS epidemic in Africa.

The move from standard-setting to achieving human rights as a reality for all the peoples of the earth will not be easy and will not happen overnight. But it is of immense significance that we enter this century with such a strong commitment to human rights and with an established framework of norms and standards in place. An opportunity exists such as never before to establish a worldwide culture of human rights. Future generations would not understand if we do not seize this opportunity.

The High Commissioner's Annual Report 1998–1999 to the Fifty-Fourth General Assembly
Introductory Statement
United Nations, New York, 4 November 1999

Chairperson, Distinguished Delegates,

It is a pleasure for me to meet again with this Committee to introduce my annual report and to discuss with you, the distinguished representatives of our member states, a subject which is at the heart of the concerns of the peoples of the United Nations: the promotion and protection of human rights.

My report covers a number of issues of importance and, together with the other human rights items and reports before this Committee, presents the wide and diverse range of human rights issues which faces the international community. This Committee, a central body in the United Nations for human rights, is uniquely situated to consider human rights from a worldwide perspective, and I would like to take this opportunity to share some reflections on the challenges which await us as we enter the next century.

Twin Challenges: Human Rights Protection and Conflict Prevention

Secretary General Kofi Annan has reminded us that we face a twofold challenge: to make the next century a century of human rights and to create a worldwide culture of conflict prevention. Both of these challenges are interrelated, and success in one will require progress in the other.

Embedding a culture of respect for human rights in the societies, institutions, and cultures of our planet is one of my prime objectives as High Commissioner. I believe we have in place the standards and proven methods to achieve that objective, if we will commit the political will and required resources.

My report surveys the international legal standards in human rights which provide detailed protection for the essential elements of human dignity, as well as the range of procedures and methods the United Nations has devised to implement those standards.

Ratification and Implementation of the Human Rights Treaties

United Nations human rights standards need to be ratified to provide the protection they were designed to give. I wish here to appeal again to all those states which have not done so to ratify those treaties. Particular attention should be given to the two International Covenants, the International Convention on the Elimination of All Forms of Racial Discrimination, the Convention on the Elimination of All Forms of Discrimination against Women, and the International Convention on the Protection of Rights of All Migrant Workers and Members of Their Families. Both the Secretary General and I have urged the ratification by all countries of the core human rights treaties by 2003, which we believe is a realistic time scale.

I very much welcome the adoption of the Optional Protocol to the Convention on the Elimination of All Forms of Discrimination against Women, which is an important step forward in the protection of the human rights of women, and I urge its early ratification and entry into force.[4]

Implementation of these treaties would go a long way toward dealing with the causes of many conflict situations we face today, which is why I give special priority to improving the functioning of the human rights treaty bodies. The work of these bodies can have a multiplier effect on the national level, leading to progressively greater respect for human rights. However, they are handicapped by being underresourced, and this issue must be addressed.

My report also deals with the Special Procedures which have their own specific contribution to make to identifying and bringing to an end serious violations of human rights.[5] As with the treaty system, we will have to make a concerted effort to improve the Special Procedures and the support we are able to give. A number of practical suggestions have been developed, and these which are reflected in my report.

Improving the functioning of the treaty system and of the special procedures will require the support and cooperation of member states, and I look forward to working together with you for that purpose.

Human Rights Defenders

Strengthening national protection and reacting to allegations of violations require the vigilant efforts of human rights defenders. Last year this Committee and the Assembly marked the fiftieth anniversary of the Universal Declaration of Human Rights by adopting a Declaration which explicitly protects those working for human rights.[6]

Here I want to express my deepest concern for human rights defenders and journalists who are imprisoned, tortured, and killed because, in carrying out the injunction of the Universal Declaration, they try to bring to light violations of human rights. A real test of our commitment to effective human rights protection will be measures taken to put the Human Rights Defenders Declaration into practice on the national level and what kind of international implementation mechanism we can put in place to protect human rights defenders.

Technical Cooperation and Regional Approaches

Building national cultures of human rights requires targeted assistance in national human rights capacity building, which is why I have given emphasis to strengthening and modernizing our program of technical cooperation. Based on national plans of action, wide involvement of civil society, and the establishment of truly independent national human rights institutions, the technical cooperation program is making a quiet but visible contribution to improving the enjoyment of human rights in many countries.

As my report shows, we have found the regional approach very productive. I want to signal here the progress made in the Asia Pacific Region in following up on their commitments in this matter. I also wish to welcome the adoption in Mauritius last April by the First Organization of African Unity (OAU) Ministerial Conference on Human Rights of the Grand Bay Declaration and Plan of Action.[7] My Office is already at work on finding ways and means to assist and support that historic document.

For Latin America and the Caribbean, I am looking forward to a visit to that region later this month and to participating in the regional workshop in Quito, Ecuador.[8] That workshop could well lay the basis for a regional strategy for Latin America and the Caribbean.

Cross-Cutting Issues

Helping states to face the challenge of effectively protecting human rights requires the United Nations to focus attention on a number of cross-cutting issues whose impacts transcend borders and where solutions require collective thinking and action.

Racial Discrimination, Racism, and Related Intolerance

No more serious danger threatens human rights today than the specter of racism. In every part of the world the virus of intolerance seeks to destroy the healthy tissues of society and causes internal and international conflict, widespread massacres, and even genocide. That is why I give such high importance to my responsibilities as Secretary General of the World Conference against Racism, Racial Discrimination, Xenophobia and Related Intolerance, which will be held in the year 2001. We are moving on a number of levels to ensure that the Conference is well prepared and that it will have a wide and lasting impact. I wish to appeal to member states to make available the necessary resources as requested in the 20 May appeal.

The World Conference against Racism will be an ideal opportunity to mobilize the local and national communities of each state in the campaign against discrimination and for the respect of the dignity of each individual. I would like to suggest that we engage civil society and the nongovernmental community in each country along with national human rights institutions in examining the question of dignity and equality. What has been achieved and what still needs to be done are two questions that they could address. The World Conference would then be able to benefit from the energy, imagination, and commitment of the people of each country in building the international response to the challenge of discrimination.

The protection of indigenous peoples is also an important matter often linked with intolerance. The International Decade of the World's Indigenous People has made some progress, but as can be seen from the Secretary General's report, much needs to be done to achieve the Decade's objectives.[9] This will require the focused action of local communities, national governments, and international organizations.

Economic, Social and Cultural Rights and the Right to Development

It would be difficult to overestimate the contribution that real respect for economic, social, and cultural rights and the human right to development could have to conflict prevention. How many of today's conflicts find their roots in peoples' struggles for recognition of their rights to economic well-being, social dignity, and respect for their own cultures?

Can we say we are respecting the right to development when, as the 1999 *State of the World's Children* report tells us, nearly a billion people, a sixth of humanity, are functionally illiterate and will enter the twenty-first century unable to read a book or sign their names and two-thirds of them are female?[10] And what about the right to food when 830 million people are chronically undernourished?

The 1999 *Human Development Report* points to the bleak reality that "more than a quarter of the 4.5 billion people in developing countries still do not have some of life's most basic choices—survival beyond age forty, access to knowledge and minimum private and public services.

Nearly 1.3 billion people do not have access to clean water.
One in seven children of primary school age is out of school.
About 840 million are malnourished.
An estimated 1.3 billion people live on incomes of less than $1 (1987 PPP$) a day."[11]

Do not these statistics prefigure grave and widespread conflicts of significant proportions? The answer to that question is that they don't have to—provided that the international community shows the leadership required for national and international action.

That is why it is essential to give the highest priority to promoting respect for economic, social, and cultural rights and the right to development. As my report shows, extensive interagency work is under way to mainstream in the spheres of development the imperative of respect for human rights. A valuable contribution to our thinking in this matter was the October 1998 Oslo Symposium on Human Development and Human Rights, which was organized jointly with the Norwegian Government and UNDP; the papers of that symposium were published recently.[12]

Rights of the Child

But the debate must be widened. It has become clear, especially in relation to the rights of the child, that the gap between policy-making in the macroeconomic sphere and in the social sphere must be closed. Decisions on macroeconomic policy such as budget deficits, interest rates, exchange rates, unemployment, and trade are too often made in ignorance and isolation from their human rights consequences. And it is left to social policy and the assistance budget to try to remedy the human suffering and dislocation those policies can cause.

This year the Commission on Human Rights discussed macroeconomic issues during a special dialogue on the rights of the child.[13] ECOSOC continued that debate.[14] The World Bank is developing the human rights elements of its policy-making. The International Monetary Fund has just made an important step in this direction in its new approach to debt relief and poverty elimination.[15]

Ten years ago the General Assembly adopted the Convention on the Rights of the Child, which combines the whole range of human rights and sets out new perspectives for the protection of the rights of children. This year we have been giving careful attention to how the various human rights bodies of the United Nations can improve their contribution to protecting child rights.

Children in Armed Conflict

Children in armed conflict and juvenile justice are two areas which have been the focus of attention. I would like to appeal here for rapid conclusion of the optional protocol raising the age of recruitment into armed forces to the age of eighteen.[16] It is, however, of great concern that in spite of the existing international norm of fifteen years, children below that age are not only recruited into armed forces but also exposed to the moral and physical dangers of combat. Arming children, directly or indirectly, should not be tolerated. I would like here to call upon countries exporting arms to undertake not to export them to countries which enroll children in armed forces in violation of their commitment under the Convention on the Rights of the Child.[17]

Juvenile justice is another important issue that requires our close attention. The Committee on the Rights of the Child has asked me to consider ways of promoting a better understanding and implementation of child rights in juvenile justice procedures. We learn almost every day of the stark abuses to which many children are subjected when confronted with the criminal justice system, and there is a clear need to better understand the underlying circumstances and identify possible remedies.

I believe that the process leading up to an international conference would enable us to make significant progress in addressing these problems. The issues should be broadened to include respect for the rights of all children who are under the authority of the state, for example those in orphanages or foster homes. I will be working closely with the Committee, UNICEF, the concerned nongovernmental organizations, and experts in examining this issue.

Preventing Massive Violations of Human Rights

Embedding a culture of human rights in the lives of individuals, social groups, government organs, and international organizations requires the patient and long-term work of building up a human rights society. Unfortunately, that ongoing work is overshadowed by the tragic situations of large-scale violations of human rights. The horrors of Cambodia, Rwanda, Democratic Republic of the Congo, Kosovo, and East Timor were brought home to us graphically by print media, radio, and television.

Why?

The public response to these terrible examples of human rights abuses, understandably, is to ask Why? Why can't more be done about gross human rights violation? Why have people in the Balkans or East Timor or Central Africa had to endure so much to secure rights about which there is a universal consensus? Why have there been genocides in Rwanda and Cambodia when the whole of the modern human rights movement is predicated on the determination, born out of the horrors of the Holocaust, that genocide would never happen again? Why cannot the international community—and the United Nations in particular—prevent these horrors from happening?

These questions are particularly poignant when we remember the warnings received of impending disaster. One year before the Rwanda crisis erupted, a report to the Commission on Human Rights had sounded the alarm. And we have known for some years of the deteriorating situation in Kosovo.

An International Mechanism for Prevention

It is here that the notion of human rights prevention comes into its own. We must raise to the international level the well-known techniques of prevention developed on the national level.

These techniques cover the whole range of prevention, including that of human rights institution building, and they include ongoing efforts within the UN system to coordinate efforts to improve early-warning and conflict-prevention capacities. But when faced with impending human rights disasters, the international community often appears unprepared and caught off-guard. Information is not in short supply; it is action that is wanting. The reports of human rights Special Rapporteurs and working groups and the reports and work of the human rights treaty bodies contain valuable sources of independent information and analysis which could help prevent disaster, if only that information could lead to action.

Could we not imagine an international mechanism which could consider that information and undertake or suggest appropriate action? That action could span the whole spectrum of established techniques of conflict prevention from quiet diplomacy, to public warnings, to action by responsible organs. To be effective, that mechanism, involving member states, would have to be able to function with discretion. This would suggest that it meet periodically in private and review information which could indicate imminent or longer-term problems. But to merit the confidence of the people, to help develop a sense of shared responsibility for the future among states, and to provide a basis for lessons learned, some public scrutiny of the work of that mechanism would have to be provided for. Could we not achieve the desired degree of transparency by making public the discussions at a set interval after each meeting, as is the practice on the national level with certain government bodies dealing with very sensitive matters?[18]

Accountability

A crucial factor in the prevention of gross violations of human rights is personal accountability and the end of impunity. I welcome the trend whereby courts are increasingly allowing the prosecution of human rights cases, irrespective of where they occurred or how much time has elapsed. I welcome, too, the fact that the international judicial machinery is finally moving into action: the setting up of ad hoc tribunals for the former Yugoslavia and Rwanda was an important step forward; and the adoption of the Statute of an International Criminal Court providing jurisdiction over the three core crimes of genocide, crimes against humanity, and war crimes was a milestone in the struggle to strengthen respect for international human rights and humanitarian law. What better way could there be to usher in an age of prevention than for states to ratify the Statute of the International Criminal Court and allow it to begin its vital work? I urge all states to ratify the Statute.

Concluding Remarks

The difficulties we face in aspiring to a worldwide culture of respect for human rights are enormous, and some would say we are naive even to take up the challenge. But after the dark days of the Second World War, the drafters of the United Nations Charter and the Universal Declaration of Human Rights took up the challenge of hope and confidence, and we have all benefited from that vision.

On that foundation a strong system of rules and procedures has been built, along with growing support of people all over the world for respect for human rights. I do not think that respect for human rights is an impossibly idealistic goal. But it will require responsible decision-making by governments. Nor do I despair of the United Nations as the focus for international human rights action. Its universality and impartiality and its ability to listen to the weakest over the influence of the strong make it indispensable.

But even more important will be the strength of civil society. As the Millennium Assembly approaches, we must develop strong and mutually reinforcing relationships with the organs of civil society to better hear the voice of "We the Peoples of the United Nations."

I now look forward to your observations and questions and to working with you toward improving respect for human rights throughout the world.

The High Commissioner's Annual Report 1999–2000 to the Fifty-Fifth General Assembly
Introductory Statement
United Nations, New York, 24 October 2000

Madame Chair, Distinguished Delegates,

It is a pleasure to be here with you again, to introduce my fourth annual report, and to discuss with you some significant developments in the field of human rights.

I must begin on a somber note. It is sad to have to report that the overall human rights situation worldwide continues to be worrying and in some areas, such as the Middle East and several parts of Africa, is worsening to a degree that gives rise to grave concern. It is a chastening environment in which the Third Committee holds its first session of the millennium. The crisis in the Middle East led to the convening of a Special Session of the Commission last week, on which I shall report to this Committee, but worsening situations in countries such as Burundi and the Democratic Republic of the Congo tend not to get the supportive human rights attention that is needed. There is a selectivity of approach and concern which is raised with me frequently on my visits to African countries and which should be addressed by this Committee, particularly as we continue our preparations for the World Conference against Racism in South Africa next year.

In summary, despite over fifty years of constructive development of international human rights norms, standards, institutions, and mandates, we are making too little progress in key areas: in the prevention of gross violations of human rights, and in the implementation in practical terms of knowledge and awareness of human rights where it really matters, at the grassroots level.

On a brighter note, the centrality of human rights to the United Nations mission was graphically illustrated at last month's Millennium Summit, notably in the Declaration adopted by world leaders.[19] The Secretary General's report, *We the Peoples,* also highlighted the fact that most people around the globe consider the protection of human rights to be the most important task of the United Nations.[20]

Not surprisingly, this increased focus has had a direct impact on the Office of the High Commissioner for Human Rights. As the number of mandates and programs has grown steadily, we have also faced an ever-larger number of requests for technical cooperation and advisory services emanating from governments all around the world. In order to deal with the evolving demands on my Office, I have initiated a management-of-change process designed to strengthen the Office as a center of excellence, particularly in the areas of performance management and strategic planning, as well as program, financial, information, and communications management.

Since the preparation of my report there have been several developments at the Commission on Human Rights which I would like to discuss.

Fifth Special Session of the Commission on Human Rights

As you are well aware, the fifth special session of the Commission on Human Rights was convened in Geneva last week to discuss the human rights implications of the outbreak of violence in the occupied Palestinian territories.[21] Special emphasis was placed on the need to put an end to violence and to restore dialogue and peace based on respect for human rights. Reference was made to the outcome of the Sharm El-Sheikh Emergency Summit. Many delegations welcomed the Secretary General's efforts in this context and underlined the relevance and importance of the Commission being seized of the matter in light of its role and mandate.

In its resolution, the Commission decided to establish a human rights inquiry commission and requested me to undertake an urgent visit to the occupied territories and to report to the fifty-seventh session of the Commission and, on an interim basis, to the current session of the General Assembly. My Office is examining the implications of the resolution. Furthermore, eight special procedures of the Commission on Human Rights were requested to carry out immediate missions to the occupied territories and also to report their findings to the Commission and the General Assembly. The Commission recommended that the Economic and Social Council meet on an urgent basis in order to act on the proposals contained in the resolution. ECOSOC is expected to meet here in mid-November.

Federal Republic of Yugoslavia

Since the preparation of my annual report, the world has celebrated the democratic election of a new President in the Federal Republic of Yugoslavia. I know that we all wish President Kostunica well as he begins the difficult task of building democratic institutions, the rule of law, and respect for human rights in his country. In this regard, I recently appointed Ambassador Amneus of Sweden as my Special Envoy on Persons Deprived of Liberty in order to address the vexed issue of prisoners, detainees and missing persons in the Federal Republic of Yugoslavia and Kosovo and to help find practical solutions. The situation in Kosovo will be a crucial test for the future of the Balkans. At its heart is the issue of respect for the human rights of all people, regardless of ethnicity.

OHCHR will continue to work in the region, together with our partners in the UN. My Office in Belgrade has been active in monitoring and protecting the rights of opinion and expression, and has done substantive work on the issue of prisoners and detainees throughout the country. The sub-Office in Podgorica contributes to early warning and conflict prevention, and in Pristina, the sub-Office has been fully involved in the monitoring of human rights violations perpetrated by all sides of the conflict.

Sierra Leone

As outlined in my report, the human rights situation in Sierra Leone continues to be a matter of serious concern. My Office is vigorously engaged there, including through its support for UNAMSIL's human rights training programs and its advocacy for the release of abductees and for humanitarian access. We are also involved in programs to strengthen civil society and activities aimed at helping victims of the conflict to rebuild their lives and their communities.

With the support of my Office, the government has made substantial progress in preparing for the establishment of a national Human Rights Commission, on which there will be a workshop shortly in Freetown. In February the Sierra Leone Parliament adopted the Statute for the Truth and Reconciliation Commission, which was drafted with assistance from my Office, and we have developed a technical cooperation project to assist the preparatory phase of the Commission.[22]

I welcome the proposed establishment of the Special Court and consider that it will play an important role in countering the climate of impunity that had, until now, persisted in Sierra Leone. My Office has commented on the draft Statute prepared by the Office of Legal Affairs and stands ready to work closely with all the relevant actors to ensure the proper functioning of the court, in compliance with the best international human rights standards.[23]

Democratic Republic of the Congo

At the invitation of the government, I paid a visit to the DRC from 1 to 3 October. I was able to visit Kinshasa, Lubumbashi, where I met with President Kabila, and Goma, which remains under the control of the main rebel movement, the Congolese Rally for Democracy (RCD), where I met with RCD President Emile Illunga.

I found that the human rights situation throughout the country has continued to deteriorate with serious, widespread, and systematic violations taking place almost on a daily basis. I noted the widespread poverty prevailing in the DRC, despite its enormous resources, and its impact on the population, in particular vulnerable groups, especially women and children. I was struck by the urgent need to restore peace and to initiate a sustainable program of development to give hope to more than fifty million Congolese who are living in terrible circumstances.

Before I left the DRC, President Kabila agreed to establish a moratorium on the death penalty, to suspend the prosecution of civilians before the

Military Court and to reform its statute so as to allow rights of defense and appeal. He also promised to carefully review a list of some two hundred arbitrarily detained individuals that I provided to him. The RCD, for its part, agreed to conduct, as soon as security conditions would permit, investigations into massacres referred to in the Special Rapporteur's reports, to facilitate the access of humanitarian agencies to vulnerable groups, and to prevent any action against representatives of civil society.

Finally, I was able to present to the major stakeholders OHCHR's subregional strategy for Central Africa and to promote the Sub-Regional Center for Human Rights and Democracy in Yaoundé, Cameroon, which will be established by the end of 2000.[24]

Chechnya in the Russian Federation

I would like to update you on the most recent developments concerning the implementation of the Resolution on the Situation in the Republic of Chechnya in the Russian Federation, adopted at the fifty-sixth session of the Commission on Human Rights.[25] I should state that Russia voted against this resolution and does not accept its terms.

I have maintained contacts with Foreign Minister Ivanov of the Russian Federation and received extensive communications from his Ministry on actions taken in the area of human rights in Chechnya. I am grateful for the information provided by the Russian authorities.

The Resolution called on the government to establish urgently a national independent commission of inquiry to investigate promptly alleged violations of human rights, to bring the perpetrators to justice, and to prevent impunity. Three separate initiatives have been taken in recent months by the Russian authorities.

The Special Representative for the protection of the human rights and freedoms of the citizens in the Chechen Republic, Mr. V. Kalamanov, has sent me two reports on his activities to date. The Special Representative says that his Office receives complaints from civilians, examines them, and forwards them to the procuracy and other appropriate agencies. Experts of the Council of Europe are working with the Office. The Special Representative notes that, as of 1 October, his Office has received 4,167 complaints on human rights abuses. Mr. Kalamanov has previously reported that over 50 percent of the appeals received were related to detention and missing family members, limitations of the freedom of movement, abuse by military servicemen and police, arbitrary arrests, beatings, and unlawful detention. The Special Representative also refers to high numbers of complaints regarding the lack of judicial institutions and legal assistance as well as extortion of money by militia for crossing checkpoints in Chechnya.

A separate body, a National Public Commission on the investigation of violations of rights and observance of human rights in the Chechen Republic, headed by M. P. P. Krasheninnikov, has been established. It is composed of a group of public figures.

A third body examining the situation is a special Commission of the State Duma, which held hearings on the economy and observance of human rights in Chechnya in September.

None of these bodies has direct investigatory or prosecution powers, and I have requested information on criminal prosecution of abuses by representatives of Russian authorities against Chechen civilians and await detailed information in response to this request.

The Russian authorities have extended invitations to the Special Rapporteur on Violence against Women and the Special Representative of the Secretary General on Children and Armed Conflict. The Special Rapporteur on Torture; the Special Rapporteur on Extrajudicial, Summary or Arbitrary Executions; and the Special Representative of the Secretary General on Internally Displaced Persons have also requested visits.

International Committee of the Red Cross (ICRC) delegates and the European Committee for the Prevention of Torture have visited places of detention inside and outside Chechnya. The Special Representative's Office has received complaints concerning 455 missing persons.

The European Court of Human Rights has received sixty cases of allegations of human rights violations against Chechens. Of these, six have so far been communicated to the Russian Government. The Government of the Russian Federation has recently instructed federal agencies to extend support to the activities of the OSCE Assistance Group, including fixing the date of the return of the Assistance Group to Chechnya.

I am very much concerned about the situation regarding the economic, social, and cultural rights of the Chechen people and in the region. The Russian authorities advise that they are allocating considerable funds to improve this situation. The humanitarian plight of the people, however, continues to be grave. There has been no significant return of displaced persons. Humanitarian agencies continue to be severely restricted in their activities because of security concerns and, sometimes, administrative reasons.

Addressing the Commission on Human Rights, I stressed the importance of a credible response from the Russian authorities commensurate with the scale of the allegations of serious human rights abuses in Chechnya. I continue to be deeply concerned and convinced of the need for these allegations to be adequately addressed. I hope that our dialogue with the Russian authorities will be helpful in this regard.

Reports also continue of serious human rights violations carried out by Chechen fighters, affecting federal and local authorities but also civilians. I am very concerned by that. However, while recognizing the need to counter terrorist activities, I reiterate that such efforts must be made in full conformity with the international human rights standards.

The Government of the Russian Federation continues its collaboration with my Office in the area of technical cooperation. In September an experts meeting was held in Moscow. This meeting launched a three-year project of technical cooperation on human rights education in Russia.

East Timor

In early August, during a visit to East Timor, I had the opportunity to meet with a wide range of East Timorese society and with international representatives, and to travel to a number of locations in and around Dili as well as Suai. Following this visit, my Office is currently finalizing a program of technical cooperation on human rights with UNTAET to provide, inter alia, human rights training to CIVPOL and support to the national truth and reconciliation process.

As we know, one of the most pressing problems concerns the situation of East Timorese refugees who are now located in West Timor. The situation of these people must be effectively and speedily addressed from the human rights perspective. I am taking steps to facilitate this process. I stand ready to cooperate with all authorities and agencies involved with a view to assisting in finding a solution.

My Office has also provided technical assistance to the Government of Indonesia to strengthen its administration of justice and capacity to support the prosecution of human rights violations, in particular in the context of the draft human rights tribunal legislation.[26] My Office is available to continue this assistance.

The Human Rights Treaty Body System

Universal ratification of the core international human rights treaties is a principal objective of the General Assembly, the Secretary General and my Office. The Millennium Assembly was an historic event, not least for stimulating ratification of these treaties. An unprecedented 273 "treaty actions" took place over those three days.

However, the question of universal ratification must not be considered in isolation from its resource implications. I draw your attention to the Annex to my report. The message it conveys is stark: unless it is adequately funded, the human rights treaty body system will not be able to fulfill its key role. I strongly urge distinguished delegates to take this matter up in their considerations under the relevant agenda item.

At the same time, treaty bodies must do their part to maximize their own effective functioning. Reform and strengthening of the treaty bodies has been the subject of numerous studies by independent scholars and initiatives by states parties, and has always been the principal focus of the meetings of chairpersons. I am pleased to advise you of two initiatives by my Office: the first-ever intercommittee meeting on harmonization of periodicity of reporting will take place early next year; and a new petitions team has been established in OHCHR to expedite the processing of individual complaints mechanisms.[27]

Globalization

Another message emerging from the Millennium Assembly was that the global context of the UN mission has changed. New opportunities and technologies are accompanied by new insecurities and fears. I draw your attention to the Secretary General's separate report on globalization, which poses some important questions and outlines the beginnings of a human-rights-based approach to finding the answers.[28]

In this context, I welcome the deepening dialogue between my Office and the World Bank. I have met with Mr. Wolfensohn and senior personnel of the Bank on a number of occasions, most recently in Prague at the annual meeting of the Bank and the IMF. I believe that the human rights community has a direct interest in seeking to foster and encourage the Bank's willingness to address human rights issues and to help clarify the implications of a rights-based approach for the work of other international institutions.[29]

UNDP Human Development Report

My Office has continued to work with our sister agencies in promoting rights-based development, and we have marked some important milestones. I warmly welcomed the publication of the United Nations Development Programme's *Human Development Report 2000,* which takes as its theme human rights.[30] It establishes once and for all that human rights and economic and social progress are inextricably linked. For far too long we have looked at development and human rights separately. This report demonstrates that they are two sides of the same coin.

The Right to Development

I am also pleased to report that the open-ended working group on the right to development made progress in September when it met to review the implementation of this right and to discuss its national and international dimensions. A harmonious and productive spirit characterized the working group, with important contributions coming from the Bretton Woods Institutions, international organizations, and states. The working group will meet for its second session in January 2001. I know that distinguished members of this Committee will want to support the practical and constructive approach which prevailed at the working group under the skillful chairmanship of Ambassador Dembri of Algeria.[31]

New Commission on Human Rights Mandates

I welcomed the appointment in August this year, by the Secretary General, of Ms. Hina Jilani as the first Special Representative for Human Rights Defenders. I view this as a particularly important mandate and would request all governments to extend to her their full cooperation. This year the Commission on Human Rights decided to underline the importance of two particular rights through the creation of new mandates on the right to food and on adequate housing as a component of the right to an adequate standard of living.[32]

Brahimi Report on Peace Operations

I welcome the recognition of the important role of human rights by the Panel on United Nations Peace Keeping Operations. The Panel's report stressed the "essential importance of the UN system adhering to and promoting international human rights instruments and standards and international humanitarian law in all aspects of its peace and security activities."[33] It recommended strengthening the capacity of OHCHR to provide support to the human rights components of UN peace operations.

My Office has been actively involved in the interagency process set up to assist the Secretary General in implementing the report's recommendations. I am convinced that enhancing OHCHR's capacity to contribute to peace operations will strengthen the sustainability of United Nations work for prevention, peace-making, peacekeeping, and peace-building.[34]

Thank you for your close attention. I would now welcome your observations and questions.

Chapter 15
Supporting United Nations Human Rights Bodies

A major expectation of the post of High Commissioner was that its incumbent would fashion the different parts of the UN human rights machinery into a coherent program that was both effective and efficient. Considerable effort was made in that direction during Mary Robinson's tenure, although progress inevitably was incremental. Much was achieved also in the strengthening of the Secretariat functions provided by the High Commissioner and her Office for UN human rights bodies.

The centerpiece of the UN human rights institutions is the Commission on Human Rights. Specifically identified in the UN Charter, the Commission is a forum of now fifty-three government representatives reflecting all regions of the world. It met first in 1946 to draft the Universal Declaration of Human Rights and in the following decades generated the corpus of international human rights treaty law. In that task it was aided by its subsidiary body, now named the Sub-Commission on the Promotion and Protection of Human Rights. The Sub-Commission consists of twenty-six independent experts elected by governments and reports to the Commission. In turn, the Commission reports to the Economic and Social Council, ECOSOC.

Apart from establishing standards, the Commission on Human Rights gradually developed a role in having these implemented and enjoyed. The protective function of the Commission came to be expressed first in its resolutions of concern over human rights violations in different countries and in the development of the "Special Procedures" whereby independent experts (Special Rapporteurs or representatives) or working groups are tasked with studying and reporting to the Commission on different human rights themes or on situations in particular countries. Despite the greater consensus achieved among states on the importance of human rights and that their protection everywhere should be a priority for the United Nations, most states resist public criticism of their own practices. They remain reluctant also to censure regional allies or powerful states. Concern over growing polarization between North and South and the need for the Commission on Human Rights to maintain its protective function were themes of Mary Robinson's last address to the Commission in 2002.

The other arm of the UN system is the human rights multilateral treaty regime. It has grown to consist of seven "core" treaties and their implementing machinery, elected committees of unpaid independent experts, known as the treaty bodies. In ratifying a human rights treaty, a country undertakes a range of commitments to ensure that the rights in question are recognized and protected at the national level, and it undertakes to report at regular intervals to the treaty-monitoring body on progress made in fulfilling the rights in question. In addition, four of the treaties have an optional procedure to allow individuals to complain to the relevant treaty committee over alleged violations of rights and freedoms. It was the practice for the High Commissioner to address opening sessions of the different treaty bodies and meetings of the Chairs of the treaty bodies. This convention served to recognize their work and to encourage cooperation between the different committees and with other parts of the UN system. It was also an opportunity to report on the constant efforts Mary Robinson spearheaded to strengthen Secretariat support for the bodies and to secure additional financial resources for their work.

Address at the Closing of the Fifty-Eighth Session of the Commission on Human Rights
Palais des Nations, Geneva, 26 April 2002

Mr. Chairman, Distinguished Delegates, Excellencies, Ladies, and Gentlemen,

This session of the Commission on Human Rights will call for deep reflection by all of us. I am convinced that everyone in this room wishes the human rights idea to triumph nationally, regionally, and internationally. How we are to achieve this is a topic that excites great passions and gives rise to agreement as well as divisions among us. Surely we agree that every effort must be made to spread a universal culture of human rights and to act to protect the victims of violations in any part of the world. That has been the policy of this Commission over the past fifty-eight sessions, and it must remain its bedrock in the future.

If the Commission were not able to act for the protection of those whose rights are being violated on a massive scale, it would lose its essence. In the aftermath of September 11, and with acute conflict and tensions in some parts of the world, we were all conscious that this could be a difficult session. But none of us could have envisaged that it would be as difficult organizationally as it proved to be.

Organizational Challenges

Following the cancellation of evening and night meetings, the Commission had to make drastic adjustments in its work. The Bureau had to meet on innumerable occasions, and the Chairman was called upon to guide the session in the face of these severe organizational difficulties. I should like to pay tribute to you, Mr. Chairman, for the wisdom and patience you demonstrated in bringing us toward a successful conclusion of the session. I should also like to pay tribute to the Members of the Expanded Bureau who had to face such unprecedented organizational difficulties due to lack of meeting services. And I am proud of the way my own team coped at every level.

It is my strong hope that such a situation will not be repeated in the future and that we can return to a Commission on Human Rights in which the voices of the Rapporteurs, the voices of national institutions, and the voices of nongovernmental organizations will be heard in fair and full measure—for they are strong voices for human rights protection. I want to encourage reflection on how this shock to the Commission's working methods points to the need to reevaluate the essential contribution that this Commission makes in giving leadership in human rights. The Rapporteurs and experts will be reflecting on all of this at their annual meeting in June this year, and the nongovernmental organizations will also be discussing their experiences at this year's Commission on Human Rights. I, for my part, pledge to work closely with the Chairperson and the Bureau over the coming months and to encourage this process of reflection.

Occupied Palestinian Territories and Israel

In addition to organizational difficulties, the Commission had to cope with acute substantive and procedural difficulties due to the worsening situation in the occupied Palestinian territories and in Israel. This was the first shadow darkening the human rights' horizon that Secretary General Kofi Annan identified when he addressed the Commission. The Commission recognized the need to respond to the severe loss of life of both Palestinians and Israelis, and to the spiraling violence that raised fundamental challenges for the observance of international human rights and humanitarian law. The Commission reviewed the situation, called for a Visiting Mission, called for and received a fact-finding report, and kept the situation under review.[1] The steps taken by the Commission stem from its commitment to protect victims of violations of human rights in a particularly difficult context.

September 11

The second shadow was the terrorist attacks of September 11 and what has happened in their aftermath. A number of strong statements during this session have affirmed the importance of upholding fully human rights and humanitarian law standards in combating terrorism. Again, my Office is ready to respond in support of any initiative that the Commission may think appropriate in order to signal clearly that human rights should not be sacrificed in the fight against terrorism.

Politicization and Prevention

When I said at the outset that this session of the Commission would call for deep reflection, I had in mind also the divisive debates and votes that have taken place with regard to situations in which it was alleged that gross violations of human rights were occurring. Let me say it openly: I hear distress and concern voiced by the human rights movement over allegations of increased politicization of issues in the Commission to the detriment of true human rights concerns. This is a time to remind ourselves of the essential role of the Commission on Human Rights in protecting human beings against gross violations through highlighting and publicizing those violations; providing a forum for victims to raise their grievances and to see their issues addressed; heeding the voice of conscience from different parts of the world; enabling NGOs to put alternative views and perspectives from those of governments; developing norms and standards; and continuing the "building blocks" protection role of the Commission. From this perspective, it is vital that Special Rapporteurs, representatives of national human rights institutions, and nongovernmental organizations are able and encouraged to undertake a dialogue with the Commission. The Commission needs to hear from them.

In the mid-1960s, as the newly independent countries entered the United Nations, they were the ones who pressed the General Assembly, the Economic and Social Council, and this Commission to deal with situations of gross violations of human rights. Developing countries led efforts for the adoption of resolution number 8 of the twenty-third session of the Commission, which remains the policy framework whereby this body engages in an annual review of situations in which gross violations of human rights are allegedly taking place and takes appropriate actions for the protection of victims. We have heard at this session the voices of some of those very developing countries arguing that there is too much criticism of them. I feel it my duty as High Commissioner to pose this question: Is it not right that when there are situations of gross violations of human rights this Commission seeks to protect the victims?

And if it is felt that the existing methods are not adequate, is there not a responsibility on the membership of this Commission to consult and to find adequate ways of helping to protect the victims of such violations? A recent report of an international commission articulated the duty of the international community to come to the protection of those whose rights are being grievously violated. They highlighted the "responsibility to protect."[2] Today, in this Commission, I ask the question How will the Commission on Human Rights, the central human rights body in the United Nations, continue to discharge this duty of protection?

We need to bear in mind that we might have reached a stage where the very success in highlighting and mainstreaming human rights issues in a more effective way could be in danger of provoking a reaction. I am particularly worried about a possible trend seeking to weaken the protection role that this Commission has been exercising. One could see this in the voting on country situations, where there has been, at this session, a preference for an approach excluding action if consensus was not possible.

The core role of the Commission in protecting human rights through drawing attention to violations and abuses must be retained. But it is clear that in the future it needs to be matched by a much more significant commitment to provide resources for technical cooperation and advisory services to assist countries in building and strengthening their national capacity in the rule of law, the administration of justice, and adherence to human rights norms and standards. Criticism will then be perceived as constructive and forward-looking, not finger-pointing in a judgmental way. Would it not be right for the Expanded Bureau, in the course of the coming year, to engage in consultations on the role of the Commission in acting for the protection of human rights and how this could be done in a manner that is equitable?

Positive Achievements

I say to all of us, without any exception: We fought for the United Nations to protect human rights. Today, as always, we must be faithful to this historic mission. Notwithstanding the difficulties experienced at the present session, including a worrying North/South divide in voting on resolutions on issues such as racism and right to development, significant progress has been made. Let me single out the resolution on enforced or involuntary disappearances, which requests an open-ended Working Group to prepare, for consideration by the General Assembly, a draft of a new, legally binding instrument.

Let me also welcome incremental progress made in the resolution on human rights of persons with disabilities. It calls on my Office to report to the fifty-ninth session of the Commission on progress in the implementation of the recommendations in the study on the Human Rights of Persons with Disabilities presented to this session. Even though I am aware that your resolution to recommend a Protocol to the Convention Against Torture, which would allow for country visits intended to prevent torture, was the subject of much debate, it is my hope that, as the process continues toward eventual adoption in the General Assembly, this will prove to be one of the important outcomes of the present session.

The resolution calling for a Special Rapporteur on the right to health continues the trend toward better implementation of economic, social, and cultural rights. Your resolutions on democracy, participation, the role of good governance in the protection of human rights, and on the role of national institutions deal with vital areas in the promotion and the protection of human rights. Your call for cooperation with thematic and country mechanisms must be heeded. Resolutions dealing with human rights in various conflict situations contain important recommendations on the advancement of human rights. The resolution on human rights in Afghanistan will give heart to the long-suffering people of that country. The emphasis you have placed on the implementation of the human rights provisions of the Bonn Agreement provides important policy guidance for the international community, and this is a priority commitment for my Office.

Without a doubt, Mr. Chairman, distinguished Delegates, progress was made at the present session. In the hope, therefore, that there will be a broad reflection over the coming months, I remind you of the way I encouraged members at the Opening of this fifty-eighth session to instill particular human rights significance into your membership of the Commission. I suggested that members might consider afresh adherence to those human rights instruments to which they are not yet party, or review their existing reporting practice or issue a standing invitation to all thematic Rapporteurs. This would be an ideal opportunity to lead by example.

Mr. Chairman, distinguished members of the Commission, Excellencies, ladies, and gentlemen, allow me to conclude these remarks by referring to the vision of one of the principal drafters of the Universal Declaration of Human Rights, Professor René Cassin. On 6 December 1947 Professor Cassin submitted a letter to the Working Party on the Implementation of Human Rights that met during the second session of the Commission. Addressing the issue of implementation, he reminded the Commission that it was essential to bear in mind that it and the organs of the United Nations should assure respect for human rights in pursuance of the Charter. It was important, he said, that the normal courts in each country be able to provide effective remedies to those whose rights are at risk.

Professor Cassin foresaw that petitions and complaints should be examined by independent persons of eminent repute appointed by the United Nations with powers of inquiry. He foresaw investigating commissions and a role for the principal organs of the United Nations, including the General Assembly, the Security Council, the Economic and Social Council, and the International Court of Justice. Professor Cassin concluded:

> Finally, I would draw the Working Parties' attention to the advisability of gradually increasing the means of implementation—by urging the importance of preventive measures which depend largely on the collaboration of states with the United Nations and the vigilance of public opinion, and means of redress, or even punishment, of the violations committed.

As we conclude this fifty-eighth session of the Commission, let us recall this vision and ask ourselves: To what extent have we been faithful to it? What more can we do to prevent gross violations of human rights? We should all be able to agree, surely, that the prevention of gross violations of human rights must be the starting point of the human rights agenda of the future. This crucial challenge should be central to our process of reflection.

Thank you.

Opening Remarks, Fifty-Third Session of the Sub-Commission on the Promotion and Protection of Human Rights
Palais des Nations, Geneva, 30 July 2001

Role of the Sub-Commission

Since its establishment, the Sub-Commission has played an important role within the United Nations in the promotion and protection of human rights. Thanks to its expertise and experience, supported by the valuable contribution of nongovernmental organizations, it has been able to provide the United Nations with useful recommendations on many issues. These include the elaboration of international standards, the development of our understanding of human rights through the study of new issues, and the prevention of violations of human rights throughout the world. On many occasions the Sub-Commission has played an important role in preparing the basis for the creation of new thematic mechanisms of the Commission on Human Rights.

Working Groups of the Sub-Commission

I would like to say a word about an aspect of the Sub-Commission which is unique in the UN's human rights program: the role of the thematic working groups—on minorities, indigenous populations, and contemporary forms of slavery. Those working groups facilitate interaction between civil society, governments, and the intergovernmental system and provide a forum for vulnerable groups which otherwise would have little or no access to the UN system.

The Working Group on Minorities is a good example. The Working Group's debate on integration and autonomy revealed the variety and complexity of situations facing minorities in different parts of the world. These discussions serve to enhance a more global understanding of the situations of peoples and groups and of the need to be more creative in finding solutions to protect and promote the rights of groups and communities.

The Working Group on Indigenous Populations has made a valuable contribution to the promotion and protection of indigenous peoples' rights in the drafting of a Declaration on the Rights of Indigenous Peoples. In recent years the Working Group has also focused on issues relating to indigenous education, language, land rights, cultural heritage, and health. The Working Group has played an important role in reviewing developments in the situation of indigenous communities throughout the world and has provided a forum for indigenous peoples from all over the world to assemble in Geneva, exchange experiences, engage in a dialogue with their respective governments, and develop joint proposals within the UN system. The Working Group should also be especially proud of its role in the creation of the Permanent Forum on Indigenous Issues, which fulfills an important objective of the International Decade of the World's Indigenous People. My Office will work hard to fulfill its mandate as lead agency in charge of implementing the resolution to set up the Permanent Forum.

Ms. Erica-Irene Daes, who chaired the Working Group on Indigenous Populations with great energy and integrity for many years, has also contributed to the preparatory process of the World Conference by specifically addressing discrimination against indigenous peoples in her reports and working papers.[3]

The Working Group on Contemporary Forms of Slavery is the only UN mechanism, which monitors compliance with Slavery Conventions and deals with a wide range of human rights concerns in this area. It has selected this year as a priority issue the trafficking in persons, in particular women and children.

Globalization and its Impact on Human Rights

As the Secretary General has noted, the overriding message to come out of the United Nations Millennium Summit last September—the largest gathering ever of heads of state and government—was the need to ensure that globalization becomes a positive force for all the world's people. At the request of the Commission on Human Rights, the Sub-Commission had earlier begun a study on the complex issue of globalization and its impact on the full enjoyment of all human rights. Much of the debate has concentrated on economic aspects. More needs to be done to improve our understanding of how the processes of globalization affect individual human rights both positively and negatively.

The approval by the Commission on Human Rights of a proposal for the Sub-Commission to host a forum on economic, social, and cultural rights, to be known as the Social Forum, is an interesting development in this area.[4] I hope that it will create a new space for dialogue and exchange, perhaps developing in a wider context the approach so successfully pioneered by the Working Group on Indigenous Populations.

Business and Human Rights

In addition to the initiative to establish the Social Forum, the Sub-Commission has continued its work to provide content to our better understanding of civil, cultural, economic, political, and social rights as well as the right to development. In that context, I note that the Sub-Commission and its sessional working group on the working methods and activities of transnational corporations have made progress in elaborating human rights guidelines for business enterprises. I commend Mr. Weissbrodt for his diligent work in preparing draft guidelines in consultation with all the main actors.[5]

The Universal Declaration of Human Rights commits every individual and every organ of society to promote and uphold the rights it enshrines. Governments have the primary responsibility for ensuring respect for human rights, but corporations, their managers, and their personnel have a strong duty to abide by the Universal Declaration and other international human rights principles in the course of their activities. Corporations have grown tremendously in the scope of their activities and their power in the world. The Secretary General has recognized the potential of corporations to play a positive role in the globalization of human rights in his Global Compact initiative.[6] With power comes responsibility. I hope that the Working Group and the Sub-Commission will help us to define more precisely that responsibility and make further progress in preparing the human rights guidelines for companies and in obtaining broad input from governments, intergovernmental and nongovernmental organizations, organizations of workers, and the business community.

Concluding Comments

I have referred to some aspects of the Sub-Commission's very diverse activities. The United Nations and the human rights community generally have long benefited from the expertise of the Sub-Commission in drafting human rights standards, increasing our understanding of new issues, and devising procedures for the protection of human rights. It goes without saying that to maintain its high standing the Sub-Commission must continue to meet the highest standards of precision and objectivity. I wish you a very successful session and look forward to working with you to achieve our shared vision of a world free from racism and all human rights abuses.

The Importance of the Independence of Special Rapporteurs and Similar Mechanisms of the Commission on Human Rights

Statement by the High Commissioner
Palais Wilson, Geneva, 16 December 1997

We have just marked the beginning of Human Rights Year leading up to the commemoration on 10 December 1998 of the fiftieth anniversary of the adoption of the Universal Declaration of Human Rights. An important focus of this year will be defending and protecting the achievements of the United Nations human rights program.

A key mechanism developed by the United Nations over the years for the promotion and protection of human rights is the system of fact-finding through independent experts designated either as Special Rapporteurs or members of working groups. These experts are charged with carefully analyzing allegations of human rights violations and government information, and informing the international community of their findings and making pertinent recommendations.

Over the years the crucial value of these procedures to saving human lives and helping resolve serious situations of violations has been fully acknowledged. The World Conference on Human Rights recognized the importance of these procedures and called for their preservation and strengthening.[7] During the coming year, I will be giving special attention to this objective.

In order to provide the international community with the independent and impartially analyzed information which is essential in human rights policy-making, the experts of the special procedures system must be secure in enjoying the privileges and immunities due to them as experts on mission for the United Nations. Member states have agreed to this by ratifying the 1946 Convention on the Privileges and Immunities of the United Nations. The International Court of Justice reaffirmed these principles in its 1989 Advisory Opinion relating to a member state's obligation under the Convention to ensure freedom of movement to a United Nations Special Rapporteur, Mr. Dumitru Mazilu.[8]

The scrupulous respect for these rights by member states is essential, and I wish to call on all states to do so fully. The Secretary General is now discussing with the Government of Malaysia application of the Convention in relation to Mr. Param Cumaraswamy, Special Rapporteur on the Independence of Judges and Lawyers. I wish to urge the government to implement fully the provisions of the Convention as a key component of international law.

Address to the Eighth Meeting of Special Rapporteurs/Representatives and Experts of the Commission on Human Rights
Palais Wilson, Geneva, 18 June 2001

Dear Friends and Colleagues,

I would like to begin by warmly welcoming you all to the Palais Wilson, particularly those among you who are attending this meeting for the first time. The addition of the mandates on human rights defenders, the rights to food, and the right to adequate housing will no doubt serve to further strengthen the United Nations human rights program. Indeed, I view the Special Procedures of the Commission as one of the main pillars of the human rights program, and as I have said on many occasions and as has been expressed in unequivocal terms in my Office's Mission Statement, OHCHR aims to provide the Special Procedures the highest-quality support.

In spite of our ongoing efforts to provide this support to you for the effective discharge of your important mandates, I am acutely aware of the difficulties, you face in doing so. I realize that many of you have conducted field missions under difficult circumstances, struggled to present reports in time for the General Assembly and the Commission, or have not always had the level of Secretariat assistance you would have hoped for.

Nonetheless, we continue to redouble our efforts on improving this situation so as to allow you all to continue with your important work and also to create a more efficient and effective system which will be able to accommodate the ever-increasing demands placed upon it as the number and scope of the mandates continue to expand.

To a large extent, some of the difficulties are as a direct result of a lack of resources. While we must address this vital issue, we would be lacking vision if we were not also attempting to seek new and more innovative ways in a change-management perspective to improve our working methods within our current level of resources. Such a dual-purpose approach has actually been our strategy, and since your last annual meeting there have been a number of significant developments which have a direct bearing on the operation of the Special Procedures system. I wish to briefly review some of these issues with you.

Special Procedures Report

Last year you discussed in detail the draft study on the strengthening of the Special Procedures system which I had commissioned, and which was completed in July 1999 by Ms. Rishmawi and Mr. Hammarberg.[9] This study draws upon consultations with all the special procedures mandate holders, with nongovernmental organizations, members of the Commission and its Bureau, staff from my Office, and me. I have fully endorsed the study's recommendations, and several proposals have been incorporated in the *Annual Appeal 2001,* which I launched in November of last year.[10] The Annual Appeal invites governments to contribute to a variety of specific activities and programs of my Office. As one of the four core elements of my program, the Special Procedures system deserves the special attention of the donor community, and it is my hope that your activities can be made more effective through the Global Appeal process.[11]

As one important step toward strengthening the special procedures, a thematic database has been developed by OHCHR in the last couple of years, with funding provided by the Ford Foundation. This system should enable you and your assistants to collect and track relevant information more easily, enhance cooperation between the various mandates, and reduce response time to requests for urgent appeals.

Change Management

Since last autumn, my Office has been engaged in a comprehensive Management of Change Process, aimed at reviewing and streamlining structures, procedures, and working conditions in our house. In January of this year, the senior management of my Office met for a weekend retreat, during which participants were able to exchange experiences and thoughts on the direction, management and mission of our Office. As one result of this exercise, a Task Force was established with a mandate to review and address issues that were raised during the retreat and later by individual staff members. Similar encouraging projects have also been initiated at the Branch level.

Quick Response Capacity

As you know, I have on repeated occasions stressed the necessity of strengthening the prevention and quick-response capacity of the Special Procedures mandates. I am pleased that a "Quick Response Desk" has been created in the thematics team at the Activities and Programmes Branch. The Desk, to which all requests for urgent action will be channeled, will evaluate and analyze the information received and coordinate appropriate responses and action. With this new mechanism, the response time to requests for urgent appeals will be significantly reduced. It is my hope that beyond and in addition to this mechanism, my Office will soon be in a position to develop an operative emergency response capacity to address effectively serious and urgent country situations. The tragedies in Kosovo, Sierra Leone, and East Timor clearly illustrate the urgent need to develop our capacity to detect emerging crisis situations, with a view to preventing gross human rights violations. I believe that the Special Procedures mechanisms have a crucial role to play in this context, and I encourage you to give particular attention to this matter in the discharge of your mandates.

Distinguished colleagues, at this juncture I would like to move on to a couple of other important and topical issues which I would like to bring to your attention. Last month the Preparatory Committee for the World Conference against Racism, Racial Discrimination, Xenophobia and Related Intolerance met for its second session here in Geneva.

I know that many of you have been closely involved in these preparations and will be taking an active role during the conference itself. I am convinced that the Special Procedures system has a key role in the continuing fight against racism and xenophobia. I do encourage all of you to reflect on how you can be a part of the Durban process, bearing in mind the specifics of the mandates entrusted to you.

I am pleased to note that, for the second consecutive year, your agenda includes the issue of "Business and Human Rights." The challenge of creating a Global Compact of shared values and principles, proposed by the Secretary General to business leaders at the World Economic Forum in 1999, is a daunting one. One of the most remarkable changes in the human rights debate in recent years has been the increased recognition of the link between human rights and business. In follow up to the Secretary General's challenge, my Office is now actively providing information and awareness-training to encourage business leaders to include human rights considerations in corporate mission statements and ethical codes. At the same time, my Office is also exploring ways in which corporations may be held accountable for human rights abuses, through the United Nations organs and procedures. It is in this second context that the Special Procedures system can play an important role, and I am pleased that some of you have already begun to consider how private business actors and the results of their actions can be considered under your respective mandates.

Finally, I wish to thank you once again for the extremely valuable and challenging work you have all been carrying out in the discharge of your mandates over the past years. I assure you that I remain committed to doing what I can to help strengthen the Special Procedures as a proactive system which not only reacts to human rights violations but is also able to take early and effective action to prevent abuses from occurring. As I mentioned earlier, appropriate funding is a prerequisite and our efforts to reach a level commensurate to your needs is a priority of my Office.

I wish you the best of success with your meeting this week.

Statement by the High Commissioner for Human Rights to the Meeting of Chairpersons of the Treaty Bodies
Palais Wilson, Geneva, 18 June 2001

Distinguished Chairpersons, Ladies, and Gentlemen,

I would like to begin by warmly welcoming you all to the Palais Wilson for this important meeting. The conventional mechanisms are one of the main pillars of the human rights program and, as I have said on many occasions and as has been expressed in unequivocal terms in my Office's Mission Statement, OHCHR aims to provide these mechanisms with the highest-quality support. In addition to its value to the members of the treaty-monitoring bodies themselves, I feel that the Chairpersons meeting provides my Office with a useful opportunity to tap into the experts' concerns and evaluate how we can improve our supporting role. I am encouraged by the productive dialogue that has been created in recent years, and I am very much looking forward to continuing this exchange with a view to achieving further positive results.

In many respects the past year has been a milestone for the human rights system as a whole. OHCHR has been deeply involved in preparatory activities for the World Conference against Racism. The road to the World Conference against Racism has not been an easy one, which has made the contributions of independent bodies and experts especially important to its success. I am convinced that the treaty-monitoring bodies have a key role in the continuing fight against racism and xenophobia, and I do encourage all of you to further reflect on the extent of your contribution to the Durban process, bearing in mind the specifics of the mandates entrusted to you.

It is also worth noting that the Commission on Human Rights, at its recently concluded session, established new mandates on the right to food and the right to adequate housing, as well as a working group to examine the issue of a possible Optional Protocol to the Covenant on Economic, Social and Cultural Rights, calling also for the designation of an independent expert. Let me also recall that this year the international community celebrates the twenty-fifth anniversary of the entry into force of the two International Covenants.

Universal Ratification of Human Rights Treaties

Of considerable importance in the context of this meeting is the appeal for universal ratification, which has received top priority within the United Nations. Indeed, at the Millennium Summit in September 2000, the Secretary General himself launched a campaign to promote ratification of the core international treaties, including all of the human rights treaties that are or will be monitored by an expert body, as well as the corresponding Optional Protocols and optional complaints procedures. An unprecedented number of states signed the recently adopted Optional Protocols to the Convention on the Rights of the Child and the Convention on the Elimination of All Forms of Discrimination against Women, and by December the latter had been ratified by a sufficient number of states to enter into force, giving advocates of women's rights throughout the world a powerful new tool to help turn these rights into reality.

In March of this year, China ratified the International Covenant on Economic, Social and Cultural Rights, bringing protection under the Covenant to the people of the most populous country in the world. Also this past March, legal questions surrounding the status of Yugoslavia were finally settled when the government officially submitted instruments of succession to many of the treaties to which the former Yugoslavia was a party, including all of the principal international human rights treaties. The appeal for ratification of all the main human rights treaties will be repeated at the fifty-sixth session of the General Assembly, with a special focus on the treaties providing protection for the rights of women.

Chairpersons, milestones are valuable because they provide an occasion to pause and take stock of progress and achievements, as well as the challenges ahead of us. While still in their infancy, the topic of "effective functioning of the treaty bodies" weighed heavily on the international agenda. A quarter of a century later this question is still very much on the minds of all those who are working toward a culture of human rights.

Improving the Effectiveness of Human Rights Treaties

The treaty bodies work in a complex web of mechanisms, programs and activities. It is a privilege of my position that I have been able to meet with many members of the human rights community in all corners of the world, and I speak with confidence when I say that the treaty bodies represent beacons of hope for many whose voices may never be heard in Geneva. The essential role of the treaty bodies, as the stewards of the treaties, as authors of jurisprudence, and as international catalysts for national change, is beyond question. But also beyond question is the fact that the potential of the treaty system has not been maximized. A number of studies undertaken in recent years have pointed to deficiencies and bottlenecks, which have been the subject of many recommendations aimed at improving the implementation of the treaties and the functioning of the treaty bodies. The various problems linked to the lack of adequate visibility of the work of treaty bodies—the reporting "burden," backlog of reports, and delays in processing individual complaints, as well as the lack of follow-up—are well known. They have been the subjects of discussions by the treaty bodies, the meeting of chairpersons, an independent expert, the Commission on Human Rights, and an independent academic study of the treaty system finalized by Professor A. Bayefsky in April 2001.[12] I am pleased to report that a number of measures are already being implemented or envisaged by the Office to help assist in further improving the functioning of the treaty bodies.

Workload

The basic underlying problem is the extremely heavy workload facing the treaty bodies. Today, the six core treaties have been ratified by a cumulative 932 states parties; the optional complaints mechanisms have been ratified by a cumulative 192 states; and 136 states have accepted the inquiry procedures—and these figures are steadily rising. The consequences of the extraordinary success of the treaty system have been a large number of reports submitted by states parties and a large number of complaints submitted by individuals, with serious backlogs accumulating as a result. This has raised alarms, not least by the treaty bodies themselves.

While the resources issue continues to be addressed, and I will mention more about this issue later, we need to do better within the parameters of the current level of resources. Indeed, the treaty-monitoring bodies and the staff servicing them deserve credit for their efforts to do so. Among specific initiatives undertaken to improve support to treaty bodies, I would like to place special emphasis on the establishment of a Petitions Team. This team will deal in an integrated manner with the communications procedures.[13]

Despite the strict mandates that they fulfill, the treaty bodies have proven to be dynamic, ready to adapt to their expanding responsibilities and to the changing world. Yet states and NGOs alike are looking to the treaty bodies to work as parts of a coherent system to make their own tasks more practicable. Organizations that work with the treaty bodies are struggling to contribute in meaningful but economical ways. And there is far to go before the treaty system will truly be accessible to the individuals it strives to protect.

Working with Partners

That leads to another factor, which is the collaboration of partners of the treaty bodies. The General Assembly, in its resolutions on the effective implementation of the treaties, recognizes the importance of UN departments and agencies, non-governmental organizations, and other organizations in the work of treaty bodies. Endeavors to engage the entire United Nations system in human rights work, which is loosely referred to as the "mainstreaming of human rights," includes efforts aimed at fully engaging them in the work of the treaty bodies. In recent years the mainstreaming exercise has come alive. Human rights have been the subject of specific guidelines issued for UN country teams. A strong human rights component in the Common Country Assessment within the UN Development Assistance Framework, which is the basis for national-level programming, works to bridge the gap that was sometimes evident between the human rights and development work of the UN system.[14] Human rights training is being conducted within many agencies, particularly the main operational agencies, and a human rights component is now a standard part of UN peacekeeping operations. Also through bilateral memoranda of understanding, OHCHR has actively worked toward facilitating and enhancing collaboration between the United Nations system and the treaty bodies. We have advanced far in establishing the links in this process, and now we must work toward ensuring effective and efficient functioning of these links.

As one of the partners of the treaty bodies, OHCHR has integrated the work of the treaty bodies in its field activities and programs. The sharing of information, both in-house and with external partners, has improved dramatically in recent years, due in no small part to the efforts just mentioned as well as the great improvements made in our use of modern information technology. The meetings that you will take part in this week will, I am sure, be enlightening in this regard: one with the special mandate-holders of the Commission on Human Rights and one with the UN departments, agencies, nongovernmental organizations, and other partners of the treaty bodies on "national implementation of the recommendations of treaty bodies."

At the same time, we must improve the outreach to the UN system, to national human rights institutions, and to nongovernmental organizations, especially those at the national level. I have been encouraged by the emerging role of national human rights institutions and nongovernmental organizations with regard to follow-up to the recommendations of the treaty bodies, and in cases where compliance is weak, their efforts can be critical. Unfortunately, noncompliance is all too common. At last count, the number of overdue reports under the treaties exceeded one thousand. A challenge for your meeting will be to find practical ways to better engage national actors.

Resources

Finally, we are only too painfully aware that none of this can function properly without adequate resources. Appropriate funding is a prerequisite and, to reach a level commensurate to your needs, is our priority. Assessing the resource needs of the treaty bodies has become an ongoing activity in OHCHR. In this we have been much aided by the treaty bodies, which have identified priority areas urgently in need of additional resources. The response from donors, although failing to fully meet the level of resources sought, has nonetheless been healthy and has resulted in considerably improved support. Nonetheless, we continue to redouble our efforts so as to allow you all to continue with your important work and also to create a more efficient and effective system, able to accommodate the ever-increasing demands placed upon it as the number of ratifications increases.

While much progress has been made with regard to all four key areas I have mentioned, clearly, serious difficulties remain. The Office will continue to work with each of the treaty bodies and will help you implement the recommendations emanating from this meeting.

Chapter 16
Working with Countries and Regions

The United Nations engagement with countries and regions on human rights issues has grown considerably over time. Indeed, the surge in demand from countries for assistance on human rights during the early 1990s was one factor that led to the creation of the position of High Commissioner. It was envisaged that a single point of authority would better service the demand for what is termed "technical assistance."

Technical assistance and capacity building can range from legislative drafting, advice on ratification of international human rights treaties, national capacity building including the training of judges, lawyers, police, and others in international human rights standards, development of national action plans for human rights, and advice on the establishment and support for national human rights institutions. By 2001 the OHCHR had technical cooperation agreements and projects in some sixty countries.

Another form of engagement with countries has led to the establishment of human rights field missions or presences. These have mostly resulted from circumstances of threatened or actual conflict. The work of field offices is varied but can include monitoring human rights violations as well as standard technical cooperation activities. In 2001 there were field presences in some twenty countries.

From the vantage point of the United Nations the world presents itself as an arrangement of regional groupings of states as well as subregional groupings and individual states large and small. An important strategy begun by Mary Robinson was to seek to promote greater attention to human rights at all these levels. At the regional level she established partnerships through Memorandums of Understanding (MOUs) with existing regional bodies with a human rights mandate and with the UN Economic Commissions in each world region. In addition she built regional profile and capacity for the Office through the appointment of full-time regional representatives. The thinking behind these steps emerges from her speeches to regional bodies. She also pioneered cooperation between OHCHR and a range of countries, including Iran and most notably China, which she visited some seven times during her term as High Commissioner.

University of Teheran Center for Human Rights Studies
Lecture
Teheran, Iran, February 2001

Ladies and Gentlemen,

It is a pleasure and honor for me to be here today to talk about the activities that my Office is undertaking with a view to promoting and protecting human rights and to listen to ideas you may have which might help us better achieve our goal.

This is the second time I have visited Iran. I was here in February 1998 for a Workshop on Regional Arrangements for the Promotion and Protection of Human Rights in the Asia Pacific region. On this occasion I am delighted to have the opportunity to come to the University and speak openly to staff and students on issues of human rights.

The Office of the High Commissioner for Human Rights

Human rights have been an integral part of the United Nations from the Charter onward. This fact was given particular recognition through the creation of the Office of the High Commissioner for Human Rights after the Vienna World Conference on Human Rights of 1993. The authority on which I operate as High Commissioner is the wide range of human rights norms which have been put on the statute book since 1945. The Universal Declaration of Human Rights was a landmark document which has given rise to over sixty human rights treaties, declarations, covenants, and codes of conduct covering almost every conceivable aspect of the individual's rights. The treaties cover issues ranging from torture to racial discrimination, from the rights of the child to discrimination against women.

The role given to me as High Commissioner by the UN General Assembly is one of human rights leadership. This we seek to do in a strategic way based on the recognition that human rights are the responsibility of all United Nations agencies and bodies. Cooperation between my Office and other UN agencies in the field is being strengthened. In recent years human rights have been integrated more and more into the development process, for example through closer ties with the United Nations Development Programme. And the presence of human rights specialists is becoming a standard feature of peacekeeping and other UN postconflict operations.

My Office promotes and protects human rights in a variety of ways. One such is a program of Technical Cooperation which responds to requests from states for technical assistance in the promotion and protection of human rights. Technical cooperation projects might include training courses for police forces, prison officials, or the legal profession as well as advisory services for the incorporation of international human rights norms and standards into national legislation. Support is also provided for the establishment of national institutions and human rights documentation centers. Financed mainly by voluntary contributions, technical cooperation is an expanding area of the United Nations human rights program.

In fact, my Office undertook a needs-assessment mission to the Islamic Republic of Iran in 1999. The purpose of this kind of mission is to have an initial overall assessment to identify possible components of a technical co-operation project. During the mission to the Islamic Republic of Iran eleven project outlines were identified in the areas of administration of justice and law enforcement, national human rights capacity building, and human rights education. My Office will continue its discussions with the Government of the Islamic Republic of Iran on these issues.

Human Rights Violations and the Rule of Law

As High Commissioner, I also listen to the voices of victims of violations of human rights and try to increase their protection. I am sure you will not be surprised to hear that I have deep concerns about human rights violations here in Iran, which I am taking the opportunity to raise with the relevant authorities.

For example, I am very concerned with the Press Law passed last year resulting in a clampdown on freedom of expression and the arrest and imprisonment of a number of journalists. I followed the student protests during last year and the heavy reprisals.

My Office receives serious reports of arbitrary arrest, unfair trials, and torture and ill treatment here in Iran. I learn of the difficulties encountered by rights defenders and I note with concern the wide use of the death penalty. These are issues that are considered and addressed by the relevant human rights mechanisms, but today I have a welcome opportunity to hear your views and comments so that I can be better informed on the realities on the ground.

Human Rights Treaty Bodies

At the institutional level, my Office supports the committees established under five of the principal international human rights treaties. The main function of the committees, also referred to as treaty-monitoring bodies, is to monitor the implementation of the respective treaties by reviewing state party reports submitted under those treaties.

In the case of the Islamic Republic of Iran, your country has ratified four of those six major international instruments: the International Covenant on Civil and Political Right; the International Covenant on Economic, Social and Cultural Rights; the Convention against Racial Discrimination; and the Convention on the Rights of the Child. It is my hope that the Islamic Republic of Iran would consider the ratification of the other two, namely, the Convention on the Elimination of All Forms of Discrimination against Women (CEDAW) and the Convention against Torture and Other Cruel, Inhuman or Degrading Treatment or Punishment.[1] I have a vivid memory of the meeting I had during my visit in 1998 with representatives of NGOs, many of them women, who raised so many interesting questions about CEDAW and the other treaties and wanted more specific information.

Complying with its reporting obligations, the Islamic Republic of Iran has submitted reports for the consideration of the respective Committees. Most recently, in June 2000 the Committee on the Rights of the Child considered the initial report of the Islamic Republic of Iran and issued its concluding observations.[2]

I am glad to see that the Islamic Republic of Iran has already taken initiatives to implement one of the major recommendations of the Committee on the Rights of the Child, the establishment of a system of juvenile justice. It is my understanding that juvenile courts have been reestablished in the Islamic Republic of Iran, that the number of juvenile judges is growing, and that provisions are made under the Third Five Year Development Plan for Juvenile Correction and Rehabilitation Centers to be created in all provinces. Judges have begun issuing alternative sanctions, such as sentencing young offenders to learn a vocation or to stay at home under the supervision of his or her parents. It is also encouraging to hear that the Judiciary of the Islamic Republic of Iran has agreed to set up a joint committee with UNICEF with the aim of drafting a Juvenile Code by the end of 2001.[3]

The Commission on Human Rights is currently monitoring the situation of human rights in fifteen countries, among them, as you probably know, the Islamic Republic of Iran. Mr. Maurice Copithorne, from Canada, reports to the Commission on Human Rights and the General Assembly on the situation of human rights in the Islamic Republic of Iran in his capacity as Special Representative of the Commission on Human Rights. His reports are public and are the basis for the discussions that take place at the Commission on Human Rights and the General Assembly.[4] Unfortunately, and unlike most of the other holders of country mandates, the Special Representative on the Islamic Republic of Iran has not been allowed to visit your country in recent years. I say "unfortunately," because I am convinced that a visit by him would contribute to a better understanding of the human rights situation in the Islamic Republic of Iran and would open the door to broader cooperation between your country and the United Nations, including my Office.

Anyone may bring a human rights problem to the attention of the United Nations, and thousands of people around the world do so every year. Three of the treaty bodies—the Human Rights Committee, the Committee against Torture, and the Committee on the Elimination of Racial Discrimination—accept and render views on individual complaints of human rights violations by those states parties which have ratified or have made a declaration recognizing the competence of the relevant treaty-monitoring body to receive and consider complaints. The Islamic Republic of Iran has not yet made such declarations. But complaints may also be directed to the thematic and country mandates of the Commission on Human Rights to which I referred previously.

I would like to emphasize that all these approaches to the promotion and protection of human rights—the provision of technical cooperation, the servicing of the human rights treaty bodies, and the servicing of the Special Procedures of the Commission on Human Rights—are interlinked and mutually reinforcing. Technical cooperation therefore goes hand in hand with the recommendations made by the treaty bodies in their examination of the state party reports, as well as the recommendations of the Special Procedures of the Commission on Human Rights.

Universality of Human Rights

At the Vienna World Conference on human rights, states reaffirmed the universality and indivisibility of human rights, as well as their commitment to the promotion and protection of those rights. In 1998, on the occasion of the fiftieth anniversary of the Universal Declaration of Human Rights, the Foreign Minister of the Islamic Republic of Iran invited my Office to facilitate a process of preparing Islamic commentaries on the Universal Declaration. As a result, my Office, in cooperation with the Organization of the Islamic Conference, held a Symposium on Islamic Perspectives on the Universal Declaration of Human Rights.[5] A distinguished group of Muslim experts were offered the opportunity to present research which expounded Islamic perspectives on human rights and recalled the contributions of Islam to the laying of the foundations of these rights. At that Symposium I learned that Islamic concern with human dignity is old; it goes back to the very beginning, but it is also dynamic. I learned that the principles of Islam relating to human dignity and social solidarity are a valuable resource from which to face the human rights challenges of today. The Islamic Republic of Iran, with its rich and ancient culture and history, can play a major role in this regard.

I welcome the commitment made by the Government of the Islamic Republic of Iran to promote respect for the rule of law, and I was encouraged by the commitment of the Iranian people to the democratic process, exemplified in the broad participation in the parliamentary elections held last year. I am aware of the difficulties and challenges ahead. It is my strong belief that in our globalized world only those countries that would let their citizens freely express themselves will be capable of preserving their identity. Only freethinking citizens, exchanging their views in an open environment, will be able to preserve a national identity capable of facing the challenges of the modern world.

Thank you for your attention. I am now open to your questions or comments.

"Punishment of Minor Crimes"
Workshop
Beijing, China, 26–27 February 2001

Excellencies, Ladies, and Gentlemen,

I am glad to return to Beijing again to address the opening session of this workshop on the theme of "Punishment of Minor Crimes." This workshop marks the first step in the implementation of the Memorandum of Understanding (MOU) on technical cooperation between my Office and the Government of the People's Republic of China.

The Memorandum of Understanding was signed on 20 November 2000. It is the expression of both parties' commitment to strengthening China's involvement in international cooperation, with the aim of improving the promotion and protection of human rights in China through, inter alia, the ratification and implementation of international human rights treaties. The MOU is not an end in itself. Its success will be judged by the practical results achieved. We must see it as the start of a qualitatively different process of cooperation between China and my Office in the field of human rights, aimed at facilitating the process of harmonization of laws and practices with international human rights standards.

Let me say a few words at the outset about international human rights norms and standards. As the Vienna Declaration of the World Conference on Human Rights 1993 state,: "Human rights and fundamental freedoms are the birthright of all human beings." These rights are distilled in an impressive body of international law as "a common standard of achievement for all peoples and all nations," in the language of the Universal Declaration of Human Rights. The rights and freedoms set forth in the Universal Declaration, the two covenants, and the other human rights treaties are to be enjoyed by all without distinction of any kind, whether of race, color, sex, language, religion, political or other opinion, national or social status, property, birth, or other status.

The task which all countries face is to implement international human rights standards and reflect them in laws and practices. In my role as United Nations High Commissioner for Human Rights, I have a particular responsibility to foster a shared commitment at the international level to further the protection and promotion of human rights and to see that commitment translated into implementation at the national level. Almost by definition, and certainly according to the Charter, the United Nations exists to promote human rights. My mandate calls on me to enhance international cooperation for the promotion and protection of human rights and to coordinate human rights promotion and protection activities throughout the United Nations system.

It is in this context that I signed the MOU on technical cooperation with China. In the course of this year, as part of the first phase of implementation of the MOU, there will be activities in the areas of human rights education, human rights and police, and punishment of minor crimes.

This workshop provides an opportunity to demonstrate the spirit of the Memorandum of Understanding in a practical way. We are meeting to share legal expertise, best practices, and comparative analysis. There is a well-known Chinese expression: "let hundreds of schools of thought flourish." In this spirit, we have gathered international experts from various countries. They are here to share with their Chinese colleagues their knowledge and experience.

I met the international and Chinese experts yesterday, and I have read the papers prepared by the international experts. The administration of justice is of the highest importance, as is evidenced by the fact that it is the subject of so many human rights standards and procedures. Indeed, it can be said that the way in which justice is administered is a key benchmark of a country's commitment to human rights. This is one of the four key areas of cooperation mentioned in the MOU.

Without prejudice to the conclusions of the workshop, I would like to share some views with you.

The objective of looking at the issue of punishment of minor crimes is to seek to identify possible ways and means of assisting China to develop law and practice in this area that are in keeping with international human rights standards. In 1998 China signed the International Covenant on Civil and Political Rights, and as part of the ratification process it will be examining in detail the requirements of articles 9 and 14 of the Covenant, which are of particular relevance to this workshop.

Punishment of minor crimes touches upon issues that are of acute concern to everyone, especially the issue of reeducation through labor. The human rights implications of the practice of administrative detention have been of major concern to my Office and to the UN's human rights mechanisms. I would refer, for example, to the views which the UN Committee against Torture gave in May 2000 on the third periodic report submitted by China. After reviewing the report, the Committee against Torture recommended that China abolish all forms of administrative detention.[6] I would also recall the view of the UN Working Group on Arbitrary Detention which deemed reeducation through labor "inherently arbitrary."[7]

The concept and practice of reeducation through labor have a long history in China. But attitudes toward the administration of justice have changed both in the world at large and here in China too. I have noticed during my visits to China the changes that are taking place every day in this country. I note with great interest your efforts to strengthen the rule of law and to build up a culture of respect for the rule of law. I can assure you of my support in this. In that context, I believe that a serious review leading to the abolition of the practice of reeducation through labor is justified. The concept of using forced labor as a punishment is against the accepted international human rights principles embodied in many international instruments. At the same time, a significant indicator of a society in which the rule of law is fully and completely respected is that citizens should be free from the threat of arbitrary detention.

China can illustrate its commitment to human rights by seriously reviewing the issue and by ensuring that its law and practices meet international standards. I understand that the issue of reeducation through labor is currently under review by the National People's Congress, particularly to ensure conformity with the Laws on Administrative Punishment and on Legislation adopted in 1996 and 2000 respectively. I hope that this workshop can contribute to the process of that review and ensure that it also conforms with the international human rights standards China has committed itself to abide by. I shall follow this process with great interest.

I would encourage the participants in this workshop to take an open-minded approach to this very timely discussion. It is important to have such a valuable opportunity to share views and practices. It is of more importance that everyone benefits from the experience. We share with our Chinese partners the wish to see concrete results from this dialogue.

I am aware that the time available for the workshop is limited—a day and a half. Three aspects of the topic will be discussed: the concept of punishment of minor crimes comparative studies and practices in regard to punishment of minor crimes in various legal systems; and protection of human rights in the context of punishment of minor crimes. There is a lot to discuss, but intensive work during the time at our disposal can bring tangible results.

My concerns focus on four areas: the fact that there is no judicial review or a process to review evidence and to allow for the presentation of a defense; the vagueness of the offenses punishable by reeducation though labor; the severity of punishment, even in comparison with criminal punishment; and the fact that local governments incorporate reeducation through labor in local regulations.

I said that I see the workshop as the start of a process of deepening dialogue and cooperation under the auspices of the Memorandum of Understanding. One of the outcomes I would welcome is that the discussions begun at this workshop be carried forward and built on. There is a lot of expertise present here today, and we should make use of that fact both for our present deliberations and in a follow-up process for the future. My Office will be happy to develop such a follow-up on issues and initiatives that emerge from the workshop. One such idea is that international and national experts will continue to follow the process closely—both the evolution of legislation in the National People's Congress and the daily practice of reeducation through labor. I am already considering the convening of a follow-up meeting with these experts in Geneva next month. I hope that through our joint efforts we can achieve our common objective: to promote and protect human rights.

I wish all of us a successful workshop, and I thank the Ministry of Foreign Affairs for the very efficient preparations.

"Human Rights Activities in the Field"
Spanish Diplomatic School, Madrid, Spain, 10 January 2000

Ladies and Gentlemen,

It is a pleasure and honor for me to be here today to talk about the activities that my Office is undertaking with a view to promoting and protecting human rights, and to listen to ideas you may have which might help us better achieve our goal.

I propose to focus on the subject of human rights field presences. The concept is relatively recent, but already field presences form an important part of the work of the Office of the High Commissioner for Human Rights and of other human rights organizations.

From an Office with most of its activities concentrated in Geneva, we have in recent years expanded considerably by establishing presences in each of the continents. By doing this, we have managed to get closer to our direct beneficiaries and consequently to have a greater impact. The establishment of field offices has also allowed us to improve our assessment of the human rights situation in a given country and hence to understand the particular needs and difficulties. This direct and continuous assessment facilitates the identification of ways whereby we can provide the support for national capacity building required in a country.

The History of Field Presences

The first human rights field presence was established in Zagreb in 1992. Two human rights officers were deployed with a mandate to provide support to the Special Rapporteur on Human Rights in the former Yugoslavia, following a recommendation of the Commission on Human Rights. In 1993 a small office was set up in Guatemala to assist the expert named by the Commission on Human Rights. A year later a fully fledged office was established in Cambodia to take over the human rights unit of the UN electoral mission in that country on the expiry of its mandate.

The 1994 genocide in Rwanda saw the biggest challenge to date to my Office. Responding to a call of the Commission on Human Rights, which was deeply concerned at the grave violations that had taken place in Rwanda, agreement was reached by my predecessor with the Government of Rwanda to set up a large human rights operation in that devastated country.

There has been a steady increase in the Office's field activities since then. From one small field presence in 1992, we can now count twenty-three field presences worldwide, the majority of them established in the African continent.

When do we establish a field presence? Why is there a field presence in a given country and not in others? What are the factors that determine the opening of a field presence?

The origins of field presences are in fact multiple. A field presence may be set up following a resolution of the Commission on Human Rights (for example, in Cambodia and the former Yugoslavia), or a resolution of the Security Council (for example, in Abkhazia-Georgia), or as a result of specific agreements with the government concerned (for example, in Colombia and Malawi). In some situations an office has been established as a response to an ongoing human rights emergency. Such was the case, for example, in Rwanda after the genocide. In other cases personnel from my Office form part of a wider UN involvement by which our expertise can combine and complement that of other UN partners, as, for example, in Angola, Sierra Leone and Liberia. We also have cooperative arrangements with other regional organizations such as the Organisation for Security and Cooperations in Europe (for example, regarding Abkhazia-Georgia) through wich each organization can bring added value for the benefit of the people of the host country.

The Mandate of Field Presences

Field presences may have a mandate to monitor the human rights situation in a given country. The monitoring of breaches of international humanitarian law might also be part of their mandate. This monitoring will lead to interventions by human rights officers vis-à-vis the local authorities with a view to preventing and protecting human rights in a given context. This should not be seen as substituting for the role of the local authorities. Far from that: our goal is to prevent human rights abuses and to encourage governmental authorities, the judiciary, and law enforcement officials to apply human rights standards and to guarantee the rule of law.

Field presences often have a monitoring mandate combined with one of providing technical assistance. In fact, both mandates are complementary as monitoring allows a better assessment of the country needs for the purposes of providing technical assistance. Also, through the provision of technical assistance, there is a constant and regular contact with the beneficiaries, resulting in a better assessment of the situation on the ground. Examples of field presences with this double mandate are our offices in Abkhazia-Georgia, Bosnia-Herzegovina, Burundi, Colombia, Croatia and the Democratic Republic of the Congo.

There are also field presences which have an exclusive technical cooperation mandate. Such is the case for our offices in Gaza, Guatemala, El Salvador, Indonesia, Malawi, Mongolia, and South Africa. The primary objective is to strengthen national capacities through human-rights-awareness programs and providing specific advice on technical issues according to the country's specific needs.

The activities undertaken by field offices are multiple: they can include the monitoring of and reporting on human rights violations and/or breaches of international humanitarian law; training of law enforcement officials including police, armed forces, and prison personnel; training of judges, lawyers, teachers, and community leaders; advice on curricula with a view to ensuring proper human rights education at all levels; trial monitoring; advice on legislation; human-rights-promotion- and -awareness campaigns; strengthening of national capacity, including direct assistance to the judiciary, national institutions, nongovernmental organizations, and civil society; monitoring displacement while promoting basic human rights standards, in particular the UN Guiding Principles on Internal Displacement;[8] and providing advice on National Plans of Action on Human Rights and National Plans of Education on Human Rights as recommended by the World Conference on Human Rights in 1993. While carrying out these activities, field offices take due consideration of the recommendations made by the treaty bodies and special mechanisms of the Commission on Human Rights with a view to facilitating their implementation.

The Colombian Office of the High Commissioner for Human Rights

Perhaps the best way of illustrating what a field presence does is to give a concrete example. Our Office in Colombia is a good case to mention as it has a broad mandate and illustrates the complementarity between monitoring and technical cooperation. Some of you may already be familiar with the activities of our Bogotá office as it was formerly headed by a distinguished Spanish diplomat, Ambassador Almudena Mazarrasa. I was deeply impressed by her commitment, and that of her colleagues, when I visited Colombia in October 1998. I would like to take this opportunity to pay tribute to the valuable support that the Spanish Government has given and continues to give to our field office in Colombia and to the work of my Office generally, and to pay tribute to the Spanish Permanent Representative in Geneva and the staff of his Mission for their support.

The office in Colombia was created following a recommendation by the Commission on Human Rights and on the invitation of the President of Colombia. Agreement on the mandate was reached in November 1996, and the first human rights officers were deployed in April 1997. The Office has a mandate to monitor the human rights situation with a view to advising the Colombian authorities on the formulation and implementation of policies, programs, and measures to promote and protect human rights. Its constant monitoring through regular visits to the field and contacts with the relevant authorities, the different parties to the conflict, the NGO community, the church, the displaced, and representatives of civil society allow the Office to have an understanding of the highly complex situation that Colombians face in their day-to-day lives. The Office, through its interventions with the authorities, exercises its preventive function by alerting them to imminent massacres or displacements of people.

Efforts are currently being undertaken to set up an alert system that will increase the Colombian authorities' capacity to intervene in time to prevent human rights violations. On several occasions the Office has been invited to present views concerning national legislation. In line with our basic premise of not seeking to substitute the responsibilities of the local authorities but to empower them by providing the relevant tools and assistance, the Office has concluded six agreements with key local authorities. These agreements aim at, for example, assisting the government to elaborate a National Plan of Action on Human Rights; improving the system of reception of complaints of the Office of the Ombudsperson; assisting the Office of the Public Prosecutor in improving the system for protection of witnesses and victims of human rights violations; the design of a computerized system within the National University to monitor the implementation of the international recommendations made by the different UN human rights mechanisms; and assisting in the elaboration of a human rights curriculum for the Judiciary School. These are just a few examples of what the Colombia Office does in terms of technical cooperation. My Office reports annually to the Commission on Human Rights on the work of the Colombia office.[9]

Development of Field Presences and Cooperation with Other UN Agencies and International Organizations

My Office's development of field presences has brought a number of challenges that we are learning to face step by step. One of our objectives is to work closely with other actors in the field of human rights, some of whom have longer experience in the field. We base our approach on an understanding of each other's mandates, capacities, and limitations. I believe we have made considerable progress in this respect.

The Office seeks to maintain contacts with all the main actors: with governments, opposition groups, nongovernmental organizations, the media, UN agencies, regional organizations, the International Committee of the Red Cross, the donor community, and above all with the host society, who is our main beneficiary. It is only through working with all the actors in a spirit of constructive dialogue and with transparency and respect for each other's mandates that we have a chance to succeed.

In this connection, my Office has concluded several Memorandums of Understanding with other United Nations partners with a view to enhancing cooperation both at headquarters and field level. Examples of this are the Memorandum of Understanding with the United Nations Development Programme and the Department of Peacekeeping Operations, with whom we have joint field operations. With UNESCO under the leadership of

Francisco Mayor, a joint letter was sent to governments with a view to enhancing efforts in the area of human rights education programs. In our office in El Salvador, for example, a National Committee for Human Rights Education composed of key national authorities has been established with a view to elaborating and implementing a National Plan of Action for Human Rights Education. Representatives of the civil society and the NGO community as well as UNESCO and UNICEF will be providing support to the Committee in the development of the Plan.

My Office continuously strives to improve the capacity of and support for field presences. We have introduced a Code of Conduct for every staff member working for our Office. We have established a project approach to all field presences with a view to encouraging serious strategic planning before going to the field. Field presences are subject to periodic evaluations as well as to internal and external auditing exercises. We have established an internal field presence task force to cope with urgent matters related to our field activities. Annual heads of field presences meetings take place in Geneva with a view to encouraging an exchange of best practices among the directors of our field offices and enhancing the dialogue between the field and headquarters. The Methodology Team at headquarters has developed a number of training manuals and guidelines with a view to giving proper, relevant tools to our officers before deployment; a systematic briefing and debriefing mechanism for all field human rights officers has been put in place. A committee for the recruitment of staff for field assignments has been established with a view to encouraging transparency in the selection process.

We are also conscious of the dangers involved in working in certain environments, notably in conflict situations or where the security situation is still precarious. The nature of our work, that of highlighting human rights violations, increases our vulnerability. I attach the greatest importance to the security of our staff, and in that connection appropriate security measures are taken before, during, and after the existence of any field operation. And it is vitally important that appropriate measures are taken to ensure that once we leave a certain country the lives of those who had particular contacts with us are not put at risk.

Field presences are costly, and funding is always an issue. All of our field presences except for the Office in Cambodia depend on extrabudgetary funding, that is, on voluntary contributions by member states. Last year, with a view to enhancing our capacity to attract contributions, my Office recruited a professional fund-raiser. Particular efforts have been undertaken to establish a system for approaching donors in a professional and transparent manner. Our first annual appeal will take place at the end of this month. I hope that governments, including Spain, will respond generously to our needs.

Field presences are not meant to stay forever in a given country. Our main goal is, in fact, to strengthen national capacity while providing the appropriate tools to improve the human rights situation. Therefore, when planning the setting up of a field presence, we should already be thinking of an exit strategy for leaving behind tangible national capacities able to develop.

Regional Cooperation

I mentioned at the beginning of my speech that my Office was examining ways to better promote and protect human rights. A strategy to which I attach particular importance is regional cooperation. We have taken a number of steps to implement regional strategies as recommended in the Vienna Declaration and Programme of Action of 1993. It was in Teheran in 1998 that a regional framework was adopted for the Asia Pacific region, bringing together representatives of governments, national institutions, and nongovernmental organizations with a view to launching a regional strategy to better promote and protect human rights. Four main pillars were considered: national plans of action; strengthening national capacity; human rights education; and economic, social, and cultural rights and the right to development. Since the Teheran meeting, several other regional meetings touching upon specific human rights matters have taken place, allowing participants to share their national experiences and to identify best practices. In each of the meetings, participants have been reporting on progress made in their respective countries since their last gathering. My Office has been servicing each of these meetings and will continue to provide technical assistance upon request of governments.

Over a month ago my Office launched a similar exercise for the Latin American and Caribbean region. The event took place in Quito, Ecuador, resulting in the adoption by consensus of relevant conclusions together with a regional framework for technical cooperation activities in that region. At this meeting I announced the appointment of my regional adviser for the Latin American and Caribbean region, former President of Chile Patricio Aylwin. Similar appointments of highly qualified regional human rights experts are being made for the other regions too.

These efforts aim at protecting and promoting human rights through the implementation of activities whether these are at a regional, subregional, or national level. To carry out these activities in the field, appropriate partnerships need to be established with key regional, subregional, or national actors. Our goal is to translate human rights standards and norms into reality by taking a very practical approach, that of empowering people and building on national capacities. To achieve this goal, we have realized that our message can be best heard if we move closer to such realities.

As diplomats you may find yourselves confronted with difficult situations you may be exposed to human rights abuses or faced with situations of conflict. We might be working in a given country where it is important for us to seek your support whether political, financial, or to bring assistance to human rights victims, for example. We will most probably meet at international conferences, meetings, or at the Commission on Human Rights. Your statements during such events can contribute to improving the human rights situation in a given country. There is a lot you can do to bring about positive change. My Office will continue in its efforts to promote and protect human rights. I am confident that you will join us in this difficult but challenging and rewarding task.

Thank you.

Celebrating the Anniversary of the Pact of San José
National Theatre, San José, Costa Rica, 22 November 1999

Secretary General of the Organization of American States, President of Costa Rica, Ladies, and Gentlemen,

It is a great honor for me, as United Nations High Commissioner for Human Rights and on behalf of the Secretary General of the United Nations, Mr. Kofi Annan, who is not able to be here today due to other commitments, to participate in the commemoration of the anniversaries of the Inter-American Commission and the Inter-American Court of Human Rights. This commemoration marks the anniversaries of two important bodies but also provides an opportunity to evaluate the realization of all human rights by all in this region and to further reinforce the ideal of establishing an effective regional human rights protection system.

During the past decades the Inter-American system of human rights protection has developed rapidly. It has been reinforced by the progress of democratization in countries of the region, including an increased awareness of common values and the need for further solidarity among states.

The Inter-American Commission on Human Rights has pioneered new approaches for conducting visits to countries and fact-finding generally. The Inter-American Court of Human Rights has also charted new paths in developing innovative jurisprudence that has helped to give meaning to the concept of the protection of human rights.

These positive developments reflect a strengthening of regional human rights norms. The establishment of a regional system is reflected in the work of the supervisory organs, their jurisprudence, their decisions, and their opinions. This progress is the result of the conviction and the commitment of those individuals, many of whom are here today, who have helped the system to expand and who continue to struggle to find a balance between the different entities comprising the system as well as to ensure its effective functioning.

It is also the result of the ideals of thousands of human rights defenders from this and other regions, and from members of the international community, who have been on the front line of the campaign against human rights violations. Their efforts too often continue to make them targets of government repression, and it is therefore our obligation to ensure that states take all necessary measures to guarantee their life and dignity. The adoption, after years of discussions, of the United Nations Declaration of Human Rights Defenders has marked an initial step in the definition of common principles for the respect of their rights. It remains our challenge to ensure that these principles are applied as the minimum guarantees for the valuable work of human rights defenders everywhere.

The adoption on 17 July 1998 of the Rome Statute of the International Criminal Court represented a milestone in international criminal law. We all hope that the establishment of the Court, which we wholeheartedly support, will effectively combat the problem of impunity, a problem that is not unknown in this region.

The idea behind the Rome Statute is to establish a standing court capable of acting on a complementary basis to the domestic organs of a state party where the state may be unwilling or unable to prosecute crimes under international law.

I strongly urge states to sign and ratify the Statute and, where necessary, to implement relevant domestic law so that the International Criminal Court can soon become a reality. There could be no clearer way of sending the message that the international community will not allow impunity in cases of crimes against humanity.

Many types of human rights violations still need to be addressed. It is vital that we continue to work toward the development of international and regional norms and the strengthening of effective international, regional, and national systems to protect persons against all forms of human rights violations.

Putting in place preventive mechanisms at the national level should be part of our early action. Strategies and programs to combat violations suffered by victims of domestic violence, by migrant workers, by victims of trafficking, by children forced into prostitution and pornography, and by refugees and displaced persons are at the core of the UN human rights program. Among preventive measures that I strongly support are the efforts of member states towards the establishment of independent, pluralistic, and effective national institutions for the protection and promotion of human rights.

In this region, I am aware that many states have established such institutions, called differently according to their national realities—*Defensorias del Pueblo*, National Human Rights Commissions, *Procuradurias de Derechos Humanos*, etc. I will meet with the Heads of these institutions of the region next week in Quito, Ecuador, where I will be attending a regional seminar organized by my Office to promote dialogue with member states with regard to technical cooperation. National human rights policies, national capacities, human rights education and training, as well as the right to development, enjoyment of economic and social rights, and other human rights issues—all of these topics will be discussed at the Quito meeting.

As the United Nations High Commissioner for Human Rights, I am committed to the enhancement of the effectiveness of the United Nations human rights machinery and to assisting member states to build national and regional capacities to promote and protect human rights.

Regional and subregional cooperation are powerful preventive forces. They enable governments to build on the experiences and best practices of countries in their region, to cooperate with neighbors and to use available resources in the most efficient way. And perhaps the greatest advantage of the regional approach is the sense of ownership and empowerment that it confers.

The International Bill of Human Rights, comprising the Universal Declaration of Human Rights and the United Nations Covenants on Civil and Political Rights and Economic, Social and Cultural Rights, serves as the global framework in which all regional and national systems for the protection of human rights function.

The United Nations recognizes the importance of regional systems and is strongly supportive of their work. My Office is also actively engaged in promoting the establishment of suitable regional systems of human rights protection such as, for example, in the Asia Pacific region. I am convinced that the achievement of international solutions can benefit from common regional goals, solidarity among countries of a particular region, similarity of national problems, and the awareness of common interests.

In the European system, the adoption of the European Convention for the Protection of Human Rights and Fundamental Freedoms by the Council of Europe in 1950 marked a particular step forward for international protection of human rights. Having established the first international complaints procedure and the first international court for the determination of human rights matters, the Council of Europe supports the most developed of the three regional systems that exist today. It nevertheless has to face the big challenge of effectively balancing its work and actions alongside the other major mechanisms of the European Union and the Organization for Security and Cooperation in Europe.

Regional cooperation in Africa is the most recently established system, with only twelve years of experience. The African system will continue to benefit from the experience of the European and the Inter-American systems. My Office is currently supporting the work of the African Commission on Human Rights and Peoples' Rights and will continue to do so.

As for the regional Inter-American system of human rights protection, whose anniversary we are celebrating here today, I have already had the opportunity earlier in my address to say how highly I regard its original and innovative character.

Our ultimate goal, to prevent human rights abuses and to enjoy a universal culture of respect for human rights, remains for all of us, as human rights advocates, a dream that is still to become reality.

I am very pleased to announce that today Dr. Pedro Nikken, the President of the Inter-American Institute of Human Rights, and I have signed a memorandum of cooperation to strengthen our initiatives on human rights promotion in the region, and I would welcome a closer cooperation between my Office and the Inter-American institutions, in particular a closer cooperation between our respective protection mechanisms in order to enhance their effectiveness and the handling of individual communications.

Let me conclude by expressing my sincere appreciation to the Government of Costa Rica for having organized this impressive event and for its support for the human rights program of the United Nations.

"Human Rights Challenges in the Asia Pacific Region"
Address at the Tenth Workshop on Regional Cooperation for the Promotion and Protection of Human Rights in the Asia Pacific Region
Beirut, Lebanon, 4–6 March 2002

Excellencies, Distinguished Representatives, Ladies, and Gentlemen,

It is a pleasure and an honor to address once again the annual Asia Pacific Workshop on Regional Cooperation for the Promotion and Protection of Human Rights. I want to warmly thank the Government of Lebanon and the UN Economic and Social Commission for West Asia (ESCWA) for their excellent cooperation in the organization of the workshop. It is especially important for me to be here today after the signing of the Memorandum of Intent between my Office and ESCWA, which has opened the door for the appointment of my two regional representatives here in Beirut alongside our representative already based in Bangkok at the Economic and Social Council for Asia Pacific (ESCAP). I see this workshop as the beginning of a fruitful cooperation with these regional economic and social commissions which will add another positive element in the step-by-step, building blocks approach so familiar to the countries of this vast and diverse region.

I am pleased that my recently appointed regional representatives for the ESCAP and ESCWA regions are here with me today. They will work in tandem with my honorary regional adviser, Mr. Justice Bhagwati, in advising on implementation of the program of action.

It might be helpful at the outset if I explain how I see the role of the regional representatives. We are in the process of appointing such representatives in all regions. Their role in the Asia Pacific, as in other regions, is to enhance OHCHR capacity to be of service and to assist you, the member states. Experience has taught our office, as is the case with other UN agencies, that presence in the region will help us in our work. It will enable us to be more efficient and more effective in responding to requests for advice. And it will ensure that we remain conscious of the need to fulfill our commitments to follow up any activities agreed upon under the Teheran Framework.[10] It is for these reasons that I have appointed regional representatives for the ESCAP and ESCWA regions. I am confident that our capacity to serve your needs will be improved and we will be better able to cooperate in concrete steps to promote and protect human rights. The regional representatives will also work closely with the UN country teams in order to ensure that a human rights perspective becomes part of the work they do, in keeping with their own respective mandates.

As a further preliminary matter, I should note that this annual Asia Pacific workshop has become a key forum for sharing human rights initiatives in the region and for enhancing regional cooperation in the field of human rights.

Human Rights Challenges in Asia Pacific and the Teheran Framework

This is a vast and vibrant region—or really six regions in one—with a rich diversity of cultures, languages, history, and ways of life. Yet it also shares many common challenges. For the poor, the overwhelming reality of their lives is the indignity of being denied almost all their rights—to food, water, health, education, housing, personal security, justice, and equality. Globalization and trade liberalization have brought wealth to many, but the gap between rich and poor—rich and poor countries, and rich and poor people within countries—is increasing. The fruits of development are not being enjoyed by all, and it is often marginalized groups who bear the brunt—women, children, minority and ethnic groups, migrants and migrant workers, indigenous people.

The Teheran Framework and its four pillars reflect a unique consensus. They are a statement by all countries in this region that human rights are a guiding light in tackling many of these challenges. They are a statement that solutions are more likely to be found if Asia Pacific states work collectively in thought and action. I am here because I share that commitment. I am here because I believe that respect for the rights set out in the Universal Declaration of Human Rights—all rights without hierarchy or preference—are necessary to achieve effective development and for all people to enjoy the benefits of globalization. As I have said before: "Poverty eradication without empowerment is unsustainable. Social integration without minority rights is unimaginable. Gender equality without women's rights is illusory. Full employment without workers' rights may be no more than a promise of sweatshops, exploitation and slavery. The logic of human rights in development is inescapable."

The phenomenon of terrorism sets many challenges to the interlinked purposes of the United Nations: international peace and security, human rights, human development, and the rule of international law. These challenges are not new, but the September 11 terrorist attacks in the United States reverberated around the world and shocked humanity.

The world has changed in many ways since September 11. But what has not changed is that a human rights approach to development is also essential in tackling the root causes of terrorism and conflict. If human rights are respected, if basic education, housing, and health care are secure, if there is freedom from personal violence and freedom for men and women to earn their living and raise their families, not only are human rights violations prevented, but conflict, terrorism, and war also can be prevented. Since September 11 I have also reiterated that it is possible to have a robust and effective action against terrorism within a commitment to upholding domestic and international standards of human rights protection. International human rights law already balances national security and respect for human rights.

Human relationships are at the heart of development. I therefore encourage you to reaffirm here in Beirut the commitment of Asia Pacific states to implement the Durban Programme of Action and to integrate its goals into all four pillars of the Framework. Fighting racism and xenophobia should be an integral part of national human rights plans of action. It should be taught in schools to build a long-term culture of human rights, it should be a plank in the strategies of national rights institutions, and it is often both a symptom and a cause of poverty.

I sincerely hope that programs under the four pillars of the Framework will help states to tackle the human rights challenges in this region. They should help to build national capacity in government and civil society. And they should strengthen institutions, such as the justice system, that are vital for countries going through a transition to democracy or which are emerging from conflict and seeking to prevent a return to cycles of violence.

Common Foundations—Treaties and Subregional Mechanisms

The Asia Pacific framework was inspired by a desire to build common human rights foundations in the region and to find ways to work together across borders and subregions. I would encourage you in two directions.

First, international human rights treaties and standards provide a common road map to tackle together the challenges I described earlier. I am encouraged that in the last two years fifty-one human rights treaties have been signed or ratified by twenty-one different states in this region. I urge you to contribute to the universal ratification of the six main human rights treaties by end 2003, a target which the Secretary General and I set at the Millennium Summit. Would it not be a powerful human rights message from Asia Pacific if by next year's meeting every state here had ratified at least two more core human rights treaties?

There is a further human rights convention I wish to mention. It is the International Convention on the Protection of the Rights of Migrant Workers and Their Families. This was adopted in 1990. Now only one more ratification is necessary for it to come into force.[11] Will one of the states in this room give life to a convention that protects a group so especially vulnerable in this globalized world? I look forward to a positive response to my challenge.

The obligation of states parties under some of the treaties to prepare reports for a treaty body is time-consuming. But it can also be a rich experience that brings together government and civil society in understanding human rights problems and potential solutions. My Office is ready to provide training and advice to any government that is serious about ratifying human rights treaties and reporting properly to the treaty bodies.

Second, I hope that every year you will take another step toward creating your own, more permanent regional or subregional human rights arrangement. I am aware of the official dialogue between ASEAN and the civil society Working Group for an ASEAN Human Rights Mechanism, on the proposal for an ASEAN human rights commission.[12] I look forward to government and NGO participants here in Beirut briefing us further on recent progress on this and similar initiatives. The Asia Pacific Forum of National Human Rights Institutions, whose members are well represented here, is an excellent example of a regional network which can enhance individual capacities and provide the space for an effective sharing of best practices.[13]

Tenth Workshop—Taking Stock

We look back on ten years of workshops and four years of the Teheran Framework. You have created a unique forum in which states have been able to come together to discuss human rights in their own region in a way that did not occur in the past. This landmark gathering is a good time to take stock, to assess the impact of our work, and to strengthen the Framework. I wish to make suggestions in four areas.

First, step-by-step change takes time, often years. I believe that this Framework should increasingly identify objectives that member states wish to achieve over a longer period with a biennial rolling program of action to work toward those goals. These annual workshops should be, in effect, review meetings where states review progress in achieving these goals and approve broad future directions. It is therefore crucial that participants in the workshops be senior officials with the necessary decision-making capacity and that the involvement of national institutions and civil society as participants be reinforced in this review process. It may be that the frequency of such review meetings should be examined. In contrast, intersessional activities should involve those who have real expertise in the subject, to exchange practical experiences, participate in training, and implement projects.

Second, workshops with participants from across the whole Asia Pacific region have been useful to explore new or difficult concepts. But in the end we must judge the success of activities by whether they lead to progress and change at the national level, creating or strengthening national capacities and infrastructures and thus affecting in a concrete way people's lives. With the vastness and diversity of this region, I believe that increasingly this Framework should concentrate principally on activities at the subregional and national levels. Workshops are not ends in themselves but rather should always be seen as part of a broader program or project to achieve real change.

Third, I encourage you to constantly evaluate and strengthen the activities under the Framework. Be guided by the spirit and the questions raised by Professor Vitit Muntarbhorn in his evaluation of the Teheran Framework. For example, four countries in the region have adopted national human rights plans of action. An evaluation of their experiences would help other states to adopt best practices and avoid the mistakes of those who preceded them.

Fourth, I believe all partners in this process should work together more closely and consistently—governments, nongovernmental organizations, national human rights institutions, my Office and other UN agencies, UN treaty bodies and thematic experts, private enterprise, and the victims of human rights violations themselves. The heart of the Framework is the commitment and hard work of states. I urge every state here to examine how it can contribute in a tangible way to the subject matter of the four pillars. It could be to host an activity, to recommend and help shape a project, to make voluntary contributions on which all the activities depend, or to offer the wisdom of your own experiences for the benefit of others.

My Office stands ready to provide the technical cooperation and advice in support of this Framework. I have already mentioned our regional representatives. I hope they will be a new source of ideas, advice, and best practice for all states.

I look to other UN agencies and global and regional financial institutions to provide technical, financial, and logistical support. I have consistently emphasized that human rights are not "owned" by any one agency. The main thrust of the Secretary General's reform process is to integrate human rights standards into all agencies, especially in the field. My office is a catalyst in that process.

This is the second year in which nongovernmental organizations and national human rights institutions have participated in a one-day premeeting and made their recommendations to the intergovernmental forum. It reflects the relevance and constructive role of civil society. I warmly welcome their presence and note how fitting it is that in this tenth anniversary year the largest number ever of national institutions from the Asia Pacific come together at this workshop. I reiterate the hope I expressed two years ago that civil society partners will be involved more in future activities under this Framework and eventually will become full participating partners in support of the intergovernmental process.

Excellencies, distinguished representatives, ladies and gentlemen, in concluding, let me reiterate that I attach great importance to this workshop and its ability to achieve tangible results for the promotion and protection of human rights in the Asia Pacific region. I would in particular emphasize the following:

First, the strong commitment of my Office to support the implementation of your deliberations with regard to future activities at the regional, subregional and national levels to further the process of regional cooperation for the promotion and protection of human rights

Second, my encouragement to all participants to consider organizing and/or hosting regional, subregional, and national initiatives with a greater involvement of national institutions and civil society and to follow up at the national level the implementation of the program that you will be adopting.

We are here today to increase and coordinate our efforts to help improve substantively the life of the peoples of this region. You can sense my enthusiasm with this approach. I count on you to make this workshop a practical step in the achievement of this objective.

Address to the Permanent Council of the Organisation for Security and Co-operation in Europe (OSCE)
Vienna, Austria, 17 July 2002

Mr. Chairman, Excellencies, Ladies, and Gentlemen,

I am very pleased to have this opportunity to meet with you here today in Vienna, and I thank you for the invitation. I last met with the OSCE Permanent Council almost exactly four years ago. Many important changes have taken place since then, both in our areas of concern and in the ways in which we work together. Nevertheless, our common commitment to the observance of human rights as an essential precondition to stability and progress in Europe remains the same. Let me begin today with my personal tribute to the vital role that the OSCE has played in enhancing security for all people living in Europe and indeed beyond. The Helsinki Final Act and the important commitments that have been made since are a continuing inspiration to the world.[14] They demonstrate the connections which should exist between respect for human rights and democracy and between conflict prevention, regional security, and economic development. When I last appeared before the Permanent Council, I expressed my great appreciation for the OSCE's original concept of security, which places human rights very much at its core. Human rights were not considered in opposition to security but instead as one of its main elements. In the aftermath of the terrible events of last September 11, as states seek effective ways to deal with the threat of terrorism, OSCE has not wavered in asserting this linkage between human rights and human security.

It has been significant over the last months that the United Nations and regional organizations in Europe and elsewhere have given the same message to their member states. That message has been that there is a duty to confront and defeat terrorism but that the actions taken by states to combat terrorism must be in conformity with international human rights and humanitarian law standards. This position was powerfully expressed by Secretary General Kofi Annan in his statement to the Security Council on 18 January this year:

> We should all be clear that there is no trade-off between effective action against terrorism and the protection of human rights. On the contrary, I believe that in the long term we shall find that human rights, along with democracy and social justice, are one of the best prophylactics against terrorism. . . . [W]hile we certainly need vigilance to prevent acts of terrorism, and firmness in condemning and punishing them, it will be self-defeating if we sacrifice other key priorities—such as human rights—in the process.

A similar message was given by the OSCE Bucharest Ministerial Declaration of 4 December 2001 and by the High Level OSCE Meeting on the Prevention and Combat of Terrorism held under the Portuguese Presidency in Lisbon on 12 June last. If I may, Mr. Chairman, I will refer particularly to your speech at Lisbon, which emphasized that the OSCE can play a major role in prevention of terrorism through its ongoing work on democratization, the rule of law, good governance, and the promotion of human and minority rights. It is in these areas also that, in cooperation with the OSCE, my Office seeks to contribute. The emphasis on prevention is equally one that we strive to promote in the work of the OHCHR.

The Summary Conclusions of the Lisbon meeting emphasized the leading role of the United Nations in combating terrorism and spoke of the strong commitment of OSCE participating states to "reinforce and develop bilateral and multilateral cooperation with the United Nations and with other international and regional organizations" in combating all forms of terrorism.

Yesterday you heard from the Secretary General of the Council of Europe, Walter Schwimmer, and no doubt he discussed the new Council of Europe Guidelines that have been drawn up to assist states in combating terrorism, while observing the core principles of the Organisation—human rights, democracy, and the rule of law.[15] The Guidelines are of potentially wider applicability than to Council of Europe member states only. Noting the cooperation envisaged at your Lisbon High Level Meeting with the Council of Europe on counterterrorism, I would ask the OSCE to encourage their application by all its member states. The OSCE Parliamentary Assembly Declaration adopted on 10 July in Berlin called on Parliaments to actively protect and promote human rights during states of emergency. The Declaration provides clear support for the implementation of the Council of Europe Guidelines by all OSCE participating states.

I believe that the reach of the Guidelines can be even wider. I urge other regional organizations in the world to examine them with a view to adopting similar provisions in the context of implementing resolution 1373 of the Security Council and upholding their regional human rights obligations.

Monitoring Antiterrorism Measures

These initiatives on human rights and terrorism are very important. But we must recognize that there is a gap in the international responses on the issue of monitoring the use of antiterrorism measures. Strong statements in support of the safeguarding of human rights standards in combating terrorism were made at this year's session of the United Nations Commission on Human Rights. But, unfortunately, the Commission was not able to agree on a proposal to establish a specific mechanism (for example, a Special Rapporteur) to monitor the impact of antiterrorism measures on human rights. As a result, there is currently no international institution with a clear mandate to assess whether measures taken and justified by a state as necessary to combat terrorism are in violation of human rights standards that that state has accepted, or which would require that derogation be made.

Last November the Director of the OSCE Office for Democratic Institutions and Human Rights (ODIHR), Ambassador Stoudmann; Secretary General Schwimmer of the Council of Europe; and I, on behalf of the OHCHR, issued a joint statement on the importance of safeguarding human rights as we strive to eradicate terrorism.[16] Thereafter we have sought to share information and enhance our capacity to monitor the human rights dimensions of actions taken to combat terrorism. More perhaps needs to be done together to ensure that information exchange continues and, above, all is acted upon. The OSCE Parliamentary Assembly Berlin Declaration reminds Parliaments of their responsibility for the oversight of executive power and the creation of law during states of emergency and other times of conflict or threats to national security. As with the Council of Europe Guidelines, I would encourage Parliaments in all countries to examine the Berlin Declaration and seek to apply its principles in scrutinizing proposed counterterrorism measures.

To sum up: hard work over fifty years by states, intergovernmental bodies, and nongovernmental organizations has developed a sophisticated system comprising human rights law, refugee law, and humanitarian law with which to curb abuses of power. Now more than ever, we must ensure that these normative frameworks are implemented and that violations of them are monitored, condemned, and addressed. In so doing we are contributing to human security and the elimination of terrorism.

Cooperation in the Field

Mr. Chairman, I would also like to take the opportunity today to recognize the OSCE's important work in the field. The OSCE has given strength to its declarations through action. This can be seen in its many field missions and presences organized from the Secretariat in Vienna, the extensive technical assistance programs of the Office for Democratic Institutions and Human Rights in Warsaw, and in the special mechanisms, including the High Commissioner on National Minorities. This has been of vital importance to all Europeans, and most of all to the victims of human rights violations. In the end, protection cannot be effective unless it is linked with development of national capacity, technical cooperation, and other forms of direct assistance. The development of this part of the OSCE's program has been one of its greatest achievements of recent years, and it has been the privilege of my Office to work closely with the OSCE on many of these activities.

Four years ago I signed an agreement on cooperation with Ambassador Stoudmann of ODIHR committing our organizations to exchanging information, developing joint projects, and providing mutual support in a range of areas. Just two months ago I reaffirmed and expanded this commitment with ODIHR in an exchange of letters with Ambassador Stoudmann. By working together with the OSCE as well as the other key regional actors, including the Council of Europe, the European Union, and the Stability Pact, we believe we can make an effective contribution.[17]

I would like to mention one area of excellent cooperation, and that is with the OSCE High Commissioner for National Minorities. His Office contributed a chapter on the experience of this pioneering institution to the recently published United Nations Guide for Minorities.[18] The High Commissioner has also participated in the Commission on Human Rights Working Group on Minorities, and further practical cooperation is planned.

We deeply appreciated the OSCE's support at the International Conference on Human Rights and Democratization, which we coorganized with the Croatian Government and the European Commission in Dubrovnik last October. One of the main aims of that event was to identify the contribution that can be made by my Office in a region in which the regional organizations play such an important role. I think we have found some useful areas in which our efforts can complement one another.

Regional Strategy of OHCHR

As I explained in Dubrovnik, my Office has made the development and implementation of regional strategies a key element in our overall approach to human rights protection and promotion. Regional strategies allow us to maximize our impact while recognizing that our capabilities are limited and that partnerships are essential. In particular, regional approaches allow us to act as catalysts, contributing to the impact of other parts of the UN system and our regional partners who are more able to engage in capacity building at the national level. A further element of our approach is to emphasize the role of civil society in the development of national capacities.

In line with this strategy, we have deployed regional representatives at the offices of the UN Regional Economic Commissions in Asia, the Middle East, Africa, and Latin America, who work with partners to mainstream human rights in a range of different programs. I have also appointed regional advisers for the different regions who provide advice to me on national and regional activities and programs. For Europe, Central Asia, and the Caucasus, my regional adviser is Ambassador Thomas Hammarberg of Sweden, who will be known to many of you.

Because of Europe's unique position as a region already benefiting from strong regional institutions, including the OSCE, we have taken a calibrated approach to our own role in the region. As I emphasized in my remarks at Dubrovnik last October, the achievement of human rights goals in Europe depends very much on a close, complementary working relationship among the European and UN partners. Our focus is on supporting the efforts of the regional organizations and not competing with, complicating, or duplicating their work. Our key areas of work embrace follow-ups to treaty body recommendations, national human rights institutions, human rights education, and national plans of action.

Central Asia

One key issue we are working on with OSCE is the promotion of human rights in the countries of Central Asia. We have conducted missions to four of the five countries over the last six months. I am pleased to report that the Governments of Kazakhstan, Kyrgyzstan, Tajikistan, and Uzbekistan enthusiastically welcomed the OHCHR delegations, and our discussions on human rights needs have been frank and constructive. I am hoping that we can engage in a similar dialogue with Turkmenistan in the near future. The aim of our initiative on Central Asia is to formulate a program to assist in the development, both at the regional and country levels, of capacities to protect and promote human rights. Among the areas we are considering are teacher training for human rights education in the schools; the development of human rights courses for lawyers, judges, police, and prosecutors; and complementary activities such as providing human rights publications and supporting human rights education initiatives. We foresee that the program might include a modest presence from OHCHR to oversee implementation, provide advice, and coordinate with other international presences in Central Asia so that we strengthen each other and avoid duplication.

We are very grateful for the support and advice that the OSCE has provided OHCHR throughout this process. The OSCE field presences in Central Asia have been very active in promoting human rights and democratic reform as crucial elements in the promotion of a holistic concept of human security, and our cooperation with them has been very fruitful. This has been particularly true in Tajikistan, where the OSCE field presence and the UN Tajikistan Office for Peace-Building support each other in implementing common human rights programs and collaborate in dealing with individual cases. I hope that our Office will continue to benefit in Central Asia from this mutually supportive cooperation with the OSCE.

Southeast Europe

Our cooperation extends to other parts of the region and to other issues. On Monday next, 22 July, in Geneva, I will join with Ambassador Stoudmann and Phillip O'Brien from UNICEF in releasing a joint report on trafficking in human beings in southeastern Europe.[19] The report covers the situations in Albania, Bosnia-Herzegovina, Bulgaria, Croatia, the Federal Republic of Yugoslavia, the former Yugoslav Republic of Macedonia, Moldova, and Romania. In addition to paying particular attention to trafficking of women and girls for commercial sexual exploitation, it also examines trafficking in children from Albania for the purposes of forced labor. We have worked closely with the OSCE on this shameful area of human rights abuse, especially in the context of the Trafficking Task Force of the Stability Pact.

We also have good cooperation with your important field presences in southeast Europe. In Bosnia Herzegovina the two organizations work closely on promoting international human rights standards through work on rule-of-law issues such as the protection of national minorities and Roma rights and the implementation of the National Plan of Action on Trafficking. There has also been joint training in UN treaty body reporting requirements.

Last month we were pleased to be invited as observers at an OSCE regional, working-level meeting in Sarajevo, which brought together some fifty staff members of the OSCE missions in Macedonia, Kosovo, the Federal Republic of Yugoslavia, Bosnia-Herzegovina, and Croatia. It is worth noting that both of our organizations are moving increasingly toward a thematic approach in southeast Europe, and it will be important that we ensure consistency and complementarity in our mutual efforts.

I should also mention our work together in Georgia, where we continue our cooperation by jointly staffing the Human Rights Office in Abkhazia as we have done since 1996. We also regularly consult together on activities in Azerbaijan, where we opened a small office earlier this year, and on the serious human rights situation in Chechnya in the Russian Federation. Another crucial programmatic area on which we exchange information is the development and strengthening of independent national human rights institutions across the region.

Mr. Chairman, I believe that one of our goals in the time ahead should be to ensure that human rights remain central to international dialogue. In this region we continue to be faced with extraordinary challenges: not only the campaign to counter terrorism, but also the reconstruction of Afghanistan, on the OSCE border, Georgia, Armenia, and Azerbaijan; peace-building in southeast Europe; and many others.

As we face up to these problems in Europe and similar problems elsewhere, I believe we must give fresh consideration to the ways in which we seek to resolve them. At the Commission on Human Rights this year, I was especially concerned at the deeply divisive debates and votes that took place on situations where it was alleged that gross violations of human rights were occurring. In my closing statement to the Commission, I expressed my concern at the increased politicization of issues in the Commission at the expense of true human rights concerns. A number of developing countries argued that there is too much criticism of them and that it is unfair. As I said in my closing address to the Commission, I feel it is my duty as High Commissioner to ask Is it not right that when human rights are at stake, human rights organizations seek to protect the victims?

I should like to ask the OSCE participating states, which represent two of the regional groupings of the Commission on Human Rights, to bring a new commitment to efforts to have a meaningful human rights dialogue in the forums, which are dedicated to that purpose, both in the UN and the OSCE. As international organizations with mandates based largely on human rights principles, it is incumbent upon the United Nations and the OSCE to provide a real opportunity for discussion of these issues, so that victims of human rights violations may raise their grievances and see their concerns addressed.

This includes ensuring a role for NGOs to put forward their views and perspectives, which may differ from those of their governments, and which may help governments and civil society in resolving human rights problems and building national capacities to protect these rights. A human rights dialogue would also benefit from the participation of national human rights institutions in intergovernmental meetings, including those of the OSCE. As we look ahead to the annual OSCE Human Dimension implementation meeting in September, I would like to underline the vital role that the OSCE has to play in promoting such dialogue.

And we should recall that such dialogue should not only encompass the identification of critical human rights situations; it should also include a commitment to provide significant resources for technical cooperation and advisory services to assist countries in building and strengthening their national capacities in the rule of law, the administration of justice, and adherence to human rights norms and standards. Criticism will then be perceived as constructive and forward-looking, not finger-pointing in a judgmental way.

Finally, Mr. Chairman, the OSCE must continue to give leadership in proposing ways to address the serious problems that all parts of Europe face, including the rising hostility toward immigrants, reflected in recent elections; the worrying rise in incidents of anti-Semitism, and at the same time, the rise in Islamophobia and anti-Arab sentiment. These concerns were focused upon at the recent OSCE Lisbon and Berlin meetings. The Declaration and Plan of Action of last year's World Conference against Racism at Durban affirmed that human diversity must be recognized as an asset, not a liability; that xenophobia must be rejected in all its forms; and that in a world which hopes to reap the benefits of globalization, a commitment to multicultural societies must be embraced. The OSCE member states have expertise in addressing these issues that can benefit the larger international community. Let me encourage you to consider sharing that expertise.

Mr. Chairman, I am very grateful for this opportunity to have shared some of my thoughts with you today. I am confident that the cooperation between our Office and the OSCE on all of these issues will continue to flourish in the time ahead.

"The Application of International Human Rights Norms by National Courts and Tribunals"
Opening Address to a Sub-Regional Workshop
Montevideo, Uruguay, 22–25 October 2001

It is a great honor for me to be here with you today and to address the opening session of this workshop. I am most grateful to the Government of Uruguay for hosting this forum and for the excellent preparation. I thank the Minister for Foreign Affairs, Dr Didier Opertti Badan, for his attendance and the support for our cooperation that his presence signifies. I am also pleased to share this opening session with Ambassador Stella Zervoudaky, the representative in Uruguay of the European Union, who will speak on behalf of the European Commission in Brussels. We have also here today Ambassador Leandro Despouy, current Chairperson of the United Nations Commission on Human Rights. It is a great pleasure to meet you in your region instead of where we usually meet, in Geneva. I am sure that the workshop will greatly benefit from your experience, knowledge, and commitment to human rights. I would also like to take the opportunity to thank the experts who will introduce the various sessions. Their recognized expertise in the subjects of the workshop will be an invaluable contribution to its success.

Let me also warmly thank our regional partner in this workshop, the American Institute for Human Rights. It is of enormous importance for the success of the workshop and for future cooperation that my Office has the Institute as an active partner. The Institute is not only the leading regional human rights institute based in the Organization of American States (OAS), but it is also known and respected worldwide for the range and quality of its research teaching and training.

Today's workshop falls within the Quito framework. The Framework of Regional Co-operation for Latin America and the Caribbean was adopted in Quito, Ecuador, in 1999 by the states of the region. It calls upon the Office of the High Commissioner for Human Rights to facilitate the exchange of experiences through meetings at the regional, subregional, and national levels. The regional workshop which we are organizing in cooperation with the Government of Argentina that will take place in Buenos Aires from 24 to 27 October on "Strategies for the Realization of Economic, Social and Cultural Rights" is another activity within the Quito framework. A regional workshop on human rights education will be held in Mexico within that framework, in cooperation with UNESCO, next month.

The Role of National Courts in Ensuring Human Rights

The focus of today's workshop is a practical one: the application of international human rights norms through national courts and tribunals. But we should reflect for a moment why it is such an important topic. We should begin by remembering that human rights are universal. They belong to all men, women, and children in the world. They are protected in our modern world by different systems—national, regional, and international. For instance, here in Uruguay there is first the national system based on your constitution and judiciary. In addition, there is a regional level of protection based on Uruguay's long membership in the OAS and Inter-American human rights treaties. Finally, we have the global human rights treaty system built by the United Nations and in which Uruguay is a full participant. All of these levels of human rights protection should reinforce and complement each other in the interest of all people who live in Uruguay. One of the best ways to ensure that we deliver the highest standards of human rights protection is to have national courts recognize and use the jurisprudence of regional and international human rights courts and bodies. The workshop will explore this subject.

I strongly believe that regional and international cooperation are essential in order to ensure respect for human rights and fundamental freedoms, and that, in turn, respect for human rights and democratic guarantees is a necessary condition for strengthening the process of integration among the countries of this region. The workshop is of particular importance because through it we are inaugurating a new subregional initiative on the protection of human rights and the consolidation of democracy. The workshop is the first activity organized by the countries of the MERCOSUR, Bolivia, and Chile. It implements in a practical way the Ushuaia protocol of 1998.[20] That Protocol recognized the link between democracy, regional economic integration, and respect for human rights. It represents an important step in the processes of cooperation between the countries of this region.

The Human Rights Pillar of MERCOSUR

This new development, the construction of a human rights pillar in MERCOSUR, can learn from the experience of the European Union. No doubt Ambassador Zervoudaky in her address will develop the parallel with the case of the European Communities leading to the European Union. The evolution of the European Union from an organization concerned only with economic integration into one in which human rights and democracy have become defining parts of its identity is certainly a positive example for MERCOSUR.

This new and exciting project began with a joint statement agreed by the countries of this region at the last session of the Commission on Human Rights. That statement emphasized the indispensable link between effective democracy and the enjoyment of all human rights. It also called for increased cooperation with my Office. I intend to ensure that your call is heard. The efforts of your countries to strengthen democracy and respect of human rights will receive increased support from my Office.

I strongly believe that my Office should make its own regional-level contribution to the promotion and protection of human rights. OHCHR already has a significant presence in the region. We have technical cooperation projects with the Governments of Argentina and Bolivia, and recently my Office has undertaken a mission to Brazil to discuss the modalities of future cooperation in the field of human rights. In this and other regions of the world we are establishing regional advisers who come from and are based in each region. In the Latin American and Caribbean region, the OHCHR human rights adviser Mr. Roberto Garreton, who is with us today, will be based in the Economic Commission for Latin America and the Caribbean (ECLAC) office in Santiago de Chile.

The Contribution of the OHCHR

Let me turn to what, specifically, my Office is contributing and hopes to contribute in its human rights work in this region. Our mandate is based on the Vienna Declaration and Programme of Action 1993, and in particular we focus on

universal ratification of international human rights instruments;
the development of national human rights action plans;
the establishment of national human rights institutions that comply with international standards;
the development of human rights education and training programs;
full attention to economic, social, and cultural rights, including the right to development;
strengthening the system of special procedures.

To work together with partners on implementing these important goals is the mission of our regional program. But in order to do this we need to construct with MERCOSUR and other regional frameworks a common human rights strategy. I would like to see as a central element of that strategy the creation of action plans on human rights at the national level as well as by the MERCOSUR. I will also raise these suggestions later in my visit to your country when I meet with the Uruguay Parliament and its human rights commission. There is no doubt that the parliaments are crucial to achieving effective national human rights strategies and infrastructures for the promotion and protection of human rights. I am also meeting with NGOs. Our experience elsewhere strongly suggests that in the development of national human rights action plans it is vital to include the voice of civil society in all its diversity.

Human Rights Promotion and Protection and National Courts

Excellencies, ladies, and gentlemen, this workshop will provide an opportunity to share legal expertise, best practices, and comparative analysis with regard to a theme which is at the very heart of human rights promotion and protection: the application of international human rights norms by national courts and tribunals.

All the countries of the region have experienced, in the recent past, the struggle for the restoration of democracy and of a fair and independent judiciary. We all know how difficult it can be for a still-fragile democracy to set up independent and effective mechanisms to ensure respect of human rights and in particular to change the judicial culture and people perception of the administration of justice. We all also know that enormous advances have been made by the countries of the region.

We now live in a global village. We can all benefit from the exchange of experience between regions on best practices in connection with the application of international human rights standards at the national level. In that connection there are two resources prepared for the workshop I would like to mention. First, you will have a compendium prepared by my Office of the General Comments and Recommendations adopted to date by the six Treaty Bodies that oversee the implementation of the major UN human rights treaties. Second, you will have a major compilation of expert analyses on the law and practice of applying international human rights norms in the countries of Latin America. This has been prepared by our partner the Inter-American Institute for Human Rights. Both should be valuable tools for the workshop discussions.

The workshop will at a later point provide an opportunity to make a first assessment of the results of the World Conference against Racism, Racial Discrimination, Xenophobia and Related Intolerance and to discuss follow-up at the regional and national levels. I hope to join the discussion in the workshop at that point. As I said at the closing session of the Durban Conference last month, I believe that the true measure of the success of the World Conference will be whether it makes a real difference in the lives of the victims of racism and discrimination. Durban must be a beginning and not an end. I am convinced the Conference documents are even more relevant after the horrific attacks on September 11 in the United States. They offer an alternative vision to hatred and destructive division between cultures and peoples. That vision is a world where all discrimination is eliminated and world cultures can live side by side in equality and peace.

Excellencies, ladies, and gentlemen, I am encouraged by the large presence of governments of the region at this workshop. It is also heartening to have representatives of national institutions and nongovernmental organizations. The energy and enthusiasm of civil society are crucial all over the world to ensure that governments respect their international human rights commitments.

One of the outcomes that I would welcome from the workshop is concrete suggestions on what happens next. How can we build together as national, regional, and international partners on this workshop? I have mentioned the need for a human rights strategy and action plans both at national and regional levels. I would like to envisage that we could agree on a review meeting on progress on any agreed strategy and action plans no later than one year ahead. OHCHR stands ready to help and to develop follow-up on the insights and initiatives that emerge from the workshop.

I wish you every success in your deliberations.

Chapter 17

Strengthening National Human Rights Protection

The concept of national human rights protections systems gained currency in the last year of Mary Robinson's tenure as High Commissioner. It was intended to capture the entirety of institutions that had or should have a role in securing domestic protection and vindication of international human rights standards.

These include courts as the primary guarantor of the rule of law. But the legislature or parliament has also a major role, one that has been encouraged greatly by the efforts of the Inter-Parliamentary Union, a body with which Mary Robinson worked closely. A new idea of the 1990s has been that of government-created, but independent, national human rights institutions or human rights commissions. Guidelines known as the Paris Principles have become the accepted minimum standards to guarantee effectiveness and independence of national institutions. While High Commissioner, Mary Robinson established a national institutions unit to support, with practical advice, their creation in all countries as well as their cooperation at regional and international levels.

The 102nd Inter-Parliamentary Conference
Berlin, Germany, 11 October 1999

Chancellor Schröder, Distinguished Guests, Ladies, and Gentlemen,

I welcome the invitation to address this important gathering. My first contact with the Inter-Parliamentary Union was in 1971, when I attended the annual meeting in Paris as a young Irish Parliamentarian. Since then the IPU has been developing its influence on the role of Parliaments worldwide.

It is fitting that parliamentarians should meet in Berlin, the new capital city which, ten years ago, witnessed one of the most remarkable democratic achievements of recent times. The unification of the German people and nation was a historic event in many respects. From a human rights perspective it represented a victory for democracy and the right of people to determine their own destiny. The positive message which went out to the world was that change, even major change, could come about in a peaceful, democratic way.

I am happy to share this platform with the President of the International

Committee of the Red Cross. The links between human rights and humanitarian crises are extremely close. Mr. Sommaruga and I recently discussed ways in which we can work even more closely together. We agreed that there is a continuum between human rights violations, conflicts, and humanitarian disasters and that there is a complementarity between the work of our two organizations.

I am particularly encouraged to see that your agenda includes issues that are fundamental to the global political, social, and economic debates of our day. The topics include peaceful coexistence; respect for ethnic, cultural, and religious minorities; ratification of the Rome Statute of the International Criminal Court; migrants; the situation in East Timor; and other equally important issues that have a direct bearing on the human rights of the people you represent.

Since I was appointed United Nations High Commissioner for Human Rights two years ago, I have been continuously confronted by the challenge of how human rights can best be secured and defended. Most people know about the gross human rights violations that are all too common in our modern world—whether in East Timor or Kosovo or Sierra Leone—but I would like to draw your attention today to less well-known forms of abuse that are all too prevalent. I refer to the countless individual communications received by my Office each day on behalf of people in detention, women who are victims of violence, children who have been abused and tortured, human rights defenders who are harassed, journalists who have been kidnapped, people who have disappeared, migrant workers who have been victimized, people who have been displaced, refugees, and indigenous people who have been intimidated.

These appeals for help not only come in ever-increasing numbers but also come from almost all the countries of the world. Most of the communications are dealt with quietly and do not come to public attention. It can be difficult, therefore, for the public to appreciate the extent and geographic spread of human rights abuses. The fact is that we are faced not only with an ever-increasing number of allegations but also with the challenge of new forms of violations.

I see my own challenge in this respect as being to ensure that these allegations are effectively investigated, to redress the wrongs suffered by the victims, and to bring the perpetrators to justice. But the biggest challenge that faces us in the field of human rights remains prevention of conflicts. We must devote more attention and resources to preventive measures; as Secretary General Kofi Annan has said, our goal must be to embark on an age of prevention.

Many actors have roles to play in human rights—governments, international development and financial institutions, NGOs, big business. Parliaments and parliamentarians have a key role to play in championing human rights, both nationally and internationally. It is parliaments that are responsible for the ratification of international human rights treaties and conventions, for the development of domestic legislation in conformity with international human rights norms, and for the adoption of policies, programs, and strategies informed by a rights-based approach.

More than that, parliamentarians can be a strong voice for those deprived of their human rights. Whether raising issues in parliament or playing an active role in Foreign Affairs or Human Rights Committees, or simply by speaking out, parliamentarians are well placed to focus public attention on rights issues, and many have done so to considerable effect.

One point that I would like to make is that human rights should not be thought of as something for other people or other countries and not for your own country or neighborhood only. Human rights are universal, and, unfortunately, so are human rights abuses. Eleanor Roosevelt, one of the chief architects of the Universal Declaration, reminded us that "human rights start in small places, close to home." That is true for all of us. Gross human rights violations do not happen overnight; they begin with discrimination and move on to more serious discrimination, then to exclusion and finally to the ultimate exclusion in the form of murder or people being driven from their homes. All of us have a duty to defend human rights and prevent this terrible process from happening.

As part of my mandate to promote and protect human rights, I attach great importance to building national capacities. During the last two years, I have given high priority to the establishment and strengthening of independent and effective national institutions for the promotion and protection of human rights. These institutions were particularly urged by the Vienna Declaration and Programme of Action of 1993. International standards for the establishment of such institutions—known as the Paris Principles—were adopted by the General Assembly later the same year and have become the benchmark for member states wishing to establish national human rights institutions.

National institutions play important roles in both developed and developing countries and should be provided with a broad mandate for the promotion and protection of human rights as well as adequate resources for their work. Recently my Office advised the British and Irish Governments on the establishment of such institutions in Belfast and Dublin, and we are currently giving support to new institutions in Sierra Leone and Rwanda, which have suffered terrible human rights violations in recent years.

As a world organization of parliaments, the Inter-Parliamentary Union is an important—indeed unique—forum for parliamentary dialogue and work for peace and cooperation among people, for the promotion of democracy, and for the defense and promotion of human rights and the protection of the rule of law. I am aware of, and applaud, the stands taken on human rights issues by the IPU over the years. In July of this year a memorandum of understanding on cooperation between the Inter-Parliamentary Union and my Office was signed by the President and the Secretary General of the IPU and myself. I strongly hope that this memorandum will facilitate cooperation between our organizations in an area of common interest for us all: the promotion and protection of human rights and fundamental freedoms.

"Protecting Human Rights: The Role and Responsibilities of the Independent Bar"
Inaugural World Conference of Barristers and Advocates
Edinburgh, Scotland, 28 June 2002

Your Lordship, the Lord Advocate; Co-Chairs of the Conference,
Distinguished Members of the Faculty of Advocates, and Members of the Bar,

Thank you for the invitation to address this Inaugural World Conference. I found it irresistible. It is an idea whose time has come, and you chose to launch it in this beautiful city of Edinburgh, a place that is rich in history and a veritable crucible of both Scottish and European civilization and culture, including the law.

When I first received the invitation I did wonder why the Australian Bar Association would want to invite me, an Irish advocate who has been out of professional service and away from the cut and thrust of the Dublin Bar for a while now, to address a conference hosted by the Faculty of Advocates in Scotland! I was intrigued to discover that this was the setting of an inaugural world conference bringing together various independent referral bars from different parts of the world: Scotland, England and Wales, Northern Ireland, Ireland, Australia, South Africa, Zimbabwe, Hong Kong, and New Zealand. A small caveat: having addressed the Bar of the High Court in Lahore, Pakistan, recently, I did ponder a little on how you select the bar associations represented here, and I would encourage you to be as inclusive as possible.

I also discovered that the theme of your inaugural conference is a subject that falls within my mandate as United Nations High Commissioner for Human Rights: the independence of lawyers.

Human Rights Advocacy

Although it has been quite a long time since I acted as an advocate in court, I will address you as an advocate of a different kind. My current job requires me to be an advocate for recognition, respect, protection, and promotion of human rights the world over, especially on behalf of the millions who are victims—or potential victims—of human rights violations. Looking at your program for this meeting, I was pleased to see that you will not only be addressing the issue of the independence of the bar, but also the role of the independent bar in promoting and protecting human rights. I would like to share some thoughts with you on both issues.

You should not underestimate the challenge. In my experience over the last five years, most victims of violations of human rights have no access to a lawyer at all. Nor do they know they have rights guaranteed under international instruments their country may have ratified. Detention without trial is common, and if a trial takes place, there may be no defense lawyer present or expected.

In this context, I believe there is an opportunity to address these broad areas at a new level in African countries arising from the commitments made in the New Partnership for African Development (NEPAD). I know that some of you have made significant individual contributions by acting as trial observers or investigators of particular problems from time to time in developing countries, and that bar associations have formed bilateral relations which can be significant. But I believe there is a new opening which arises from the way in which African leaders in the NEPAD have prioritized their commitment to strengthening the administration of justice and rule of law and adhering to international human rights norms and standards. They have also proposed a mechanism of African peer review to monitor progress.

The priority given to these key areas stems from the direct link now made by African countries between strengthening human rights protection and human development. The problem is that, despite the priority given, African countries will not be able to prioritize domestic resources because these will be needed to service the debt burden, tackle HIV/AIDS, and provide better education, health care, infrastructure, etc. Hence the challenge to the international community, both at the official level of governments and international institutions and at the level of professional bodies such as yours. Could I suggest that a constructive outcome of this inaugural meeting might be the establishment of a task force to examine how representatives of independent bars might provide intellectual and professional support to this aspect of NEPAD? My Office would be very pleased to work closely with you on such a project.

The Independence Principle

A system based on respect for the rule of law needs not only strong independent and impartial judges and prosecutors, but also strong and independent lawyers who are able to pursue their work freely and without fear of reprisals. When I served on the advisory board of the International Commission of Jurists, I became familiar with the work of the Centre for the Independence of Judges and Lawyers and its annual reports on *Attacks on Justice: The Harassment and Persecution of Judges and Lawyers*, which bring home the scale of the problem in different regions of the world.

You have asked me to speak about human rights. Let me challenge you, and begin with a quote from Eleanor Roosevelt, who chaired the first UN

Human Rights Commission that which drafted the Universal Declaration of Human Rights:

> Where, after all, do universal human rights begin? In small places, close to home—so close and so small that they cannot be seen on any maps of the world. . . . Unless these rights have meaning there, they have little meaning anywhere. Without concerted citizen action to uphold them close to home, we shall look in vain for progress in the larger world.

What "concerted action" are your bar associations taking in this regard? I was encouraged by some of the ideas of the Australian Law Commission in its report *Managing Justice: A Review of the Federal Civil Justice System.* I note the recommendations on how local bars can expand access to justice by preparing pamphlets explaining how lawyers bill their clients; what one can expect from an initial consultation, pro bono work, etc. Pricing policy can also be important in determining whether people can afford the services of independent advocates! Is it not also the responsibility of the independent bar to ensure that access to justice, especially for the indigent, is treated as a human right to be defended?

International Human Rights Foundations

Enough of this cross-examination! Nor do I propose to lecture you on human rights, but just to reflect briefly on what we have gained in over half a century. The UN Charter and the Universal Declaration of Human Rights adopted by the General Assembly in 1948 gave a vision of a world grounded in good governance, democracy, the rule of law, and respect for human rights. The Universal Declaration was transformed into binding international law in 1976 when two covenants, the International Covenant on Civil and Political Rights and the International Covenant on Economic, Social and Cultural Rights, entered into force. These treaties and the Universal Declaration, known collectively as the International Bill of Human Rights, are the cornerstone of the remarkable body of international and regional instruments, well over seventy in number, which form the basis of international human rights law and regulate the fundamental rights and freedoms of all individuals.

The regime of international human rights law established by these instruments is now recognized as a part of the national legal order in many jurisdictions in the world. Here in the United Kingdom, for example, the enactment of the Human Rights Act 1998 brought into the domestic law of the various jurisdictions of the United Kingdom the rights provided for under the European Convention on Human Rights. In a number of other common law jurisdictions represented in this conference, various constitutional provisions or judicial mechanisms have similarly ensured the domestication of international human rights law in the national legal system. A good example is the Constitution of South Africa of 1996, which explicitly incorporates international human rights law as part of the law of South Africa.

The Office of the High Commissioner for Human Rights

Let me now introduce briefly the Office of High Commissioner for Human Rights. It was established by the General Assembly in 1993 to give leadership in the promotion and protection of human rights, democracy, and the rule of law. I would add that, in its evolution, the mandate of this Office has also come to encompass the prevention of violations of human rights. So, you could say that my task as High Commissioner for Human Rights is to be an advocate for all aspects of human rights: the promotion of these rights, the prevention of violations of these rights, and the protection of those who have become victims of these violations. In this task, my Office has over the years paid particular attention to the challenge of protecting the independence of judges, prosecutors, and lawyers and speaking out whenever their ability to exercise their professional responsibilities in true independence was threatened or comprised by governments and other actors. We recognize that violations of the independence of the judiciary and of lawyers are, in fact, violations of the international legal obligation incumbent upon governments to respect such independence and amount to violations of international human rights law.

Global Pool of Precedent

Recently I addressed the World Association of Women Judges at their conference in Dublin on a related subject and advanced two propositions.[1] First, I argued that the global human rights cause set out in the Universal Declaration has reached a certain maturity and that that maturity should allow us to think in terms of a single system of universal rights protection where distinctions that have been drawn in the past between national and international law need to be rethought. Second, and following upon the first proposition, I argued that human rights protection is not the work of two unconnected systems—the international and the national—but rather that it is a shared enterprise with interlocking and reinforcing national and international dimensions.

What does this mean for the independent bar in the national jurisdictions? I think it means, among other things, that the regime of international human rights law is not a strange and far-off terrain for the independent lawyer practicing within the jurisdiction of his or her own national territory. Increasingly the independent lawyer has to deal with human rights questions, whether at the criminal bar or commercial bar, or in matters involving trade or environmental disputes or, more obviously, in the context of constitutional litigation. Human rights have ceased to be a "fringe activity." As put by Lord Goldsmith QC and Nicholas Cowdrey QC in their article "The Role of the Lawyer in Human Rights": "[Human rights] is an area of law which is fundamental to everyone and which permeates all legal activity, economic and social, in public law and in private."[2] I would add that it has become part of the professional duty of judges, prosecutors and lawyers to explore the full potential of human rights law and to use their competence to ensure that the rule of law prevails as our guiding pillar in the democratic societies in which we live. Your work as lawyers must thus constitute the pillar of an effective legal protection of human rights which alone can ensure the protection of the individual against the abuse of power by those in authority.

International Human Rights Courts

The interconnectedness of the international human rights system and national legal systems also manifests itself in the emergence of international or regional human rights courts in which national independent lawyers are increasingly involved. The European Court of Human Rights in Strasbourg and the Inter-American Court of Human Rights are the best known. The establishment of similar regional human rights courts has been mooted elsewhere, for example the proposed African Court of Human and Peoples' Rights, whose protocol has already been signed and ratified by a number of African states, and the proposed regional human rights court for the Southern African Development Community (SADC).[3]

There are other judicial and quasi-judicial mechanisms established within the UN in which the independent lawyer is playing a critical role, as advocate or in some other expert capacity. And then, of course, there are the ad hoc tribunals created to deal with the atrocities in the former Yugoslavia and in Rwanda. These have shown us the inter-linkages between the national and the international. The atrocities may have been perpetrated in a national context, but the crimes committed are condemned as crimes against international human rights law and international humanitarian law. The accused standing trial in these tribunals may be citizens of individual countries—and in one case so far a former head of state—and the lawyers prosecuting and defending them may originate from different bars in different countries. But the common denominator is that the trials are aimed at securing justice based on internationally accepted norms and standards of international law. The recently established International Criminal Court (ICC) will build on this work.

Role of the Independent Lawyer

What, then, is the role of the independent lawyer in the challenge of upholding the rule of law and international human rights standards in the context of his or her work not only in the national courts but also in these international tribunals?

It was put simply by UN Secretary General Kofi Annan a few years ago when he said: "The rule of law is essential to peace, development and the realization of human rights. The practice of law is a privilege, but a privilege that carries with it a heavy responsibility to ensure respect for the law."[4]

One way that legal practitioners—independent lawyers—can ensure respect for the law is for them to engage effectively with the challenge of promoting and protecting human rights, not only for their immediate clients but also for the benefit of society at large. This requires better familiarization with the content of international human rights law. Yet, not long ago the Special Rapporteur on the Independence of Judges and Lawyers made the sad observation that recent experience has shown that in many countries bar associations are not responding to this expectation. He went on to note that:

> While in a few countries where the regime is repressive, fears of reprisal are real, yet in many other countries there appears to be an apathy coupled probably with the association being more concerned with addressing commercial and more materialistic aspects of the profession and embroiled in external politics and factionalism.[5]

The Special Rapporteur concluded that there was a need to sensitize bar associations not only on their roles in the advancement of the independence of their profession, but also on their role in the protection of judicial independence and human rights generally.

The Special Rapporteur on the Independence of the Judiciary and Lawyers

The Special Rapporteur I am referring to is the distinguished Malaysian lawyer Param Cumaraswamy, who is no doubt known to some of you.[6] Since 1994, when the Commission on Human Rights established his mandate, Param Cumaraswamy has worked actively to defend the independence of both the judiciary and lawyers and has reiterated the need for independent lawyers to take their roles and responsibilities in defending human rights and the rule of law more seriously. This appeal to independent lawyers to face up to these responsibilities is based on agreed international principles. The Basic Principles on the Role of Lawyers, adopted by the Eighth United Nations Congress on the Prevention of Crime and the Treatment of Offenders in 1990, provide the basis. These principles recognize, inter alia, that "Adequate protection of the human rights and fundamental freedoms to which all persons are entitled, be they economic, social and cultural, or civil and political, requires that all persons have effective access to legal services provided by an independent legal profession."[7]

Taken as a whole, the Basic Principles provide a range of rights and freedoms, together with duties and responsibilities that are incumbent upon lawyers. Among these is Principle 14, which states that in protecting the rights of their clients and in promoting the cause of justice, lawyers shall also "[seek] to uphold human rights and fundamental freedoms recognized by national and international law." The responsibility of lawyers to uphold the promotion and protection of human rights is reiterated in Principle 23, which also guarantees the right of lawyers, like other citizens, to freedom of expression, belief, association, and assembly.

In brief, then, I would remind you that your obligation to act to uphold nationally and internationally recognized human rights is clear. Like judges and prosecutors, you play a crucial role in the administration of justice and in the prevention of impunity for human rights violations. While the states' duty is to secure your independence, your principal obligation is to act in such a way that democracy and the rule of law, essential for the survival and good ordering of the state itself, are preserved.

Respect for the independence of lawyers must also come from the standards of the Bar itself, in tackling corruption, bias, and unethical or unprofessional conduct and promoting values of independence, integrity, propriety, and professional competence. I have no doubt that these are among the issues that you will be addressing in your discussions in this conference.

Your conference represents a new beginning—a bringing together from different countries and jurisdictions of independent bars that share a common professional vision and a common legal tradition. This is yet another manifestation of the recognition of the need for lawyers to reposition themselves to play their part in today's increasingly globalized world. But, of course, your deliberations at this conference have a resonance that goes farther and wider than the legal jurisdictions of countries represented here. And in this, you are not alone.

I was pleased to learn of another international conference of independent lawyers which took place recently in Montreal. The gathering drew together some three hundred lawyers from eighty countries to discuss the formation of an International Criminal Bar Association, which will aim at acting on behalf of accused persons appearing before the International Criminal Court, due to become operational in The Hague next year.

The proposed International Criminal Bar and other international bar associations bringing together the world community of independent lawyers will have a particular responsibility to work toward the common objective of ensuring the protection of their own independence, the integrity of the national and international justice systems, and the protection of human rights and fundamental freedoms, including the right to fair trial and legal representation of those individuals accused of the most abominable crimes, whether in national or international tribunals.[8]

Indeed, this responsibility must be to the fore at a time when the challenge of confronting the scourge of terrorism has created an environment in which some argue that choices have to be made between our security and our civil liberties. This we must resist strongly. Those who committed the terrorist attacks in the United States on September 11 were enemies of freedom and democracy, with no respect for the sanctity of human life and the values of human rights. But it would be a tragedy if the response to this assault on our common humanity were to entail an erosion of the very human rights and values which we have painstakingly constructed. The fight against terrorism should never be an excuse for the diminution of human rights. This is the message I have reiterated time and again since the events of September 11, and which I wish to urge members of the independent bars to take back with them at the conclusion of this conference.

Let me conclude by referring to some of the practical work my Office is doing to promote and protect the independence of lawyers. In addition to supporting the Special Rapporteur, we are engaged in a number of technical cooperation programs through which we conduct training courses and workshops for legal professionals, including judges, prosecutors, and lawyers. In the last year training programs have been undertaken in South Asia, the Arab and Andean regions, Cambodia, and East Timor. My Office is preparing in conjunction with the International Bar Association resource materials and a training manual for such human rights courses and workshops.

On that practical note, I wish your new Association well. I hope as it grows it will look to the Office of the High Commissioner in Geneva as a partner in its human rights work.

International Coordinating Committee of National Institutions for the Promotion and Protection of Human Rights
Farewell Address
Palais des Nations, Geneva, 17 April 2002

Distinguished Members of the International Coordinating Committee,
Ladies, and Gentlemen,

It is a pleasure to be with you again at your Annual Meeting held in parallel to the fifty-eighth session of the Commission on Human Rights. I am particularly pleased to welcome here Mr. Gils Robles, the Council of Europe's Commissioner on Human Rights.

This year's Commission on Human Rights is proving a challenging one in many ways. Some of these challenges will impact directly on your work. Regrettably, we have seen a number of the meetings of the Commission cancelled, due to budgetary constraints, with the broad agenda of the Commission having to be completed in much less time than initially planned. Tomorrow you will take the floor before the Commission for one hour. I share your disappointment that your time has been reduced.

However, how the time will be used has been entrusted to your Committee, and I am confident that you will encourage an effective use of it—limited though it may be. Over the past five years I have consistently reaffirmed my commitment to the establishment and strengthening of effective, independent, pluralist, and accessible national institutions established in conformity with the internationally accepted standards—the Paris Principles.[9] I have not wavered, nor have the Special Adviser and the National Institutions Team, from reenforcing the importance of full compliance with these Principles.[10] I again urge your Committee and those institutions with which you are associated to remain vigilant in this regard. Your credibility and your participation in United Nations forums depend on it.

A Review of Progress

As I come toward the end of my term as High Commissioner, I want to take this opportunity to review with you some of the important steps I have witnessed regarding national institutions over the past five years. There has been a definite, marked increase in interest by member states in establishing national human rights institutions following the adoption of the Paris Principles in 1993. While there is not yet an independent national institution in each state, there is one in every corner of the globe—from Mongolia to New Zealand, Denmark to South Africa, Argentina to Canada. These institutions can serve as examples for states and civil society beginning the process of establishing national institutions. We have drawn on your experience in guiding their establishment and development. Our most recent challenge is in Afghanistan, where we have been active in assisting the establishment of a National Human Rights Commission. We are working in support of a national Working Group, with preliminary assistance from practitioners from the Human Rights Commissions of Sri Lanka and Malaysia. This sharing of best practices and experiences can be reinforced through the regional groupings of national institutions that have developed. Since 1996 we have seen the work, mandate, and structure of the Asia Pacific Forum of National Human Rights Institutions strengthen. The planned move of the Forum into a more central location in the heart of the region will contribute to this further strengthening.

The First General Assembly of the Americas Network of National Institutions, in Jamaica, has resulted in a similar structure being established, with the Mexican Human Rights Commission acting as the Network's ad interim Secretariat. I was pleased to read that the promotion and protection of the rights of indigenous peoples will form a part of the Network's standard program of work. In the Caribbean, my colleagues have been working with the new subregional association of national institutions as they have developed their constitution—which includes a major focus on human rights.

In Africa, the nucleus for an African Secretariat to support the national institutions of this large continent is taking shape. OHCHR stands ready to support this Secretariat and the activities that it plans to undertake, within the resources we have available.

Within Europe, the Danish Centre for Human Rights has been active in coordinating the various efforts throughout the continent. In November in Ireland and Northern Ireland, I note that you will hold your regional conference with the support of the Council of Europe. This conference will address issues related to asylum seekers, the role of national institutions in postconflict situations, and international cooperation. I look forward to my Office playing an active role in this important Conference, continuing to strengthen our cooperation and building on the presence of Mr. Robles here today.

At the international level, I applaud your efforts at finding consensus in your work. No better example exists than your joint statement to the World Conference against Racism, Racial Discrimination, Xenophobia and Related Intolerance. Many of you were involved in the Conference preparations by undertaking practical initiatives and stimulating local awareness of the vast number of issues within the Durban agenda. You contributed constructively to many of the parallel events organized during the Conference and addressed the plenary in your own right. And you have provided effective follow-up through a number of activities, including the very thorough discussion during your Sixth International Conference just completed.

National Institutions and the Treaty Bodies

You have expressed considerable interest in strengthening your relationship with the United Nations treaty bodies. Support to the treaty bodies is a core area of the work of OHCHR. There has been considerable progress in the attention paid by treaty bodies to national institutions. This has been reflected in consultations by the treaty bodies with national institutions in gathering information in relation to the state party reports—though this can be considerably strengthened; including national institutions in the review process of state party reports; and in the important follow-up to the Concluding Observations of the treaty bodies.

A number of treaty bodies have supported the efforts of national institutions, as evidenced in the recent General Recommendation of the Committee on the Elimination of Racial Discrimination.[11] They have called on states to provide the necessary resources to your institutions, without compromising your independence. They have also called into question government interference in your work and therefore can be guarantors of your existence when you might come under attack from your governments—a phenomenon we know is not restricted to any particular geographic region. I therefore applaud your call at your International Conference for a more formal relationship between the treaty bodies and national institutions and assure you that my Office will assist you in this regard.

I encourage you to use all the resources at your disposal to exchange national, regional and international best practices. I was delighted to launch recently your impressive Web site, financed by my Office and developed with the assistance of the Danish Centre for Human Rights.[12] This Web site is your window to the world to give those not aware of your work the chance to become so. It also provides an innovative and cost-effective way to exchange experiences among yourselves.

Disability Rights

I have always looked to national institutions to help lead the way on a number of important human rights issues. The challenges facing national institutions are many, as they are for those whom you seek to serve. In this context, I have encouraged you from time to time to focus on several specific issues. Last year one particular area was HIV/AIDS and the effects this pandemic is having on every society. This year I have been encouraged to see not only your active response to our request for information for our disability study, but also your own discussion on disability rights and enhancing the work of national institutions in their promotion and protection. I look forward to vigorous participation by national institutions and NGOs in the process of preparing a new International Convention on the Rights of People with Disabilities.[13]

While the work of national institutions is now on a solid footing within my Office, through the efforts of the Special Adviser and a small National Institutions Team, a major issue remains the need for resources to respond to requests from your ever-expanding group. I therefore again call upon you to encourage your governments to provide appropriate support to my Office in this area.

Mr. Chairman, let me conclude my final address, as High Commissioner for Human Rights, to the International Coordinating Committee of National Institutions by saluting you warmly and emphasizing the value of your work. I thank you for your strong expressions of support through the years. It has been a pleasure for me to get to know many of you and see your important work firsthand. I wish you all the best in your endeavors and assure you that whatever I may do in the future, you will still hear my voice in support of your work.

Thank you.

V
Continuing Challenges

Chapter 18

Mainstreaming Human Rights

On his appointment as Secretary General in 1997, Kofi Annan initiated major reform of the UN Secretariat. One such reform called for human rights to be integrated or mainstreamed into all the activities of the United Nations, a task that he decided would be led by the High Commissioner for Human Rights. This important boost for the priority of human rights principles and values coincided with the appointment of Mary Robinson. It was to be her most challenging institutional task during her tenure as High Commissioner. OHCHR developed working relationships and understandings with the UN Executive Committees, different UN agencies, and with the Bretton Woods institutions, in particular the World Bank. There followed the conceptual advance of specifying "rights based" approaches and their gradual adoption in some fields of UN work. The examples given here concern development, poverty, human rights fieldwork in peacekeeping and peace building, and environmental protection. Mary Robinson's efforts to encourage mainstreaming in many other areas are to be found in speeches in other chapters.

"Bridging the Gap between Human Rights and Development: From Normative Principles to Operational Relevance"
World Bank Presidential Fellows' Lecture
Washington, D.C., USA, 3 December 2001

Mr. President,

When I was invited to give a Presidential Fellows' Lecture, I accepted readily. Months ago the date was put firmly in my diary. It fitted the closer links that had been developing at many levels between the World Bank and my Office. The Bank has been an active participant in workshops and seminars we have organized. It has supported the work of the human rights treaty bodies and working groups, such as the Working Group on the right to development, and has been a resource for us. It was a timely invitation to try to bring all this together and see how we might deepen further the relationship.

That was before September 11. The terrible attacks in the United States on that day have altered the landscape in ways we are still trying to assess. Of one thing we can be certain, they have brought home dramatically the urgency of addressing the problem of world poverty, the divides in our world, and the need for an ethical globalization drawing on the international human rights norms and standards.

In the days following September 11 my colleagues and I brainstormed on the human rights perspective. We concluded that, based on the existing jurisprudence, the attacks on innocent civilians in the twin towers in New York constituted a crime against humanity. As such, there was an obligation on all states to cooperate to bring the perpetrators to justice. That justice could be either before a national court, such as the courts of the United States where the attack took place, or before a specially established international court. Characterizing the attacks as a crime against humanity isolates the perpetuators in a significant way—you cannot purport to commit a crime against humanity in the name of any religion. Furthermore, the approach is focused on going after individual perpetrators and bringing them to justice.

There is another linkage to be made with an event that concluded on 8 September. As the gavel come down on the adoption of the Durban Declaration and Programme of Action, I knew we had achieved an important breakthrough for human rights and in combating racial discrimination, xenophobia, and intolerance. Three days later one of my first thoughts was that this antidiscrimination agenda would be more vital and needed than ever.

So, with this added sense of urgency and gravity, let me explain the work of our Office and how we see the potential for a still closer working relationship with you.

Under the terms of my mandate, I have the "principal responsibility for United Nations human rights activities." I would describe the role of my Office as needing to be catalytic, to strive to be a center of excellence, to add value to the knowledge base about international human rights, and to network efforts worldwide on the protection and promotion of human rights. It also has the duty to support the entire UN human rights machinery.

In 1997 the reforms of the Secretary General brought a new dimension of work. Those reforms designated human rights as an issue cutting across the four substantive fields of the UN's activities, including development cooperation. Thus, a major task for the United Nations, and in particular my Office, is to facilitate the integration of human rights fully into all of the Organization's work, including the field of development.

What Can Human Rights Offer Development?

The main issue I want to address today is a challenge faced by human rights agencies, including my own Office, by other United Nations bodies, and indeed by donor and developing countries as well as nongovernmental actors working in development or human rights. What can human rights offer to development work? How can those who are working for universal observance of human rights impact effectively on poverty—itself a violation of human rights—powerlessness, and the conflict and human suffering which poverty underpins?

To begin with, perhaps I should try to answer a prior question. What has the activity of promoting and protecting human rights got to do with development? Are these not wholly different fields of national and international endeavor? What does it add to try to relate them?

The UN's mainstreaming reforms see human rights as both a means and an end of development. Furthermore, under international human rights principles, the individual, and by extension the impoverished community in which she or he lives—and which is the focus of development strategies and policies—are entitled to the same respect for human dignity as are those human beings who have the good fortune to live in countries classified as developed. They are entitled to expect of their governments the same commitment to protect their rights, whether individual or communal. Even though the states in which they live may not have the resources to guarantee those rights as effectively as richer and more developed countries, they have the same internationally endorsed entitlement to policies which will protect and realize their rights, including through international assistance, as any other human beings on the planet.

We owe this thinking on the relationship between development and human rights largely to countries of the South. When the newly independent countries of the 1960s and 1970s joined the United Nations, they took the promise of universal human rights principles and insisted that they were applied to the conditions of their peoples. Despite serious problems of governance, and often of corruption, the belief was there. From their efforts came the UN Declaration on the Right to Development of 1986. From that deeply influential statement—adopted in Cold War conditions—has come the current thinking of a rights-based approach to development that seeks to bring about the promise of universal human rights and dignity.

The international human rights documents, including the Declaration on the Right to Development of 1986, are replete with references to the interdependent or mutually reinforcing relationship that exists between all categories of rights—by which I mean civil, political, economic, social, and cultural rights—within national protection systems. But these documents go one step further. They express the further requirement for effective enjoyment of those rights, whether a country is developing or developed, of a participatory democracy, based on the rule of law, as the only system of government that can ensure the implementation of all categories of rights. In short, the framework of values that guides a human rights approach to development is one that builds on development as a process committed to the guarantee of all human rights, the rule of law, and democracy.

This holistic view is surely not far removed from the approach of the World Bank in its actual practice on development. But history records a gulf between development and human rights specialists and advocates. This, at least in part, may have had to do with the dominant professions that became engaged in both fields. There was a time—it may still be the time—when human rights discourse was almost always that of the diplomats, lawyers, and philosophers, while development thinking and writing was the domain of economists and other social scientists. This inheritance, and hopefully its demise, is captured in a comment in the Human Development Report 2000:

Until the last decade human development and human rights followed parallel paths in both concept and action—the one largely dominated by economists, social scientists, and policy-makers, the other by political activists, lawyers, and philosophers. They promoted divergent strategies of analysis and action—economic and social progress on the one hand, political pressure, law reform, and ethical questioning on the other.[1]

In its *Annual Report 2001*, the World Bank illustrates how that gap is being closed:

Poor people often lack legal rights that would empower them to take advantage of opportunities and protect them from arbitrary and inequitable treatment. They, more than any other group in society, are adversely affected by laws permitting discrimination, deficient laws and institutions that fail to protect individual and property rights, and insufficient enforcement of these laws, as well as other barriers to justice.[2]

This assessment of the effects of poverty is little different from a human rights analysis which defines poverty as "the sustained or chronic deprivation of the resources, capabilities, choices, security and power necessary for the enjoyment of an adequate standard of living and other civil, cultural, economic, political and social rights." It is clear that there is convergence. The challenge is to use a common analysis and multidisciplinary and multisectoral approaches to achieve development and poverty reduction.

If these assumptions about the convergence and complementarity of human rights and development are shared, the issue remains: How in practical terms are we to make it work? How has human rights thinking moved from the affirmation of principles in the Universal Declaration of Human Rights, and developed through treaties and legal standards, to operational approaches which contribute to development?

At the Millennium Summit, the General Assembly pledged to "spare no effort to free our fellow men, women and children from the abject and dehumanizing conditions of extreme poverty, to which more than a billion of them are currently subjected." There was also an explicit recognition of the link between the realization of the right to development and poverty reduction.

The process of making relevant operationally a human-rights-based approach to poverty reduction is at the beginning stage. It is a story with many chapters and an increasing range of actors working to achieve rigorous and operationally specific human-rights-based approaches to their work.

Rights-Based Approaches

Rights-based approaches to development may be seen as the operational expression of the inextricable link between development and human rights. A rights-based approach is a conceptual framework for the process of human development that is normatively based on international human rights standards and operationally directed to promoting and protecting human rights. The rights-based approach integrates the norms, standards, and principles of the international human rights system into the plans, policies, and processes of development. The norms and standards are those contained in the wealth of international treaties and declarations that I have mentioned. The principles in question are participation, empowerment, accountability, nondiscrimination, and express linkages to international human rights norms and standards. But it should be emphasized that at the heart of a human rights approach must be the legal character of the international treaties that create rights and duties.

Drawing from existing research and development experience, we might say that a human rights approach provides

enhanced accountability;
higher levels of empowerment, ownership, and free, meaningful, and active participation;
greater normative clarity and detail;
easier consensus and increased transparency in national development processes;
a more complete and rational development framework;
integrated safeguards against unintentional harm by development projects;
more effective and complete analysis; and
a more authoritative basis for advocacy.

Rights also lend moral legitimacy and the principle of social justice to development objectives and help shift the focus of analysis to the most deprived and excluded, especially to deprivations caused by discrimination. A human rights approach involves attention being directed to the need for information and a political voice for all people as a development issue. It believes that civil and political rights should be acknowledged in practice as well as in theory as integral parts of the development process, and that economic, social, and cultural rights should be recognized and implemented as human rights, rather than shrugged off as fanciful ideals or abstract absolutes.

Of these various principles, in my view the most defining attribute of human rights in development is the idea of accountability. I have in the past called for a more critical approach to the integration of human rights into the work of development—one that asks hard questions about obligations, duties, and action. All partners in the development process—local, national, regional, and international—must accept higher levels of accountability. Establishing ways to operationalize and evaluate institutions and mechanisms for accountability in development programming is therefore a defining challenge in the years ahead. I recognize the important conceptual work produced by the World Bank in this area.

However, while much in the field of human rights and development is now settled on a level of general principle, expectations can be too high. A human-rights-based approach in any given set of circumstances

provides an analytical and procedural framework, including participation, for the consideration of the complex issues involved in the development equation, rather than definitive answers; it will not necessarily shed light on the requisite or even the best policy mix, and the discussion of trade-offs will always be a difficult one;

should not rely on unrealistic assumptions concerning the practical value of formal redress through legal processes and institutions; human rights need to be seen as open-textured and flexible and capable of policy application in diverse situations in ways not limited to adjudication in courts and tribunals.

Human Rights and Development in Practice

I would like to share with you some examples of the work OHCHR and others are doing to bridge this gap between the conceptual and programmatic domains, through concrete research and practice.

At the Interagency Level

Under the 1997 reforms, many important initiatives have been undertaken at the interagency level, including working with the United Nations Development Group to incorporate human rights standards in the Common Country Assessment and United Nations Development Assistance Framework (CCA/UNDAF).[3] Similar efforts have been made under the UN Strategy for Halving Extreme Poverty by 2015 and its Options for Action.[4] We have been involved also in the preparation of human rights guidelines for UN Resident Coordinators as well as in encouraging various other initiatives directed at human rights integration.[5] The Human Rights Strengthening (HURIST) joint program between my Office and UNDP is an important and practically oriented laboratory for the learning and dissemination of such lessons and shared experiences.[6]

Gender

Gender is an issue that both human rights and development experts have recognized belatedly as a necessary component of their work. Internationally adopted human rights standards can provide useful guidance in improving women's rights, and a major focus of international human rights law has been discrimination. Currently 168 states have undertaken to apply the Convention on the Elimination of All Forms of Discrimination against Women.[7] Ratification of this and other legal standards on gender equality and on the rights of women provide a reference and a means of avoiding cultural-sensitivity traps.

The Bank's work on poverty reduction strategies points out that "gender-sensitive development strategies contribute significantly to economic growth as well as to equity objectives." The Bank's recent, and excellent, report *Engendering Development* sums up much of the growing evidence on the extent to which gender disparities lead to economically inefficient outcomes and result in slower growth and lower levels of welfare.[8]

Some dimensions of the impact of gender on economic growth and development have long been recognized. Improving access to education for girls and women reduces child mortality and improves the nutritional status of children, and improving gender equality in secondary education has been linked to increases in per capita income. When women lack the right to inherit or to own property, the resulting rigidities in gender roles influence the effectiveness of development strategies. For example, women who do not own land or whose low social status limits their access to agricultural extension services have less opportunity to increase productivity. Let us keep in mind that the two core human rights instruments that provide the framework for achieving gender equality are the Convention for the Elimination of Discrimination against Women (CEDAW) and the Convention on the Rights of the Child. Dare I pose the question Have members of the Board of the Bank examined the small print of these documents?

HIV/AIDS

Appreciation of the linkages between health and human rights as complementary approaches to the advancement of human well-being is growing. There is greater recognition of the centrality of human rights to global health challenges, and increased attention is being given to the accountability of states under international law for issues related to health. And there is recognition of the need to address the right to health in light of the social and economic conditions that allow people to lead healthy lives, such as access to safe drinking water, food and nutrition, housing, and to education and information related to health matters—including sexual and reproductive health.

In many respects HIV/AIDS has broken new ground for a better understanding of these linkages. A lack of respect for human rights is linked to virtually every aspect of the AIDS epidemic, from the factors that cause or increase vulnerability to HIV infection, to discrimination based on stigma attached to people living with HIV/AIDS, to the factors that limit the ability of individuals and communities to respond effectively to the epidemic. This link is apparent in the disproportionate incidence and spread of the disease among certain groups, including, in particular, people living in poverty. It is also apparent in the fact that the overwhelming burden of the epidemic today is borne by developing countries, where the disease threatens to reverse vital achievements in human development. There is clear evidence that where individuals and communities are able to realize their rights—to education, free association, information, and most importantly, nondiscrimination—the incidence and impact of HIV and AIDS are reduced.

We have also seen a growing commitment by states to the promotion and protection of human rights in relation to global health issues. At the General Assembly Special Session on HIV/AIDS, for example, states committed themselves to the realization of human rights as an essential part of the international response to the pandemic.[9] At the World Conference against Racism, states recognized the need to address the impact of racism as a determinant of health status and access to health care, including measures to prevent genetic research from being used for discriminatory purposes.

The Declaration on the TRIPS (Trade Related Aspects of Intellectual Property Rights) Agreement and Public Health adopted in Doha sent an important signal regarding the need to balance intellectual property rights against public health priorities for developing countries.[10] The Declaration stresses the need for TRIPS to be interpreted in a manner "supportive of WTO members' right to protect public health" and to promote access to medicines, particularly with regard to HIV/AIDS, tuberculosis, malaria, and other epidemics.

Mr. President, I would like to return to the events of September 11 and conclude with some reflections. I read your recent newspaper article, which carried the headline "Rich Nations Can Remove World Poverty as a Source of Conflict."[11] As I hope will have been clear from what I have said, I agree with the analysis and prescription. We must, as you said, fight poverty and exclusion worldwide. I would add only the issues of nondiscrimination and dialogue. Globalization was addressed recently at the World Conference against Racism in Durban, South Africa. While noting the positive opportunities offered by globalization, the Conference Programme of Action warned that globalization can also aggravate poverty, underdevelopment, marginalization, social exclusion, cultural homogenization, and economic disparities along racial lines.

The Durban Conference expressed determination to ensure that the economic growth resulting from globalization is channeled to eradicate poverty, inequality, and deprivation. A central element in the new globalization must be the fight against all forms of intolerance. That requires intensifying dialogue between all cultures and regions. The events of September 11 have made this all the more urgent.

Amartya Sen wrote recently that the central issue, directly or indirectly, in the growing skepticism about the global order is inequality—between as well as within nations. To address that inequality I believe we need what Guy Verhofstadt, the Prime Minister of Belgium and current President of the European Union, has called ethical globalization.[12] For me, the foundations of ethical globalization are the international human rights standards making all rights available to all.

I believe there is convergence of thinking between the human rights agenda and the World Bank agenda. The bridge is built. We are dealing with the same intractable challenges to human betterment but from different approaches and with different resources. Lawyers should not be the only voice in human rights and, equally, economists should not be the only voice in development.

Recently I was glad to accept the invitation by the Bank to endorse the third volume of the *Voices of the Poor: From Many Lands.*[13] One testimony contained in this third and last volume of the series touched me particularly. Fernando from Brazil said: "In a *favela* people have no idea of their rights. We have police discrimination; the politicians abuse us, and others use their knowledge to take advantage of us. So I want to know all about rights and obligations." Together we must ensure that his testimony is heard.

Thank you.

"A Human Rights Approach to Poverty Reduction Strategies"
Preface to the OHCHR Draft Guidelines
10 September 2002

Eradicating poverty must be our first goal in this new millennium. Governments have committed themselves to taking action through strategies and programs that aim to reduce poverty and eliminate extreme poverty. The denial of human rights is inherent in poverty, something which is powerfully recorded in recent studies, such as *Voices of the Poor.*[14] Poverty cannot be banished without the realization of human rights. In the words of the Human Development Report 2000: "A decent standard of living, adequate nutrition, health care, education and decent work, and protection against calamities are not just development goals—they are also human rights."[15]

In a letter dated 6 July 2001, the Chair of the United Nations Committee on Economic, Social and Cultural Rights asked the Office of the High Commissioner to develop guidelines for the integration of human rights into poverty-reduction strategies. In response to this request, I asked three experts—Professors Paul Hunt, Manfred Nowak, and Siddiq Osmani—to prepare draft guidelines and in the process to consult with national officials, civil society, and international development agencies, including the World Bank. This publication contains the results of their work.

I have commented before that

> Lawyers should not be the only voice in human rights and, equally, economists should not be the only voice in development. The challenge now is to demonstrate how the assets represented by human rights principles, a form of international public goods, can be of value in pursuing the overarching development objective, the eradication of poverty.[16]

In elaborating the Draft Guidelines, the authors have taken up the challenge of bridging the divide between a normative approach and a development economist's approach to the concept and content of poverty. The text draws on both the experience of the international human rights system over the last fifty years and more recent scholarship by social scientists.

At the same time the experts have helped to clarify what a rights-based approach to development means in practice. The Draft Guidelines therefore contribute to a major task facing the United Nations, and in particular OHCHR, that of integrating human rights into all of the Organization's work, including the goal of eradicating poverty.

We are well embarked upon the United Nations Decade for the Eradication of Poverty (1996–2007). The General Assembly, in establishing the Decade, called upon "the United Nations system . . . to participate actively in the financial and technical support of the Decade . . . with a view to translating all measures and recommendations into operational and concrete poverty eradication programs and activities." It also urged "the strengthening of international assistance to developing countries in their efforts to alleviate poverty." I believe the draft guidelines make a valuable contribution to realizing the goals of the Decade.

I hope also that the Draft Guidelines will strengthen implementation of the Millennium Development Goals. They provide ample illustration of how attention to human rights can reinforce each of the eight development goals.

National and international strategies addressing poverty reduction need to take into account the human rights dimension of poverty and its remedies. The draft guidelines are intended to assist countries, international agencies, and development practitioners to translate human rights norms, standards, and principles into pro-poor policies and strategies. I hope that they will become a practical tool to implement human rights approaches to poverty reduction at the country level.

I encourage governments, nongovernmental organizations, and international development agencies to test and pilot the Draft Guidelines and to contribute what is learned from that experience when, as is proposed, they are reviewed in 2003.

"Strengthening Human Rights Field Operations"
Address to the International Human Rights Symposium
Bonn, Germany, 26 May 1998

Excellencies, Ladies, and Gentlemen,

I would like to consider today the profound importance of conducting human rights work in the places where people live. Our presence in the field allows us to understand the true state of human rights in a society: it gives substance to the words of governments, faces to the victims of rights violations, and immediacy to the actions of human rights workers.

Daily contacts in the field—in the form of dialogue with officials, information sharing with NGOs, meetings with individual victims—help us to learn about the unique qualities of different societies. Of course, our hope is that the societies learn too: that the meaning of human rights is appreciated at a deeper level, that human rights violations decrease, that the threat of conflict—whether internal or external—is reduced. Human rights fieldwork presents the opportunity for a remarkable synergy, between a society and its international professionals working together with members of that society, for the advancement of human rights. In recent years the Office of the High Commissioner for Human Rights has increasingly devoted its efforts to fieldwork in that broad sense, as we have established presences in Rwanda, Burundi, the Democratic Republic of Congo, Colombia, El Salvador, Guatemala, Togo, Liberia, Angola, Malawi, and Georgia and expanded and developed others in Gaza, Cambodia, Mongolia, Bosnia and Herzegovina, Croatia, and the Federal Republic of Yugoslavia. There is clearly momentum toward more fieldwork by my Office, and this is why the subject of today's conference is so timely.

Indeed, much remains to be done to assure the quality and effectiveness of our fieldwork and to establish consistent methodologies. This is an area of activity, in fact, that is still quite young and in the process of being shaped. The basic prerequisites for effective human rights field operations in the full sense have been well cataloged by a number of concerned parties, and I trust their conclusions will be given due consideration at this symposium. Among these studies I would pay special tribute to the work of the Aspen Institute in the United States, which benefited from the contributions of some among us here today.[17] The Institute's findings, which I firmly endorse, include the need for clear methodologies and, more specifically, for careful planning, training, the identification of stable funding sources, recruitment of persons experienced in human rights work, and a practice of recording the "lessons learned" from completed operations to benefit those of the future. There is a need to strike a balance between monitoring and advisory activities, with a focus on institution building. It has been suggested that there should be a specialized field-mission unit within my Office to ensure a consistent approach, and indeed, our new structure now includes a team dedicated to the refinement of field methodologies. We must work for the implementation of all of the fine suggestions made so far in this area.

Today, however, I would like to concentrate on a different but related topic: the relationship between human rights fieldwork and peacekeeping operations. There is a profound connection, as I have often emphasized, between a society's respect for human rights and the security of that society's people. Human rights fieldwork can, in fact, make an important contribution to international peace and security. This is a principle that I believe has not yet been accepted widely. Too often we look at the question of respect for human rights in isolation: Do a country's laws comport with its international obligations? Are persons imprisoned for their beliefs? Is the right to economic opportunity recognized, the right to be free from discrimination? The implications of the answers to these questions extend beyond the integrity of the particular government in question: they touch on that society's very stability, and the stability of societies in its neighborhood.

Human rights violations, I have argued, are frequently the root causes of conflict and humanitarian crises. The deprivation of human rights takes from people an integral part of their lives, their sense of dignity and self-worth—a loss which humans are deeply disposed to resist. And they do resist. They fight. They even take up arms and make war.

If we wish to eliminate the root causes of conflict, as we are all committed to do, then we must ensure respect for human rights in the field, in societies around the world, in a real way which affects people's lives. It is for this reason, I believe, that we must integrate human rights work into peacekeeping, peacemaking, and postconflict peace-building.

Part of addressing root causes of conflict lies in improved respect for human rights. If we understand and accept this principle, then we will greatly enhance the value of human rights operations—and peacekeeping operations—in countries around the world. The ways in which human rights concerns intersect with peacekeeping operations will inevitably vary according to mandates, political realities, practical considerations on the ground. But I should like to propose several principles today, on which I hope we could all agree, to bring human rights and peacekeeping closer together.

Human Rights Concerns Should Be Integrated into Early-Warning and Preventive Action

My Office, as the institution of the UN mandated to ensure human rights protection and promotion, has emphasized the value of early-warning and preventive action to deter human rights violations and defuse situations which may escalate into armed conflict. The information and findings of UN human rights experts (Rapporteurs, representatives, members of human rights treaty bodies), together with those of UN human rights field offices, can be an important part of the early-warning mechanisms of the UN as a whole. As we are in the process of starting a review of the human rights machinery, it is essential to keep in mind two important objectives: that this information from UN human rights experts is readily accessible, and that progress, or lack of progress, in human rights can be quantified and measured, thus allowing some degree of benchmarking, possibly country by country.

OHCHR recognizes that the wealth of information at its disposal can be useful to the DPKO, DPA, and OCHA, as well as to the Executive Committees of the UN.[18] I would like to ensure that in the context of the existing mechanisms of coordination we have (the Inter Agency Standing Committee (IASC), Executive Committees, etc.) we identify, perhaps on a monthly basis, potential crisis situations—situations that could result in gross violations of human rights, threats to international peace and security, shocks to the international conscience. This information, considered together with that of DPA, DPKO, OCHA, UNHCR, and others, could

strengthen the early warning capacity of the UN;
enhance the substantive exchanges between the UN offices mentioned above and other concerned parties, including governments; and
integrate human rights concerns before crises arise and thus prepare the ground for effective cooperation both in preparedness and in responses to crises within the UN.

Beyond the point of warning, the actual deployment of human rights field monitors or advisers may in some cases be part of a strategy for preventive action (not too different from the concept of preventive deployment in the Agenda for Peace effectively used already in the context of the former Yugoslav Republic of Macedonia).[19] This may, for example, be the case in Kosovo, in the Federal Republic of Yugoslavia, where the Contact Group has expressed support for an increased presence of my Office. Any such action should normally take place in full cooperation with DPKO, DPA, and OCHA, further developing the UN's collegiate capacity in prevention.

Human Rights Concerns Should Be an Element of Crisis Response

I would argue that, at the point at which a peacekeeping operation is proposed to the Security Council, the human rights dimension, including a gender perspective, should automatically be a part of planning, requiring close cooperation between DPKO, DPA and our Office. While the need and opportunity to include human rights officers or advisers within different peacekeeping operations will vary, an explicit human rights strategy should be part of the planning of any peacekeeping presence. Such a strategy should normally cover advice, training, and, together with UNDP, institution building and, when mandated by the Security Council or determined by the Secretary General, also monitoring.

It is a fact that there has been, and will continue to be, resistance from some member states on the Security Council to the integration of human rights into peacekeeping mandates. It is to be hoped that the proper reflection of the human rights dimension in reports of the Secretary General to the Council will win increasing recognition of its integral relationship to peace and security. When states insist that human rights mandates be kept separate from peacekeeping mandates, the responsibility on us is all the greater to ensure that integrated planning within the Secretariat results in a coordinated UN strategy on the ground.

UN peacekeeping operations should be held to the highest standards of conduct, and strong adherence to human rights standards will enhance the operation's standing—and its credibility—with governmental and other actors. I would like to see a human rights component included routinely in any peacekeeping operation launched by the United Nations. This has been the subject of some debate, with the view advanced that human rights concerns should, at least in some cases, be divorced from the main focus of activities of peacekeeping operations.

Put simply, I believe that this view is mistaken. A human rights unit in a peacekeeping operation can provide valuable information to the mission's leadership on progress achieved to improve respect for human rights and, therefore, lessen the possibility of a setback to efforts to achieve peace. In a peacekeeping operation's later stage, its human rights institution-building activities can be the key to the mission's ultimate success, ensuring that the gains achieved are safeguarded well into the future by building an effective national human rights infrastructure.

It is thus important to integrate human rights concerns from beginning to end: to include human rights experts in preparatory missions prior to peacekeeping operations; to integrate human rights units—with equal standing to other mission elements—into ongoing peacekeeping operations; and to emphasize as part of an exit strategy the establishment of solid national institutions, to ensure the long-term success of the operation. This last point should always be addressed in cooperation with UNDP, which is already present in the country and can coordinate UN action there.

In the arrangements made to integrate human rights components into peacekeeping operations, several factors should be taken into account:

The overall authority of the Chief of the Mission, normally a Special Representative of the Secretary General or SRSG, should be recognized and human rights activities should be coordinated, with a close working relationship established between the human rights unit and others with connected mandates, either inside (for example, CIVPOL) or outside (for example, UNDP, UNHCR) the peacekeeping operation itself.

While the use given to human rights information assembled by missions may vary (with different policies prevailing, for example on public statements), the integrity of the monitoring and reporting processes should always be protected.

The human rights unit should receive guidance and support from OHCHR, using the knowledge and experience gained from similar operations elsewhere and from other mechanisms of the UN human rights system.

Administrative support to the units should be provided efficiently and cost-effectively, with a priority equal to that of other nonmilitary components.

There Should Be Human Rights Training for All Participants in Peacekeeping Operations

In connection with the applicability of humanitarian law in peacekeeping operations, it should be noted that at present the Status of Forces Agreements (SoFAs) include the following procedures: the forces shall observe the principles and spirit of the general international conventions applicable to the conduct of military personnel. The international conventions referred to above include the four Geneva Conventions of 12 August 1949 and their additional protocols and the UNESCO Convention of 14 May 1954 on the Protection of Cultural Property in the event of armed conflict. The SoFAs should therefore make it a practice to include in their articles also an explicit reference to the International Bill of Human Rights and the importance of women's rights as human rights. UN peacekeeping operations should provide for the training of all UN personnel in international human rights and gender standards as well as in the respect of basic international human rights law by UN peacekeeping forces themselves. This can be accomplished, for example, by including such training in programs organized at the national level by countries providing peacekeeping personnel. Training should also be organized routinely immediately upon deployment in the country of operation, as part of the induction program for newly appointed peacekeepers.

Human rights training is especially important in the context of civilian police contingents of peacekeeping missions who are consistently assigned specific human rights tasks. Indeed, CIVPOL officers are, in every sense, human rights monitors. In El Salvador, with ONUSAL, the responsibilities of CIVPOL included monitoring the human rights record of police forces; similar responsibilities were assigned to CIVPOL in Cambodia, Mozambique, Croatia, and elsewhere, including in Bosnia and Herzegovina today, where the International Police Task Force (IPTF) is responsible for monitoring the action of local police and investigating alleged human rights violations. Many of these operations, indeed, have had their own human rights offices.

OHCHR has pursued a vigorous program of human rights training for military and civilian personnel for peacekeeping missions. Our first such training was held in 1994 in Mozambique, for civilian police of UNOMOZ. Other training has been conducted for CIVPOL in the former Yugoslavia. Comprehensive training programs for military officials have been or are held at the UN Staff College in Turin. OHCHR is also developing a human rights manual for trainers of peacekeeping forces, in cooperation with DPKO, which will be made available to governments and others involved in such training. Furthermore, it is essential to ensure that all staff members of the UN, particularly those in the humanitarian sector and engaged in the field, have a much greater knowledge of the human rights standards, mechanisms, and procedures. Improved communication on human rights with our Office, and an integrated approach by all of us, is the key to greater effectiveness of the whole UN human rights machinery in its ability to know, assess, and respond to human rights needs.

Stable Funding for Human Rights Operations Must Be Identified

While my Office is optimistic about our ability to obtain the necessary voluntary funds for field activities, our experience with HRFOR in Rwanda has shown that voluntary contributions are probably not an adequate funding basis for large human rights field operations. The integration of human rights components into peacekeeping operations carries the natural advantage that funding is obtained through assessed contributions. As DPA has advocated, there should also be an effort to persuade the General Assembly to provide an adequate funding basis for missions not classified as peacekeeping operations, and therefore not funded from special accounts. A discussion on these objectives, and feasible interim devices, would be welcome.

Peacekeeping Should Always Lead to Postconflict Peace-Building

The value of technical cooperation programs aimed at strengthening democratic and human rights institutions, the rule of law, and popular human rights awareness has long been recognized. This value is enhanced when such programs are implemented in war-torn societies that are on the road toward peace. In this context technical cooperation becomes reinforcement, strengthening the fragile institutions built by the parties and their international partners in the aftermath of war. Just as one would not use bricks without mortar, we should not invest in peacekeeping operations without adding an element for long-term human rights protection.

My Office participated in a very interesting meeting organized by the World Bank in Paris last month on Post Conflict Reconstruction, which for the first time brought together the humanitarian, the development, and the human rights institutions as well as major bilateral and multilateral donors in order to discuss openly how to develop more effective strategies to deal with the aftermath of conflict as well as to address the root causes of humanitarian crises. An informal network has been created which may pave the way to greater coordination at ground level in reconstruction efforts. With respect to technical cooperation in human rights, I have endeavored to strengthen our own programs in advisory services and technical cooperation, including the promotion of democratic institutions, development and human rights, women's rights and gender issues; human rights support to parliament; constitutional assistance; human rights training; legislative reform assistance; administration of justice; establishing or strengthening national human rights institutions; training of police and prison officials; assistance on specific human rights issues; the implementation of comprehensive national plans of action for the promotion and protection of human rights; and the implementation of projects related to economic, social, and cultural rights, including the right to development.

The strategy is to link with partners engaged in similar programs and indeed not to reinvent the wheel! Priority consideration is being given to requests for cooperation with respect to programs that strengthen national human rights capacities and national human rights institutions and infrastructures. Close cooperation with DPA (given its lead responsibility for post-conflict peace-building), DPKO, OCHA, and UNDP is essential to ensure the effectiveness of the overall program.

Technical cooperation programs will typically need to be sustained beyond the mandates of peacekeeping operations. Cambodia is an example of the human rights work of the peacekeeping operation continuing beyond the mission's expiration. These programs should eventually be integrated into the developmental work of UNDP under the good governance program. We have also concluded that, where monitoring is mandated by the competent legislative organ, a dual approach to human rights fieldwork combining monitoring and reporting, on the one hand, and technical cooperation programs, on the other, is the best approach for carrying out effective human rights work, whether in the context of peacekeeping operations or not.

Ladies and gentlemen, it remains to be seen whether the proposal for routine inclusion of human rights components in UN peacekeeping operations will be adopted, but I believe it is essential that a clear decision on this matter is taken soon. In the meantime, we must aspire to the highest standards of achievement and efficiency for the field operations that we currently maintain. Our recent experience has shown us ways to improve our performance in the field, and we are working now, in OHCHR, to implement these ideas as swiftly as resources allow. It is my hope that this conference will yield conclusions that will help us in our efforts to strengthen human rights field operations. If our work in this field is truly to have the effect of improving respect for human rights in the places where people live, then we must enhance the capacity of the international community—the capacity to investigate, resolve, and prevent human rights violations at their source.

World Summit on Sustainable Development
Address to Plenary Session
Johannesburg, South Africa, 26 August–5 September 2002

The Earth Summit at Rio de Janeiro has been an essential reference point for this Summit on Sustainable Development.[20] Rio did produce a conceptual breakthrough in that the natural world was added to the social and economic dimensions of development to give us the concept of sustainable development.

I should like to recall another reference point which is also important for the Johannesburg Summit deliberations, and that is the World Conference on Human Rights which took place the following year, 1993, in Vienna. The understandings reached at that Conference added new dimensions to the concept of development, namely human rights and democracy. In so doing, the Conference was reaffirming core ideas of the 1986 Declaration on the Right to Development. Vienna confirmed an international consensus that economic, social, and cultural rights were individual human rights to be given equal weight to civil and political rights, and that both sets of rights were universal, interdependent, and indivisible. It also declared that democracy, development, and respect for human rights were interdependent and mutually reinforcing. Vienna confirmed the recognition that the promotion and protection of human rights in all countries is a legitimate concern of the international community.

These understandings have had a singular influence on development policies and programs since, as have the commitments at Rio. A human rights approach to development is being adopted increasingly by development agencies and donors as well as in development work. This was reflected in the *Human Development Report 2000*, a landmark statement on the human-rights-based approach to development. As the Report noted, "Poverty eradication is a major human rights challenge of the 21st Century. A decent standard of living, adequate nutrition, health care, education, decent work, and protection against calamities are not just development goals—they are also human rights."[21]

The *Report* is equally clear on the importance for development of guaranteeing civil and political rights—freedom of speech, association, and participation—to empower poor people to claim their social, economic, and cultural rights. Meanwhile the recognition of the linkage between democracy and development has led to the emphasis in development practice over the last decade on building democratic institutions, the rule of law, and effective legal systems that function to protect the human rights of all without discrimination.

Human Rights and the Environment

I would like now to turn to the relationship between human rights and the environment.

The Rio Declaration and Agenda 21 did not contain many explicit references to human rights.[22] Nor did Vienna have many references to the environment. The Rio Summit in retrospect may have placed too much emphasis on environmental sustainability without regard to the human dimension, while the Vienna World Conference may be faulted for having placed too little. But it is a positive gain to note that in the decade since then, there has been continuous progress in bringing together the human and environmental dimensions within the concept of sustainable development.

An example of that progress was the Expert Seminar convened by OHCHR and the United Nations Environment Programme (UNEP) in January 2002.[23] Its aim was to review and assess progress achieved since Rio and Agenda 21 in promoting and protecting human rights in relation to environmental questions. A pamphlet on the experts' conclusions has been published jointly by OHCHR and UNEP for this Summit.

Reading the seminar's conclusions, it is striking how at every level—international, regional, national—there is a greater appreciation than ever before of the nexus between human rights and environmental themes, especially when considered in the context of sustainable development.

At the international level, a number of important human rights treaties take into account the environmental dimensions of human rights.[24]

At the regional level, a number of instruments have addressed the linkages, again with an emphasis on information and participation. I would single out the 1998 Aarhus Convention on Access to Information, Public Participation and Access to Justice in Environmental Matters.[25] It illustrates how procedural rights to information and participation help protect human rights and the environment at the same time. Mention should also be made of the experience of the European and inter-American human rights systems, which have increasingly interpreted environmental degradation in human rights terms.[26]

It is at the national level, however, that some of the most striking developments have taken place. The right to a healthy environment has been formally recognized in over ninety national constitutions enacted since 1992. Often the right is made expressly justiciable. In other countries, especially in South Asia and Latin America, constitutional rights to life, health, and family life have been interpreted as embracing environmental factors.

I would identify the prime goal for the immediate future as to achieve a deeper understanding of the links between human rights and environmental protection. It will involve a significant effort on the part of both human rights and environmental practitioners to come to grips with the values, methodologies, and comparative advantages of each other. It will also involve a continued effort on the part of institutional actors—such as my Office and of the United Nations Environment Programme—to foster this understanding. The draft Plan of Action of the Conference has paragraphs that seek further cooperation between UNEP and OHCHR. I call for the final adoption of those paragraphs.[27]

Let me end with words from my friend and colleague, the Executive Director of UNEP Klaus Töpfer:

> The contribution of environmental protection to the realization of basic human rights, and the role of human rights in protection of the environment are undeniable. Substantive rights such as the right to food, health, and the right to life itself will not materialize for all of the world's inhabitants unless we maintain a clean and healthy environment with a sustainable base of environmental and natural resources. Certainly, the full potential of human rights cannot be realized when an increasing portion of the world's inhabitants find their human potential constrained by a polluted and degraded environment and are relegated to hopelessness in extreme poverty.[28]

Chapter 19

Terrorism, Peace, and Human Security

When she was President of Ireland, Mary Robinson was the first head of state to visit Rwanda after the genocide. Her personal experience of meeting its victims affected her deeply. As High Commissioner, the experience of witnessing, firsthand, civilian suffering in other conflicts, whether in Chechnya, Sierra Leone, the Occupied Palestinian Territories, East Timor, Colombia, or the Balkans, drove her to constantly argue for more emphasis by the international community on the prevention of conflict. For her, respect for human rights and humanitarian law, accountability for atrocities, and the imperative of development were all necessary means to ensure sustainable peace. (See also Chapters 12 and 14.) She had the opportunity to present these views to the United Nations Security Council for the first time in 1999. This was a significant step in itself. It reflected recognition by the Security Council of the links between international peace and security, and human rights and human security. It also was an acknowledgment of the importance of the position of High Commissioner for Human Rights in advancing these related goals.

The horrific attacks on the United States on September 11, 2001, brought a different form of political violence—international terrorism—into world focus. In the aftermath of those attacks, crimes against humanity as Mary Robinson characterized them, her concern that human rights should not be sacrificed in the legitimate and necessary responses to the challenge of terrorism was a consistent, if not always welcomed, injunction. The shadow over human rights was an image she used to express her concern over the immediate and longer-term effects of unchecked counterterrorism measures on states' commitment to human rights and the rule of law. Her views on the prevention of terrorism mirror her views on the prevention of other forms of violence, concern for the victims, the need to ensure accountability of the perpetrators under the law, the need to build a culture of tolerance and human rights, and the need to address underlying causes.

"Protection of Civilians in Armed Conflict"
Statement to the Security Council
United Nations, New York, 16 September 1999

Mr. President,

I warmly welcome this opportunity to address members of the Security Council. I wish to express my appreciation to the Council for having commissioned this report on the protection of civilians in armed conflict and thank the Secretary General for an excellent, clear, and concise document.

I am pleased to be here with you today as the report raises issues close to my heart. The report accurately reflects the innumerable challenges which the United Nations faces in its work and so many of the human rights issues which my staff and I address on a daily basis. My Office is more than willing to play its part in implementing the report's constructive recommendations on the effective implementation of international human rights, humanitarian and refugee law, and on the prevention of gross violations of human rights so crucial to national and regional stability and thus to international peace and security.

As High Commissioner for Human Rights, I have assumed a burden of listening: listening to the pain and anguish of victims of violations; listening to the anxieties and fears of human rights defenders. I am glad to share this burden with you today, members of the Council, because you have the power and possibilities to alleviate the pain and to prevent some of the anxieties being realized.

I refer to East Timor first because the terrible events of recent days are so fresh in my mind.[1] The awful abuses committed in East Timor have shocked the world—and rightly so since it would be hard to conceive of a more blatant assault on the rights of hundreds of thousands of innocent civilians. The murders, maimings, rapes and countless other atrocities committed by the militias with the involvement of elements of the security forces were especially repugnant because they came in the aftermath of the freely expressed wishes of the East Timorese people about their political future. I saw evidence of a well-planned and systematic policy of killings, displacement, destruction of property, and intimidation. There must be accountability for the grave violations committed in East Timor. My recommendation is the establishment of an international commission of enquiry to gather and analyze evidence of the events in East Timor.

What happened in East Timor is a graphic example of the plight of civilians in conflict situations. And East Timor is just the latest example. In the former Yugoslavia, I met women and girls who had been sexually assaulted, raped, and forced into sexual slavery.[2] In Sierra Leone, I met children whose arms or legs had been brutally cut off during the civil war.[3] I listened to accounts of children being abducted by rebels and sent to training centers or directly to the battlefront. Children were forced to attack their own villages and families and commit the most horrendous atrocities. Many of these child soldiers have been killed, while others were maimed and psychologically scarred for life. In Colombia and Cambodia, human rights defenders vividly described the climate of violence in which they were carrying on their activities at great personal risk. Reports from Angola tell how rebels provoked a mass movement of displaced persons desperate to reach the relatively safe haven of provincial capitals.

Mr. President, it had been expected that the collapse of superpower rivalry would lead to a reduction in conflict, but the decline in interstate fighting has been more than made up for in the growth of vicious internal conflicts, often unpredictable and volatile. These are conflicts that drag on for years without settlement or that flare up afresh when peace seemed to be at hand. The village has become the battlefield and the civilian population the primary target. Girls and women are routinely subjected to sexual abuse and gender-based violence. Children are recruited and kidnapped to become child soldiers, forced to give violent expression to the hatreds of adults.

Both the Secretary General's report and my own experiences bring home the reality: civilians are no longer just victims of war: today they are regarded as instruments of war. Starving, terrorizing, murdering, raping civilians—all are seen as legitimate. Sex is no defense, nor is age; indeed, it is women, children, and the elderly who are often at greatest risk. That is a strange, terrible state of affairs in the year after we commemorated the fiftieth anniversary of the Universal Declaration of Human Rights.

Conflicts almost always lead to massive human rights violations but also erupt because human rights are violated due to oppression, inequality, discrimination, and poverty. These conditions are exacerbated when the state is too weak or unable to address them efficiently. Human rights violations are thus both a consequence of and a contributing factor to instability and further conflict. And, as a result of globalization and increasing interdependence between states, conflicts that are essentially internal often have spill-over effects beyond national borders.

As so clearly underscored by the Secretary General in his report, there is an intrinsic link between systematic and widespread violations of the rights of civilians and the erosion of international peace and security. For example, in Iraq and the former Yugoslavia, the Security Council has recognized that the repression of the civilian population has led to consequences that threatened peace and security in the region. Human security has become synonymous with international security. Human security can only be guaranteed through the full respect of all fundamental rights. This intrinsic link demands the attention and action of the Security Council in the field of human rights protection and the prevention of massive and gross violations.

The first need today is not that we write new laws, but that we implement what already exists in the field, close to the victims and where it really matters. To this end, I wish to express my support for those recommendations in the report which call on states to ratify all of the international instruments in the areas of human rights, humanitarian, and refugee law; to withdraw reservations, and most importantly, to comply fully with their provisions. Could we not also take the concrete step of raising the minimum age for participation in hostilities to eighteen years?

A serious issue that must be addressed is accountability. We are increasingly being faced with the dilemma of having to stop atrocities being committed and seeking avenues for the peaceful settlement of conflicts, on the one hand, while needing to hold accountable and punish the perpetrators of human rights violations, on the other. To grant amnesty to the authors of the most atrocious crimes for the sake of peace and reconciliation may be tempting, but it contradicts the purpose and principles of the United Nations Charter as well as internationally observed principles and standards. For these reasons, the recommendations in the Secretary General's report on enforcing accountability for war crimes and on measures to deter and contain those guilty of egregious human rights violations are especially important.

I wish to commend the Security Council for having established the two ad hoc tribunals for the former Yugoslavia and Rwanda. I warmly welcome the adoption of the Statute of the International Criminal Court providing jurisdiction over the three core crimes of genocide, crimes against humanity, and war crimes. We must move forward now and ensure that our collective support for the establishment of an effective International Criminal Court will, through the speedy ratification of its Statute, be a significant milestone in the struggle to strengthen respect for human rights and humanitarian and refugee law.

Mr. President, the best protection for civilians in armed conflict is prevention. By addressing the root causes of conflict and seeking to defuse tensions, the atrocities and violations of fundamental rights committed during armed conflict can be prevented. The major building blocks for peacebuilding and reconciliation are good governance, the rule of law, respect for human rights, a strong civil society, and institutions which can guarantee an environment conducive to stability and peace.

The Security Council has a vital role to play both in the prevention stage and, should that fail, in the deployment of peacekeepers to minimize the impact of conflict on civilians. I welcome the fact that the Security Council is looking to adapt its methods of work to focus on the goal of better protecting individuals in the face of this formidable challenge.

After reading the Secretary General's report and hearing his presentation today, nobody could any longer complain that they did not realize how bad the situation facing civilians in today's armed conflicts was. It should be our collective goal to implement the recommendations of the report and so develop enforceable mechanisms for the protection of civilians in armed conflict. This is the only way we will deliver on our promises to guarantee a life of respect, dignity, and human rights for all.

"What Prevention Requires"

Address to the Washington Conference on Atrocities Prevention and Response

United States Holocaust Memorial Museum, Washington, D.C., USA, 28 October 1999

I would like first of all to congratulate Harold Koh, his colleagues, and all those involved in preparing this timely conference. It is timely because we continue to see, every day, the catastrophic effects of not preventing atrocities and how vital it is, when they occur, that the response be swift and effective.

The place we are meeting in, the Holocaust Museum, reminds us of the worst manifestation of human tyranny. The word "genocide" is often misused and has even become debased through overuse. In the case of the Holocaust, it is entirely appropriate since it was nothing less than an attempt to obliterate the Jewish people from the earth.

But our being here also reminds us that the people who drafted the Universal Declaration of Human Rights did so at a time when the world was still trying to come to grips with the horrors of the Holocaust. The drafters of the Universal Declaration were idealists who sought to learn from the terrible human rights abuses committed during the war by setting out in clear language the rights which all of us have simply by virtue of being human. We should take heart from their vision—and from their practical single-mindedness. They had a vision, but they also had their feet firmly on the ground, as is shown by the fact that the Universal Declaration, born out of a determination that the world would never again experience genocide, has stood the test of time and has been the source of an impressive body of human rights law.

Alas, it has not prevented genocide. Earlier this week I had a meeting in Geneva with some of the members of the Eminent Persons Group established by the Organization of African Unity to see what lessons we could learn from the genocide in Rwanda. One of the lessons must be to resource preventive capacity in regional institutions, such as the Conflict Prevention Unit of the OAU, as well as equipping the UN human rights mechanisms to function at full effectiveness. In large part this is simply a resources issue because targeted resources could transform existing underfunded mechanisms into an effective early-warning system.

Before addressing the aims of the conference, let me say what I feel the conference should not be. It should not be a forum where like-minded countries, NGOs, and international organizations all agree around the table that prevention is very important and then we go away and nothing happens. It would be difficult to find anybody who would disagree with the proposition that atrocities should be headed off before they happen. But that has not resulted in an end to atrocities and mass killings in many parts of the world.

There is no shortage of examples where failure to take preventive action has resulted in atrocities. This year we have seen what happened in East Timor and Kosovo, not to mention the dozen or so continuing conflicts in Africa. In none of these cases could it be said that the outside world was ignorant of what was happening; on the contrary, with modern communication there are few parts of the world that escape the eye. Even as we meet today, atrocities are being committed or are imminent.

I would draw attention to two cases in particular where the warning signs are unmistakable: the Great Lakes region and the former Yugoslavia. As you are aware, reports coming from the Great Lakes region speak of a dangerously unstable state of affairs. Despite the high expectations raised by the signing of the Lusaka Peace Agreement, fighting continues in the Democratic Republic of Congo, with reports of widespread human rights abuses. In Burundi, attacks on the capital and elsewhere have cost the lives of hundreds in the past three months alone, including UN workers whose only aim was to bring humanitarian help to the region. The danger of more widespread conflict flaring up again is clear: Yet can we say that international attention is really focused on the problems of the region?

In the former Yugoslavia the situation remains critical too. Three months after the fighting ended in Kosovo, attacks against the Serb and Roma population are ongoing; houses are burned down or forcibly occupied; people are driven out or killed. The plight of Montenegro draws little attention, but it is clear that the potential exists there for another outbreak of conflict. Has nothing been learned from the international community's experiences in the rest of the former Yugoslavia? Or is it the case, as some allege, that we only take action to address human rights violations after the violations have been perpetrated?

If this conference is to be successful, it will have to address the issues that lie at the heart of prevention and devise ways of putting more emphasis on, and more resources into, prevention. Discussion should include the policy and financial implications of really putting prevention into practice, the hard choices that fall to be made, and the shortfall between what we say should be done and what has happened in practice.

A Culture of Prevention

My view of prevention is simple: I see it as the most important task of the Office of the High Commissioner for Human Rights. The rationale for prevention has been well described by the Swedish Foreign Minister, Anna Lindh.[4] I have quoted her before and make no apologies for doing so again, as it seems to me she hit the nail on the head:

> In all cultures and every society, prevention is something normal. Measures are taken to avert crop destruction by flood or rodents. Cattle are protected from predators. Warning signals are placed at rail crossings and air traffic is controlled to avoid accidents. Insurance policies are developed in almost all areas of human activity. All this is the result of preventive thinking, based on the assumption that accidents and disasters can be avoided, if you think ahead while preparing for the worst. . . . It is high time to transfer and strengthen the sophisticated preventive habits we know so well at home into the field of international security.[5]

It is not as if the value of prevention has not been highlighted over the years. Prevention was the central theme of the lengthy study of conflict done by the Carnegie Commission when some of the great thinkers of the day looked at the root causes of conflict.[6] That thought-provoking report came to three central conclusions: that deadly conflict is not inevitable; that the need to prevent deadly conflicts is increasingly urgent, and that preventing deadly conflict is possible. What the study tells us is that we should not be put off by the doomsayers who insist that conflict and violence are the natural lot of the human race and will never be eradicated.

Nor should we be deterred by the risk of failure. If we look at failures of prevention in the past, what becomes apparent is that many were put into effect too late or were halfhearted, the equivalent of bringing a leaky bucket to a fire that is already threatening to blaze out of control. Prevention is by no means a new concept, but there are many cases where insufficient attention and resources have been devoted to prevention, only for the cost of repairing the damage afterwards, to exceed preventive costs many times over.

Strategies of Prevention

The challenge we face is to put strategies in place that will be effective in preventing atrocities from occurring. I see four essential strategies that are complementary and interrelated. All are predicated on my belief that strengthening the culture of human rights and respect for others in societies is the bedrock on which the issue of prevention is based:

first, economic and social development programs which have human development as their chief focus and which are capable of improving the lot of the poorest;
second, accountability;
third, strengthening capacity, that is, support for participatory systems of government, for democracy, the rule of law, the judiciary, for national human rights institutions; and
fourth, human rights education.

Economic, Social, and Cultural Rights

All of these strategies are important, but I place economic and social development at the top of the list because I see it as of fundamental significance and because it receives less attention than the others. To be frank, I feel that rich countries are often guilty of doublespeak when they talk to the developing countries about rights issues. The rich countries urge that civil and political rights be observed, and they are properly critical of abuses where they occur. But when it comes to economic, social, and cultural rights of poorer countries and the right to development, they have a good deal less to say. Yet those rights are enshrined just as clearly in the Universal Declaration and in the international covenants and declarations of the United Nations as civil and political rights are. Not only that, but the international community has repeatedly affirmed its support for these rights at numerous international conferences—at Cairo, Beijing, and Copenhagen, to name only three.

The problems of extreme poverty and economic and social imbalances are getting worse, not better. The human rights so many take for granted—freedom of speech and religion, the right to a fair trial—cannot flourish where people are deprived of access to food, to health care, to education. And it is the abuse of these essential rights that leads inexorably to atrocities and gross violations. Atrocities do not suddenly happen; they start with minor discrimination; that leads to worse forms of discrimination, which turn into exclusion and finally the ultimate exclusion by which people are driven from their homes and murdered.

Focused, human-centered development programs have a key role to play in preventing atrocities. Yet the readiness of rich countries to abide by their solemn undertakings to assist in development is weakening. It is simply not credible to talk about human rights and prevention and at the same time to cut aid budgets.

The irony is that aid budget cuts are taking place just when it seems that some crucial lessons are being learned by the donor agencies. There is a new focus on the human-centered approach to development that recognizes that improving the individual's lot is a more important objective than simply striving for better GNP growth. Professor Muhammud Yunus, founder of the Grameen Bank in Bangladesh, states in the latest Human Development Report:

> When I was arguing that helping a one-meal family to become a two-meal family, enabling a woman without a change of clothing to afford to buy a second piece of clothing, is a development miracle, I was ridiculed. That is no development, I was reminded sternly. Development is growth of the economy, they said; growth will bring everything. We carried out our work as if we were engaged in some very undesirable activities. When UNDP's Human Development Report came out we felt vindicated. We were no longer back-street operators, we felt we were in the mainstream.[7]

I am pleased to see the new awareness of the human dimension of development in the strategies of UNDP, the World Bank, and other development agencies and that cooperation between my Office and these agencies has increased markedly.

Accountability

Accountability for atrocities is an indispensable weapon in preventing further human rights violations. I believe that movement toward the establishment of effective machinery to punish those guilty of crimes against humanity is irreversible. The setting up of an International Criminal Court is the logical next step following the work done by the Rwanda and former Yugoslavia Tribunals. I welcome the adoption of the Rome Statute, and I appreciate that the United States is working closely with the growing international consensus. I hope that the United States will throw its support behind the Court and play the lead role on this, just as it has on so many human rights issues over the years. A clear message should go out: nobody who commits atrocities should expect to get away with it. That is true whether the crimes are committed in the former Yugoslavia, in Cambodia, in Chile, or in any other part of the world. And it is true of East Timor, where the International Commission of Inquiry called for by the Commission on Human Rights has been formed and has begun its work.

Ratification of the Rome Statute will be a challenging test of the international community's resolve to put the legal mechanisms on a sound basis. At the same time, we must remain open to the possibilities of different ways of securing justice and accountability, bearing in mind the harsh reality of many political and postconflict situations. The magnitude of the problems facing countries in postconflict situations can be so great that the normal processes of justice are simply not feasible. I think, for example, of the present situation in Sierra Leone. The people of Sierra Leone have experienced atrocities on a scale and of a brutality that are scarcely imaginable. The campaign of terror was purposely aimed at the civilian population. The number of deaths will never be known, nor the number of those deliberately maimed and raped. And the people of Sierra Leone have had to endure the further indignity that the outside world has shown little interest in their awful plight.

The amnesty provision contained in the Lomé Peace Agreement of 7 July was not something that the United Nations favored, and a reservation was entered when the agreement was signed, pointing out that there could be no amnesty for the grossest crimes amounting to crimes against humanity. When I visited Sierra Leone last June, I called for the establishment of a Commission of Inquiry to investigate the massive human rights violations which have taken place. My Office has maintained contacts at a number of levels with the Sierra Leone authorities to seek ways of ensuring that there is accountability for the atrocities that took place. In particular, I have sent consultants to assist in the establishment of a Truth and Reconciliation Commission. I have also sent my adviser on national human rights institutions to explain the principles that make such bodies effective.

Because the issues raised in Sierra Leone are so important, I have commissioned a distinguished African jurist to carry out an examination of the nexus between a possible Commission of Inquiry and the Truth and Reconciliation Commission that is being established. I believe this study may have a broader relevance in addressing conflicts in Africa.[8]

Rwanda is another country trying to come to terms with a very bloody past, the genocide of 1994. Five years on, the problems regarding the administration of justice and gross overcrowding of jails remain acute. Of even more long-term importance, for both the country and the region, is the task of embedding a culture of human rights. My Office has been supportive of the establishment of a National Human Rights Commission and we participated in a useful workshop last month in Kigali. Special Representative Michel Moussali, in his current report to the General Assembly, draws attention to an idea raised by the Rwandan Government of resorting to a system of participatory justice, incorporating the ancient traditional system of justice known as *Gacaca*, to bring to light the full truth about the heinous crimes committed in Rwanda and to administer justice to those responsible. The Special Representative felt that the government's initiative was an interesting approach and worth pursuing, and a number of donors, including the United States, are supportive. If this initiative respects human rights norms and is effective in addressing the problem of Rwanda's huge prison population—currently numbering some 130,000—then it is worth close examination.[9]

What these approaches have in common is the search for effective ways of breaking the cycle of impunity. It is not enough that societies recover from atrocities; lessons must be learned and ways found to ensure that they will not recur. Facing up to the reality of what has happened and rendering justice to the perpetrators are vital components in the process whereby societies can come to terms with atrocities and move on.

Capacity Building

The third strategy I wish to emphasize is capacity building, both in regional organizations and at the national level. There are clear linkages between participatory democracies and freedom from atrocities. It cannot be said that there has never been a case in history where two democracies have gone to war, but it is certain that the likelihood of conflict and gross human rights abuses is far greater where participatory democracy is absent. Most of the worst atrocities have happened where there are totalitarian regimes that refuse to answer to their citizens. It behooves us, therefore, to put resources into measures that support the establishment and consolidation of democracy, and to resource regional organizations to have preventive strategies in their regions.

Capacity building is a growing area of work for my Office. We now have technical cooperation programs with fifty-five countries and field presences in twenty-three. The countries we are assisting range from Nepal to Guatemala, from Bhutan to Azerbaijan. An example of the ways in which we can help is support for national human rights institutions. We have received requests from over forty countries wishing to establish human rights institutions. I have mentioned our support in this area for Sierra Leone and

Rwanda. Another example I would mention is South Korea. A few weeks ago I visited South Korea, where I met President Kim Dae-jung, who has championed the cause of a national human rights institution. I stressed to the Korean officials I met, as I do to all governments, that there are certain basic requirements for national human rights institutions to be effective: notably that they must be genuinely independent and have powers consistent with a capacity to discharge their functions.

Human Rights Education

And finally I would mention human rights education. The first step in establishing a human rights culture is to know what your rights are. There is still a great ignorance in many societies of even the basics of human rights. We are halfway through the UN Decade of Human Rights Education, and my Office is engaged in quite a number of initiatives aimed at tackling the information deficit. I see human rights education as an empowering instrument which enables individuals to understand and fight for their own rights as well as the rights of others.

Responding to Atrocities

I am conscious that the title of this conference is Atrocities Prevention and Response, and that I have spent most of my time talking about prevention. That is because I strongly believe that prevention is all-important. Even after atrocities have happened, the need for preventive measures is still great. Coming back to the Report of the Carnegie Commission, the areas of preventive action which they identified included measures after conflict has broken out—namely, preventing the further spread of conflict and preventing the reemergence of conflict in the aftermath of a peace settlement. Both are situations with which my Office is familiar.

One concrete measure that could be taken is to respond to the growing international movement for the protection of children in armed conflict. The human rights impacts of armed conflict are particularly horrific when visited upon these most vulnerable members of the civilian population. A whole generation risks being blighted by this terrible phenomenon. I give my wholehearted support to the campaign to end the use of child soldiers. At three regional conferences this year organized by the Coalition to Stop the Use of Child Soldiers, in Mozambique, in Uruguay, and most recently, in Berlin, many governments—and even some national liberation movements—expressed support for raising the age limit for the recruitment of children into armed forces from fifteen to eighteen. It is my sincere hope that governments—including that of the United States—will translate these expressions of support into solid commitment next year through the adoption of an Optional Protocol to the Convention on the Rights of the Child and so demonstrate that children have no place in armed conflict.[10]

The best response we can make to atrocities is to learn from them, to resolve to address the underlying root causes, and above all, to prevent them from happening again. Kofi Annan has laid down the challenge to us in calling for an age of prevention. That requires effective strategies, and I have outlined the ones I see as being important. But it calls for more: it calls for imagination and a change of mindset. It can be hard to persuade people of the value of a preventive approach because the results may not be visible or newsworthy—a conflict avoided, an atrocity prevented. But if we could go away from this conference with a firm resolve to devote to preventive measures even a fraction of the attention and resources that are poured in after atrocities occur, we would have made a good start.

"Human Rights in the Shadow of 11 September"
Fifth Commonwealth Lecture
London, UK, 6 June 2002

Secretary General, Excellencies, Ladies, and Gentlemen,

Last week we watched a simple, poignant ceremony at Ground Zero in New York. The completion of the physical clear-up after the outrage of the terrorist attacks on the World Trade Center was marked by the removal of the last piece of steel draped in a black cloth. For those relatives who had no body to bury, it was intended to provide a form of closure, a ceremony seeking to help in the painful healing process.

It is time, also, to take stock of the impact of those attacks and their aftermath on human rights. Writing last February, Michael Ignatieff put it starkly: "The question after September 11 is whether the era of human rights has come and gone."[11]

Not gone, is my response, but we are challenged in new ways to respond to profound concerns over human security in our world today. My own sense is that there is an enormous responsibility to uphold rigorously international human rights standards, recognizing that they, too, are the object of terrorist attacks. At the same time, I believe there must be more commitment to the implementation of those standards in practice through strong support for human rights capacity building at the national level.

I was very pleased, therefore, to accept the invitation of the Secretary General, Don McKinnon, and the Director of the Commonwealth Foundation, Colin Ball, to give this fifth Commonwealth Lecture. It is an opportunity I value, to bring my own thoughts together and to benefit from your comments, reactions, and questions.

The Commonwealth is committed to developing solidarity between the peoples of developed and developing states through economic, social, cultural, and humanitarian cooperation. It is committed to conflict resolution on the basis of shared values and principles of human rights and democracy as laid out in the Harare Declaration. Continuing membership is dependent on acceptance of those values and principles. Those whose membership is withdrawn or temporarily suspended, are actively encouraged to come back in. It is literally an organization in which common values and common principles are promoted for the Commonwealth or the common good.

My Office works closely with you on national capacity building in some of the smallest and poorest member countries in the Caribbean, the South Pacific, and Southern Africa. I have some other suggestions for cooperation to which I will return. And I should add that I have a similar wish for continued practical cooperation with *La Francophonie*!

The theme of my lecture is straightforward. We, meaning "We the Peoples of the United Nations," must renew, in the aftermath of September 11, our belief in the vision of the founders set out in the UN Charter of 1945. That vision is of a world in which the scourge of war and terrorism is banished and in which universal peace is achieved through our collective commitment to the purposes of the Charter.

Those purposes can be summarized as four: international peace and security, economic and social development, the promotion and protection of human rights, and strengthening the rule of international law. No alternative model of world order has emerged to supercede that of the UN Charter. Indeed, its principles were reaffirmed in the Millennium Declaration of September 2000 at the largest gathering of world leaders in history.

We need no reminding today of the urgency of implementing these interconnected ideals and goals, as two Commonwealth members, India and Pakistan, stand poised for open conflict. Or if we think of the continuing conflict in the Middle East or, less often referred to, the devastating conflict in the Democratic Republic of the Congo involving six other African countries and in which it is estimated that over two million people have been killed since 1990. Such complex and deadly disputes divert vital resources and attention from development and cause immense human suffering and violation of human rights.

A Crime against Humanity

Language is vital in shaping our reaction to a critical event. The words we use to characterize the event may determine the nature of the response. In the immediate aftermath of September 11, I described the attacks on the World Trade Center as constituting a crime against humanity. It is worth recalling why that description is appropriate. First of all, the September 11 attacks were mainly aimed at civilians. They were ruthlessly planned and their execution timed to achieve the greatest loss of life. Their scale and systematic nature qualify them as crimes against humanity within existing international jurisprudence.

There are other characteristics of the attacks that should be noted. They were carried out by individuals, not by the security forces of any state. The attacks were, as I have said, aimed primarily at civilians, but they were aimed also at the open democratic society that is the United States. Their purpose was to destabilize the society through terrorizing its people, a purpose that thankfully was not achieved. Those who carried out the attacks were non-nationals, and in that sense what occurred was international. Although at the international level agreement has not yet been reached on a precise definition, the attacks made by members of Al-Qa'eda undoubtedly fall within any conceivable definition of terrorism.

There is a duty on the entire world community of states to find and punish those who plan and facilitate such crimes. One positive institutional development we should note is the coming into force of the Statute of the International Criminal Court. It is the first instrument to codify the elements of a crime against humanity. It establishes individual criminal responsibility for such crimes whether these are state sanctioned or the acts of groups. The universal ratification of the Statute is an important goal for the world community. Seventeen Commonwealth states have ratified and twenty-one more have signed the International Criminal Court Statute. I join the call made by the Commonwealth heads of government for all member states to ratify. We must equip ourselves with the means to deal with crimes such as those of September 11 in the future.

International cooperation and resolve are vital in combating those who plan acts of terrorism. The United Nations Security Council has taken important steps in this direction. In Resolution 1373 of 28 September, it imposed a new international legal obligation on states to cooperate against terrorism, taking language from existing international conventions. All states are required to take a wide range of legislative, procedural, economic, and other measures on preventing, prohibiting, and criminalizing terrorist acts. These measures are designed to deny space, money, support, and haven to terrorists; to establish a network of information sharing and cooperative action; and to end the impunity of perpetrators of terrorist acts. As you will know, the Commonwealth leaders issued a statement pledging support for the implementation by its members of Resolution 1373 on 25 October last.

The Security Council noted with concern the close connection between international terrorism and transnational organized crime, such as illicit drugs, money laundering, illegal arms trafficking, and illegal movement of nuclear, chemical, biological, and other potentially deadly materials. These criminal activities also include illegal trade in precious metals and minerals, and in people smuggling and trafficking in women and children. Criminal networks prey on weak states, and their activities induce conflict, corruption, and misery in many developed and developing countries. They bring out a human rights challenge that has yet to be fully faced, that of the accountability of the nonstate actor. Confronting and defeating these threats will require deeper and more sustained international cooperation.

To oversee implementation of Resolution 1373, a Counter Terrorism Committee, chaired by UK Ambassador Sir Jeremy Greenstock, was established. This month states will begin a second round of reporting to the Committee on their ongoing efforts to implement the resolution.

The War against Terrorism

Despite efforts to frame the response to terrorism within the framework of crimes under national and international law, an alternative language has emerged post-September 11. That language, which has shaped to a much larger extent the response at all levels, has spoken of a war on terrorism. As such, it has brought a subtle change in emphasis in many parts of the world; order and security have become the overriding priorities. In the past, the world has learned that emphasis on national order and security often involved curtailment of democracy and human rights. As a result, a shadow has been cast.

This shadow can be seen in official reactions that at times have seemed to subordinate the principles of human rights to other more "robust" action in the war against terrorism. There has been a tendency to ride roughshod over—or at least to set on one side—established principles of international human rights and humanitarian law. There has been confusion on what is and what is not subject to the Geneva Conventions of 1949. There have been suggestions that the terrorist acts of September 11 and their aftermath in the conflict in Afghanistan demonstrated that the Geneva Conventions were out of date.

Evidence has been gathered by human rights NGOs, most recently by Amnesty International's Report 2002, that post-September 11 certain nonviolent activities have been considered as terrorism in some countries and excessive measures have been taken to suppress or restrict individual rights including privacy rights, fair trial, political participation, freedom of expression, and peaceful association.[12] Regulations controlling surveillance are being lifted, and the right to asylum is being severely restricted.

NGOs have been consistent in asserting that human rights are not in opposition to security but, on the contrary, one of its aspects. They have reminded states that there is no logic in discarding the very values that—in principle—they are fighting to ensure. Yet, our Office is flooded with calls from human rights defenders around the world drawing attention to new restrictions and oppressive measures.

It is essential that the actions taken by states to combat terrorism be in conformity with international human rights standards. Secretary General Kofi Annan powerfully expressed this duty in his statement to the Security Council on 18 January this year:

> We should all be clear that there is no trade-off between effective action against terrorism and the protection of human rights. On the contrary, I believe that in the

long term we shall find that human rights, along with democracy and social justice, are one of the best prophylactics against terrorism. . . . while we certainly need vigilance to prevent acts of terrorism, and firmness in condemning and punishing them, it will be self-defeating if we sacrifice other key priorities—such as human rights—in the process.

Strong statements in support of this view were also heard at this year's session of the United Nations Commission on Human Rights. But there were troubling signs as well. The Commission chose not to take specific action or undertake any new initiatives to monitor the impact of antiterrorism measures on human rights. Currently, there is no international institution with a clear mandate to assess whether measures taken and justified by a state as necessary to combat terrorism are in violation of human rights standards which that state has accepted, or which would require that a derogation be made. The Counter Terrorism Committee does not believe this to be part of its mandate.

My Office has been consulting with regional human rights organizations such as the Council of Europe, the ODIHR Unit of the OSCE, the OAS, and OAU to share information and enhance our capacity to monitor the human rights dimensions of actions taken to combat terrorism.[13] We also encourage UN human rights mechanisms such as Special Rapporteurs to deal vigorously with the issues that fall within their mandates.

In August of last year the Human Rights Committee, which monitors state compliance with the International Covenant on Civil and Political Rights, adopted its General Comment 29 on Article 4, on derogations and human rights in states of emergency.[14] The Committee marked the boundaries between legitimate balancing of rights and security, and impermissible or excessive limitation of rights. It offers very useful guidance in the current context.

Although abuses of emergency powers occurred before September 11, they were clearly criticized as impermissible measures. The great concern now is that where mature democracies blur the lines or set a bad example, undemocratic regimes consider they are given a green light to pursue repressive policies, secure in the belief that any excesses will be ignored. It thus becomes more difficult to secure conformity with basic standards and safeguards against abuse of power.

These very standards were set in place to respond to brutal conflicts and violations of human rights. Hard work over fifty years by states, intergovernmental bodies, and nongovernmental organizations has developed a sophisticated system comprising human rights law, refugee law, and humanitarian law with which to curb abuses of power. Now, more than ever, we must ensure that these normative frameworks are not only implemented but also linked closely so that they support each other.

It is of particular concern that the post-September 11 environment is reinforcing a fortress mentality within Europe. As controls are tightened, there is a coarsening of debate and of language used in speaking of asylum seekers and immigrants in Europe. This together with the resurgence of anti-Semitism and the rise in Islamophobia are challenges that must be faced by European leaders and citizens alike.

The declaration and action agenda from last year's Durban World Conference against Racism affirmed that human diversity must be recognized as an asset, not a liability; that xenophobia must be rejected in all its forms; and that in a world which hopes to reap the benefits of globalization, a commitment to multicultural societies must be embraced.

Building Comprehensive Human Security

If the immediate challenge for the human rights movement is to maintain the integrity of international human rights and humanitarian law norms in the light of heightened security tensions, there is also a long-term agenda: that is to build a world of true human security. One positive result of the tragedy of September 11 should be that we gear ourselves to respond to the call of the UN Secretary General when he urges us to make this century the age of prevention, rather than reaction.

It is important that there be more recognition of the links between development, human rights, and democracy and their necessary connection to security. The very real security fears of New Yorkers and others in the developed world are matched by the different—but equally immediate—insecurity of persons in the developing world. The 1994 UN *Human Development Report* reminded us that "human security is not a concern with weapons—it is a concern with human life and dignity," and it identified seven specific human security components: economic, food, health, environmental, personal, community, and political security.[15]

This approach not only gives security a human face and puts the emphasis back on the protection of individual human beings, but it also supports the principle of the indivisibility of rights. Furthermore, it underlies the original vision of the UN Charter, which was powerfully and influentially restated in the 1997 Carnegie Commission Report *Preventing Deadly Conflict.*[16] Its basic conclusion is that conflict, human rights violations, underdevelopment, and poverty cannot be decoupled. Security requires a comprehensive strategy that seeks to address root causes. Violent conflict is best prevented, as the Report notes: "[B]y creating capable states with representative governance based on the rule of law, with widely available economic opportunity, social safety nets, protection of fundamental human rights, and robust civil societies."

Another recent authoritative study on the point, the report of the International Commission on Intervention and State Sovereignty titled *The Responsibility to Protect,* reminds us of

> growing and widespread recognition that armed conflicts cannot be understood without reference to such root causes as poverty, political repression, and uneven distribution of resources. "Every step taken towards reducing poverty and achieving

> broad-based economic growth," the Secretary General has stated in his recent report, "is a step toward conflict prevention." Preventive strategies must therefore work "to promote human rights, to protect minority rights and to institute political arrangements in which all groups are represented." Ignoring these underlying factors amounts to addressing the symptoms rather than the causes of deadly conflict.[17]

The need for practical capacity building implied by this approach spans the full range of human rights concerns—from civil liberties and democratic institution building to action on concerns such as environmental degradation, poverty, underdevelopment, and infectious disease.

We are witnessing real breakthroughs in some of these areas: in the funding necessary to combat HIV/AIDS and in increased funds to meet the Millennium Development Goals on education and health, stimulated by the welcome involvement of the private sector. A similar approach is needed in capacity building to strengthen the administration of justice, rule of law, and adherence to human rights standards in developing countries. The best antidotes to extremism are the right to freedom of expression and opinion and an independent media.

The Commonwealth Human Rights Initiative report of last year on Human Rights and Poverty Eradication provides a range of practical measures to instill a human-rights-based approach in poverty-eradication efforts.[18] I strongly commend them and urge member states to implement them.

The Commonwealth, with its large African membership, has an important role to play in working with the New Partnership for Africa's Development, the Africa-owned and -led regional economic and social plan of action. That role was recognized at the Heads of Government Meeting in Australia when all Commonwealth institutions were called upon to assist with implementation. For the United Nations, too, NEPAD presents a concrete opportunity to contribute. The goals of NEPAD are in large part those agreed on in the Millennium Declaration.

The implementation of NEPAD provides an historic opportunity for African states and peoples to reinforce the protection and promotion of human rights, making this a fundamental principle for sustainable development, human security, social justice, and adherence to good governance and the rule of law.

Concluding Remarks

In conclusion, I want to reiterate that despite worrying challenges, we have the possibility of positive change. I believe there is an opportunity to develop a new and deeper realization of the links between human rights, democracy, and development in our world and to move from the rhetoric of prevention to real action.

We now understand in a more profound way that no nation can isolate or exclude itself from the effects of global problems of endemic poverty and conflict. In essence, the tragedy of September 11 must spur renewed action on all these fronts. Deprivation and denial of rights in the world can no longer be viewed simply as holding a moral claim on us all: they must now be seen as crucial battlefields for the security of all. If it is to succeed in its goal of ensuring greater human security, combating terror must also be a war on disadvantage, discrimination, and despair.

There has been much debate on the physical form of a memorial to the victims of September 11 who died when an outrageous attack was made on their lives and on the values of an open and democratic state. There is perhaps no more fitting memorial, no more lasting testament to those who lost their lives, than for world leaders to commit to the implementation of a broader vision of security through justice and equality.

To take inspiration from the words of Seamus Heaney, we have the opportunity, coming out of this terrible shadow, to make good on the vision of the founding fathers of the United Nations:

Once in a lifetime
the longed-for tidal wave
of justice can rise up
And hope and history rhyme.[19]

Chapter 20

Ethical Globalization

The idea of an ethical foundation to globalization came to express Mary Robinson's belief in the need for a new global order built on respect for human rights as both moral and legal obligation. As she says below: "It would be a profoundly humane ethics shepherding a humane globalization and not an ethics simply playing catch-up to self-interested and blundering economic and military forces." Advocacy for an ethical globalization has become her main project following the completion of her term as United Nations High Commissioner for Human Rights.

"Ethics, Human Rights and Globalization"
Second Global Ethic Lecture
University of Tübingen, Germany, 21 January 2002

Introduction

The invitation to give the second Global Ethic Lecture at the University of Tübingen was irresistible. Linking human rights with ethics and globalization represents, I believe, a connection whose time has come. And yet, the task is daunting. Every day brings further evidence of the unacceptable divide in our world, the harsh statistics of millions living in extreme poverty and enduring conflict. The increasing frustration and disillusionment with market-led globalization is evidenced by the protests at the G8, WTO, EU, and other Summits.

We are at the edge of a big idea: the shaping of ethical globalization. But how? What are the components, the linkages, and the energies that need to be harnessed? And what better place to pose such questions than here in Tübingen?

I would like to express deep appreciation to the Rector, Professor Schaich, for his warm welcome and to thank my friend Professor Hans Küng for this invitation. He was the first to introduce me to the concept of a global ethic. I am a great admirer of his lifelong commitment to bringing people of different spiritual traditions and backgrounds together around the values that unite us as one human family.

A year ago, as my colleagues and I were working to build public support for the World Conference against Racism, we looked to the unique role of faith leaders in promoting greater tolerance and respect. Many of the religious and spiritual leaders who had participated in the Millennium World Peace Summit joined together against prejudice and intolerance. Their statements are collected in a book entitled *Sacred Rights.*[1] I see their willingness to contribute to the values of the World Conference as a significant expression of Hans Küng's vision of a global ethic that undergirds international efforts to protect the human rights of every individual.

A similar commitment has been reflected in the results of the UN Year of Dialogue among Civilizations, 2001. Hans Küng was one of the Eminent Persons who contributed to the consultations during that Year. With the other members of the group he has just published an assessment, Crossing the Divide: The Dialogue among Civilisations.[2]

In preparing my remarks for today, I was reflecting on the fact that nearly ten years have passed since the adoption of two important international declarations, one by the world's governments, the other by the world's religious leaders. The two texts I am referring to are Declaration and Programme of Action of the World Conference on Human Rights, adopted in Vienna in June 1993, and Declaration of the Religions for a Global Ethic, adopted in Chicago just five months later.[3] These documents were, in many ways, ahead of their time in addressing what world leaders at the UN Millennium Summit identified as the central challenge we face today: ensuring that globalization becomes a positive force for all the world's people.

It is a measure of the rapid pace of social change that neither document refers specifically to the term "globalization," which has today become so central to our attempts at describing our times. However, I believe that both offer the vision and the proposals needed to guide our response to the growing "backlash against globalization."

I would like to do two things in my lecture. The first is to explore the linkages between ethics and human rights in general terms. What is the relationship between ethics and rights, and how do they both link to values, morality, and to law? It is not only an interesting intellectual exercise to analyze these concepts; it is also directly relevant to the world of action and to policy choices we face as individuals, as citizens of different countries, and as world citizens. Second, I will address the challenges of globalization. What role can ethics and human rights play in a world of greater inequality within as well as between nations?

Here and now we are already embraced by the three formidable terms of my title: ethics, globalization, and human rights. To simplify, I have an ethical responsibility to speak as truthfully as I can to you, who have a right to hear my considered views on this topic in a manner intelligible to you but also consistent with what I might say in Tokyo as well as in Togo, or Tübingen, or in any other setting on the globe. Whatever the situation, there is no escaping the moral or ethical responsibility of the speaker, the rights and indeed duties of the audience to listen carefully and fairly, and, nowadays, on such a major topic, the global implications of the speech. I stress this rather obvious point to help root our occasion in this actual concrete situation and to avoid the mystification which the title itself or indeed the necessary abstractions in its development might produce. Ethics, human rights, and globalization are part of our everyday experience, and to that we must continually return.

Ethics and Morality

In general, as well as in academic discourse, the terms "ethics" and "morality" operate at times interchangeably and at other times distinctively. For our purposes it will be convenient to use ethics in the more concrete sense of ethical decision and action, with morality and its cognates used in a more fundamental and abstract sense.

Among other descriptions, that of the human being as a moral or ethical being, as one who makes ethical decisions and performs ethical actions, good or bad, is universally acceptable. So the range of ethics and morality is as broad as the human race, however diverse the view may be as to what in particular areas of human activity is adjudged to be morally acceptable or unacceptable, good or bad, right or wrong.

Ethics is therefore often the product of particular traditions of a community, either a particular society or portion of society, or more widely, it is the product of the particular history of large numbers of societies, allowing us to speak of the ethics of the human community. At this most basic level ethics, human rights, and the developing global interactions of the whole human race are intimately intertwined.

Ethics must be connected to morality. Ethics without morality is empty. Unless this link is there, people inside certain communities fall into the delusion of thinking that their own ethical codes exhaust all there is to morality in general. They allow their own ethics to masquerade as true morality. One flagrant example of this was the South African Immorality Act under apartheid. That law enshrined a racist ethical code of the dominant white community that proclaimed interracial marriages as immoral.

The collapsing of ethics into morality is also a source of the complaint of cultural imperialism behind some interpretations of international human rights instruments—for example, the assertion that one category of rights, civil and political, is more important than other categories, such as social or labor rights. Or, indeed, the reverse proposition, which is also advanced. It can amount to a covert effort to smuggle a particular ethics into a universal order and to call the result universal morality. The starting position must be that of the Universal Declaration of Human Rights, which proclaimed the entitlement of all human beings everywhere to all rights. That essentially moral position was reaffirmed, as I have said, in the Vienna Declaration of 1993.

Values

At a more abstract level than morality and ethics we could place values. Values are the building blocks of both morality and of ethics. Thus, a significant achievement of the Millennium Summit of the General Assembly, held in September 2000, the largest gathering of heads of states ever to have taken place, was to agree on a number of fundamental values essential to international relations in the twenty-first century.[4] These are freedom, equality, solidarity, tolerance, respect for nature, and shared responsibility. I will return to these values later and to the commitment in the Millennium Declaration "to ensure that globalization becomes a positive force for all the world's peoples."

Human Rights and Law

Moving now to human rights: in our hierarchy they seem to occupy an intermediate stage between values and moral foundations and the immediate personal decisions, which concern ethics. In this they are akin to law, particularly international law, and yet not to be identified simply with law. Law is nevertheless an indispensable part of the picture. It is a necessary complement to both morality and ethics. This is not simply because it is a coercive instrument sometimes necessary to get a set of moral and ethical values to work. It is also because it is a crucial element in the ongoing, *dynamic* relationship between ethics and morality.

Law, especially through the jurisprudence of the courts, introduces the element of open-ended, continuing investigation into the meaning of moral and ethical values as they deal with new circumstances that no one could predict when covenants, and rules, were first drawn up. This allows both ethics and morality to evolve to meet modern times. The field of bioethics is a current example. My Office has invited experts on bioethics to convene in Geneva later this week for a consultation on moral and ethical issues arising from developments in biotechnology, and to address the manner in which the international human rights system should respond.[5] So, the traffic is not just one-way: human rights law does not simply translate morality and ethics into a rule; it also provides the impetus to fresh development of morality and ethics.

Global Ethics and Global Human Rights

To sum up: we can say that values, morality, ethics, law, and human rights are all linked in a complex normative cluster. We need to do further thinking about that cluster. The events of September 11 and their aftermath underline the urgency of that thinking. It may be helpful to explore the topic further here, not least because one of its major navigators in recent decades has been Professor Küng. His explorations into the most difficult terrain of world religions and their associated moralities have opened the way to dialogue and convergence at the spiritual sources of morality and civilization. In addition, by promoting a coalition between religious believers of very different traditions, nonbelievers and religious agnostics, in search of a moral consensus on a number of fundamental issues, he has furthered the prospects of the global conversation that is essential to a globalizing ethics—if one may use the phrase—and to the global ethos that will make human rights more comprehensible, complete, and defensible around the globe.

In that work Professor Küng has laid great stress on peace between the religions and the nations and on nonviolent means in promoting a free and just society. I am reminded of Virginia Woolf's challenge to apply innovative thinking: "We can best help you prevent war, not by repeating your words and repeating your methods, but by finding new words and creating new methods."[6]

With his further insistence on the value of truth and truthfulness, Hans Küng's work suggests an important grouping of values which should offer further possibilities of grounding such a universal or global ethic. Truth, freedom, justice, and peace, along with the other values declared at the Millennium Summit—equality, solidarity, tolerance, respect for nature, and shared responsibility among the nations for economic and social development—are being recognized and practiced or violated in different ways in the most diverse situations around the world. In their further elaboration through continuing dialogue, the framework of ethical globalization could emerge, in which human rights—civil and political, social, economic, and cultural—are enjoyed without discrimination, become part of the rules of the road we must travel together. It would be a profoundly humane ethics shepherding a humane globalization and not an ethics simply playing catch-up to self-interested and blundering economic and military forces.

The very call to truth is also a call to defend freedom of expression and of search for truth, a call to listen to the truth traditions of others and to be open to being enriched by them. Such call to ever-fuller truth excludes both fanaticism and indifference, as Professor Küng points out. Such a moral call and response can be pursued effectively only where other moral values such as freedom and justice are fully honored.

Together they find more concrete expression in the language of human rights. For their proper implementation freedom, justice, and their embodiment in human rights require and promote solidarity between all humans on the basis of the inviolable and equal dignity of each. The establishment of such a peaceful, just, and free society on earth constitutes the present political challenge and ethical obligation of the human race. It also represents the commitment of world leaders in the Millennium Summit. The practical question then is how we may hold the international community to those commitments.

Globalization

In his report to the UN Millennium Summit, Kofi Annan described the world of globalization

> as a new context for and a new connectivity among economic actors and activities throughout the world. Globalization has been made possible by the progressive dismantling of barriers to trade and capital mobility, together with fundamental technological advances and steadily declining costs of transportation, communication and computing. Its integrative logic seems inexorable, its momentum irresistible.[7]

But we all know that, despite its momentum, concerns about its impact continue to grow. The report notes that the increasing backlash against globalization has come about, first, because its benefits and opportunities have been so highly concentrated among a relatively small number of countries and are spread unevenly within them. Further, its costs are unevenly distributed, with developing countries and countries with economies in transition bearing the brunt of those costs. More broadly, globalization has come to mean greater vulnerability to unfamiliar and unpredictable forces that can bring on economic instability and social dislocation. As the report puts it: "There is mounting anxiety that the integrity of cultures and the sovereignty of states may be at stake. Even in the most powerful countries, people wonder who is in charge, worry for their jobs and fear that their voices are drowned out in globalization's sweep."[8]

Where do we go from here? In straightforward terms, the task is to create the momentum to implement the Millennium Declaration's commitment to make globalization a positive force for all the world's people, to make it inclusive and equitable.

Prime Minister Tony Blair, who gave the first Global Ethic Lecture last year, spoke in similar terms when he saw the way forward in developing a doctrine of international community based on a foundation of mutual rights and responsibilities.[9] His steps toward that community include the need for rich countries to meet what he termed their moral obligation to the poor countries, and in the long term their self-interest, in freeing up trade in agricultural goods. He also called for much more radical action on debt relief and environmental protection, in particular tackling global warming through implementing the Kyoto Protocol.

A similar message is to be found in an interesting book, *An Open Letter on Globalization—The Debate.*[10] The book arose from an initiative of the Prime Minister of Belgium, Guy Verhofstadt, as President of the European Council. He wrote an open letter to antiglobalization protesters. In the letter he conceded that the protesters might be asking many of the right questions. But did they have the right answers? He later convened a conference in Ghent to which he invited a number of globalization critics and others, including myself. What emerged as a consensus was the need for a new approach, which Guy Verhofstadt termed "ethical globalization."

Human Rights and Globalization

Building an ethical and sustainable form of globalization is not exclusively a human rights matter, but it must include the recognition of shared responsibility for the universal protection of human rights. That responsibility is shared by all of us—individuals, the religions, corporations, states, international financial institutions and the United Nations. Over fifty years ago the drafters of the Universal Declaration of Human Rights stressed the link between respect for human rights and freedom, justice, and peace in the world and called for a just international and social order. That Declaration also affirmed that the true meaning of human rights is one that embraces duties and community as well.

What is emerging is the need for globalization as an economic process to be subject to moral and ethical considerations and to respect international legal standards and principles. I want to illustrate how a new alignment between the framework of international human rights law and that of globalization can be advanced. Let me mention a few examples of how a human-rights-based approach could help develop thinking and action toward an ethical globalization.

World Trade

My first example concerns the international rules regulating trade. The 144 members of the World Trade Organization have all ratified at least one human rights instrument. All but one have ratified the Convention on the Rights of the Child, and 112 have ratified the International Covenant on Economic, Social and Cultural Rights. When negotiating and implementing international rules on trade liberalization, these governments should bear in mind their concurrent obligations to promote and protect human rights, mindful of the commitment made in the Vienna Declaration 1993 that "human rights are the first responsibility of governments."

While the World Trade Organization agreements provide a legal framework for the economic aspects of the liberalization of trade, the norms and standards of human rights balance this by offering a legal framework for trade liberalization's social and ethical dimensions.

What does that mean in practice? It means answering questions such as

Is trade truly free and fair? The developing countries have heard many promises over the years but have too often found that, in practice, access to markets where developing countries hold competitive advantages has been denied.

Do intellectual property rules consider the cultural rights of indigenous and local communities?

Are intellectual property rules conducive to ensuring access to drugs under the World Health Organization essential drug list?

AIDS/HIV

On this last question let us consider the issue of AIDS. First clinically encountered in 1981 in San Francisco as a disease of gay men, it is now endemic in practically every country and mainly in the heterosexual community. For all the virus's own neutrality as between nationality, class, and gender, it is now dominantly infecting and affecting the poorer classes and countries in the developing world, with women increasingly the more vulnerable. Sub-Saharan Africa has been devastated, and many Asian, Caribbean, East European, and even Latin American countries are following in Africa's footsteps.

A lack of respect for human rights is linked to virtually every aspect of the AIDS epidemic, from the factors that cause or increase vulnerability to HIV infection, to discrimination based on stigma attached to people living with HIV/AIDS, to the factors that limit the ability of individuals and communities to respond effectively to the epidemic. Our work and that of others have shown that emphasis on the human rights of victims can make a great difference. Let me explain.

Human tragedies of this kind, although not normally on this scale, are often the first disturbers of moral conscience and the first prompters of moral response. Given the global range of the pandemic, only a global response will be effective. In the search for a global ethic, a very practical beginning might be made by analyzing the dimensions of the pandemic with, for example, people living with HIV/AIDS in Zambia, their carers and others responsible. These dimensions of the pandemic would uncover the deeper roots in cultural practices and in the multiple economic, social, and health privations. As these are only in part locally or nationally generated and, particularly in the economic sphere, are of international origin in even the most remote Zambian village, one is rapidly entangled in the inequities of world trade and the failure of international aid.

Lack of adequate nutrition, of basic medicines, of clean water, of elementary education, of suitable employment, of equality for women, among a multitude of other privations, increase the vulnerability of these poor people to HIV and AIDS. The poverty deprives them in turn of the means of treatment and care which are available to the wealthy. And just as poverty makes them more vulnerable to HIV, so infection and disease in turn increase their poverty through extra medical costs, loss of income, funeral costs, and so on. If one were to trace on the globe the lines of the privations contained in the UNDP Human Development annual reports, they would coincide almost exactly with the line of infection by HIV.

Starting from HIV/AIDS in our hypothetical Zambian village, with its immediate appeal to the moral conscience, one could begin to discern, step by painful step, the elements of a global morality, or at least of the requirements of a humane moral response which would have worldwide implications and operate at every level of individual and social human existence from biological and physical through the relational, intellectual, and spiritual. It may be the task of some of those already living with AIDS and of those living with them and caring for them to help articulate the global moral range of the seemingly menial tasks and restricted lives in which they are involved. The insights of the poor, deprived, and suffering are essential to our enterprise of developing a globalizing ethic with a human rights component. People living with HIV/AIDS and their associates could be one matchless source.

On the positive side, there is progress in recognizing global responsibilities. Recent proposals have highlighted the need for increased cooperation around key areas. The World Health Organization Commission on Macroeconomics and Health, led by Harvard economist Jeffrey Sachs, has proposed that rich countries spend an extra one-tenth of 1 percent of their economies on the health of the poor. If all wealthy countries cooperated, this would add $38 billion a year to health spending by 2015. The commission argues that if that money went to poor nations that also spent more and improved their health care systems, these countries would see at least $360 billion a year in economic gains, lifting millions of people out of poverty and saving an estimated eight million lives a year. UK Chancellor Gordon Brown has proposed a US$50 billion a year investment fund for development targeted at building the capacity of developing countries to improve education and health systems.[11]

A practical expression of cooperation and shared responsibility repeatedly called for is that developed countries should halt the slide in Official Development Assistance and become true development partners for the Least Developed Countries by lifting the burden of debt.

TRIPS and AIDS

The debate over access to HIV/AIDS drugs in developing countries has highlighted the potential conflicts between the intellectual property rights of pharmaceutical companies, which are vital for innovation and research, and the rights of people facing life-threatening disease to adequate health care. Making globalization respond to the needs of all people means finding ways to address this conflict.

The World Trade Organization's Declaration on the Trade Related Aspects of Intellectual Property Rights (TRIPS Agreement) and Public Health adopted in Doha in 2001 sent an important signal regarding the need to balance intellectual property rights against public health priorities for developing countries. The Declaration stresses the need for TRIPS, which covers patents, to be interpreted in a manner "supportive of WTO members' right to protect public health" and to promote access to medicines, particularly with regard to HIV/AIDS, tuberculosis, malaria, and other epidemics.

The Global Compact

A key characteristic of economic globalization is that the actors involved are not only states but also private powers in the form of multinational or transnational corporations. It is now the case that more than half of the top economies in the world are corporations, not states, and international investment is increasingly private. Thus, a new challenge is to ensure that such powerful actors in the globalized economy are accountable for the impact of their policies on human rights and human lives.

One initiative in which my Office is deeply involved concerns the encouragement of an ethical approach by private business enterprises to their activities. The UN Global Compact, which was formally launched by the Secretary General in July 2000, is becoming an overall framework through which the UN is pursuing its engagement with the private sector. It is worth noting that it involves the encouragement of self-regulation, or ethics, to uphold human rights and environmental standards rather than legally binding regulation. However, we should also note that there is considerable debate over whether such ethical codes can be fully effective. There is a trend toward holding companies accountable through legal rules for the human rights and environmental impact of their policies.[12]

Another critical area where the private sector must play a bigger role, if globalization is to benefit more people, is employment generation. There are an estimated sixty-six million unemployed young people in the world today making up more than 40 percent of the world's total unemployed. What future can they expect without the opportunity of decent work? To highlight the urgency of the problem, the ILO estimates that the global economy will need to accommodate half a billion more people in developing countries over the next ten years.

The UN has launched a Global Agenda for Employment as a way to focus the energies of UN agencies, the Bretton Woods Institutions, national governments, employers, and trade unions on addressing these challenges.[13]

Conclusion

Rereading the Millennium Declaration and assessing it in the aftermath of September 11, I am struck by the fact that we have no need for new pledges and commitments. They are all there in solemn language.

We need something more prosaic: implementation, implementation, implementation! One of the attributes of the human rights system is that it is refining its capacity to measure progress through monitoring steps taken by states to implement their commitments. Here, too, the rigor of a legal regime can help to underpin the values of ethical globalization. The next phase must be less aspirational, less theoretical and abstract, and more about keeping solemn promises made.

Appeal at the World Social Forum
Porto Alegre, Brazil, 31 January 2002

This is a critical moment in the debate on globalization. The World Social Forum is establishing itself firmly on the international stage, while the World Economic Forum continues to command attention even as it meets in New York this year. As these two apparently opposing perspectives on the world take center stage once again, the time has come to move beyond the arguments for or against globalization.

Globalization is a reality; it is not new, and it is not going away. It is within our power, however, to ensure that it becomes a positive force for all the world's people.

Although globalization is not new, a "globalized" civil society movement, with tremendous potential to effect change, is. I call on other global actors—corporations, governments, and the international financial organizations—to join with globalized civil society and share responsibility for humanizing globalization. The tools to do so already exist, and they include the extensive body of international human rights legal standards.

As part of the shaping of ethical globalization, we need to work together to identify the steps at the local, national, regional, and international levels to make human rights part of the decision-making of governments, international organizations, the private sector, and wider civil society. This has become all the more vital at this time of great uncertainty for human rights. The aftermath of September 11 has raised concerns about the danger of limiting fundamental freedoms in response to the need to combat terrorism. It has also made the issues we addressed in Durban last September at the World Conference against Racism even more relevant. We are one human family in a small and integrating planet. What alternatives have we but to promote respect, tolerance, and solidarity among all of us?

Building an ethical and sustainable form of globalization is not exclusively a human rights matter, but human rights do provide a legal, analytical, and procedural framework—including the critical role of participation—to address the complex issues raised. As they elaborate international trade and financial regimes, governments should bear in mind their concurrent obligations to promote and protect human rights, together with the commitment made at the Vienna World Conference on Human Rights that "human rights are the first responsibility of governments." It means, for example, that in discussing agricultural agreements, states should be examining the impact of trade liberalization on the right to food and the right to development; or, in dealing with the intellectual property rights of pharmaceutical companies, vital for innovation and research, and the rights of people facing life-threatening diseases, they should ensure the right of access to adequate health care.

Globalization as an economic process must be subject to the moral and ethical imperatives to which the international human rights instruments give legal expression. Human rights are more than just good ideas or distant goals. States have freely accepted the obligations under human rights treaties and have agreed to be held accountable for their implementation. Human rights provide a rigorous framework to empower people from around the world to harness the energies of the global movement and shape a new globalization that benefits all people.

I would appeal to those gathered at the World Social Forum:

to take the debate where it counts—into the sphere of obligations accepted by governments—and call for implementation in all contexts, including the WTO;

to engage other sectors of society—including the private sector—to ensure that they respect human rights and are not complicit, directly or indirectly, in human rights violations; and

to encourage the private sector to work with local civil society to build support for accountable and efficient governance.

An ethical globalization is our best hope for building bridges of respect and understanding between people of different cultures, traditions, and walks of life. It is our best hope for shining the light of public scrutiny on those who would violate the rights of individuals and groups. It is our best hope for expanding freedom and democracy to every corner of the globe.

Farewell Speech to Staff of the Office of the High Commissioner for Human Rights

Palais Wilson, Geneva, 10 September 2002

I would like to thank all those involved in organizing this occasion. Yesterday I bade farewell to our New York colleagues, and this is the last time I will address you as High Commissioner for Human Rights. It is both a sad and a proud occasion for me.

It is sad because the past five years have been both difficult and eventful and I have had the privilege of working with so many wonderful friends and colleagues. I feel a deep sense of pride in what you represent. People outside Palais Wilson do not realize how hard you work or the dedication which you show to the cause of human rights. But I have seen that for myself, and I appreciate your dedication and hard work. I wish to express my deep gratitude to all of you. It would simply not have been possible to do the job without your support and cooperation.

Somebody wrote that the High Commissioner should wake up each morning thinking of human rights. In my experience in the job, it has been difficult not to wake up in the morning thinking of all that needs to be done—even to avoid lying awake in the middle of the night thinking about that has not been easy! I know that for you, too, the burden has been heavy and that many have gone the extra mile for the human rights cause.

One great consolation to me as I leave Geneva is that I am leaving a strong, invigorated team in place in the Office of the High Commissioner. The fight for human rights will not be over next week or next month or next year. So we need to have the best people in place, committed to carrying on this vital work. And it has encouraged me greatly to watch the team here grow in strength and efficiency. The Office is well placed now to carry on the fight.

I think that a lot of progress has been made in recent years in strengthening human rights. But I will not conceal from you that my concern about the future of human rights has grown over the past year. I am conscious that this is an uncertain time for those who champion the rights of the individual. Some voices are heard suggesting that after the terrible attacks in the United States on September 11, human rights are somehow less important, that the security imperative outweighs other considerations. I do not believe that.

On the contrary, in combating terrorism the full range of human rights must be observed.

It is a time for those who believe in human rights to keep their nerve. Human rights are not expendable, whatever the circumstances. And I strongly believe that human rights will endure.

It has been a privilege to serve as United Nations High Commissioner for Human Rights. Ever since the General Assembly approved the Secretary General's nomination, I have been deeply conscious of the trust that the international community placed in me. I have tried to live up to that trust. This job is not an easy one.

Whether as High Commissioner or as a colleague working in this Office here in Geneva, in New York, or in the field, everyone shoulders a heavy responsibility. The hopes of the desperate land on our desks. Often they cannot find a remedy from their own national courts or administrations. Their only hope of justice lies with the international community and institutions such as the Office of the High Commissioner. They look to us as their last hope. That is a basic reality that has guided me during the five years in this position and has motivated me in speaking out when the occasion required, even if what I had to say was not always popular.

There is a saying that if you want to succeed you should speak softly but carry a big stick. The High Commissioner for Human Rights has no big stick except the appeal to the moral conscience of the world. I have tried to speak softly, but clearly, to governments, though from time to time I have found that the only way to get a result is to raise my voice a bit!

At the same time, I have urged from the start that the full range of human rights—economic, social, and cultural as well as civil and political—must be our goal. We need a rounded human rights agenda which takes account of the needs of all. That agenda, I may add, is a most valuable asset in the fight against terrorism.

I will return to the impact of September 11 because the implications of that terrible event must be faced up to squarely. But I would like to spend some time identifying those areas where it seems to me that progress has been made over the past five years and to look at the potential for building on that progress and the obstacles that lie ahead.

When I take stock of where human rights stand today, the first thing I would mention is the fact that human rights are now firmly on the agenda of the international community. If one thinks back twenty years to arguments about whether human rights were universal, whether they could be made operational, whether they have a serious place in the conduct of international relations, one would have to conclude that human rights have indeed come a long way. Most governments today will at least acknowledge that human rights have a role to play. Unfortunately that does not necessarily mean that they will observe human rights standards. You will often still hear governments arguing that they must place other factors first. The difference is that today those sorts of claims go against the tide of opinion. There is much greater recognition now of the centrality of human rights and the immense benefits a rights-based approach brings. That is a big step forward.

Our mandate is to give leadership in human rights, and I am glad we are doing so by being operational in the field. We are a small UN Office, so it is necessary to be strategic. But I am conscious of the different ways in which we have become operational. Last month I was able to assess the impact of the work of our colleagues in the Office in Cambodia, to visit East Timor again and see how the human rights unit in UNTAET had developed, and to meet Nick Howen in Bangkok and hear his views as regional representative for Asia on what our priorities should be.

After that I traveled with colleagues to the Sustainable Development World Summit in Johannesburg. Thanks to well-prepared speeches and speaking notes, I was able to make substantive and relevant interventions on issues such as the right to water, HIV/AIDS, human rights and sustainable development, corporate responsibility and human rights, and the environment. The human rights message was getting across—and it was badly needed. When I met civil society NGOs—environmental and development activists, as well as human rights activists—they expressed deep appreciation of the leadership our Office was giving. The civil society message was clear: no sustainable development without human rights.

Another advance I see is the consolidation of international human rights legislation. The momentum in this area was clearly shown at the Millennium Summit, which saw 273 signatures, ratifications of or accessions to major human rights treaties and instruments undertaken by 84 states. The entry into force of the Optional Protocols to CEDAW and to the CRC on the involvement of children in armed conflict and sale of children, child prostitution, and child pornography were particularly satisfying examples. It is worth recalling how difficult the process was in each of those cases and that many thought success would never come. But it did come, and that is further proof that determination and perseverance can achieve results that make an enduring impact. It would be a wonderful advance if the one remaining ratification needed to bring the Convention on Migrant Workers into effect could be obtained in the coming weeks.

Getting treaties enacted and ratified is, of course, only the start. We must redouble our efforts in the time ahead to ensure that the legislation is put into practice, and that civil society plays its full part in ensuring implementation of these commitments.

I would like to say a special word here about the International Criminal Court. All of us should warmly welcome the fact that the ICC has become a reality. I find it particularly welcome that the statute contains provision for the prosecution of rape as a war crime. Having an independent court will bring the perpetrators of human rights violations to account. Above all, it will have a deterrent effect on those contemplating such violations. As I said yesterday in New York, I regret the current attempts to undermine the legitimacy and effectiveness of the ICC, but I believe they will be short term, and that the ICC will prove its worth many times over.

A further area of progress has been in the mainstreaming of human rights in the work of the United Nations as a whole and in that of other international organizations. As in the other areas I have mentioned, there is room for improvement here also. But it is remarkable to see bodies such as UNDP and the World Bank take on the human rights dimensions when in the past they might have tended to regard these as difficult and sensitive. I am convinced that mainstreaming of both human rights and strong gender perspective is the key to making human rights acceptable everywhere, and I hope that the beginnings we have made will be built on.

Let me say a word about the role of the United Nations in protecting human rights, a role that I believe is absolutely crucial. When I first took on the job of High Commissioner, I expressed misgivings about the UN. Over five years as High Commissioner, I have seen some positive developments, though I will say frankly that I would like to have seen more. What I am more and more convinced of is how important it is that the world has a United Nations that is efficient, aware, and responsible. The UN is unique because it, alone among international organizations, can claim universal legitimacy.

I have made a number of proposals for strengthening the role of human rights within the UN. One specific proposal is that human rights guidelines be drawn up for use in implementation of the Millennium Development Goals agreed on in the wake of the Millennium Declaration. Another idea I have suggested to the Secretary General is to mark next year's tenth anniversary of the Vienna Conference by devising a methodology to monitor progress made in reaching human rights goals. An Annual UN Progress Report on Human Rights, carried out by independent experts, would bring an external view to bear on progress and on the challenges for the implementation of the Millennium Declaration human rights goals.

And the United Nations needs to look ahead to issues such as bioethics and the human rights dimension of scientific and technological developments, to issues which deserve more attention, such as the rights of the disabled and the use of the Internet and information technology to promote respect for human rights.

As in all of its activities, the UN must demonstrate that its approach to human rights is effective and can bring real improvements to people's lives. I wish my successor well in pursuing this goal.

I want to make special mention of human rights defenders. I need not stress to you the pivotal role that human rights defenders play. But this is a good time to put on record how much I, and the international community, owe to the thousands of women and men who have stood up for the rights enshrined in the Universal Declaration. Progress has been made through the appointment of the Secretary General's Special Representative for Human Rights Defenders, and Hina Jilani is doing excellent work in that capacity. Human rights defenders need our special care and attention as they stand in the front line of the struggle. It has been a privilege for me to get to know so many of them, to see their courage and perseverance, and to hope that we can maintain the link in the future.

The chief threats to human rights can be seen in those forces which are the opposite of its strengths. For example:

that governments will only pay lip service to their human rights commitments and will not live up to them;
that international organizations may falter in their mainstreaming of human rights and gender;
that the vigilance of civil society will be relaxed, the security argument bowed to.

I am confident that together we can deal with all of these threats. The continued vigilance of civil society, is a key factor. I have always found it natural to link my work with civil society and I was glad to have the occasion in New York, yesterday, to express my deep appreciation for the support I have received from the NGO community over the past five years. I was concerned at the last session of the Commission on Human Rights that the voices of NGOs were not allowed to be heard as much as in the past. I urge NGOs to carry on their work and to focus activities not only on governments, but also on other key players, such as the business community, who have such a powerful role.

Returning to September 11: I said at the start that I was apprehensive about the impact the aftermath has been having on human rights. At the annual meeting of the Special Rapporteurs and Chairs of the Treaty Bodies which took place recently in Geneva, it was striking how many reports had come in from around the world on the erosion of civil liberties in the guise of combating terrorism. And it was noticeable and worrying at the last session of the Commission that the pressure for action in some of the worst cases of human rights abuses was less strong this year.

Responding to terrorism will remain a major focus of international affairs over the coming years. But we must all continue to insist on respect for basic rights and fundamental freedoms in countering terrorist threats. We should not hesitate to draw attention to the relevant international standards and in particular to the nonderogable rights that must be protected at all times.

The happier side of my departure from Geneva is that I will take away with me so many precious memories. As a private citizen, I will remain committed to the cause of human rights. An area I am particularly interested in is the place of human rights in the globalized world and how we can work toward ethical standards of globalization. A related issue of vital importance is national capacity building. When we look back at the history of the human rights movement, it is inevitable that we pay tribute to the extraordinary vision of Eleanor Roosevelt, who recognized that what the world needed was a universal, indivisible law on human rights. Now what is needed above all is the building up of national protection systems to ensure implementation of agreed human rights law. That fits well with one of my favorite Eleanor Roosevelt quotes: that human rights begin “in small places, close to home.”

Ethical globalization, national capacity building—these are linked areas where I see great challenges for all who are interested in human rights. I intend to devote time to developing ideas for strengthening these areas as part of the overall goal of embedding a culture of human rights.

Once again, my thanks to all of you for your support, and my best wishes to my successor Sergio Vieira de Mello and to you all in the struggle that lies ahead. As High Commissioner, I have been conscious that the human rights mandate, more than any other, reflects who are the source and who should be the focus and inspiration of the United Nations, as reflected in the opening words of the Charter: *We the peoples . . .*

Thank you.

Afterword

The two biggest tributes that a person can be accorded are recognition by peers and the legacy of having made a difference. Few are fortunate enough to achieve one of the two. Even fewer merit both.

Mary Robinson is an exceptional woman who is universally recognized as a powerful force for the promotion and protection of human rights and widely regarded as a moral voice for those who are denied these rights. She has made a difference in the lives of people everywhere, from the biggest metropolis to the most remote village. Her work as United Nations High Commissioner for Human Rights won her the admiration of her supporters and the respect of her critics.

A wise man once said, "Always do right. This will gratify some people and astonish the rest." Mary Robinson has been doing right for many years. When she encountered problems, she presented solutions. When she saw injustice, she acted to correct it. When she saw despair, she offered hope. Her moral principles and her sense of right and wrong never fell victim to political expediency.

This is a legacy which she can rightly be proud of, one that belongs not just to her but to all of us, particularly to those thousands of human rights defenders who continue her work on the ground, where it matters most, day in and day out. It is a legacy which is reflected well in the eloquent and passionate speeches and statements included in this book. This collection offers an excellent opportunity to understand what she sought to achieve as High Commissioner and gives a good insight into Mary Robinson the public figure.

I am privileged to be asked to offer my thoughts on this book, which is certain to serve as an excellent resource for the work of the Office of the High Commissioner for Human Rights. It will also help to make the work of the United Nations in defense of human rights better understood and appreciated by opinion makers, governments, and the public.

Louise Arbour
United Nations High Commissioner for Human Rights

Appendix 1

Key International Legal Instruments

1945 Charter of the United Nations signed on 26 June 1945

1948 Universal Declaration of Human Rights, General Assembly resolution 217 A (III) of 10 December 1948

1948 Convention on the Prevention and Suppression of the Crime of Genocide, 78 *UNTS* 277

1949 Geneva Convention I for the Amelioration of the Condition of the Wounded and Sick in Armed Forces in the Field, 75 *UNTS* 31

1949 Geneva Convention II for the Amelioration of the Condition of the Wounded, Sick and Shipwrecked Members of Armed Forces at Sea, 75 *UNTS* 85

1949 Geneva Convention III Relative to the Treatment of Prisoners of War, 75 *UNTS* 135

1949 Geneva Convention IV Relative to the Protection of Civilian Persons in Time of War, 75 *UNTS* 285

- 1977 Geneva Protocol I Additional to the Geneva Conventions of 12 August 1949, and Relating to the Protection of Victims of International Armed Conflicts, 1125 *UNTS* 3

1950 European Convention on the Protection of Human Rights and Fundamental Freedoms, *European Treaty Series* No. 5

1951 Convention on the Status of Refugees, 189 *UNTS* 150

- 1967 Protocol Relating to the Status of Refugees, 606 *UNTS* 276

1966 International Convention on the Elimination of All Forms of Racial Discrimination, 660 *UNTS* 195

1966 International Covenant on Economic, Social and Cultural Rights, 993 *UNTS* 3

1966 International Covenant on Civil and Political Rights, 999 *UNTS* 171

- Optional Protocol to the International Covenant on Civil and Political Rights 999 *UNTS* 171
- Second Optional Protocol to the International Covenant on Civil and Political Rights, 6 *ILM* 383

1968 Proclamation of Tehran, Final Act of the International Conference on Human Rights, A/CONF.32/41 of 13 May 1968

1969 American Convention on Human Rights, *O.A.S. Treaty Series* No. 36

1979 Convention on the Elimination of All Forms of Discrimination against Women, 1249 *UNTS* 13

1999 Optional Protocol to the Convention on the Elimination of All Forms of Discrimination against Women, General Assembly resolution 54/4 of 15 October 1999, A/RES/54/49

1981 African Charter on Human and Peoples' Rights, OAU Document CAB/LEG/67/3 rev. 5, 21 *ILM* 58 (1982)

1981 Declaration on the Elimination of All Forms of Intolerance and of Discrimination Based on Religion or Belief, General Assembly resolution 36/55 of 25 November 1981, A/RES/36/55

1984 Convention against Torture and Other Cruel Inhuman and Degrading Treatment or Punishment, 1984 *ILM* 1207

1989 United Nations Convention on the Rights of the Child, General Assembly resolution 44/25 of 20 November 1989, A/RES/44/25

2000 Optional Protocol to the Convention on the Rights of the Child on the Involvement of Children in Armed Conflicts, General Assembly resolution 54/263 of 25 May 2000, A/RES/54/263

2000 Optional Protocol to the Convention on the Rights of the Child on the Sale of Children, Child Prostitution, and Child Pornography General Assembly resolution 54/263 of 25 May 2000, A/RES/54/263

1990 International Convention on the Rights of Migrant Workers and Members of Their Families, General Assembly resolution 45/158 of 18 December 1990, A/RES/45/158

1990 Beijing Declaration and Platform for Action, Fourth World Conference on Women, 15 September 1995, A/CONF.177/20

1992 Declaration on the Rights of Persons Belonging to National or Ethnic, Religious and Linguistic Minorities, General Assembly resolution 47/135 of 18 December 1992, A/RES/47/135

1993 Vienna Declaration and Programme of Action, A/CONF.157/23 12 July 1993

1998 Aarhus Convention on Access to Information, Public Participation and Access to Justice in Environmental Matters

1999 Worst Forms of Child Labour Convention, ILO No. 182, 38 *ILM* 1207 (1999)

2000 Protocol to Prevent, Suppress and Punish Trafficking of Persons, Especially Women and Children, supplementing the United Nations Convention against Transnational Organised Crime, General Assembly Resolution 55/25 of 15 November 2000, A/RES/55/25

2002 Durban Declaration and Programme of Action of the World Conference against Racism, Racial Discrimination, Xenophobia and Related Intolerance and the provisions of General Assembly resolution 56/266 of 27 March 2002, A/RES/56/266

Appendix 2

High Commissioner for the Promotion and Protection of All Human Rights

General Assembly resolution 48/141 of 20 December 1993

The General Assembly,

Reaffirming its commitment to the purposes and principles of the Charter of the United Nations,

Emphasizing the responsibilities of all States, in conformity with the Charter, to promote and encourage respect for all human rights and fundamental freedoms for all, without distinction as to race, sex, language or religion,

Emphasizing the need to observe the Universal Declaration of Human Rights[1] and for the full implementation of the human rights instruments, including the International Covenant on Civil and Political Rights,[2] the International Covenant on Economic, Social and Cultural Rights,[2] as well as the Declaration on the Right to Development,[3]

Reaffirming that the right to development is a universal and inalienable right which is a fundamental part of the rights of the human person,

Considering that the promotion and the protection of all human rights is one of the priorities of the international community,

Recalling that one of the purposes of the United Nations enshrined in the Charter is to achieve international cooperation in promoting and encouraging respect for human rights,

Reaffirming the commitment made under Article 56 of the Charter to take joint and separate action in cooperation with the United Nations for the achievement of the purposes set forth in Article 55 of the Charter,

Emphasizing the need for the promotion and protection of all human rights to be guided by the principles of impartiality, objectivity and non-selectivity, in the spirit of constructive international dialogue and cooperation,

1. Resolution 217 A (III).
2. See resolution 2200 A (XXI), annex
3. Resolution 41/128, annex

Aware that all human rights are universal, indivisible, interdependent and interrelated and that as such they should be given the same emphasis,

Affirming its commitment to the Vienna Declaration and Programme of Action,[4] adopted by the World Conference on Human Rights, held at Vienna from 14 to 25 June 1993,

Convinced that the World Conference on Human Rights made an important contribution to the cause of human rights and that its recommendations should be implemented through effective action by all States, the competent organs of the United Nations and the specialized agencies, in cooperation with non-governmental organizations,

Acknowledging the importance of strengthening the provision of advisory services and technical assistance by the Centre for Human Rights of the Secretariat and other relevant programmes and bodies of the United Nations system for the purpose of the promotion and protection of all human rights,

Determined to adapt, strengthen and streamline the existing mechanisms to promote and protect all human rights and fundamental freedoms while avoiding unnecessary duplication,

Recognizing that the activities of the United Nations in the field of human rights should be rationalized and enhanced in order to strengthen the United Nations machinery in this field and to further the objectives of universal respect for observance of international human rights standards,

Reaffirming that the General Assembly, the Economic and Social Council and the Commission on Human Rights are the responsible organs for decision- and policy-making for the promotion and protection of all human rights,

Reaffirming the necessity for a continued adaptation of the United Nations human rights machinery to the current and future needs in the promotion and protection of human rights and the need to improve its co-ordination, efficiency and effectiveness, as reflected in the Vienna Declaration and Programme of Action and within the framework of a balanced and sustainable development for all people,

Having considered the recommendation contained in paragraph 18 of section II of the Vienna Declaration and Programme of Action,

1. *Decides* to create the post of the High Commissioner for Human Rights;
2. *Decides* that the High Commissioner for Human Rights shall:
   (*a*) Be a person of high moral standing and personal integrity and shall possess expertise, including in the field of human rights, and the general knowledge and understanding of diverse cultures necessary for impartial, objective, non-selective and effective performance of the duties of the High Commissioner;
   (*b*) Be appointed by the Secretary-General of the United Nations and

4. A/CONF.157/24 (Part I), chap. III.

approved by the General Assembly, with due regard to geographical rotation, and have a fixed term of four years with a possibility of one renewal for another fixed term of four years;

(*c*) Be of the rank of Under-Secretary-General;

3. *Decides* that the High Commissioner for Human Rights shall:

(*a*) Function within the framework of the Charter of the United Nations, the Universal Declaration of Human Rights,[1] other international instruments of human rights and international law, including the obligations, within this framework, to respect the sovereignty, territorial integrity and domestic jurisdiction of States and to promote the universal respect for and observance of all human rights, in the recognition that, in the framework of the purposes and principles of the Charter, the promotion and protection of all human rights is a legitimate concern of the international community;

(*b*) Be guided by the recognition that all human rights—civil, cultural, economic, political and social—are universal, indivisible, interdependent and interrelated and that, while the significance of national and regional particularities and various historical, cultural and religious backgrounds must be borne in mind, it is the duty of States, regardless of their political, economic and cultural systems, to promote and protect all human rights and fundamental freedoms;

(*c*) Recognize the importance of promoting a balanced and sustainable development for all people and of ensuring realization of the right to development, as established in the Declaration on the Right to Development;[3]

4. *Decides* that the High Commissioner for Human Rights shall be the United Nations official with principal responsibility for United Nations human rights activities under the direction and authority of the Secretary-General; within the framework of the overall competence, authority and decisions of the General Assembly, the Economic and Social Council and the Commission on Human Rights, the High Commissioner's responsibilities shall be:

(*a*) To promote and protect the effective enjoyment by all of all civil, cultural, economic, political and social rights;

(*b*) To carry out the tasks assigned to him/her by the competent bodies of the United Nations system in the field of human rights and to make recommendations to them with a view to improving the promotion and protection of all human rights;

(*c*) To promote and protect the realization of the right to development and to enhance support from relevant bodies of the United Nations system for this purpose;

(*d*) To provide, through the Centre for Human Rights of the Secretariat and other appropriate institutions, advisory services and technical and financial assistance, at the request of the State concerned and, where appropriate, the regional human rights organizations, with a view to supporting actions and programmes in the field of human rights;

(*e*) To coordinate relevant United Nations education and public information programmes in the field of human rights;

(*f*) To play an active role in removing the current obstacles and in meeting the challenges to the full realization of all human rights and in preventing the continuation of human rights violations throughout the world, as reflected in the Vienna Declaration and Programme of Action;[4]

(*g*) To engage in a dialogue with all Governments in the implementation of his/her mandate with a view to securing respect for all human rights;

(*h*) To enhance international cooperation for the promotion and protection of all human rights;

(*i*) To coordinate the human rights promotion and protection activities throughout the United Nations system;

(*j*) To rationalize, adapt, strengthen and streamline the United Nations machinery in the field of human rights with a view to improving its efficiency and effectiveness;

(*k*) To carry out overall supervision of the Centre for Human Rights;

5. *Requests* the High Commissioner for Human Rights to report annually on his/her activities, in accordance with his/her mandate, to the Commission on Human Rights and, through the Economic and Social Council, to the General Assembly;
6. *Decides* that the Office of the High Commissioner for Human Rights shall be located at Geneva and shall have a liaison office in New York;
7. *Requests* the Secretary-General to provide appropriate staff and resources, within the existing and future regular budgets of the United Nations, to enable the High Commissioner to fulfil his/her mandate, without diverting resources from the development programmes and activities of the United Nations;
8. *Also requests* the Secretary-General to report to the General Assembly at its forty-ninth session on the implementation of the present resolution.

Notes

Introduction

1. The term of office provided for the post is four years and is renewable once. In 2001 Mary Robinson had announced that she would not seek a second term. She thereafter agreed with the Secretary General to continue for a fifth year, which ended on 11 September 2002. See further below.

2. For biographies, see Olivia O'Leary and Helen Burke, *Mary Robinson: The Authorised Biography* (London: Hodder & Stoughton, 1998); John Hogan, *Mary Robinson: A Woman of Ireland and the World* (Niwot, Colo.: Roberts Rinehart, 1997).

3. At the end of her term in September 2002, Mary Robinson issued a press release setting out her own summary of her achievements: Mary Robinson, *Ten Priorities as United Nations High Commissioner,* Geneva, 10 September 2002.

4. *Supra* note 2.

5. Mary Robinson, "Daunting Challenges Lie Ahead after Difficult but Rewarding Year," *The Irish Times,* 13 October 1998.

6. Peter Capella and Ewen MacAskill, "Robinson Quits UN Job Citing Lack of Funds," *The Guardian,* 20 March 2001.

7. Peter Capella, Owen Boycott, and Rosie Cowan, "Leaders United to Get Robinson to Stay," *The Guardian,* 4 April 2001.

8. A. J. Hobbins, "Humphrey and the High Commissioner: The Genesis of the Office of the High Commissioner for Human Rights," *Journal of the History of International Law* 3 (2001): 37–74. On the post of High Commissioner, see A. Clapham, "The High Commissioner of Human Rights," in P. Alston, ed., *The United Nations and Human Rights* (Oxford: Clarendon Press, 2004); A. Clapham, "Creating the High Commissioner for Human Rights: The Outside Story," *European Journal of International Law* 5 (1994): 556–68; B. G. Ramcharan, *The United Nations High Commissioner for Human Rights: The Challenge of International Protection* (The Hague: Martinus Nijhoff, 2002); P. Alston, "Neither Fish nor Fowl: The Quest to Define the Role of the UN High Commissioner for Human Rights" *European Journal of International Law* 2 (1997) 321–35. See also B. Mukherjee, "United Nations High Commissioner for Human Rights: Challenges and Opportunities," in G. Alfredsson et al., eds., *International Human Rights Monitoring Mechanisms* (The Hague: Martinus Nijhoff, 2001); United Nations, *The High Commissioner for Human Rights: An Introduction,* HR/PUB/HCHR/96/1 (Geneva: UNHCHR, 1996).

9. High Commissioner for the promotion and protection of all human rights, General Assembly resolution 48/141 of 20 December 1993, A/RES/48/141, 7 January 1994. The full text of the resolution establishing the mandate of the High Commissioner is set out in Appendix 2.

10. Kofi Annan, *Renewing the United Nations: A Programme for Reform*, Report of the Secretary General, A/51/950, 14 July 1997. See also *Strengthening the United Nations: An Agenda for Further Change*, Report of the Secretary General, A/57/387, 9 September 2002.

11. Mary Robinson, *Realizing Human Rights: "Take Hold of It Boldly and Duly . . ."* DPI/1937/E (New York: United Nations Department of Public Information, 1998).

12. *Supra*, at note 5.

13. See especially Chapter 18.

14. Vienna Declaration and Programme of Action, World Conference on Human Rights, Vienna, 14–25 June 1993, A/CONF.157/24.

15. Vienna Declaration, paragraph 5.

16. On cooperation with UNDP, see UNDP, *Human Rights and Human Development: Human Development Report 2000* (New York: United Nations Department of Public Information and Oxford University Press, 2000).

17. See further Chapter 1.

18. United Nations Millennium Declaration General Assembly resolution 55/2 of 8 September 2000, A/RES/55/2, 18 September 2000. The Millennium Development Goals (MDGs) are drawn from the Declaration and commit states to a series of development targets to be met by 2015; see www.un.org

19. See Afterword.

20. See especially Chapter 16.

21. Ian Martin, "A New Frontier: The Early Experience and Future of International Human Rights Field Operations," Papers in the Theory and Practice of Human Rights No. 18 (Colchester: Human Rights Centre, University of Essex, 1998).

22. Amnesty International, "A High Commissioner for Human Rights: Time for Action," Vol. IOR 41/35/93 (1993).

23. *The High Commissioner for Human Rights: An Introduction*, HR/PUB/HCHR/96/1 (Geneva: United Nations, 1996).

24. It was a dimension of the tragedy of the death of Sergio Vieira de Mello that the Office of High Commissioner was denied the likely major impact of his vast humanitarian operational experience on the further integration of fieldwork into the mandate of the High Commissioner.

25. For the range of OHCHR projects and programs of technical assistance that were in place at the end of Mary Robinson's tenure of the post, all funded through voluntary contributions by donor states, see OHCHR Annual Report 2001, Geneva.

26. See Chapter 16.

27. Annual Appeal for 2001, overview of activities and financial requirements (Geneva: OHCHR, 2001); see also Annual Reports 2001, 2002, and 2003.

28. On the Global Compact, see Chapter 13.

29. See Chapter 12.

30. See Chapter 19.

31. *Realizing Rights: The Ethical Globalization Initiative*, is intended to bring "key stakeholders together in new alliances to integrate concepts of human rights, gender sensitivity and enhanced accountability into efforts to address global challenges and governance shortcomings"; see www.eginitiative.org.

Chapter 1. A Personal Vision

"Realizing Human Rights: 'Take Hold of It Boldly and Duly . . .'"

Oxford University's Romanes Lecture is an annual event provided for by a fund established by George John Romanes in 1891. This lecture was later published by the United Nations Department for Public Information: Mary Robinson, "Realizing Human Rights: 'Take Hold of It Boldly and Duly . . .'" (New York: United Nations Department of Public Information, 1998), DPI/1937/E.

1. Lord Jenkins of Hillhead, *The Chancellorship of Oxford: A Contemporary View with a Little History (Romanes Lecture, 1996)* (London: Clarendon Press, 1997).

2. The Vienna Declaration and Programme of Action, adopted by the World Conference on Human Rights on 25 June 1993, A/CONF.157/23, 12 July 1993, Para. 1.

3. Mary Robinson visited Somalia in 1992 to highlight the famine and violence affecting the population following the overthrow of Siad Barre. She later published a moving diary of the visit: Mary Robinson, *A Voice for Somalia* (Dublin: O'Brien Press, 1992). In 1994 she visited Rwanda as Irish President; see Olivia O'Leary and Helen Burke, *Mary Robinson: The Authorised Biography* (London: Hodder & Stoughton, 1998).

4. United Nations member states are organized into five unofficial but powerful regional groups through which much diplomacy and bargaining take place. Representation on UN committees and bodies is arranged through the regional groups. The groups are Africa Group, Asia Pacific, Group of Latin America and Caribbean states, Eastern Europe, and Western European and Others.

5. High Commissioner for the promotion and protection of all human rights, General Assembly resolution 48/141 of 20 Decemeber 1993, A/RES/48/141, 7 January 1994. The full text of the resolution establishing the mandate of the High Commissioner is set out in Appendix 2.

6. The Fourth World Conference on Women, Beijing, China, 4–5 September 1995; Report of the Fourth World Conference on Women, A/CONF.177/20, 17 October 1995, www.un.org/womenwatch/daw/beijing.

7. Proclamation of Teheran, Final Act of the International Conference on Human Rights, Tehran, 22 April to 13 May 1968, A/CONF. 32/41 of 13 May 1968.

8. Kofi Annan, *Renewing the United Nations: A Programme for Reform*, Report of the Secretary General, A/51/950, 14 July 1997, para. 201, action 15(b).

9. *Human Rights Questions: Comprehensive Implementation of and Follow-up to the Vienna Declaration and Programme of Action,* Report of the High Commissioner for Human Rights, A /53/372 of 11 September 1998.

10. Annan, *Renewing the United Nations*, paras. 59–60.

11. Philip Alston, "Neither Fish nor Fowl: The Quest to Define the Role of the UN High Commissioner for Human Rights," *European Journal of International Law* 8:2 (1997): 321.

12. Annan, *Renewing the United Nations*, paras. 78–79.

13. A. Frankovits, E. Sidoti, and P. Earle, *The Rights Way to Development: A Human Rights Approach to Development Assistance, Policy and Practice* (New South Wales: Human Rights Council of Australia, 1998).

14. Rosalyn Higgins, *Problems and Process: International Law and How We Use It* (Oxford: Clarendon Press, 1994), pp. 1–2.

"The Universal Declaration of Human Rights: A Living Document"

The Third Symposium on Human Rights in the Asia Pacific Region was hosted by the Japanese Ministry of Foreign Affairs and the United Nations University from 27 to 28 January 1998. Held to mark the fiftieth anniversary of the Universal Declaration of Human Rights, it explored ways and means to advance international commitment and cooperation in promoting and protecting human rights in the Asia Pacific region.

This address was the first of a number of commemorative speeches that Mary Robinson made at events throughout the world in the anniversary year. Other speeches or statements commemorating this anniversary were:

"Statement on the Importance of the Independence of Special Rapporteurs and Similar Mechanisms of the Commission on Human Rights," 16 December 1997. This text is included in Chapter 15.

"Commencement Address at Harvard University," Harvard University, USA, 4 June 1998.

"The Universal Declaration of Human Rights: Hope and History," address to the Oslo Conference on Freedom of Religion or Belief, University of Oslo, Norway, 14 August 1998. This text is included in Chapter 3.

"The Universal Declaration of Human Rights: A Living Document," keynote address, Forum 98: *50 Years after the Universal Declaration of Human Rights*, Geneva, 28 August 1998.

"Statement at the European Regional Colloquy organized by the Council of Europe," Strasbourg, France, 2 September 1998.

"Human Rights: Challenges for the 21st Century," First Annual Dag Hammarskjöld Lecture, Uppsala, Sweden, 1 October 1998.

"The Mortal Power of Affirmation," United Kingdom United Nations Association and United Nations Information Centre's celebration of the fiftieth anniversary, London, UK, 30 November 1998.

"Translating Words into Action," meeting of the General Assembly to commemorate the fiftieth anniversary of the Universal Declaration of Human Rights, United Nations, New York, 10 December 1998.

Message on the Fiftieth Anniversary of the Universal Declaration of Human Rights, the Fiftieth Anniversary of the Universal Declaration of Human Rights 1948–98, Human Rights Day, 10 December 1998.

"The Business Case for Human Rights," an article published in *Visions of Ethical Business*, The Financial Times, Management, in association with Pricewaterhouse Coopers and the Council on Economic Priorities (Europe).

15. Proclamation of Teheran, Final Act of the International Conference on Human Rights, Teheran, 22 April to 13 May 1968, A/CONF. 32/41 of 13 May 1968.

16. The quotation is from Nelson Mandela's message to the Commemorative Workshop on the Universal Declaration of Human Rights, Warsaw, Poland, 30–31 January 1997.

17. The InterAction Council drafted a Universal Declaration of Human Responsibility in September 1997. The intent was that the Declaration would be adopted by the UN General Assembly on the fiftieth anniversary of the Universal Declaration. However, this did not occur. The text of the proposed declaration can be found at www.interactioncouncil.org.

Acceptance of the Erasmus Prize

The *Praemium Erasmianum* is an annual award founded by Prince Bernhard of the Netherlands. Its purpose is "to honor persons or institutions that have made an exceptionally important contribution to European culture, society or social science."

18. Hugo Grotius, *On the Law of War and Peace*, trans. A. C. Campbell (Ontario: Kitchener, 2001).

19. From a speech by Seamus Heaney at a protest rally against continuing violence in East Timor, held in Dublin, Ireland, on 11 September 1999. Published in: *East Timor, Indonesia and the World Community: Resistance, Repression and Responsibility Special Edition of the Bulletin of Concerned Asian Scholars* 32, 1–2 (2000).

20. Dag Hammarskjöld, *Markings*, trans. Leif Sjoberg and W. H. Auden (London: Faber and Faber, 1964).

21. See further Chapter 9 on the Assisting Communities Together (ACT) program.

22. Aung San Suu Kyi, *Freedom from Fear* (New York: Penguin, 1991).

Chapter 2. The Struggle against Racism

The Third Decade to Combat Racism and Racial Discrimination and the convening of the World Conference against Racism, Racial Discrimination, Xenophobia and Related Intolerance, were agreed on in General Assembly resolution 53/132 of 9 December 1998, A/RES/53/132, 23 February 1999.

"The Global Impact of Racism"

Mary Robinson was the first recipient of the William J. Butler Human Rights Medal, established by the Urban Morgan Institute for Human Rights to honor those who work tirelessly in the service of human rights.

1. *Ocalan v. Turkey,* Judgment of the European Court of Human Rights, 12 March 2003.

"Combating Intolerance"

At the invitation of Swedish Prime Minister Göran Persson, the governments of more than fifty states took part in the Stockholm International Forum on Combating Intolerance held on 29 and 30 January 2001. Mary Robinson contributed this keynote speech. A Declaration on Combating Intolerance adopted by the Forum was submitted to the United Nations World Conference against Racism. The subject of the previous year's international forum was the Holocaust.

2. Seamus Heaney, *Crediting Poetry: The Nobel Lecture 1995* (Oldcastle, Co. Meath: Gallery Books, 1995).

3. This speech was given by Nobel Peace Laureate Elie Wiesel at the ceremony commemorating the fiftieth anniversary of the liberation of Auschwitz: www.pbs.org/eliewiesel/life/auschwitz.html.

4. The Working Group delivered this statement during an Informal Consultation held from 15 to 16 January 2001 in Geneva in the lead-up to the World Conference on Racism: www.icare.to/ngo-working-group.html.

5. The Sweden 2000 Institute is a diversity consultancy based in Gothenburg, Sweden: see www.sverige2000.se.

6. For the full text of the declaration *Tolerance and Diversity: A Vision for the 21st Century*, see www.unhchr.ch/html/racism/00-vision.html.

Elimination of Racism and Racial Discrimination

The World Conference against Racism, Racial Discrimination, Xenophobia and Related Intolerance, Conference Report, A/CONF.189/12, 25 January 2002: www.unhchr.ch/html/racism.

"United to Combat Racism: A Youth Vision"

Held from 26 to 27 August 2001, in the lead up to the World Conference against Racism, the International Youth Summit enabled eight hundred Youth Representatives to participate directly in the World Conference. Forty of the Youth Representatives, drawn from all world regions, drafted a parallel Youth Declaration during the Conference. It is available from the WCAR NGO Forum Web site: www.racism.org.za.

7. After the September 11, 2001 attacks the Children's Summit was postponed. It was held in May 2002, see Chapter 10.

8. The Voices of Victims Special Forum was organized by the International Human Rights Law Group (now Global Rights) in collaboration with the South

Africa Human Rights Commission, UN treaty bodies, and national institutions. It ran from 1 to 6 September 2001 in Durban. See International Human Rights Law Group, *Voices: A Special Forum on Comparative Experiences of Racism* (Washington: International Human Rights Law Group, 2001). The event can be viewed at www.vodium.com/mediapod/hrlawgroup/voices1

Chapter 3. Women's Rights Are Human Rights

The number of states parties to the Convention on the Elimination of All Forms of Discrimination against Women and its Optional Protocol continue to rise. As of 9 June 2004 there were 177 and 60 states parties, respectively.

Women's Rights Are Human Rights

The speech was delivered at the Afghanistan National Workshop on Women's Rights, 8 March 2002, organized by Simar Samar, Minister for Women of the Interim Administration of Afghanistan. Its themes were echoed in Mary Robinson's message as High Commissioner for International Women's Day in 2002.

1. Secretary General's Message to the Brussels Summit, SG/SM/8066 AGF/173, 4 December 2001.
2. Beijing Declaration and Platform for Action, Fourth World Conference on Women, A/CONF.177/20, 15 September 1995.
3. Security Council Resolution 1325, S/Res./1325 of 31 October 2000.
4. Joint Declaration of the Special Rapporteurs on Women's Rights, Ms. Marta Altolaguirre, Special Rapporteur on Women's Rights of the Inter-American Commission on Human Rights; Ms. Radhika Coomaraswamy, Special Rapporteur on Violence Against Women, Its Causes and Its Consequences of the UN Commission on Human Rights; Ms. Angela Melo, Special Rapporteur on the Rights of Women in Africa of the African Commission on Human and Peoples' Rights: www.cidh.org/declaration.women.htm.
5. The Afghan Women's Summit for Democracy, 4–5 December 2001, adopted the Brussels Proclamation: www.un.org/womenwatch/afghanistan.
6. The Roundtable on Building Women's Leadership in Afghanistan, convened by UNIFEM and the Government of Belgium, Brussels, 10–11 December 2001, adopted the Brussels Action Plan: www.unifem.org.au/actplan.doc.

"Women, Human Rights and Sustainable Development in the 21st Century"

The Gala Dinner for African Women Leaders in Pretoria on 31 August 2002, hosted by First Lady Zanele Mbeki, was the culmination of a South African Women's Forum workshop that ran parallel to the World Summit on Sustainable Development in Johannesburg. The workshop was held to remedy a perceived lack of attention to women's issues in the Draft Plan of Implementation to be discussed at the World Summit. The women leaders present at the dinner included not only ministers and parliamentary leaders but also representatives of grassroots organizations.

7. Beijing Declaration and Platform for Action, Fourth World Conference on Women, A/CONF.177/20, 15 September 1995.
8. World Bank, *World Development Report 2000/2001: Attacking Poverty* (Oxford: Oxford University Press, 2001), p. v.
9. On human trafficking, see further Chapter 5.
10. NEPAD is considered in more depth in Chapter 8.

World Rural Women's Day Message

The celebration of World Rural Women's Day, launched at the Beijing Conference, includes awards for women's creativity in rural life. Every year some thirty laureates are honored for work in their communities. The six referred to in the speech were Rahamata Savagado of Burkina Faso, Isadora Garcia of Honduras, Anita Hayes from Ireland, Rape Veizaj of Albania, and a representative of the Bolivian organization Hornos. Some 240 women have been direct beneficiaries of this initiative since its inception.

Realizing Women's Human Rights, the Challenges

As part of the five-year review of the Beijing Declaration and Platform of Action OHCHR convened in-house workshops on current gender issues as well as supporting regional and international events connected to the Review. The Beijing+5 Review, a United Nations General Assembly Special Session entitled "Women 2000: Gender Equality, Development and Peace for the Twenty-first Century," was held in New York from 5 to 9 June 2000. Part of this event was the Division for the Advancement of Women (DAW) and UNIFEM cosponsored panel at which Mary Robinson gave this speech. The text reflects the content of "Building on Achievements: Women's Human Rights Five Years after Beijing," the paper submitted by OHCHR to the Special Session.

Further detail of the events and debates can be found in the Beijing+5 outcome document: United Nations, *Women 2000: Gender Equality, Development and Peace for the Twenty-First Century* (New York: United Nations, 2000).

11. DAW, the Division for the Advancement of Women, is within the Department of Economic and Social Affairs of the UN Secretariat. UNIFEM is the United Nations Development Fund for Women. See also the Inter-Agency Network on Women and Gender Equality: www.un.org/womenwatch.

12. Beijing Declaration and Platform for Action, Fourth World Conference on Women, 15 September 1995, A/CONF.177/20.

13. The Asia Pacific Forum of National Human Rights Institutions' Regional Workshop on the Role of National Human Rights Institutions in Advancing the International Human Rights of Women, held in Suva, Fiji Islands, from 5 to 7 May 2000; Concluding Statement and Recommendations: www.nhri.net.

Chapter 4. Eliminating Religious Discrimination and Intolerance

"Sacred Rights: Faith Leaders on Tolerance and Respect"

On 15 June 2001 Mary Robinson delivered this speech at the launch of the following book: David Finn, with Mary Robinson, *Sacred Rights: Faith Leaders on Tolerance and Respect* (New York: Ruder Finn Press, 2001). This publication was compiled by the Millennium World Peace Summit of Religious and Spiritual Leaders in cooperation with OHCHR for the World Conference on Racism.

"Human Rights, Hope and History"

The Oslo Conference on Freedom of Religion or Belief was hosted by the Norwegian Council of Religious and Humanist Communities with a focus on freedom of religion and belief and the Universal Declaration of Human Rights. It resulted in the adoption of the Oslo Declaration on Freedom of Religion or Belief and the establishment of the Oslo Coalition on Freedom of Religion or Belief. The Oslo Coalition facilitates a number of projects with the goal of increasing religious tolerance: www.oslocoalition.org.

1. Vàclav Havel's speech was delivered to the fifty-fourth session of the Commission on Human Rights marking the fiftieth anniversary of the Universal Declaration of Human Rights, in Geneva, on 16 March 1998.

2. United Nations Declaration on the Elimination of All Forms of Intolerance and of Discrimination Based on Religion or Belief, General Assembly resolution 36/55 of 25 November 1981, A/RES/36/55.

3. Hans Küng, *A Global Ethic for Global Politics and Economics* (Oxford: Oxford University Press, 1998).

4. The Parliament of World's Religions initiative is led by the Council for Parliament of World's Religions. Parliaments of World's Religions have been held in Chicago, 1893; Chicago, 1993; Cape Town, 1999; and Barcelona, 2004.

5. Excerpt from "From the Republic of Conscience," in Seamus Heaney, *Opened Ground: Poems 1966–1996* (London: Faber and Faber, 1998).

"Seminar on Enriching the Universality of Human Rights: Islamic Perspectives on the Universal Declaration of Human Rights—Personal Impressions"

The seminar was facilitated by the Office in response to a request from Iran for such an event. It was attended by twenty experts on Islam chosen by the Organization of Islamic Conference to represent its sixty-six member states. A second such conference was held in 2002.

Chapter 5. Combating Other Discrimination and Exclusion

"Honoring Human Dignity and Worth"

The annual Kennedy Foundation International Awards were established by the Kennedy Foundation in 1962 to recognize outstanding research, education, public policy, and advocacy that improve the lives of people with intellectual disabilities and their families.

1. John F. Kennedy remarks made at the White House to members of the American Legion, 1 March 1962. See John F. Kennedy, *Public Papers of the Presidents of the United States: John F. Kennedy; Containing the Public Messages, Speeches, and Statements of the President, 1961–1963*, vol. 2 (Washington, D.C.: Government Printing Office, 1962), p. 185.

2. United Nations Declaration on the Rights of Mentally Retarded Persons General Assembly resolution 2856 (XXVI) of 20 December 1971.

3. Principles for the Protection of Persons with Mental Illness and for the Improvement of Mental Healthcare, General Assembly resolution 46/119 of 17 December 1991.

4. Standard Rules on the Equalization of Opportunities for Persons with Disabilities, General Assembly resolution 48/96, annex, of 20 December 1993.

5. Committee on Economic, Social and Cultural Rights, General Comment No. 5, E/1995/22.

6. The Special Olympics is a continuous international program of sports training and athletic competition for persons with intellectual disabilities and was founded

by Eunice Kennedy Shriver. The first Special Olympics took place in Chicago in 1968 with one thousand athletes from the USA and Canada. Since then it has grown rapidly and now involves almost 1.4 million participants in 150 countries: www.specialolympics.org.

7. Very Special Arts (VSA) was founded in 1974 by Jean Kennedy Smith as a nonprofit organization aimed at "creating a society where people with disabilities can learn through, participate in, and enjoy the arts." Some five million people from more than sixty countries participate annually in VSA arts programs: www.vsarts.org.

8. Gerard Paul Fougerouse, *The United States in a Wheelchair* (1993): www.gerard-fougerouse.org.

9. John F. Kennedy speech made on signing the Maternal and Child Health and Mental Retardation Bill into Law, 24 October 1963: Kennedy, *Public Papers of the Presidents of the United States*, vol. 3, p. 881.

"The Human Rights Dimensions of Disability"

Following Commission on Human Rights resolution 2000/51, increased cooperation between the High Commissioner and the Special Rapporteur on Disability led to the commissioning of this study. Mary Robinson made these remarks at a meeting hosted by OHCHR to present the preliminary findings of the study to an audience of representatives of states, civil society, and intergovernmental agencies. See Gerard Quinn and Theresa Degener, *Human Rights and Disability: The Current Use and Future Potential of United Nations Human Rights Instruments in the Context of Disability*, HR/PUB/02/1 (New York and Geneva: United Nations, 2002).

10. Note 4, *supra*.

11. Human Rights of Persons with Disabilities, Commission on Human Rights resolution 2000/51, E/CN.4/RES/2000/51, 25 April 2000.

12. Human Rights of Persons with Disabilities, ECOSOC decision 2000/268, E/DEC/2000/268, 28 July 2001.

13. Deborah Birmingham, *Advocacy: A Rights Issue, A Reflection Document* (Dublin: The Forum of People with Disabilities in Dublin, 2001).

14. Comprehensive and integral international convention to promote and protect the rights and dignity of persons with disabilities, General Assembly resolution 56/168 of 19 December 2001, A/RES/56/168.

15. The Ad Hoc Committee was established by General Assembly resolution 56/168 of 19 December 2001, A/RES/56/168. OHCHR was involved in the initial meeting of the Ad Hoc Committee held from 29 July to 9 August 2002 and has continued to play an active role in the drafting of the Convention. For updates on the draft convention, see: www.ohchr.org/english/issues/disability/convention.htm.

Marking the Fiftieth Anniversary of the Refugee Convention

The Ministerial Meeting of State Parties commemorated the fiftieth anniversary of the adoption of the 1951 Convention and resulted in the adoption of the Declaration on International Protection, Ministerial Meeting of States Parties to the 1951 Convention and/or its 1967 Protocol Relating to the Status of Refugees, reprinted in *International Journal of Refugee Law* 14, 1 (2002): 169–72.

16. The San Remo Declaration on the Principle of Non-Refoulement 2001 adopted by the XXVth Round Table on Current Problems of International Humanitarian Law. The Round Table was organized by the International Institute for Humanitarian Law and UNHCR to mark the fiftieth anniversary of the 1951

Convention. The Declaration states that the non-*refoulement* principle is customary international law.

17. UNHCR Note on International Protection, A/AC.96/951, 13 September 2001.

"Ratify the Migrants Convention Now!"

The International Convention on the Protection of the Rights of All Migrant Workers and Members of Their Families, General Assembly resolution 45/158 of 18 December 1990, A/RES/45/158, entered into force on 1 July 2003, three months after achieving twenty ratifications. By March 2004 there were twenty-five states parties.

18. The Committee on the Protection of the Rights of All Migrant Workers and Members of Their Families, the body that monitors implementation of the Convention, held its inaugural meeting 1–5 March 2004 in Geneva.

19. Kofi Annan, Statement for International Migrants' Day, 18 December 2001. Full text is available from the OHCHR Web site: www.ohchr.org.

"Combating Trafficking in Human Beings—A European Convention?"

Work on this Council of Europe Convention discussed by Mary Robinson at this panel is being undertaken by the Committee on Action against Trafficking in Human Beings (CAHTEH), which was due to complete work on a European Convention on Action against Trafficking by the end of 2004. The European Convention would build on the principles agreed in the Protocol to Prevent, Suppress and Punish Trafficking in Persons, Especially Women and Children, Supplementing the United Nations Convention against Transnational Organized Crime. That Protocol entered into force on 25 December 2003.

20. Traffic in Women and Girls, Commission on Human Rights resolution 2001/48 of 24 April 2001, E/CN.4/Res/2001/48, especially para. 5. See also Traffic in Women and Girls, General Assembly resolution 55/67 of 4 December 2000, A/RES/55/67, paragraph 2.

21. The IGO Contact Group on Human Trafficking and Migrant Smuggling was established in March 2001 to promote cooperation and collaboration among intergovernmental organizations. It includes representatives of OHCHR, the International Labour Organization, the International Organization for Migration, and the United Nations High Commissioner for Refugees. Other members now include the International Migration Policy Programme and the Council of Europe. The Coordinator of the Geneva-based NGO Caucus against Trafficking participates in an observer capacity. The Group was led by OHCHR for its first year. In March 2002 UNHCR and ILO jointly took on this position. The IGO Group seeks to strengthen individual and collective capacities of member organizations in the areas of trafficking and smuggling through the sharing of information as well as through the development and implementation of joint initiatives.

22. The Protocol to Prevent, Suppress and Punish Trafficking in Persons, Especially Women and Children, supplementing the United Nations Convention against Transnational Organized Crime, General Assembly resolution 55/25 of 15 November 1999, A/RES/55/25.

Address to the National Assembly of Cambodia

For the full text of this speech, see www.ohchr.org. Recommended Principles and Guidelines on Human Rights and Human Trafficking were produced by OHCHR and presented to ECOSOC in May 2002, E/2002/68/Add.1.

23. Barbara Limanowska, *Trafficking in Human Beings in Southeastern Europe: A UNICEF, UNOHCHR and OSCE-ODIHR Joint Report* (New York: UNICEF, 2002): www.unhchr.ch/women/trafficking.pdf.

24. Protocol to Prevent, Suppress and Punish Trafficking in Persons, Especially Women and Children, supplementing the United Nations Convention against Transnational Organized Crime, General Assembly resolution 55/25 of 15 November 1999, A/RES/55/25. Optional Protocol to the Convention on the Rights of the Child on the involvement of children in armed conflict, General Assembly resolution 54/263 of 25 May 2000, A/Res/54/263, entered into force on 12 February 2002.

World AIDS Day

See International Guidelines on HIV/AIDS and Human Rights, Commission on Human Rights resolution 1997/33 of 11 April 1997, E/CN.4/RES/1997/33. The Guidelines were developed jointly by UNAIDS and OHCHR in September 1996 and revised in 2002. The 2002 revision was of guideline 6 on access to prevention treatment, care, and support. Mary Robinson participated in the General Assembly Special Session on HIV/AIDS, 25–27 June 2001. See OHCHR Issue Paper: *A Human Rights-Based Approach to HIV/AIDS*, June 2001. See also "OHCHR/UNAIDS/WHO Panel Event, 5 September 2001, "Exploring the link: HIV/AIDS, stigma, discrimination and racism," Opening Remarks; "Realizing the Right to Health," Opening Statement: Panel discussion, fifty-eighth session of the Commission on Human Rights, Geneva, 3 April 2002.

25. From Peter Piot's statement to the World Conference against Racism, Plenary Session, 4 September 2001. Full text is available from the OHCHR Web site: www.ohchr.org.

26. World Trade Organization Declaration on the Trade Related Aspects of Intellectual Property (TRIPS) Agreement and Public Health (Declaration of Doha), WT/MIN(01)/DEC/2, adopted 14 November 2002.

27. The Guidelines were developed at the Second International Consultation on HIV/AIDS in 1996 and were published jointly by OHCHR and UNAIDS in 1998.

Chapter 6. Human Rights Defenders

"New Protection for Human Rights Defenders"

On the same day that Mary Robinson spoke at this conference on the draft UN Declaration on Human Rights Defenders, Jorge Ortega, a prominent Colombian trade unionist and human rights defender, was assassinated. The High Commissioner returned to the conference the following day to publicly condemn those responsible. See OHCHR Press Statement, "High Commissioner for Human Rights Ends Her First Visit to Colombia," 26 October 1999.

1. Declaration on the Right and Responsibility of Individuals, Groups and Organs of Society to Promote and Protect Universally Recognized Human Rights and Fundamental Freedoms, General Assembly resolution 53/144 of 9 December 1998, A/RES/53/144, 8 March 1999.

2. Human Rights Defenders, Commission on Human Rights resolution 2000/61 of 27 April 2000, E/CN.4/RES/2000/61. The resolution calls for the creation of a Special Representative of the Secretary General to oversee compliance with the Declaration on Human Rights Defenders.

"Linking the National and the International: A Challenge for Human Rights Defenders"

The Dublin Platform for Human Rights Defenders, from 17 to 19 January 2002, at which this speech was delivered marked the launch of a new Irish NGO: FrontLine, the International Foundation for the Protection of Human Rights Defenders

3. Further details about the work of FrontLine can be found on their website: www.frontlinedefenders.org. The Observatory for the Protection of Human Rights Defenders established by FIDH (International Federation for Human Rights) and OMCT (World Organisation against Torture) also work in this field: www.omct.org.

4. Security Council Resolution 1373 of 28 September 2001 obliges all UN member states to take a range of measures to combat terrorism and to submit reports to the Security Council Counter Terrorism Committee.

5. Joint statement by Mary Robinson, UN High Commissioner for Human Rights, Walter Schwimmer, Secretary General of the Council of Europe; and Ambassador Gérard Stoudmann, Director of the OSCE Office for Democratic Institutions and Human Rights, 29 November 2001: www.ohchr.org.

6. Human Rights Committee General Comment No. 29, States of Emergency (Article 4) of 14 July 2001, CCPR/C/21/Rev.1/Add.1, 31 August 2001.

7. Kofi Annan opening a high-level General Assembly debate on 10 November 2001. The full statement is available from www.ohchr.org. The Secretary General, in his report to the General Assembly, proposed to establish a panel of eminent persons to review the relationship between the United Nations and civil society: *Strengthening of the United Nations: An Agenda for Further Change*, A/57/387 and Corr. 1, 9 September 2002. The panel he convened completed their report in June 2004: *We the Peoples: Civil Society, the United Nations and Global Governance*, Report of the Panel of Eminent Persons on United Nations–Civil Society Relations, A/58/817, 7 June 2004. Its recommendation—that the United Nations should make full use of NGOs, the private sector, parliamentarians and local authorities—were fully consonant with Mary Robinson's views voiced in this and many other speeches.

8. Angelina Acheng Atyam on receiving a United Nations Human Rights Prize in 1998. The prize is granted annually in accordance with General Assembly Resolution 2217 of 19 December 1966, A/RES/21/2217.

Chapter 7. Economic, Social, and Cultural Rights

"Promoting Economic, Social, and Cultural Rights"

1. China ratified the International Covenant on Economic Social and Cultural Rights on 27 June 2001.

2. The Teheran Framework for Technical Co-operation in the Asia Pacific region was the name given to the agreement on intergovernmental cooperation under OHCHR auspices on human rights in the Asia Pacific region, endorsed in Teheran on 2 March 1998.See Report of the Secretary General to the fifty-fourth session of the Commission on Human Rights E/CN.4/1998/50, 12 March 1998. See also Chapter 16.

3. The Vienna Plus Five International NGO Forum on Human Rights, Ottawa, Canada, 22–24 June 1998. See *Human Rights Tribune Special Edition: Vienna Plus Five International NGO Forum* 5: 3 (July 1998): www.hri.ca/tribune.

4. Habitat International Coalition's Housing and Land Rights Network is an international movement of over four hundred organizations and individuals working in the field of human settlements: www.hic-mena.org. For FoodFirst Institute

for Food and Development Policy, see: www.foodfirst.org. For FoodFirst Information and Action Network, see www.fian.org.

5. The General Comments of the Committee on Economic, Social and Cultural Rights are contained in International Human Rights Instruments—Compilation of General Comments and General Recommendations Adopted by the Human Rights Treaty Bodies, HRI/GEN/1/Rev.5, 26 April 2001.

6. The draft optional protocol remains under consideration by the Commission on Human Rights.

7. The Beijing Plan of Action was agreed at the Eighth Workshop on Regional Cooperation for the Promotion and Protection of Human Rights in the Asia Pacific Region, Beijing, China, 1–3 March 2000, E/CN.4/2000/102 annex.

8. Workshop for Judges on the Justiciability of Economic, Social and Cultural Rights in South Asia was held in New Delhi, 17–18 November 2001.

"The World Food Summit: Five Years Later"

This event, attended by heads of state and government, was a five-year review hosted by FAO at its Rome headquarters to assess the progress made since the World Food Summit 1996. Mary Robinson's report to the World Food Summit+5 is available from the Web site: *www.unhchr.ch/html/menu2/WFS.doc.* Three expert meetings to prepare this submission were held between 1997 and 2001 and included the contribution of the Special Rapporteur on the Right to Food, Professor Zeigler. See Food and Agriculture Organization, *Report of the World Food Summit: Five Years Later; Part One* (Rome: FAO, 2002): www.fao.org/worldfoodsummit.

9. Committee on Economic, Social and Cultural Rights, General Comment 12, Right to Adequate Food (Article 11), E/C.12/1999/5. See also Mary Robinson, "The Human Right to Food and Nutrition," Symposium, Geneva, 12 April 1999.

10. The Norwegian initiatives include the passing of the 1999 Human Rights Act which grants the force of law to major human rights instruments, including the International Covenant on Economic, Social and Cultural Rights. Additionally the Minister of Agriculture prepared *White Paper No. 19 on Agricultural Food Production* outlining a rights-based agricultural policy. These and other examples are detailed in the High Commissioner's Report to the World Food Summit+5 referenced in the head note above.

11. By way of example, the Constitution of South Africa (secs. 28, para. 1 [c], and 35; para. 29) codifies the right to food with resultant obligations on the state in certain circumstances. Concerning the right to housing, the South African Constitutional Court held that while the economic, social and cultural rights protected by the Constitution are subject to progressive realization, the Court retains the power to consider whether reasonable steps are being taken toward their realization. See *Government of the Republic of South Africa v. Irene Grootboom and Others*, 4 November 2000; Order of the Supreme Court of India of 23 July 2001, on the matter of Writ Petition (Civil) No. 196 of 2001 (*People's Union of Civil Liberties v. Union of India and Others*).

"The Human Right to Adequate Housing—Practical Aspects"

This was Mary Robinson's opening statement to a joint OHCHR/HABITAT expert group meeting on practical aspects of the human right to adequate housing, Geneva, 9 March 1999.

12. International Labour Organization, R115: Workers' Housing Recommendation, adopted on 28 June 1961: www.ilo.org/ilolex/english/recdisp1.htm.

13. The post of Special Rapporteur on the Right to Housing was created in 2000

by the Commission on Human Rights. Question of the realization in all countries of the economic, social and cultural rights, Commission on Human Rights resolution 2000/9 of 17 April 2000, E/Cn.4/Res/2000/9.

14. 1996 Revised European Social Charter, *European Treaty Series* 163.

15. The Centre on Housing Rights and Evictions (COHRE) plays an influential role in specifying the elements of the right to housing and in campaigning over violations: www.cohre.org.

16. The Practice of Forced Evictions: Comprehensive Human Rights Guidelines on Development-Based Displacement, adopted by the Expert Seminar on the Practice of Forced Evictions Geneva, 11–13 June 1997, E/CN.4/Sub.2/1997/7.

17. Ibid.

Chapter 8. The Right to Development

Working Group on the Right to Development, Commission on Human Rights

The Working Group and the Independent Expert on the Right to Development were established in 1998 by ECOSOC resolution 1998/269 endorsing resolution 1998/72 of the Commission on Human Rights.

1. The Social Summit+5, twenty-fourth Special Session of the General Assembly, Geneva, 26 June-1 July 2000, General Assembly resolution S-24/2, A/Res/S-24/2.

2. Declaration on the Right to Development, General Assembly resolution 41/128 of 4 December 1986, A/Res/41/53.

3. In fulfillment of para. 3(c) of her mandate and Right to Development, Commission on Human Rights resolution 1998/72 of 22 April 1998, E/CN.4/RES/1998/72, Mary Robinson submitted a number of reports to the Commission on Human Rights on her Office's activities to advance the right. See Report of the High Commissioner for Human Rights on the Right to Development, E/CN.4/1999/19, 3 February 1999 Interim Report of the High Commissioner for Human Rights on the Right to Development, E/CN.4/1999/WG.18/3, 20 August 1999; Right to Development—Report of the High Commissioner for Human Rights, E/CN.4/2000/20, 21 December 1999: The Right to Development—Report of the High Commissioner for Human Rights, E/CN.4/2000/WG.18/CRP.2, 12 September 2000; The Right to Development—Report of the High Commissioner for Human Rights, E/CN.4/2001/25, 5 January 2001; The Right to Development—Report of the High Commissioner for Human Rights, E/CN.4/2002/27, 27 November 2001.

4. New Partnership for African Development (NEPAD) Document, OAU Declaration 1(XXXVII), July 2001, para. 43: www.uneca.org/nepad and www.nepad.org.

5. See Chapter 20. This session of the World Economic Forum took place in New York from 31 January to 4 February 2002; the World Social Forum was held on the same dates in Porto Alegre, Brazil. See www.weforum.org and www.forumsocialmundial.org.br.

6. Right to Development, General Assembly resolution 53/155 of 9 December 1998, A/RES/53/155, 25 February 1999.

7. World Trade Organization Declaration on the TRIPS Agreement and Public Health (Declaration of Doha), adopted 14 November 2002, WT/MIN(01)/DEC/2.

8. Fourth report of the Independent Expert on the right to development, Mr. Arjun Sengupta, submitted in accordance with Commission resolution 2001/9 to the Commission on Human Rights, open-ended working group on the right to development, E/CN.4/2002/WG.18/2, 20 December 2001.

9. The Right to Development—Report of the High Commissioner for Human Rights, E/CN.4/2002/27, 27 November 2001.

10. This lecture is included in Chapter 18.

"Challenges for Human Rights and Development in Africa"

This speech was given at a panel on "Poverty and Racism: Challenges for Human Rights and Development in Africa," which Mary Robinson chaired. The event was organized by the United Nations Economic Commission for Africa (UNECA) to examine the theme, Human Rights in Africa: Implications of the Durban Declaration and the New Partnership for Africa's Development (NEPAD) for the Organization of African Unity and United Nations Agencies.

11. Organization of African Unity Convention on the Prevention and Combating of Terrorism adopted by the OAU 35th Summit, Algiers, July 1999. It entered into force 6 December 2002 and had thirty-four ratifications as of July 2004.

12. The World Bank, *World Development Report 2000/2001: Attacking Poverty* (Oxford: Oxford University Press, 2001).

13. Poverty and the International Covenant on Economic, Social and Cultural Rights, Statement adopted by the Committee on Economic, Social and Cultural Rights, E/C.12/2001/10, 4 May 2001.

14. Poverty and the ICESCR, para. 8.

15. Poverty and the ICESCR, para. 11.

16. For Mary Robinson's foreword to the Draft Guidelines, *A Human Rights Approach to Poverty Reduction Strategies*, see Chapter 18.

17. World Bank, *World Development Report 2000/2001*, p. 117.

18. The World Conference against Racism, Racial Discrimination, Xenophobia and Related Intolerance, Conference Report, A/CONF.189/12.

19. Millennium Declaration, General Assembly resolution 55/2 of 8 September 2000, A/Res/55/2, 23 September 2000.

20. David Dollar and Paul Collier, *Globalization, Growth, and Poverty: Building an Inclusive World Economy* (Oxford: Oxford University Press, 2001).

21. Grand Bay (Mauritius) Declaration and Plan of Action adopted by the First OAU Ministerial Conference on Human Rights in Africa, Grand Bay, Mauritius, 12–16 April 1999.

22. Africa Dialogue II, "Promoting Justice and Reconciliation in Africa: Challenges for Human Rights and Development," organized by the Office of the High Commissioner for Human Rights in collaboration with the International Criminal Tribunal for Rwanda, held in Arusha, Tanzania, 24–26 May 2002: www.unhchr.ch/html/menu6/africandialogue2.doc.

23. African Regional Dialogue I, "Human Rights, the African Union and the New Partnership for Africa's Development," 5–7 November 2001. General Report, prepared by Rapporteur General, Professor Shadrack Gutto: www.unhchr.ch/html/menu6/Africadialog1.htm.

"The United Nations Millennium Development Goals—A New Challenge for International Cooperation"

This speech was prepared for the building-dedication ceremony of the Watson Institute for International Studies at Brown University, Providence, Rhode Island. The Millennium Development Goals are drawn from the United Nations Millennium Declaration of 18 September 2000, General Assembly resolution A/55/L.2. More information and progress reports are available at www.un.org/millenniumgoals.

24. High Level Panel on Financing for Development, *High Level Panel on Financing for Development* (New York: United Nations Department of Public Information, 2001); see www.un.org/reports/financing.

25. United Nations Financing for Development Conference, 18–22 March 2002, Monterrey, Mexico. The Conference Report, A/Conf.198/11, is available from www.un.org/esa/ffd.

26. "Financing a World Fit for Children," speech by Chancellor of the Exchequer Gordon Brown, United Nations General Assembly Special Session on Children, in New York on 10 May 2002. For the full text see www.ukun.org.

Chapter 9. Human Rights Education

"The Universal Declaration of Human Rights Is the Most Universal Document in the World"

1. United Nations Decade of Human Rights Education (1995–2004), General Assembly resolution 49/184 of 23 December 1994, A/RES/49/184, 6 March 1995.

"Promoting Human Rights Education"

Mary Robinson gave this speech at the annual event to mark Human Rights Day organized by OHCHR for all UN agencies based in Geneva. The contribution of human rights education to a culture of peace was discussed, and a human rights education database hosted by the Office was launched: www.unhchr.ch/hredu.nsf.

2. The definition of human rights education is taken from the preamble to the General Assembly resolution, note 1, *supra*.

3. Mid-term evaluation of the Decade on Human Rights Education to the General Assembly in September 2000: United Nations Decade for Human Rights Education (1995–2004), A/55/360, 7 September 2000.

4. Her statement to the Youth Conference can be found in Chapter 2.

"Human Rights Education in Primary and Secondary Schools"

Mary Robinson opened this Beijing Workshop on a visit to China that was planned to consolidate the cooperation begun the year before with the signing of a Memorandum of Understanding between the Chinese Government and OHCHR.

5. Note 1, *supra*.

6. The Sub-Regional Training Workshop on Human Rights Education in Northeast Asian Schools, Seoul, Republic of Korea, 1–4 December 1999.

Chapter 10. Children's Rights

Worst Forms of Child Labour Convention

This address was delivered at the eighty-seventh session of the International Labour Conference, held from 1 to 17 June 1999. The Conference adopted the Convention concerning the Prohibition and Immediate Elimination of the Worst Forms of Child Labour (ILO No. 182), 38 *International Legal Materials* 1207 (1999). It entered into force on 19 November 2000.

1. Rights of the Child, Special Dialogue on Children was held in Geneva on 14 April 1999, during the fifty-fifth session of the Commission on Human Rights. The

Summary Record of the meeting is contained in E/CN.4/1999/SR.32 of 10 May 1999.

2. The meeting referred to was of a working group of the Commission on Human Rights. See "Message on the Adoption of the Text of Draft Optional Protocol," included in this chapter.

Optional Protocol on Involvement of Children in Armed Conflict

The Optional Protocol to the Convention on the Rights of the Child on Involvement of Children in Armed Conflict was adopted and opened for signature, ratification, and accession by General Assembly resolution A/RES/54/263, 25 May 2000. The Protocol entered into force on 12 February 2002.

Address to the General Assembly Special Session on Children

The Special Session on Children was held from 8 to 10 May 2002 to review progress under the Declaration and Plan of Action of the 1990 World Summit for Children. The renewed commitment of those present to children's rights is recorded in the outcome document: A World Fit for Children, A/RES/S-27/2 of 11 October 2002.

3. World Declaration on the Survival, Protection and Development of Children of the World Summit for Children, 30 September 1990, and its Plan of Action, endorsed by the General Assembly: World Summit for Children resolution 45/217 of 21 December 1990, A/RES/45/217. The Declaration and the Plan of Action are available at www.unicef.org/wsc.

4. As of June 2004 the number of states parties to the Convention on the Rights of the Child had risen to 192.

5. The testimonies mentioned were heard during the presentation of the Report of the Secretary General of the United Nations to the Security Council on the Protection of Civilians in Armed Conflict, S/1999/957, 8 September 1999. See also Chapter 19.

6. The Special Session of the General Assembly on HIV/AIDS, 25–27 June 2001, New York, adopted the Declaration of Commitment on HIV/AIDS: Global Crisis—Global Action, Special Session resolution 26/2 of 27 June 2001, A/RES/S-26/2, 2 August 2001.

7. The study was requested in The Rights of the Child, General Assembly resolution 56/138 of 19 December 2001, A/RES/56/138, 15 February 2002. A report detailing the work done so far on this study was submitted in early 2004: Rights of the Child: Progress Report of the Secretary-General on the Study on the Question of Violence against Children, E/CN.4/2004/68, 27 January 2004.

8. "A World Fit for Us," the message of the Children's Forum held prior to the Special Session. Is available from www.unicef.org/specialsession.

Chapter 11. Minorities and Indigenous Peoples

Message on Minorities' Rights Day, India

This message was sent to the celebration of the first Minorities' Rights Day in India. This national day was initiated by Professor Tahir Mahmood, Chair of the National Commission on Minorities, and was intended to mark the adoption by the United Nations General Assembly of the Declaration on Minorities' Rights as well as raising awareness of minority rights issues in India.

1. United Nations Declaration on the Rights of Persons Belonging to National or Ethnic, Religious and Linguistic Minorities, General Assembly resolution 47/135 of 18 December 1992, A/Res/47/135.

Protection of Minorities and Other Vulnerable Groups

This regional seminar had the title "Protection of Minorities and Other Vulnerable Groups through Strengthening Human Rights Capacity at National Level." It was one of a number of regional seminars promoted by Mary Robinson in the lead-up to the World Conference against Racism and in her capacity as its Secretary General.

2. See Hurst Hannum, ed., *Documents on Autonomy and Minority Rights* (Dordrecht: M. Nijhoff, 1993).

3. Advisory Opinion of 21 June 1971 on *The Legal Consequences for States of the Continued Presence of South Africa in Namibia (South West Africa) notwithstanding Security Council Resolutions*, 276 (1970), ICJ Judgment (1970). See also Nigel Rodley, "Human Rights and Humanitarian Intervention: The Case Law of the World Court," 38 *International Comparative Law Quarterly* 256 (1989).

4. The Migrant Workers Convention came into force on 1 July 2003.

5. Note 1, *supra*.

6. The Council of Europe instruments include the Framework Convention for the Protection of National Minorities 1994, which entered into force on 1 February 1998. By 2004 it had thirty-five states parties. See further www.coe.int. The 1990 OSCE Copenhagen Commitments include extensive provisions on national minorities, but the main OSCE contribution has been the creation of the Office of the High Commissioner on National Minorities. It was established in 1992 to identify and seek early resolution of ethnic tensions. See further www.osce.org.

7. Report of the World Conference to Combat Racism and Racial Discrimination, Geneva, 14–25 August 1978, E.79.XIV.2.

8. Report of the Second World Conference to Combat Racism and Racial Discrimination, Geneva, 1–12 August 1983, E.83.XIV.4 and corrigendum.

9. The World Conference against Racism, Racial Discrimination, Xenophobia and Related Intolerance, Durban, 31 August–8 September 2001, Declaration and Programme of Action, A/CONF.189/12, 25 January 2002.

United Nations Permanent Forum on Indigenous Issues

The Permanent Forum on Indigenous Issues within the United Nations, an initiative begun at the 1993 Vienna World Conference on Human Rights, was approved on 28 July 2000 (Economic and Social Council Resolution, E/RES/2000/22). The Forum was given financial and secretariat support by the OHCHR in its initial stages. It is now serviced by the Department for Economic and Social Affairs. The Permanent Forum met for the first time in New York from 11 to 23 May 2002 and has met annually since then: www.un.org/esa/socdev/unpfii.

10. The International Decade of the World's Indigenous People (1995–2004), General Assembly resolution 48/163 of 21 December 1993, A/RES/48/163, 18 February 1994. The High Commissioner for Human Rights was appointed as Coordinator of the Decade by General Assembly resolution 52/108 of 12 December 1997, A/RES/52/108,18 February 1998.

11. The Working Group on Indigenous Populations was established by the Sub-Commission on the Promotion and Protection of Human Rights. The Working Group has provided a forum for the world's indigenous peoples for over twenty years. The Working Group on Indigenous Populations was first proposed by the

Sub-Commission, in resolution 2 (XXXIV) of 8 September 1981. It was endorsed by Commission on Human Rights resolution 1982/19 of 10 March 1982 and authorized by Economic and Social Council resolution 1982/34 of 7 May 1982. In 1985 the United Nations Voluntary Fund for Indigenous Populations was established to assist representatives of indigenous communities and organizations to participate in the deliberations of the Working Group. Since 1996 the Working Group has worked on a thematic basis, addressing a specific issue at each session. Reports of the Working Group are available from the OHCHR Web site: www.ohchr.org.

12. Mary Robinson was made an Honorary Chieftain of the Choctaw Nation in 1992 when she was President of Ireland, the first woman to have such a title granted to her. The honor was bestowed at an event in Dublin to commemorate the 145th anniversary of a donation made by the Choctaw Nation to the people of Ireland during the famine of 1848.

13. United Nations Institute for Training and Research: www.unitar.org.

14. The interagency support group includes OHCHR, UNDP, Habitat, UNFPA, UNEP, WHO, UNITAR, DPI, WIPO, UNHCR, FAO, UNESCO, ILO, UNICEF, CBD, and the World Bank. The secretariat functions for the Permanent Forum are provided by the UN Department of Economic and Social Affairs, Division for Social Policy and Development: www.un.org/esa.

Chapter 12. Human Rights after Conflict

"Building the Rule of Law after Conflict"

This presentation was made at a conference, "Building Justice: A Conference on Establishing the Rule of Law in Post-Conflict Situations," organized by the United Nations Office at Vienna and the Austrian Ministry of Foreign Affairs. The Conference focused on case studies of Albania, Angola, Bosnia, and Mozambique.

1. Kofi Annan, statement to the opening of the fifty-fourth session of the Commission on Human Rights on 16 March 1998.

2. Anatole France, *The Red Lily*, trans. Winifred Stephens (London: John Lane, 1930).

"Developing a Human Rights Culture in Southeast Europe"

The Peace Implementation Council (PIC) was established to implement the 1995 Dayton Peace Agreement on Bosnia and Herzegovina. The Humanitarian Issues Working Group was absorbed by the PIC and gives guidance to the Council on humanitarian issues.

3. In 1999 the European Union initiated the Stability Pact for South Eastern Europe "to foster peace, democracy, respect for human rights and economic prosperity in order to achieve stability in the whole region": www.stabilitypact.org.

"Universal Jurisdiction and Combating Impunity"

The Princeton Project on Universal Jurisdiction was designed to clarify and formulate principles on universal jurisdiction in international criminal law. It was sponsored: the Program in Law and Public Affairs and the Woodrow Wilson School of Public and International Affairs, Princeton University; the International Commission of Jurists; the American Association for the International Commission of Jurists; the Netherlands Institute of Human Rights; and the Urban Morgan

Institute for Human Rights. Mary Robinson's video message was published as the foreword to The Princeton Project, *The Princeton Principles on Universal Jurisdiction* (Princeton, N.J.: Princeton University Office of University Printing and Mailing, 2001).

4. Declaration on the Protection of All Persons from Enforced Disappearances, General Assembly resolution 47/133 of 18 December 1992, A/47/49 47.

5. Inter-American Convention on Forced Disappearance of Persons, *International Legal Materials* 33 (1994): 1429, entered into force 28 March 1996.

6. Draft International Convention on the Protection of All Persons from Enforced Disappearance, Sub-Commission resolution 1999/24 of 26 August 1999, E/CN.4/SUB.2/RES/1999/24.

7. United Nations Convention against Transnational Organized Crime, General Assembly resolution 55/25 of 15 November 2000, A/Res/55/25, 8 January 2001.

8. *The Case Concerning the Arrest Warrant of 11 April 2000 (Democratic Republic of Congo v. Belgium)* (14 February 2002), International Court of Justice, General List No. 121.

9. International Law Association, London Conference 2000, "Final Report on the Exercise of Universal Jurisdiction in Respect of Gross Human Rights Offences by the Committee on International Human Rights Law and Practice": www.ila-hq.org.

10. *R v. Bow Street Stipendiary Magistrate and others,* ex parte *Pinochet Ugarte* [1998] 3 WLR 1456; *R v. Bow Street Stipendiary Magistrate and others,* ex parte *Pinochet Ugarte (No.2)* [1999] 2 WLR 272; *R v. Bow Street Stipendiary Magistrate and others,* ex parte *Pinochet Ugarte (No.3)* [1999] 2 WLR 827.

"Transitional Justice: Defining the Quality of Indonesia's Future Democracy"

The Indonesian National Commission on Human Rights, Komnas HAM, hosted the workshop at which this speech was delivered.

Opening of the National Parliament of the Democratic Republic of East Timor

For one of Mary Robinson's last public speaking commitments as High Commissioner, she returned to East Timor and spoke at the opening of the national parliament, an occasion of great hope that was in stark contrast to her first visit to the region in 1999.

"Breaking Down the Walls of Silence"

Mary Robinson spoke at the first thematic public hearing of the Truth and Reconciliation Commission. The final report of the Commission was released on 28 August 2003: www.cverdad.org.pe. Sections of the report in English translation have been made by the International Centre for Transitional Justice at www.ictj.org/americas/peru.asp.

Chapter 13. Business and Human Rights

"Profitable Partnerships: Building Relationships That Make a Difference"

The annual Business for Social Responsibility Conference is one of the largest international gatherings of professionals involved in corporate social responsibility: www.bsr.org.

1. Mike Moore, "Challenges for the Global Trading System in the New Millennium," speech to the Council on Foreign Relations, Washington, D. C., 28 September 1999: www.wto.org/english/news_e.htm.

2. The Fair Labor Association: www.fairlabor.org.

3. Social Accountability International, *Social Accountability 8000* (New York: SAI, 2001).

4. Global Sullivan Principles for Social Responsibility: www.globalsullivanprinciples.org.

5. Insan Hitawasana Sejahtera, *Peduli Hak: Caring for Rights* (Jakarta: IHS, 1999). Reebok commissioned Insan Hitawasana Sejahtera, an Indonesian social science research and consultancy organization, to report on working conditions in two of their factories in Indonesia. The full report is available from the Centre for Research on Multinational Corporations: www.somo.nl/monitoring/resource.htm.

6. For details of the Global Compact, see www.unglobalcompact.org and the speech "Beyond Good Intentions: Corporate Citizenship for a New Century," included in this chapter.

7. The ILO Declaration was adopted in 1998. It commits member states to respect and promote principles and rights in four categories, whether or not states have ratified the relevant Conventions. The categories are freedom of association and the effective recognition of the right to collective bargaining, the elimination of forced or compulsory labor, the abolition of child labor, and the elimination of discrimination in respect of employment and occupation: www.ilo.org.

8. At the 1992 Earth Summit in Rio de Janeiro, the international community adopted Agenda 21, the first global plan of action for sustainable development: www.un.org/esa/sustdev.

"Beyond Good Intentions: Corporate Citizenship for a New Century"

Mary Robinson gave this inaugural lecture of the Royal Society Arts and Manufactures (RSA) World Leaders Lecture series. The Global Compact, discussed in this lecture, was announced by Kofi Annan at the World Economic Forum on 31 January 1999. Its operational phase was launched the following year. For more information, see the Web site www.unglobalcompact.org.

9. Kofi Annan, *We the Peoples* (New York: United Nations Department of Public Information, 2000), p. 7.

10. Kofi Annan, *We the Children: End-Decade Review of the Follow-up to the World Summit for Children* (New York: UNICEF, 2002). See also Chapter 10.

11. Mary Robinson was awarded the Albert Medal of the Royal Society of Arts in November 2001 in recognition of her work on the Global Compact.

12. The Institute of Directors, established in 1903, is one of the largest gatherings of business directors in Europe: www.iod.com.

13. Roger Cowe, "Firms 'Need Forcing' to Do the Right Thing," *The Observer*, 14 October 2001: observer.guardian.co.uk/business.

14. For more information on the Global Reporting Initiative, see www.globalreporting.org.

15. Workshop on Indigenous Peoples, Private Sector Natural Resource, Energy and Mining Companies and Human Rights, Geneva, 5–7 December 2001. See Report of the Workshop, presented to the twentieth session of the Working Group on Indigenous Populations of the Sub-Commission on the Promotion and Protection of Human Rights, 22–26 July 2002, E/CN.4/Sub.2/AC.4/2002/3, 17 June 2002.

16. International Council on Human Rights Policy, *Beyond Voluntarism: Human Rights and the Developing International Legal Obligations* (Versoix, Switzerland: International Council on Human Rights Policy, 2002).

17. The norms were finally agreed by the Sub-Commission in 2003: Norms on the responsibilities of transnational corporations and other business enterprises with regard to human rights, Sub-Commission resolution 2003/12, 26 August 2003, CN.4/Sub.2/2003/12/Rev.2.

18. See Chapter 20.

Chapter 14. The High Commissioner and the United Nations Human Rights System

"Human Rights Today"

This lecture was given by Mary Robinson after receiving an honorary doctorate from the University of Leuven on the occasion of its 575th anniversary.

1. Kofi Annan, *Renewing the United Nations: A Programme for Reform*, Secretary General's Report, A/51/950, 14 July 1997.

2. Workshop on the Promotion and Protection of Human Rights in the Latin American and Caribbean Region, Quito, Ecuador, 29 November to 1 December 1999. For the conclusions, see www.unhchr.ch/html/menu6/qutocncls.

3. The Rome Statute of the International Criminal Court 2187 *United Nations Treaty Series* 90, entered into force on 1 July 2002.

The High Commissioner's Annual Report 1998–1999 to the Fifty-Fourth General Assembly

The speech was on introducing her 1998–1999 Annual Report, A/54/36, 23 September 1999, to the General Assembly.

4. The Optional Protocol to the Convention on the Elimination of Discrimination against Women, adopted by General Assembly resolution 54/4 of 6 October 1999, A/RES/54/4, entered into force on 22 December 2000.

5. Special Procedures is the generic name given to the collection of individual experts and groups appointed by the Commission on Human Rights to report on a range of human rights concerns.

6. The Declaration on Human Rights Defenders, General Assembly resolution 53/144 of 10 December 1998, A/RES/53/144. See further Chapter 6.

7. Organization of African Unity Grand Bay (Mauritius) Declaration and Plan of Action CONF/HRA/DECL (1).

8. Note 2, *supra.*

9. The High Commissioner was appointed Coordinator of the International Decade of the World's Indigenous People (1995–2004). See also Chapter 11.

10. UNICEF, *The State of the World's Children 1999: Education* (New York: UNICEF, 1998).

11. UNDP, *Human Development Report 1990: Globalization with a Human Face* (Oxford: Oxford University Press, 1999).

12. Symposium on Human Development and Human Rights, Oslo, 2–3 October 1998.

The Symposium discussed experiences on operational implications of mainstreaming human rights priorities and concerns into United Nations development work. It was jointly organized by OHCHR and UNDP, with the Royal Ministry of Foreign Affairs of Norway. The Symposium was also a contribution to the fiftieth anniversary of the Universal Declaration of Human Rights.

13. Rights of the Child, Special Dialogue on Children was held in Geneva on 14 April 1999, during the fifty-fifth session of the Commission on Human Rights. The Summary Record of the meeting is contained in E/CN.4/1999/SR.32 of 10 May

1999. See further The Rights of the Child, Commission on Human Rights resolution 1999/80 of 28 April 1999, E/CN.4/RES/1999/80.

14. Poverty eradication and capacity building, ECOSOC resolution 1999/5 of 23 July 1999, E/RES/1999/5.

15. At their 1999 Annual Meetings, held in Washington, D. C., from 25 to 30 September 1999, the IMF and World Bank agreed to place poverty reduction at the center of their work and, when working with poor countries, to embark only on programs that address the issue. For further information on the meetings and their outcomes, see www.imf.org/external/am/1999/index.htm.

16. Optional Protocol to the Convention on the Rights of the Child on the Involvement of Children in Armed Conflicts, General Assembly resolution 54/263 of 25 May 2000, A/RES/54/263.

17. Following her term as High Commissioner for Human Rights, and as Honorary President of Oxfam International, Mary Robinson has been involved in the Control Arms Campaign calling for greater international regulation in the form of an arms trade treaty. www.controlarms.org.

18. Kofi Annan picked up this idea in his speech to the 2004 Stockholm International Forum. Speaking on 7 April 2004 at an event to commemorate the tenth anniversary of the Rwandan genocide, the Secretary General announced that he would create the post of Special Adviser on the Prevention of Genocide. Juan E. Méndez was appointed to this post on 12 July 2004. See Kofi Annan's opening address to the Stockholm International Forum, Preventing Genocide, 26 January 2004: www.preventinggenocide.com.

The High Commissioner's Annual Report 1999–2000 to the Fifty-Fifth General Assembly

This speech was made when Mary Robinson presented her 1999–2000 Annual Report, A/55/36, 17 October 2000, to the General Assembly.

19. Millennium Declaration, General Assembly resolution A/55/L.2, 8 September 2000.

20. Kofi Annan, *We the Peoples: The United Nations in the 21st Century* (New York: United Nations Department of Public Information, 2000); www.un.org/millennium/sg/report.

21. The mission was conducted from 8 to 16 November 2000. The High Commissioner visited Israel and the Occupied Palestinian Territories, and Egypt and Jordan. The report of her visit was presented to the Chairman of the General Assembly on 27 November 2000.

22. The Truth and Reconciliation Commission of Sierra Leone called for in Article XXIV of the Lomé Peace Agreement was established by an Act of Parliament on 22 February 2000 and was inaugurated on 5 July 2002. The final report of the Commission was expected to be released in October 2004. The Commission became operational toward the end of 2002. News of the progress of the TRC can be found on the International Center for Transitional Justice's Web site: www.ictj.org, or from the Irish Centre for Human Rights: www.nuigalway.ie/human_rights.

23. The Special Court for Sierra Leone was established pursuant to Security Council resolution 1315 of 14 August 2000 by the signing of the Agreement between the United Nations and the Government of Sierra Leone on the Establishment of a Special Court for Sierra Leone on 16 January 2002. The first trial began on 3 June 2004. For further information on the Court and the proceedings before it, see www.sc-sl.org.

24. The Sub-Regional Center for Human Rights and Democracy in Yaoundé,

Cameroon, began its activities in March 2001 Mary Robinson spoke at its official inauguration in June 2002.

25. The Situation in the Republic of Chechnya of the Russian Federation, Commission on Human Rights resolution 2000/58 of 25 April 2000, E/CN.4/RES/2000/58.

26. See also Chapter 12.

27. See Chapter 15.

28. Secretary General's report on Globalization: Globalization and Its Impact on the Full Enjoyment of all Human Rights, A/55/342, 31 August 2000, requested by General Assembly resolution 54/165 of 24 February 2000, A/RES/54/165.

29. Mary Robinson gave a Presidential Lecture at the World Bank in November 2001; see Chapter 18.

30. United Nations Development Programme, *Human Development Report 2000: Human Rights and Human Development* (New York: Oxford University Press, 2000). This edition of the annual report highlighted the role of the "Seven Freedoms" in understanding the relationship between human rights and development, and it contained a Special Contribution from Mary Robinson entitled *Universality and Priorities.*

31. See further Chapter 8.

32. Following the resolutions of the Commission on Human Rights, Jean Ziegler of Switzerland and Miloon Kothari of India were appointed as Special Rapporteurs on, respectively, the right to food and the question of adequate housing. See United Nations Press Release: "Human Rights Commission appoints Experts on Right to Food, Adequate Housing," 12 September 2000.

33. The Report of the Panel on United Nations Peace Keeping Operations, "The Brahimi Report on Peace Operations," A/55/305-S/2000/809, 21 August 2000: www.un.org/peace/reports/peace_operations.

34. See Chapter 18.

Chapter 15. Supporting United Nations Human Rights Bodies

Address at the Closing of the Fifty-Eighth Session of the Commission on Human Rights

The Commission on Human Rights meets annually in Geneva for six weeks in March and April. For an account of the fifty-eighth session of the Commission on Human Rights, see Rachel Brett, *Snakes and Ladders: Report on the 58th Session of the Commission on Human Rights* (Geneva: Quaker United Nations Office, 2002).

1. The Human Rights Situation in the Occupied Palestinian Territory, Report of the High Commissioner to the Commission on Human Rights, E/CN.4/2002/184, 24 April 2002.

2. International Commission on Intervention and State Sovereignty, *The Responsibility to Protect: Report of the International Commission on Intervention and State Sovereignty* (Ottawa: International Development Research Centre, 2001); www.dfait-maeci.gc.ca/iciss-ciise.

Opening Remarks, Fifty-Third Session of the Sub-Commission on the Promotion and Protection of Human Rights

The Sub-Commission meets annually in Geneva for three weeks in July and August.

3. The World Conference against Racism, Racial Discrimination, Xenophobia and Related Intolerance, Durban, South Africa, 31 August to 7 September 2001.

On Mary Robinson's position as Secretary General of the World Conference, see Chapter 2.

4. Mary Robinson spoke to the World Social Forum in Porto Alegre, Brazil, in January 2002; see Chapter 20.

5. The Working Group on the Working Methods and Activities of Transnational Corporations of the Sub-Commission adopted the norms at its twenty-second meeting, on 13 August 2003. Norms on the responsibilities of transnational corporations and other business enterprises with regard to human rights, adopted by the Sub-Commission on the Promotion and Protection of Human Rights resolution 2003/12 of 26 August 2003, E/CN.4/Sub.2/2003/12/Rev.2.

6. On the Global Compact, see further Chapter 13.

The Importance of the Independence of Special Rapporteurs and Similar Mechanisms of the Commission on Human Rights

This statement by the High Commissioner was made in response to legal proceedings brought against the Special Rapporteur on the Independence of the Judiciary by judicial authorities in Malaysia over remarks he made in a published interview. The question of the scope of immunity attaching to a Special Rapporteur in the exercise of official functions was referred by ECOSOC to the International Court of Justice. See International Court of Justice, *Advisory Opinion of 29 April 1999 on the Difference Relating to Immunity from Legal Process of a Special Rapporteur of the Commission on Human Rights,* General List No. 100.

7. The Vienna Declaration and Programme of Action, adopted by the World Conference on Human Rights on 25 June 1993, confirmed by General Assembly resolution A/CONF.157/23, 12 July 1993.

8. International Court of Justice, *Advisory Opinion of 15 December 1989 on the Applicability of Article VI. Section 22, of the Convention on the Privileges and Immunities of the United Nations,* International Court of Justice Reports 1989, p. 187.

Address to the Eighth Meeting of Special Rapporteurs/Representatives and Experts of the Commission on Human Rights

9. Thomas Hammarberg and Mona Rishmawi, "Capacity Building to Strengthen the Special Procedures System of the United Nations Human Rights Programme" (unpub. ms., Commissioned by the OHCHR, 1999).

10. Office of the High Commissioner for Human Rights, *Annual Appeal 2001: Overview of Activities and Financial Requirements* (Geneva: OHCHR, 2001).

11. The UN Global Appeal or Humanitarian Appeal is an annual appeal to donors by a number of UN departments and agencies including the OHCHR and is coordinated by the Office of Humanitarian Affairs.

Statement by the High Commissioner for Human Rights to the Meeting of Chairpersons of the Treaty Bodies

12. Anne Bayefsky, *The UN Human Rights Treaty System: Universality at the Crossroads* (The Hague: Kluwer Academic Publishers, 2001).

13. The Petitions Team was created in December 2000 when the High Commissioner reorganized the Support Services Branch of OHCHR.

14. The Common Country Assessment (CCA) and the Development Assistance Framework (UNDAF) were both introduced as part of Kofi Annan's 1997 reforms. The UNDAF facilitates strategic coordination between the various UN agencies operating in a country. The Framework contains common objectives, common strategies,

and a common time frame to enable a more coherent approach to development assistance in a country. The Framework is designed with reference to the findings of the CCA. The CCA uses a common set of indictors based on internationally agreed declarations, goals, and programs of action. See further: www.ohchr.org/english/issues/development/index.htm.

Chapter 16. Working with Countries and Regions

University of Teheran Center for Human Rights Studies

Mary Robinson spoke at the University of Teheran, shortly after inauguration of the Center for Human Rights, during her visit to Iran for the Regional Preparatory Meeting of the World Conference against Racism.

1. Iran has yet to ratify either the Convention on the Elimination of All Forms of Discrimination against Women or the Convention against Torture and Other Cruel, Inhuman or Degrading Treatment or Punishment.

2. Initial reports of states parties due in 1996: Iran (Islamic Republic of), CRC/C/41/Add.5, 23 July 1998; Concluding Observations of the Committee on the Rights of the Child: Iran (Islamic Republic of), CRC/C/15/Add.123, 28 July 2000.

3. The Draft Country Programme Document for the Islamic Republic of Iran, E/ICEF/2004/P/L.21, 31 March 2004, prepared for the 2004 Annual Session of the Executive Board of UNICEF, states at para. 15: "Technical support was also provided to the development of a draft juvenile justice code, which has been accepted by the Judiciary but not yet approved by the Parliament, and advocacy for the re-establishment of juvenile courts in Tehran."

4. Maurice Copithorne, Special Representative on the Situation of Human Rights in the Islamic Republic of Iran of the Commission on Human Rights, made three reports to the Commission between 1999 and 2001: E/CN.4/1999/32; E/CN.4/2000/35; and E/CN.4/2001/39.

5. Mary Robinson's reflections on the Symposium on Islamic Perspectives on the Universal Declaration of Human Rights are included in Chapter 4.

"Punishment of Minor Crimes"

This two-day workshop in Beijing was the first activity undertaken after the signing of a technical cooperation agreement between the OHCHR and the Government of the People's Republic of China in November 2000.

6. Third periodic reports of states parties due in 1997: China, CAT/C/39/Add.2, 5 January 2000; Conclusions and recommendations of the Committee against Torture: China. A/55/44, paras. 106–45, 9 May 2000.

7. This opinion of the Working Group on Arbitrary Detention is taken from the Report of the Working Group on Arbitrary Detention, Visit to the People's Republic of China, E/CN.4/1998/44/Add.2, 22 December 1997, paras. 93–99.

"Human Rights Activities in the Field"

The number of field presences continues to rise; each of these reports regularly to the Office. Regional reports are available on the Office's Web site, and the most recent report of the Colombian Office, in Spanish, can be found on their Web site: www.hchr.org.co.

8. Further Promotion and Encouragement of Human Rights and Fundamental Freedoms, Including the Question of the Programme and Methods of Work of the Commission Human Rights, Mass Exoduses and Displaced Persons (UN Guiding

Principles on Internal Displacement), E/CN.4/1998/53/Add.2, 11 February 1998; Report of the Representative of the Secretary General, Mr. Francis M. Deng, submitted pursuant to Commission resolution 1997/39.

9. Report of the United Nations High Commissioner for Human Rights on the Human Rights Situation in Colombia (1997), E/CN.4/1998/16, 9 March 1998. For subsequent reports, see the Colombia Office's Web site: www.hchr.org.co/documentoseinformes/publico.php3.

Celebrating the Anniversary of the Pact of San José

The American Convention on Human Rights (OAS Treaty Series No. 36), also known as the Pact of San José, was promulgated in Costa Rica in 1969 and came into force in 1978 on achieving eleven ratifications.

"Human Rights Challenges in the Asia Pacific Region"

This Workshop on Regional Cooperation for the Promotion and Protection of Human Rights in the Asia Pacific Region was hosted by the Asia-Pacific Forum of National Human Rights Institutions. The Forum was established in 1996.

10. The Teheran Framework for Technical Cooperation in the Asia Pacific region is annexed to the Report of the Secretary General to the fifty-fourth session of the Commission on Human Rights, E/CN.4/1998/50, 12 March 1998. The Framework enshrines the commitment of the thirty-six states present to work for the promotion and protection of human rights by sharing experiences and expertise. The Framework was concluded at the Sixth Workshop on Regional Arrangements for the Promotion and Protection of Human Rights in the Asian and Pacific region held in Teheran, Islamic Republic of Iran, from 28 February to 2 March 1998.

11. The International Convention on the Rights of Migrant Workers and Their Families came into force on 1 July 2003.

12. ASEAN, the Association of South East Asian Nations, was established in 1967 to promote regional economic, social, and cultural cooperation.

13. The Asia Pacific Forum of National Human Rights Institutions was established after the first regional meeting of national human rights institutions, which took place in 1996; see www.asiapacificforum.net.

Address to the Permanent Council of the Organisation for Security and Co-operation in Europe (OSCE)

Composed of representatives of the fifty-five participating states, the Permanent Council of the OSCE meets weekly. Mary Robinson spoke to the Council on a number of occasions, this being the last.

14. Helsinki Final Act 1975 of the Organisation for Security and Co-operation in Europe (formerly the Conference for Security and Cooperation in Europe): www.osce.org/docs/english/summite.htm.

15. Directorate General of Human Rights of the Council of Europe, *Guidelines on Human Rights and the Fight against Terrorism* (Strasbourg: Council of Europe, 2002). The *Guidelines* were adopted by the Committee of Ministers on 11 July 2002 at the 804th meeting of the Ministers' Deputies.

16. Joint statement by Mary Robinson, UN High Commissioner for Human Rights; Walter Schwimmer, Secretary General of the Council of Europe; and Ambassador Gérard Stoudmann, Director of the OSCE Office for Democratic Institutions and Human Rights, on terrorism and human rights was issued on 29 November 2001 and is available in full from www.ohchr.org.

17. The European Union created the Stability Pact for South Eastern Europe in

1999 "to foster peace, democracy, respect for human rights and economic prosperity in order to achieve stability in the whole region." For more information, see www.stabilitypact.org.

18. United Nations Guide for Minorities, HR/P/UNG/2, published by the OHCHR, in 2002.

19. Barbara Limanowska, *Trafficking in Human Beings in Southeastern Europe: A UNICEF, UNOHCHR and OSCE-ODIHR Joint Report* (New York:UNICEF, 2002); see www.unhchr.ch/women/trafficking.pdf.

"The Application of International Human Rights Norms by National Courts and Tribunals"

This workshop was held by Bolivia, Chile, and the countries of MERCOSUR with the support of the OHCHR in partnership with the Inter-American Institute of Human Rights and the United Nations Development Programme. The conclusions of the workshop called for continued technical cooperation between OHCHR and MERCOSUR. MERCOSUR, Mercado Común del Cono Sur (Southern Cone Common Market), consists of Argentina, Brazil, Paraguay, and Uruguay and was established in 1991 by the Treaty of Asunción. Since its beginnings as a vehicle for a common market, MERCOSUR has developed and expanded beyond economic cooperation. The "Political MERCOSUR" includes Bolivia and Chile in addition to the original four states and exists as a mechanism for political consultation.

20. 1998 Ushuaia Protocol on Democratic Commitment in MERCOSUR, Bolivia, and Chile. This Protocol confirms that functioning democratic institutions constitute an indispensable precondition for the existence and development of integration between the six states party to it.

Chapter 17. Strengthening National Human Rights Protection

The 102nd Inter-Parliamentary Conference

The Inter-Parliamentary Union was founded in 1889 and is based in Geneva. It has long been an important global force in support of international human rights. See www.ipu.org.

"Protecting Human Rights: The Role and Responsibilities of the Independent Bar"

The Inaugural World Conference of Barristers and Advocates, instigated by the Barristers and Advocates Forum of the International Bar Association, was held from 27 to 29 June 2002. It was attended by members of all the independent referral bars of the world and resulted in the Edinburgh Declaration. The Declaration defends the independence of courts and of the legal profession throughout the world. A follow-up conference took place in Capetown in April 2004.

1. The International Association of Women Judges (IAWJ) met in Dublin from 22 to 26 May 2002 for their Sixth Biennial Conference, which had the theme of "Judicial Creativity." For more information about the work of the IAWJ see www.iawj.org.

2. Lord Goldsmith and Nicholas R. Cowdrey, "The Role of the Lawyer in Human Rights," *HRI News* 4: 2 (1991): 1.

3. The Protocol to the African Charter on Human and Peoples' Rights on the Establishment of an African Court on Human and Peoples' Rights, 9 June 1998,

OAU/LEG/EXP/AFCHPR/PROT (III), established the framework for the African Court of Human and Peoples' Rights. It has not yet entered into force.

4. Kofi Annan, foreword to *Global Law in Practice: 50th Anniversary of the International Bar Association*, ed. J. Ross Harper (The Hague: Kluwer Law International, 1997), pp. v–vi.

5. Param Cumaraswamy, "The UN Special Rapporteur on the Independence of the Judges and Lawyers," *CIJL Yearbook*, 7 (1999): 63, pp. 81–82.

6. Param Cumaraswamy completed his term as Special Rapporteur in 2003. The current Special Rapporteur is Leandro Despouy (Argentina).

7. Basic Principles on the Roles of Lawyers, adopted by the Eighth United Nations Congress on the Prevention of Crime and the Treatment of Offenders in Havana, Cuba, 27 August–7 September 1990.

8. The International Criminal Bar has now come into existence and held its first General Assembly in Berlin from 22 to 23 March 2003: www.bpi-icb.org.

International Coordinating Committee of National Institutions for the Promotion and Protection of Human Rights

9. The Paris Principles (the Principles Relating to the Status and Functioning of National Institutions for Protection and Promotion of Human Rights), a comprehensive set of recommendations about the functions, role, status, and composition of national human rights institutions, arose out of an international workshop facilitated by the Centre for Human Rights in October 1991 in Paris. They subsequently received endorsement by the Commission on Human Rights (E/Cn.4/1992/54, 3 March 1992) and the General Assembly (A/RES/48/134, 20 December 1993).

10. The Special Adviser was Brian Burdekin, former Federal Human Rights Commissioner of Australia and a recognized world authority on national institutions.

11. Committee on the Elimination of Racial Discrimination General Recommendation No. 28: Technical assistance of 19 March 2002, included in Report of the International Committee on the Elimination of Racial Discrimination, A/57/18, 1 November 2002.

12. The National Human Rights Institutions Forum: www.nhri.net

13. See further Chapter 5.

Chapter 18. Mainstreaming Human Rights

"Bridging the Gap between Human Rights and Development: From Normative Principles to Operational Relevance"

Under the Presidential Fellows Programme, for which this lecture was delivered, eminent thinkers and leaders are invited by the World Bank's President (currently James Wolfensohn) to speak on topics of their choosing.

1. UNDP, *Human Development Report 2000* (New York: United Nations Department of Public Information and Oxford University Press, 2000).

2. The World Bank, *The World Bank Annual Report 2001* (Washington, D.C.: The World Bank, 2001), p. 59.

3. The Common Country Assessment (CCA) and the Development Assistance Framework (UNDAF) were both introduced as part of Kofi Annan's 1997 reforms; see www.unhchr.ch/development/mainstreaming.html.

4. Halving Extreme Poverty: An Action Strategy for the United Nations, ACC/2000/15, approved on behalf of the Administrative Committee on Coordination

(ACC) by the Consultative Committee on Programme and Operational Questions (CCPOQ), seventeenth session, New York, 20–22 September 2000.

5. The UN System and Human Rights: Guidelines and Information for the Resident Coordinator System, ACC/2000/7, approved on behalf of the Administrative Committee on Coordination (ACC) by the Consultative Committee on Programme and Operational Questions (CCPOQ), sixteenth session, Geneva, February–March 2000. The Guidelines are available at accsubs.unsystem.org/ccpoq/documents/manual/human-rights-gui.pdf.

6. HURIST, the joint OHCHR and UNDP Human Rights Strengthening program, was developed to support the implementation of the UNDP's human rights policy as presented in, United Nations Development Programme, *Integrating Human Rights with Sustainable Human Development: A UNDP Policy Document* (New York: UNDP, 1998). Further information about the program and the latest HURIST status reports are available from either www.unhchr.ch/development/hurist.html or www.undp.org/governance/hurist.htm.

7. As of June 2004 this had risen to 177 states parties to the Convention on the Elimination of All Forms of Discrimination against Women.

8. World Bank, *Engendering Development: Through Gender Equality in Rights, Resources and Voice* (Oxford: Oxford University Press, 2001).

9. General Assembly Resolution of Commitment on HIV/AIDS, A/Res/S-26/2.

10. Declaration on the TRIPS Agreement and Public Health adopted in Doha, 14 November 2001, Wt/MIN(01)/DEC/2.

11. James Wolfensohn, "Rich Nations Can Remove World Poverty as a Source of Conflict," *International Herald Tribune*, 6 October 2001.

12. Guy Verhofstadt, "The Paradox of Anti-Globalisation: An Open Letter," 26 September 2001, published, among other places, in *The Guardian*, 28 September 2001. This open letter was discussed during the International Conference on Globalization, at the University of Ghent, Belgium, 30 October 2001, at which Mary Robinson spoke. For further information on this event, see www.globalisation debate.be/2001.

13. Deepa Narayan (dir.), *Voices of the Poor*, vol. 3 (New York: World Bank and Oxford University Press, 2002).

"A Human Rights Approach to Poverty Reduction Strategies"

The Draft Guidelines were developed by the OHCHR with the support of Professor Paul Hunt, Professor Manfred Nowak, and Professor Siddiq Osmani in 2002. The Draft Guidelines call for people, as the bearers of rights, to be the central focus of policies, programs, and projects aimed at reducing poverty.

14. Deepa Narayan (dir.), *Voices of the Poor*, vols. 1–3 (New York: World Bank and Oxford University Press, 2001, 2002).

15. UNDP, *Human Development Report 2000* (New York: United Nations Department of Public Information and Oxford University Press, 2000), p. 8.

16. From the World Bank Presidential Lecture included in this chapter.

"Strengthening Human Rights Field Operations"

The International Human Rights Symposium of 26 May 1998 was organized by the German Government to mark the fiftieth anniversary of the adoption of the Universal Declaration of Human Rights.

17. The Aspen Institute, "Voices from the Field: Learning from the Early Work of Comprehensive Community Initiatives" (1997): www.aspeninstitute.org. The Aspen Institute was founded in 1950 as a nonprofit organization that aims to "foster enlightened leadership, the appreciation of timeless ideas and values, and open-minded dialogue on contemporary issues."

18. DPKO is the Department of Peacekeeping Operations; DPA is the Department of Political Affairs; and OCHA is the Office Coordinating Humanitarian Affairs. Details of the work of each of these departments is available from www.un.org.

19. An Agenda for Peace, Preventive Diplomacy, Peacemaking and Peacekeeping, Report of the Secretary General, pursuant to the statement adopted by the Summit Meeting of the Security Council on 31 January 1992, A/47/277-S/24111, 17 June 1992, published as Boutros Boutros-Ghali, *An Agenda for Peace* (New York: United Nations, 1992): www.un.org/Docs/SG/agpeace.html.

World Summit on Sustainable Development

The World Summit on Sustainable Development was held in 2002 to review progress made since the Earth Summit in Rio de Janeiro in 1992. Information on the World Summit can be found in The Report of the World Summit on Sustainable Development, A/CONF.199/20, and its Corrigendum, A/CONF.199/20/Corr.1. The Office of the High Commissioner for Human Rights submitted a background paper, "Human Rights, Poverty Reduction and Sustainable Development: Health Food and Water," which is available from www.ohchr.org/english/about/publications/papers.htm.

20. At the 1992 Earth Summit in Rio de Janeiro, the international community adopted Agenda 21, the first global plan of action for sustainable development: www.un.org/esa/sustdev.

21. UNDP, *Human Development Report 2000: Human Rights and Human Development* (New York: Oxford University Press, 2000), p. 8.

22. The Rio Declaration formulated the link between human rights and the environmental protection element of sustainable development largely in procedural terms. Public participation was also emphasized in Agenda 21(chap. 23). Otherwise, Agenda 21 provided a limited number of direct references to human rights, notably with respect to youth, women, and indigenous peoples (chap. 24.1, chap. 25.8, and chap. 26.1–2).

23. Science and the Environment, Commission on Human Rights decision 2001/111 of 25 April 2001, E/CN.4/DEC/2001/111, requested the OHCHR and the United Nations Environment Programme (UNEP) "to review and assess progress achieved since the United Nations Conference on Environment and Development in promoting and protecting human rights in relation to environmental questions and in the framework of Agenda 21." This review took the form of a joint UNEP/OHCHR Expert Seminar on Human Rights and the Environment, which took place in Geneva on 16 January 2002, immediately preceded by a preparatory meeting of experts held 14–15 January 2002. The resultant report was delivered to the fifty-eighth session of the Commission on Human Rights: Report of the Joint OHCHR/UNEP Seminar on Human Rights and the Environment, E/CN.4/2002/WP.7. Further information about the work of the UN Environment Programme can be found at: www.unep.org.

24. The Convention on the Rights of the Child and ILO Convention No. 169 concerning Indigenous and Tribal Peoples in Independent Countries, OHCHR/UNEP Seminar Report. See also the work of the Special Rapporteur of the Commission on Human Rights on Adverse Effects of the Illicit Movement and Dumping of Toxic and Dangerous Products and Wastes on the Enjoyment of Human Rights: www.ohchr.org.

25. 1998 UN-ECE Convention on Access to Information, Public Participation and Access to Justice in Environmental Matters (the Aarhus Convention), ECE/CEP/43: www.participate.org/convention/convention.htm.

26. For the European Court of Human Rights, see *Zander v. Sweden* (1993),

concerning the probable pollution of a drinking-water well from a nearby dump; and *López Ostra v. Spain* (1994), in which the court recognized that "severe environmental pollution may affect individuals' well-being and prevent them from enjoying their homes in such a way as to affect their private and family life adversely." For the Inter-American Commission, see *Yanomami v. Brasil*, Resolution 12/85, Case 7615, 5 March 1985.

27. Plan of Implementation of the World Summit on Sustainable Development, Report of the World Summit on Sustainable Development, A/CONF.199/20, para. 154: "Strengthen cooperation between the United Nations Environment Programme and other United Nations bodies and specialized agencies, the Bretton Woods institutions and the World Trade Organization, within their mandates."

28. Klaus Töpfer, speech to WSSD, 2 September 2002; see www.joburgsummit.co.za/Jowsco/news.

Chapter 19. Terrorism, Peace, and Human Security

Protection of Civilians in Armed Conflict

This speech was delivered to the Security Council when it met to consider the Report of the Secretary General of the United Nations to the Security Council on the Protection of Civilians in Armed Conflict, S/1999/957, 8 September 1999.

1. Mary Robinson visited Indonesia, where she spoke to evacuated UNAMET staff from 12 to 13 September 1999, less than two weeks after the 30 August ballot and in the midst of the escalating atrocities. See OHCHR Press Release, "Human Rights High Commissioner Welcomes Indonesian Decision on Peacekeepers in East Timor and Recommends International Probe," 14 September 1999.

2. Mary Robinson visited a number of countries in the Balkans from 2 to 13 May 1999. See OHCHR Press Release, "High Commissioner for Human Rights Calls on Yugoslav Government to end 'Vicious Abuses' in Kosovo and Commit to Return of Refugees and Displaced Persons," 13 May 1999.

3. Mary Robinson visited Sierra Leone from 24 to 25 June 1999. See OHCHR Press Release, "High Commissioner for Human Rights Calls for Urgent Attention to Situation in Sierra Leone," 25 June 1999.

"What Prevention Requires"

4. Anna Lindh, Swedish Foreign Minister and a friend of Mary Robinson, was murdered in Stockholm on 11 September 2003. The Anna Lindh Programme on Conflict Prevention was launched in Stockholm on the first anniversary of her death. See: www.ui.se.

5. Anna Lindh, "Create a Worldwide Culture of Conflict Prevention," International Herald Tribune, 18 September 1999.

6. Carnegie Commission on Preventing Deadly Conflict, *Preventing Deadly Conflict: Final Report* (New York: Carnegie Corporation of New York, 1998).

7. UNDP, *Human Development Report 1999: Globalisation with a Human Face* (New York: United Nations Department of Public Information, 1999), p. 15.

8. As Mary Robinson envisaged, a two-pronged approach to discovering the truth and combating impunity was pursued with a Truth and Reconciliation Commission (TRC) and a hybrid national/international court. The Truth and Reconciliation Commission of Sierra Leone called for in Article XXIV of the Lomé Peace Agreement was established by an Act of Parliament on 22 February 2000 and was inaugurated on 5 July 2002. The final report of the commission was released in October 2004. It became operational toward the end of 2002, the same

year that the officials for the Special Court for Sierra Leone arrived in Freetown. News of the progress of the TRC can be found on the International Center for Transitional Justice's Web site: www.ictj.org; or the Irish Centre for Human Rights' Web site: www.nuigalway.ie/human_rights. The Special Court for Sierra Leone was established pursuant to Security Council resolution 1315 of 14 August 2000 by the signing of the Agreement between the United Nations and the Government of Sierra Leone on the Establishment of a Special Court for Sierra Leone on 16 January 2002. The first trial began on 3 June 2004. For further information on the Court and the proceedings before it, see www.sc-sl.org.

9. The law on Gacaca Tribunals was passed in January 2000 and they are now operating throughout Rwanda. For further information, see www.inkiko-gacaca.gov.rw.

10. Optional Protocol to the Convention on the Rights of the Child on the Involvement of Children in Armed Conflicts, General Assembly resolution 53/263 of 25 May 2000, A/RES/54/263, entered into force on 12 February 2002.

"Human Rights in the Shadow of 11 September"

Mary Robinson devoted her 2002 Report to the General Assembly, subtitled "Human Rights a Uniting Concept," to an extensive assessment of the subject of human rights and terrorism, E/CN.4/2002/18, 27 February 2002.

11. Michael Ignatieff, "Is the Human Rights Era Ending?," *The New York Times*, 5 February 2002.

12. Amnesty International, *Amnesty International Report 2002* (London: Amnesty International, 2002).

13. Joint statement by Mary Robinson, UN High Commissioner for Human Rights; Walter Schwimmer, Secretary General of the Council of Europe; and Ambassador Gérard Stoudmann, Director of the OSCE Office for Democratic Institutions and Human Rights on terrorism and human rights, 29 November 2001, available from www.ohchr.org.

14. Human Rights Committee, General Comment No. 29, States of Emergency (Article 4) CCPR/C/21/Rev.1/Add.11.

15. UNDP, *Human Development Report 1994: New Dimensions of Human Security* (New York: United Nations Department of Public Information, 1994).

16. Carnegie Commission on Preventing Deadly Conflict, *Preventing Deadly Conflict: Final Report* (New York: Carnegie Corporation of New York, 1997).

17. International Commission on Intervention and State Sovereignty, *The Responsibility to Protect* (Ottawa: International Development Research Centre, 2001), para. 3.18.

18. Commonwealth Human Rights Initiative, *Human Rights and Poverty Eradication—A Talisman for the Commonwealth* (London: Commonwealth Human Rights Initiative, 2001).

19. Seamus Heaney, *The Cure at Troy: After 'Philoctetes' by Sophocles* (Lawrence Hill, Derry: Field Day, 1990), p. 77.

Chapter 20. Ethical Globalization

"Ethics, Human Rights and Globalization"

The Global Ethic Foundation is dedicated to intercultural and interreligious research and is founded on the ideas of the theologian Hans Küng. This speech was delivered as the Foundation's second Global Ethic Lecture. See further www.weltethos.org.

1. Mary Robinson's remarks at the launch of this publication are included in Chapter 4.

2. Hans Küng, Giandomenico Picco, Kamal A. Aboulmagd, et al., *Crossing the Divide: Dialogue among Civilizations* (South Orange, N.J.: The School of Diplomacy and International Relations, Seton Hall University, 2001).

3. Declaration Towards a Global Ethic Adopted by the Parliament of World's Religions, Chicago, 1993, published by the Global Ethic Foundation.

4. United Nations Millennium Declaration, General Assembly resolution 55/2 of 8 September 2000, A/RES/55/2, 18 September 2000.

5. The High Commissioner's Expert Group on Human Rights and Biotechnology, convened in accordance with Commission on Human Rights resolution 2001/71, met in Geneva from 24 to 25 January 2002. Their mandate was to consider the area in which the OHCHR might best provide follow-up to UNESCO's Universal Declaration on the Human Genome and Human Rights. The conclusions of the Expert Group were finalized in July 2002 and presented to the fifty-ninth Commission on Human Rights (Human Rights and Bioethics, E/CN.4/2003/98, 10 February 2003). These conclusions and further information regarding the work of the OHCHR on bioethics and related issues can be found at www.unhchr.ch/biotech.

6. Virginia Woolf, *Three Guineas* (San Diego, Calif.: Harcourt Brace Jovanovich, 1966).

7. Kofi Annan, *We the Peoples* (New York: United Nations Department of Public Information, 2000), p. 9.

8. Ibid., p. 10.

9. The first Global Ethic Lecture, "Values and the Power of Community," delivered by Tony Blair on 30 June 2000 is available from the Global Ethic Foundation's Web site: www.weltethos.org.

10. Guy Verhofstadt, "The Paradox of Anti-Globalisation: An Open Letter," 26 September 2001, published, among other places, in *The Guardian*, 28 September 2001. This open letter was discussed during the International Conference on Globalization, at the University of Ghent, Belgium, 30 October 2001 at which Mary Robinson spoke. For further information on this event, see www.globalisationdebate.be/2001.

11. Gordon Brown outlined the idea of an "International Development Trust Fund" or "International Financing Facility" in a series of speeches starting in 2001including at the annual meetings of the World Bank and the IMF. For the most recent International Finance Facility Proposal, issued in April 2004, see www.hm-treasury.gov.uk.

12. Mary Robinson's ideas about the Global Compact are explored more fully in Chapter 13.

13. The ILO's report *A Global Agenda for Employment* was discussed at the Global Employment Forum in Geneva, held from 1 to 3 November 2001. The Global Agenda was subsequently adopted by seven hundred political and economic leaders. For further information, see www.ilo.org/public/english/employment/geforum.

Appeal at the World Social Forum

The World Social Forum established in 2001 brings together people from civil society organizations who are critical of the direction globalization is taking. It offers an alternative vision of globalization to that of the World Economic Forum, based in Davos, Switzerland. In January 2002 Mary Robinson as High Commissioner, attended the second World Social Forum meeting in Porto Alegre Brazil. She then traveled to New York, where, in a gesture of support following September 11, the World Economic Forum convened.

Index

Editorial Acknowledgments

This book grew out of the experience of serving for one year (2001–2) as senior adviser to Mary Robinson, United Nations High Commissioner for Human Rights. My eyes were opened to the scale of what this new UN institution for the promotion and protection of human rights was entrusted to deliver. A year was long enough to absorb also the depth of commitment not of the High Commissioner alone, but also of the staff in the Office of the High Commissioner for Human Rights (OHCHR). Drawn from all over the world and based in Geneva, New York, and the field, they sought under Mary Robinson's leadership to defend and to advance the mission of "All Rights for All."

I am indebted to many for encouragement, advice, and assistance. The book has the good will of Mary Robinson and all the staff who served under her. In particular, I would like to thank Robert Husbands, Cecilia Canessa, Mona Rishmawi, José Díaz, Lisa Oldring, and Maria Francisca Ize-Charrin. Lisel Holdenreid and Michelle Bologna, former interns in Geneva, and Rigmor Arden, a graduate student at the University of Essex, contributed to fact checking and editing. My research assistants at different points, Nuala Ni Mhuircheartaigh and Laurel Townhead, made indispensable contributions; the book would never have been completed without their efforts. I would like also to acknowledge the valuable advice of Ambassador Ronan Murphy of Ireland, who preceded me as senior adviser, and that of Stefanie Grant, former Head of the Research and Right to Development Branch in OHCHR.

I am grateful to Bill Butler and the Paul Shurgot Foundation for a grant that supported my research assistants, and to Bert Lockwood, series editor, for his encouragement. I would like to thank too the skilled staff at the University of Pennsylvania Press. The project was my own idea, and any defects remain my responsibility.

Kevin Boyle